The Diabetes Prevention & Management Cookbook

Your 10-Step Plan for Nutrition & Lifestyle

Johanna Burkhard and
Barbara Allan, RD, CDE

D1319461

For complete cataloguing information, see page 384.

Disclaimer

This book is a general guide only and should never be a substitute for the skill, knowledge, and experience of a qualified medical professional dealing with the facts, circumstances and symptoms of a particular case.

The nutritional, medical and health information presented in this book is based on the research, training and professional experience of the authors, and is true and complete to the best of their knowledge. However, this book is intended only as an informative guide for those wishing to know more about health, nutrition and medicine; it is not intended to replace or countermand the advice given by the reader's personal physician. Because each person and situation is unique, the author and the publisher urge the reader to check with a qualified health care professional before using any procedure where there is a question as to its appropriateness. A physician should be consulted before beginning any exercise program. The author and the publisher are not responsible for any adverse effects or consequences resulting from the use of the information in this book. It is the responsibility of the reader to consult a physician or other qualified health care professional regarding his or her personal care.

The recipes in this book have been carefully tested by our kitchen and our tasters. To the best of our knowledge, they are safe and nutritious for ordinary use and users. For those people with food or other allergies, or who have special food requirements or health issues, please read the suggested contents of each recipe carefully and determine whether or not they may create a problem for you. All recipes are used at the risk of the consumer.

We cannot be responsible for any hazards, loss or damage that may occur as a result of any recipe use.

For those with special needs, allergies, requirements or health problems, in the event of any doubt, please contact your medical adviser prior to the use of any recipe.

Design and production: Daniella Zanchetta/PageWave Graphics Inc.
Editor: Sue Sumeraj
Recipe editor: Jennifer MacKenzie
Nutrient analysis: Barbara Selley, RD, and Cathie Martin, BSc (H.Ec.), Food Intelligence
Proofreader: Sheila Wawanash
Indexer: Gillian Watts
Photographers: Mark T. Shapiro and Colin Erricson *(for Creamy Tuna Pasta Bake)*
Associate photographer: Matt Johannsson *(for Creamy Tuna Pasta Bake)*
Food stylist: Kate Bush and Kathryn Robertson *(for Creamy Tuna Pasta Bake)*
Prop stylist: Charlene Erricson

Cover image: Quinoa Tabbouleh (page 239)

iStockphoto.com images: Multigrain Granola and Fruit Parfait©iStockphoto.com/Pullia; Quinoa Tabbouleh ©iStockphoto.com/1MoreCreative; and Salmon with Balsamic Maple Glaze©iStockphoto.com/Chuck Place.

We acknowledge the financial support of the Government of Canada through the Book Publishing Industry Development Program (BPIDP) for our publishing activities.

Published by Robert Rose Inc.
120 Eglinton Avenue East, Suite 800, Toronto, Ontario, Canada M4P 1E2
Tel: (416) 322-6552 Fax: (416) 322-6936
www.robertrose.ca

Printed and bound in Canada

1 2 3 4 5 6 7 8 9 MP 21 20 19 18 17 16 15 14 13

Contents

Acknowledgments

We dedicate this book to each and every person managing prediabetes or diabetes. The long hours we spent in the kitchen and in front of the computer will be worth it if you benefit from the information while enjoying the delicious food!

This book has been enriched by the exceptional efforts of several people, and we wish to express our gratitude first to the team at Robert Rose: our supportive publisher Bob Dees; our super editor Sue Sumeraj for her incredible attention to detail and for keeping this project on track in her usual congenial style; and home economist Jennifer MacKenzie, who shared her expert cooking knowledge to ensure accuracy and clarity in the recipes. We also appreciate the contribution of Marian Jarkovich, Director of Sales and Marketing, and Martine Quibell, Manager of Publicity, for all of their diligent work to promote the book in North America and beyond. And designer Daniella Zanchetta at PageWave Graphics did a marvelous job integrating all of the visual material with the text.

We're especially indebted to Barbara Selley, RD, of Food Intelligence and her associate, Cathie Martin, BSc (H.Ec.), for their excellent and thorough work on the nutritional analyses of recipes and their assistance with menus and other diabetes-related information.

A special thanks to Sharon Zeiler, RD, Senior Manager, Diabetes Education and Nutrition, Canadian Diabetes Association (CDA), and the volunteer dietitians affiliated with the CDA who reviewed the book and provided insight and constructive feedback.

Barbara Allan would especially like to thank Johanna for inviting her to be part of this exciting and unique project. The collaboration provided Barbara with a new format to share her passion for diabetes education and expand her limits as a dietitian. She also extends sincere gratitude to Sue Sumeraj, who was a very patient teacher to this first-time book writer! Furthermore, Barbara is grateful for the support and encouragement of her family and friends, and especially her dear kids, Aidan and Madelyn.

Johanna Burkhard would like to express her appreciation to her spouse, Ron, for his constant encouragement, quick wit and humor throughout the project, and to her children, Nicole and Patrick, who have been such an inspiration with their healthful approach to living.

Most importantly, we dedicate this book to each and every person managing prediabetes or diabetes. The long hours we spent in the kitchen and in front of the computer will be worth it if you benefit from the information while enjoying the delicious food!

Introduction

Diabetes, one of the most common non-contagious diseases, is a health crisis around the globe. An estimated 366 million people had diabetes in 2011, and the prevalence of diabetes is projected to get much worse. By 2030, it is estimated that 552 million people will have diabetes.

This constitutes a health crisis because diabetes is a dangerous disease. Uncontrolled, it can cause kidney failure, heart attack, stroke, blindness, amputation and an early death. The monetary cost of diabetes is in the billions of dollars, but the human cost is beyond measure.

There is no cure for diabetes. Once diagnosed, it must be managed to reduce the risk of these serious complications, with daily attention to healthy eating, exercise, medication, blood glucose monitoring, foot care and regular visits with a health care team.

Before diabetes is diagnosed, many people transition through a "prediabetes" stage, in which blood glucose is elevated but is not high enough to be considered diabetes. Prediabetes is itself a health hazard, as it is linked to heart disease and stroke. And it, too, is a common condition: about 35% of U.S. adults have prediabetes, contributing to 280 million cases around the world.

Despite these gloomy statistics, there is much hope. Research is proving that people with prediabetes can take steps to reduce their risk of diabetes, heart disease and stroke. And those same steps can help people with diabetes to thrive and lead fulfilling lives. These steps are outlined in this book, along with many strategies and recommendations to help you achieve them. We will teach you how to make the right food choices, explain why eating a healthy diet is the best defense against disease and provide you with recipes for delicious meals and snacks. In addition, we offer the latest information on exercise, stress management, medications and so much more. Everything is presented in a straightforward way to cut through the confusion.

The Diabetes Prevention and Management Cookbook is special because it blends the expertise of a Certified Diabetes Educator, who is also a Registered Dietitian, with that of a food and cooking expert. Barbara Allan has over 20 years of experience working with people who have diabetes and prediabetes. She will guide you, step by step, toward a lifestyle that manages blood glucose, blood pressure and cholesterol

Did You Know?

Globally, 8.3% of people have diabetes and 6.4% have prediabetes.

People with prediabetes can take steps to reduce their risk of diabetes, heart disease and stroke.

Did You Know?

In the United States and Canada, there are approximately 30 million people with diabetes and 85 million people with prediabetes. Added together, this is more than 30% of the population.

Enjoy the delicious recipes and harness the power of whole foods, whatever your health goals may be.

A diagnosis of diabetes or prediabetes can be upsetting. Let the facts assure you that good health is possible, whether you are aiming to prevent or manage diabetes.

while supporting a healthy weight. Johanna Burkhard is a bestselling cookbook author who brings a whole foods approach to this book. Maximum nutrition and taste is her goal, using natural ingredients you have on hand. All recipes have been created, tested and retested until they met specific nutrition guidelines. Best of all, they have been assembled into a delicious prescription for health: a 28-day menu with meals and snacks you can customize to your needs.

You will also enjoy this book if you are interested in food that tastes good and is good for you. You don't need to have a diagnosis of diabetes or prediabetes to benefit from the recipes, menu plans, tips and health information it contains. If, however, you are managing your cholesterol, blood pressure or weight, this book will be even more valuable.

A diagnosis of diabetes or prediabetes can be upsetting. Let the facts assure you that good health is possible, whether you are aiming to prevent or manage diabetes. Information is power. Information turned into delicious meals is even more powerful!

Part 1

Lifestyle for Diabetes Prevention and Management

Chapter 1
Understanding Diabetes

Did You Know?

Diabetes is formally called diabetes mellitus. *Diabetes* is Greek for "siphon" and *mellitus* is from the Latin word for "honey." Diabetes mellitus is therefore named for one of its symptoms: the production of large amounts of sugar-containing urine.

Diabetes is a complex problem that affects millions of people around the world. It is an ancient disease, but even today scientists do not know exactly what causes it. At present, there is no cure. Diabetes is very dangerous, causing an increased risk of atherosclerosis, heart attack, stroke, kidney failure, amputation, blindness and death. Thankfully, diabetes can be well managed to reduce the risk of these serious complications. Read on to learn more about diabetes and how to take care of yourself.

Complications of Diabetes

Diabetes is a major cause of:

- cardiovascular disease (including atherosclerosis, heart attack and stroke)
- kidney disease (including kidney failure)
- blindness
- amputation
- erectile dysfunction
- depression

Did You Know?

Glucose is a sugar that is a key source of energy for our bodies and brain. Glucose is found in foods we eat, either as natural or added sugar or as part of starchy foods (such as bread, rice and potatoes).

What Is Diabetes?

Very simply, diabetes is high blood sugar (glucose). It is diagnosed with a blood glucose test. Some people are surprised to discover they have diabetes, as they have been feeling fine. Others may be very sick, with symptoms such as frequent urination, thirst and weight loss. Although each person's experience is different, all diabetes is caused by a lack of insulin, insulin that doesn't work well or a bit of both.

The Three Types of Diabetes

There are three main types of diabetes: type 1, type 2 and gestational (GDM).

When a person makes little or no insulin, he has type 1. This condition usually develops in people who are 30 years of age or younger, but it can occur at any time. People with type 1 experience powerful symptoms (see box, below), so they do not go undiagnosed. About 5% to 10% of people with diabetes have type 1. They manage this condition with a healthy lifestyle and insulin.

> **With type 2 diabetes,** there may be no symptoms. That's why it is so important to be screened regularly.

Symptoms of Diabetes

- Excessive thirst and urination
- Excessive hunger and loss of weight without trying
- Feeling more tired than usual
- Blurred vision
- Slow healing of cuts or sores
- Dry, itchy skin
- Bladder, urinary tract or vaginal infections
- Sexual dysfunction

With type 2 diabetes, there may be no symptoms. That's why it is so important to be screened regularly.

The cause of type 1 diabetes is not known for certain. Most likely an infection or other "intruder" causes the body to mistakenly destroy its own insulin-producing cells. There is no cure for type 1, nor is there a way to prevent it, although researchers are working hard on these challenges.

Type 2 diabetes and GDM are different conditions but with some key similarities. In either case, insulin is not working well (called insulin resistance) and/or is not in sufficient supply to keep blood glucose levels normal. In pregnancy, some insulin resistance is expected, as the placenta makes hormones that work against insulin. As long as the pancreas can create enough extra insulin to counteract this, blood glucose levels remain normal. In up to 18% of pregnancies, however, the pancreas cannot keep up, and GDM is the result. GDM must be expertly managed through diet and exercise to protect the health of the developing baby. In

Did You Know?

Insulin is a hormone made by the pancreas. It has many roles, but is best known for keeping blood glucose levels steady. Insulin works all day, and especially after meals, to help glucose enter the body's cells, where it can be stored or used for energy.

some cases, insulin injections are needed. GDM usually goes away after the birth of the baby but is likely to recur in future pregnancies. Women who have had GDM have an increased risk of developing type 2 and need to be screened regularly.

A third to half of people with type 2 diabetes are undiagnosed.

Insulin Resistance

Insulin is a very powerful hormone. It keeps blood glucose in check and also helps cells store fat and amino acids (components of protein). "Insulin resistance" (IR) is the term used when insulin is not working as well as it should. Exactly why this happens is unknown. When insulin stops working effectively, the pancreas needs to produce more insulin to compensate. This means people with IR actually make more insulin than people without IR. IR is found in people with prediabetes, diabetes, obesity and polycystic ovarian syndrome, and may be found in people with high blood pressure and abnormal blood fats.

Type 2 is the most common type of diabetes (90% to 95% of cases). It is seen mostly in older people, but children and teens can develop it too. It occurs when gradually worsening insulin resistance and a dwindling insulin supply cause the blood glucose level to go up. This can take months or years, so symptoms can be subtle or nonexistent. In fact, a third to half of people with type 2 diabetes are undiagnosed. Once discovered, type 2 is managed with a healthy lifestyle, medications and, sometimes, insulin.

What Causes Type 2 Diabetes?

The exact cause of type 2 diabetes is a mystery. In almost every case, there are several factors working together. As mentioned above, one of the factors is insulin resistance. Insulin resistance means the pancreas is making insulin but the insulin does not work well. This causes the pancreas to work harder to make *more* insulin.

Ongoing insulin resistance puts a strain on the pancreas. Over time, this overtaxed organ may produce less insulin. If it does, blood glucose levels creep up. Diabetes happens at the union of excess insulin resistance and reduced insulin production. Research suggests that the pancreas is working at only 50% when blood glucose has reached diabetic levels.

Is Inflammation the Root of Insulin Resistance?

We know insulin resistance is a cause of diabetes, but what causes insulin resistance? New research suggests that inflammation in fat cells is a culprit.

Inflammation is a process that helps the body heal itself, but if it becomes chronic, it can cause damage. Some scientists think insulin resistance is linked to the presence of inflammatory cells, called macrophages, in fat tissue. Macrophages are immune cells that normally respond to infections, but in obese people, macrophages move into the fat tissue, where they cause inflammation and release cytokines. Certain cytokines cause cells to become resistant to the effects of insulin.

Although much more research is needed, this finding provides another incentive to eat well, be active and reduce body fat.

Age also plays a role, perhaps because things just don't work as well as they should when we get older. Some people gain weight as they age. They may also be less active. Weight gain and lack of activity promote insulin resistance. Diabetes also runs in families and in certain ethnic groups, pointing to a strong genetic (inherited) cause.

Indeed, there are many risk factors for diabetes:

The exact cause of type 2 diabetes is a mystery. In almost every case, there are several factors working together.

Risk factors for type 2 diabetes

- Having a mother, father, brother or sister with type 2 diabetes
- Having a history of prediabetes
- Having a history of GDM or a large baby (9 pounds/ 4 kilograms or more at birth)
- Being 40 or more years of age
- Having high blood pressure or high cholesterol levels
- Having polycystic ovarian syndrome

- Being of Aboriginal, African, Asian, South Asian or Hispanic heritage
- Having schizophrenia
- Having acanthosis nigricans (soft, dark, velvety skin patches)
- Being overweight, especially around the middle

As you can see, some of the risk factors are inherited, so you cannot change them. Others, such as high blood pressure or overweight, can be managed with a healthy lifestyle (and sometimes medication). The more risk factors you can control, the better your chance of preventing diabetes.

Keep in mind that having one or several of these risk factors doesn't mean that you will definitely get type 2 diabetes; it simply means you are more at risk for it. On the other hand, some people with none of these risk factors develop diabetes.

What Is Prediabetes?

Prediabetes increases your risk for type 2 diabetes, heart attack and stroke, but these problems are not inevitable. Read on to learn what you can do.

Type 2 diabetes takes months or years to develop. During this period, prediabetes may be diagnosed. In prediabetes, the pancreas gradually makes less insulin, with resulting higher than normal glucose levels. Prediabetes is also called "impaired fasting glucose (IFG)" or "impaired glucose tolerance (IGT)" depending upon which glucose level is high.

Besides being a step on the road to type 2, prediabetes is linked to heart and blood vessel disease, including heart attack and stroke.

Hyperglycemia and Hypoglycemia

Another word for high blood glucose is "hyperglycemia." *Hyper* means "high," *glyc* indicates "glucose," and *emia* means "in the blood." On the flip side is *hypo*glycemia, or blood glucose that is too low. People with diabetes take steps to lower their blood glucose, but they may sometimes overshoot the mark. This is usually the result of certain medications or insulin. To learn more about hypoglycemia prevention and treatment, see page 130.

How Are Diabetes and Prediabetes Diagnosed?

All adults should have their blood glucose measured regularly, at least every three years once they reach their 40s. Some physicians will recommend earlier or more frequent testing, depending upon how many risk factors a person has.

If you have prediabetes, have your blood glucose measured at least once every year.

Glucose Testing Methods

There are several ways to measure glucose. Each one involves giving a blood sample, and each test has its own cut-off for normal, prediabetes or diabetes. To confirm a diagnosis, it is usually necessary to have high blood glucose on two separate days.

- *Fasting test:* Blood glucose is measured first thing in the morning, after you haven't eaten for at least eight hours.

- *Two-hour, 75-gram glucose tolerance test:* After fasting glucose is measured, a sweet-tasting drink containing 75 grams of glucose is consumed (this is about the same amount of sugar as that found in two cans of soda). The blood glucose is measured two hours later.

- *Hemoglobin A1c (HbA1c or glycated hemoglobin) test:* Glucose is a sugar, and sugar is sticky. Glucose in the blood sticks to, or "glycates," many body cells. When it sticks to the hemoglobin portion of a red blood cell, the compound is called hemoglobin A1c. Since red blood cells live for two to three months, your HbA1c reflects your overall glucose control during that timeframe. If blood glucose levels have been generally normal, HbA1c will be in the normal range. If you have had high blood glucose, your HbA1c will be high too. Results are given as a percent, to show what percent of hemoglobin has become glycated.

Did You Know?

Because HbA1c is an estimate of your glucose control over the past two to three months, it is not affected by what you ate recently. In fact, you do not even have to fast before checking your HbA1c.

Blood glucose can also be measured with a "casual," or "random," glucose test, measured at any time of the day and unrelated to eating or drinking. A casual test might be done if diabetes is highly suspected, as with people who are experiencing symptoms of weight loss and extreme thirst and urination. Diabetes is confirmed when these symptoms are backed up by a result of 200 milligrams per deciliter or greater (in the U.S.), or 11.1 millimoles per liter or greater (in Canada).

Find Your Glucose Level

In the United States, glucose is measured in milligrams per deciliter (mg/dL), while in Canada, it is measured in millimoles per liter (mmol/L). To convert mg/dL to mmol/L, divide the mg/dL figure by 18.02. (Example: 200 mg/dL ÷ 18.02 = 11.1 mmol/L.) To convert mmol/L to mg/dL, multiply the mmol/L figure by 18.02. (Example: 11.1 mmol/L × 18.02 = 200 mg/dL.)

U.S.	Fasting (mg/dL)	Glucose Tolerance (mg/dL)	Hemoglobin A1c (%)
Normal	maximum 99	maximum 139	maximum 5.6
Prediabetes	100–125	140–199	5.7–6.4
Diabetes	126 or higher	200 or higher	6.5 or higher
Canada	Fasting (mmol/L)	Glucose Tolerance (mmol/L)	Hemoglobin A1c (%)
Normal	maximum 6.0	maximum 7.7	maximum 5.9
Prediabetes	6.1–6.9	7.8–11.0	6.0–6.4
Diabetes	7.0 or higher	11.1 or higher	6.5 or higher

Note: There is some debate about the cut-off for prediabetes. In the United States, prediabetes is diagnosed with a *lower* blood glucose level than in Canada, as 100 mg/dL is equal to 5.6 mmol/L. Likewise, in the U.S., a normal fasting glucose is a maximum of 99 mg/dL (5.5 mmol/L); in Canada, a fasting glucose of 5.6 to 6.0 is considered an "increased risk of diabetes."

How Can Diabetes Be Prevented?

> **Reduce your risk** of diabetes by eating well, being active and managing stress.

It should now be clear that diabetes is very common and very serious. If your blood glucose is presently normal, that is good news. Continue to have it measured at least every three years or as your physician recommends. Reduce your risk of diabetes by eating well, being active and managing stress. You will find our 10-step approach (beginning on page 38) very useful in achieving those goals. Then, let the menu plans and recipes bring variety and spice to your day.

If you have prediabetes, a number of major research studies have proven it is possible to return to normal blood glucose levels, or at minimum, remain prediabetic without developing diabetes outright. These research studies offer great hope for our future ability to stop the global tidal wave of glucose disorders. Here is a summary of influential diabetes prevention studies from around the world.

Advanced Glycation End Products (AGEs)

It is well known that high blood glucose is one of the causes of diabetes complications, but just how does glucose harm us? One of the routes is through "glycation" (also called "glycosylation"). Glucose is a sugar, and sugar is sticky. Glucose sticks to, or glycates, many cells in the body. The combination of glucose and protein in the cell is called an advanced glycation end product, or AGE. Hemoglobin A1c (see page 13) is an example of an AGE.

Although glycation is normal to some extent, high blood glucose can allow this process to go unchecked. Glycated cells do not work exactly as they should. Most diabetes complications are at least partly due to AGEs. Keeping blood glucose in the target range reduces glycation, providing yet another reason to manage your diabetes as well as you can.

Some foods we eat also contain AGEs. When sugar is mixed with protein and fat — and especially when this combination is cooked for a long time or at a high temperature — AGEs are formed. How you prepare food and how much you eat plays a direct role in the amount of AGEs in your body. You will find tips on reducing AGEs in your cooking on page 266.

Did You Know?

Smoking raises AGE levels in the body. Tobacco contains compounds called pre-AGEs, but when tobacco is burned, AGEs are formed. AGE levels in cigarette smokers are significantly higher than those in nonsmokers, and diabetic smokers have been found to have greater AGE deposition in their arteries and eyes.

The Da Qing IGT and Diabetes Study

In 1986, a study of 577 people with impaired glucose tolerance began in the city of Da Qing, China. Participants were divided into four groups. Each group followed a different plan: a normal lifestyle plan (the control group), a healthy diet plan, an exercise plan, or a diet plus exercise plan. Those in the healthy diet group were encouraged to eat more vegetables and less sugar, and to drink less alcohol. They were also encouraged to lose weight if their BMI was greater than 25 (see page 94). The exercise group was instructed to aim for 20 minutes a day of moderate activity, such as walking. The diet plus exercise group followed both regimens.

By the end of the six-year study, almost 70% of the control group had developed diabetes, compared to about 44% of the healthy diet group, about 41% of the exercise group and about 46% of the diet plus exercise group.

The researchers concluded that diet and/or exercise led to a significant decrease in the development of diabetes. As if this isn't remarkable enough, 20 years later those groups were *still* healthier. A follow-up study conducted in 2006 found that 80% of the diet and/or exercise groups had eventually developed diabetes, compared to 93% of the control group. For many of the people in the study, six years of healthy habits paid off 20 years later!

A Study of Japanese Men with IGT

In Tokyo, 458 men with impaired glucose tolerance were assigned to either a normal lifestyle or one designed to reduce their weight through diet and exercise. As Japanese people are generally lighter than Caucasians, the control group aimed to maintain their BMI at 24, while the weight loss group aimed for a BMI of 22 or less. After four years, about 9% of the control group had developed diabetes, versus only 3% of the weight loss group. This translates into a 67% lower risk for the weight loss group, with an average weight loss of *only 5 pounds (2.3 kg)*.

The Finnish Diabetes Prevention Study

This study examined 522 overweight middle-aged people with prediabetes. The group was divided in half. The control group was given general advice on a healthy lifestyle. The other group received individual nutrition counseling and did strength training three times per week. On average, the participants in the latter group lost 8 pounds (3.6 kg) each — about 5% of their body weight. By the end of the four-year study, 11% of this group had developed diabetes, compared to 23% of the control group. This is the same as a 58% reduction in the risk of developing diabetes.

The STOP-NIDDM Trial

This study looked at the effect of acarbose, a diabetes medication that helps reduce the rise in blood glucose after meals. The study randomly assigned 1,368 people with prediabetes, in nine countries, to use either acarbose or a placebo. They were followed for about three years. After the study, participants had a glucose tolerance test and were examined for hypertension, atherosclerosis, stroke and other health conditions. Those who had taken acarbose were found to be 25% less likely to develop type 2 diabetes, 34% less likely to develop hypertension and 49% less likely to have heart and blood vessel problems.

The Diabetes Prevention Program

This U.S. study was special for several reasons: it was the largest diabetes prevention study ever undertaken, with 3,234 participants; it included people from various ethnic groups, reflecting the higher risk of diabetes in these populations; and it compared the effects of a healthy lifestyle with those of medication in slowing the development of diabetes in people with impaired glucose tolerance.

Each participant was provided with general guidelines on healthy eating, was encouraged to exercise for at least 30 minutes, five days per week, and was advised to avoid excessive alcohol. Smokers were encouraged to quit. Then the participants were divided into four groups:

- The "lifestyle intervention group" was given a lot of support, including individual and group nutrition education, supervised fitness classes, goal-setting workshops and regular checkups. This support allowed participants to lose 7% of their body weight.

- The second group started taking metformin, a diabetes medication that reduces insulin resistance.

- The control group took placebo pills.

- The fourth group started taking the drug troglitazone; however, researchers were forced to abandon this part of the study because the drug caused serious adverse side effects.

After an average follow-up of about three years, 11% of people in the control group had developed diabetes, compared to 8% of the metformin group and 5% of the lifestyle intervention group. In other words, the people in the lifestyle intervention group reduced their risk by 58%, while those in the metformin group reduced theirs by 31%.

It is interesting that both the Diabetes Prevention Study in Finland and the Diabetes Prevention Program in the U.S. found that a healthy lifestyle could reduce the risk of developing diabetes by the same 58%. It is also interesting that, in the

Did You Know?

People with prediabetes are likely to develop type 2 within 10 years unless they take steps to prevent or delay it.

Both the Diabetes Prevention Study in Finland and the Diabetes Prevention Program in the U.S. found that a healthy lifestyle could reduce the risk of developing diabetes by the same 58%.

U.S. study, lifestyle changes were found to reduce diabetes risk better than medication. Also worth noting is how well older adults did in the lifestyle intervention group: people 60 years and up reduced their risk of developing diabetes by 71%.

Diabetes Prevention Program Outcomes Study

As with the Da Qing study, the Diabetes Prevention Program had a follow-up study. As the original program came to an end, all participants who decided to stay on (88% chose to) were provided with group education to help them follow the lifestyle intervention program. The original lifestyle group kept up their usual efforts, and the metformin and placebo groups began more regular exercise and attempted to lose 7% of their weight. Those in the metformin group continued to use the drug.

Participants were followed for an average of 10 years. Although everyone was now maintaining a healthy lifestyle, the study showed that the original lifestyle intervention group continued to stay the healthiest. By the end of 10 years, that group had 43% less diabetes than the original placebo group. Older participants (over 60 years of age) did even better, with a 49% reduction in their risk. Meanwhile, the metformin group reduced their risk by 18% (note that these participants had now been on metformin for an average of 13 years).

The Bottom Line

These studies tell us that type 2 diabetes can be prevented or delayed with lifestyle changes and medication. A healthy lifestyle includes regular exercise (about 150 minutes per week), a small weight loss (5% to 7% of body weight) and a lower-fat and higher-fiber diet. Medications such as acarbose and metformin can also be helpful (see page 129 for more information on the risks and benefits of various medications, so you can make an informed choice).

Now to turn research into action! With the results of the diabetes prevention studies in mind, we have developed a practical, easy-to-follow 10-step program that will help you prevent or delay type 2 diabetes if you have been diagnosed with prediabetes. If you already have diabetes, these steps will help you manage it.

Step 1: Eat three meals a day, spread 4 to 6 hours apart.
Step 2: Limit carbohydrate to 45 to 75 grams per meal.

Step 3: Choose low- and medium-GI foods most often.
Step 4: Choose healthy fats.
Step 5: Eat low-fat protein at every meal.
Step 6: Aim to limit sodium to 1500 milligrams per day.
Step 7: Choose low-carbohydrate, low-calorie beverages.
Step 8: If you are overweight, lose 5% to 10% of your weight.
Step 9: Aim for 30 minutes of exercise a day.
Step 10: Get 7 to 9 hours of sleep and safeguard your mental health.

These steps are specially designed to prevent and manage diabetes, but anyone can benefit!

In chapter 3, each step is explained in detail so you'll understand exactly what to do and why. This knowledge will enable you to live in the "real world," making choices that work for you. Because healthy eating is so important, we've also provided menu plans and over 150 recipes that meet strict nutrition guidelines. These recipes and menus will take the burden of meal planning off your shoulders, giving you one less thing to worry about — we've figured everything out for you! Even better, the recipes are absolutely delicious, proof that you don't have to sacrifice taste to improve your health.

It is important to note that these steps will not prevent diabetes for all people, or for their entire lifespan. Just as some people develop diabetes for no obvious reason, some people get the disease despite their best efforts to prevent it. This is discouraging, but it underlines the fact that diabetes is a complex condition. Take heart in knowing that a healthy lifestyle is rewarding in and of itself.

If you already have diabetes, these steps will help you with your overall health. Diabetes affects many parts of the body and is often associated with other conditions, including high blood pressure, excess weight and heart disease. Any steps you take to manage your diabetes will likely help those conditions too. As inspiring as this may be, there is more! Managing is one thing; *thriving* is quite another. A healthy lifestyle will allow you to thrive with diabetes and enjoy life to the fullest.

Managing your diabetes is one thing; *thriving* is quite another. A healthy lifestyle will allow you to thrive and enjoy life to the fullest!

If You Have Type 1 Diabetes

This book is dedicated to the prevention and management of type 2 diabetes, but all of the nutrition information can be adapted for people with type 1. After all, regular meals and snacks, with a moderate amount of low-glycemic-index (low-GI) carbohydrates, are the basis for any diabetes menu. Work with your health care provider to ensure that you are getting enough calories and to see if you have specific needs for protein, fat or sodium that differ from what is provided by our menus (explained on page 138). Be especially watchful for hypoglycemia if you increase your fiber intake, switch to lower-GI carbohydrates or increase your activity. Talk to your health care team about your plans.

Otherwise, we invite you to enjoy delicious, easy-to-prepare meals while benefiting from advice on exercise, stress management, the value of quality sleep and many other tips and strategies for successful diabetes management.

If You Have Had Gestational Diabetes

Women with GDM follow a special moderate-carb, low-GI diet to manage their glucose levels and achieve an appropriate weight gain. After delivery, blood glucose levels usually return to normal, but GDM can recur in future pregnancies and is a warning that type 2 diabetes could be around the corner.

If you have had GDM, you have a special opportunity to safeguard future pregnancies and reduce your risk of type 2. Keep following the principles of diet and exercise you learned when you had GDM. In addition to a healthy lifestyle, stay on top of your glucose control by getting checked at these key times:

- *At six to 12 weeks after delivery:* Have a glucose tolerance test. (In Canada, test at six weeks to six months.)

- *Every three years:* Assuming the above test was normal, have your fasting glucose or glucose tolerance tested at least once every three years (more often if you have additional risk factors).

- *When you are planning another pregnancy:* Have a glucose test before you start trying to conceive.

- *When you are pregnant again:* Consider having a glucose tolerance test at the end of the first trimester. If it's normal, retest at 24 to 28 weeks.

Stick with the Program

Because of your GDM, you have a unique insight into how to feed yourself and your family. When you were managing GDM, you learned to eat low-GI foods such as brown rice and whole-grain pasta, breads, crackers and flours. You kept portions of starchy carbohydrates to about 1 cup (250 mL), and enjoyed sensible servings of fruit and milk. You likely ate larger portions of vegetables. You learned the importance of eating regular meals, including breakfast. You avoided or strictly limited sugary foods and drinks.

You likely felt so good eating this way that you promised to keep it up after delivery. In truth, this needs to be your menu for life: it is your diabetes prevention strategy and a healthy diet for the whole family.

For Yourself, for Your Kids

Children born to mothers with GDM have a higher risk of diabetes themselves, and a higher risk of being overweight. It is essential to feed them plenty of healthy food and give them every opportunity to be active. We all love to indulge our children with junk food, but there has to be a limit. Save sugary sodas and candy for special occasions. Avoid candies and drinks that masquerade as fruit, such as gummies, "drinks" and "ades." Offer real fruit and vegetables at meals and snacks. Serve whole-grain bread, crackers and cereal. Ask anyone who cares for your kids to respect your wishes.

Teach your children to read labels so you can find healthy choices together. Involving them in the process will get them on board much more easily. Resist the "pester power" of kids who have seen one too many commercials for the latest sugary cereal. At the store, let them pick from a selection of cereals *you* think is okay. Since it's your money, you have a say!

> ## SOUND BITE
>
> *When I was diagnosed with GDM, I was annoyed I had to cut out sweets and limit my weight gain. Wasn't I eating for two now? But after a while, I could see how much better my blood sugar was. Eating smaller meals more often and choosing low-GI carbs did the trick. I also felt really good. My dietitian encouraged me to stick with this eating pattern after my baby was born, and I promised myself I would!*
>
> *— Perdita, 25*

Chapter 2
Nutrition 101

Did You Know?

The term "whole foods" means foods that have had little or no processing and that contain no added ingredients, such as preservatives, sugar or salt. Examples of whole foods include raw fruits and vegetables, legumes, nuts and seeds, fresh cuts of meat and whole grains.

Starting with the right **ingredients makes it easier to take good care of your body.**

Next to air and water, food is life itself. Food provides energy and nutrients for growth and repair, and the right food can mean the difference between poor and good health. Food is enjoyed for its taste, texture and smell, and is an essential part of holidays and celebrations. Eating is something we do virtually every day of our lives.

These days, there is much confusion about what is the "best" food. Many people find it frustrating trying to keep up with all the nutrition advice they hear. Others put their health at risk by consuming an abundance of "empty calorie" foods like soda pop, candies, pastries, sugary cereals and salty snacks. Many of us have become overfed but undernourished.

There is no one best diet for everyone, but modern science is finding new reasons why we should eat like our grandparents. In other words, researchers can now tell us exactly why eating three meals a day, including breakfast, is good for us. There is proof that cooking at home, and enjoying the company of others while dining, contributes to better physical and mental health, and that eating in a non-rushed, non-stressed way leads to better digestion and greater satisfaction. There is mounting evidence that wholesome, less processed foods are essential, as is an abundance of vegetables and fruits.

That's why this book takes a whole foods approach to cooking and eating. While we don't ask you to prepare everything "from scratch," starting with the right ingredients makes it easier to take good care of your body. Our tips, recipes and menus will help you *thrive* while on your journey to prevent or manage diabetes.

Macronutrients and Micronutrients

Food is made up of macronutrients and micronutrients. The macronutrients are carbohydrate, fat and protein. The micronutrients are vitamins, minerals and phytochemicals. It can be useful to know these terms, as most packaged foods list them on their labels (see page 30 for information on reading labels).

Macronutrients

Macronutrients give us energy and building blocks to grow and repair our body. Carbohydrate (often called "carb") is broken down into glucose (the main energy source for the body) and fiber (which helps keep the digestive system running smoothly). Fat is a source of energy, and stored fat is used to cushion our organs (and our tailbone!). Protein is a source of energy and plays an integral role in making skin, hair, organs and most other tissues.

> **Macronutrients give us** energy and building blocks to grow and repair our body.

Nutrient Requirement Terms

U.S. and Canadian scientists work together to determine how much of each macro- and micronutrient we need on a daily basis, as well as guidelines for water and fiber. The most recent comprehensive report of our requirements is called the *Dietary Reference Intakes* (2006, with updates for calcium and vitamin D in 2010), published by the Institute of Medicine. This report is used by health and nutrition experts to guide the public. Some terms you may have heard of come from this report:

- *Recommended Dietary Allowance (RDA):* The daily nutrient intake that should meet the needs of almost all healthy people for a given age, sex and life stage.
- *Estimated Average Requirement (EAR):* The average daily nutrient intake level that is estimated to meet the requirements of 50% of the healthy individuals for a given age, sex and life stage.
- *Acceptable Intake (AI):* The recommended daily intake used when an RDA cannot be determined. It is based on observed intakes or estimated intakes of apparently healthy people.
- *Tolerable Upper Intake Level (UL):* The highest daily nutrient intake that is unlikely to cause adverse effects to almost all individuals in the general population.

The next time you eat something healthful, take a moment to reflect — not just on the taste but also on the benefits you are giving your body. There are thousands of nutrients in food, doing you a good turn today and for a lifetime.

Did You Know?

Our grandparents knew that eating carrots was good for the eyes. Today, we know that the phytochemical beta carotene is the reason. In the eye, beta carotene is converted to a form of vitamin A called retinal, which then binds to a protein called opsin. This molecule resides in the light-sensitive rods and cones of the retina. When exposed to light, the retinal sends a signal to the optic nerve, and then to the brain, allowing us to see. People who are low in beta carotene (or vitamin A) will experience poor night vision and, if the deficiency becomes severe, can even become blind.

Carbohydrate-rich foods include breads and cereals, rice, potatoes, yams and other root vegetables, fruit, milk and sugar. Fat can be added to meals as butter, margarine, mayonnaise or oil, or may already be present in food (as in marbled meat). Protein is found in meat, fish, poultry, eggs, cheese, legumes, nuts and tofu. Many foods contain more than one of the macronutrients, and some, such as milk and nuts, contain all three.

All of the macronutrients are absolutely vital for health. The optimal mix of macronutrients has been debated over the last 30 years. Low-carb diets have been in and out of fashion. Some people follow very low-fat diets. We believe in avoiding extremes, so our meals provide a reasonable amount of all macronutrients.

Each of the macronutrients is discussed in more detail later in the book: carbohydrates in Steps 2 and 3 (pages 44–62); fat in Steps 4 and 5 (pages 63–80); and protein in Step 5 (page 74).

Micronutrients

Micronutrients are tiny catalysts for millions of essential chemical reactions that take place in our bodies. They include vitamins (such as vitamin A, thiamin, niacin, vitamin C and vitamin D), minerals (such as calcium, magnesium, iron

A Whole Foods Approach

With our nutrition knowledge growing all the time, it is an exciting era for eaters! It can also be confusing. Do you need to take a vitamin pill that "now contains lutein"? Is it a good idea to eat foods fortified with fish oil? We do not have the definitive answers to these questions, but we do feel confident about the power of whole foods. Foods that are less processed retain more of their natural goodness, including fiber, vitamins, minerals and phytochemicals, and these marvelous nutrients are proven fighters against diabetes, hypertension, heart and blood vessel disease, obesity, Alzheimer's disease, osteoporosis and cancer. As helpful as vitamin and mineral supplements can be, no supplement will ever be able to provide the thousands of phytochemicals found in whole grains, vegetables, fruit, nuts and legumes.

and zinc) and phytochemicals (special health-promoting plant compounds). There are thousands of phytochemicals, and more are being discovered all the time. You may have heard of beta carotene (found in carrots) and lycopene (found in tomatoes). As scientists discover these compounds, manufacturers are quick to add them to foods and supplements. This creates many new options for consumers, but keep in mind that whole foods are still the most nourishing choice (see "A Whole Foods Approach," opposite).

Food Guides

Dietary reference intakes tell us how much of all the different nutrients we need. It would be difficult for individuals to keep track of all of these, however, so health authorities create food guides. Guides are found in most countries around the world. Food guides usually group foods according to which nutrients they contain, and tell people how many servings to have from each group. We have considered the United States Department of Agriculture's MyPlate and Health Canada's Eating Well with Canada's Food Guide in writing this book.

MyPlate divides food into five groups: grains, vegetables, fruits, dairy and protein. Canada's Food Guide divides food into four groups: grain products, vegetables and fruit, milk and alternatives, and meat and alternatives.

Food guides are changed every few years as new research becomes available. The most recent food guides, on which this book is based, emphasize lots of vegetables and fruit, whole grains, lean protein foods and low-fat dairy products and alternatives. We have adapted the food guides for people with diabetes and prediabetes, building menus that are very low in sodium, saturated fat and trans fat while providing a specific amount of calories, protein and carbohydrates.

You can find the USDA's MyPlate at www.choose myplate.gov and Health Canada's Eating Well with Canada's Food Guide at http://hc-sc.gc.ca/fn-an/food-guide-aliment/index-eng.php.

U.S. and Canadian Food Groups

MyPlate	Canada's Food Guide	Examples
Grains	Grain Products	Bread, cereal, pasta, rice, tortillas, roti, crackers
Vegetables Fruits	Vegetables and Fruit	Vegetables, fruits and their juices
Dairy	Milk and Alternatives	Milk, yogurt, soy milk, kefir, cheese
Protein	Meat and Alternatives	Meat, fish, poultry, tofu, legumes, nuts and nut butters

How Much Should I Eat?

As mentioned above, each of the macronutrients provides food energy, also known as calories or kilocalories. The amount of food energy we need is based on many things. Men generally need more calories than women, younger people need more calories than older people, and active people need more calories than sedentary people. Those who want to lose weight will need to eat 300 to 500 calories less than usual and/or increase their activity. Having an idea of your energy needs will help you decide how much to eat.

The wholesome, appetizing meals and snacks in this book are customizable to your energy needs. You can create your own combination of meals (and snacks, if needed), keeping in mind that:

- The daily menu plans (pages 148–155) provide 1600 calories per day (in three meals).
- Each breakfast provides about 400 calories.
- Each lunch provides about 550 calories.
- Each dinner provides about 650 calories.
- Snacks provide 100 to 200 calories each.

If you require only 1600 calories, the daily menu should be enough for you. If you need 1800 calories, add two 100-calorie snacks or one 200-calorie snack. If you need 2200 calories, add three snacks of 200 calories each. If you need more than this, you may decide to have more than one serving of a given recipe.

Energy Needs for Men (in Calories)

Age	Sedentary, Wanting Weight Loss	Sedentary, Wanting Weight Maintenance	Active, Wanting Weight Loss	Active, Wanting Weight Maintenance
19–30	2100	2500	2500	3000
31–50	1900	2300	2400	2900
51–70	1700	2100	2100	2600
71+	1600	2000	2000	2500

Note: The weight-loss columns are 400 to 500 calories less than the maintenance levels.

Energy Needs for Women (in Calories)

Age	Sedentary, Wanting Weight Loss	Sedentary, Wanting Weight Maintenance	Active, Wanting Weight Loss	Active, Wanting Weight Maintenance
19–30	1600	1900	1900	2300
31–50	1600	1800	1800	2200
51–70	1600	1700	1700	2100
71+	1600	1600	1600	2000

Note: The weight-loss columns are 300 to 400 calories less than the maintenance levels, except for women over 30. We encourage this group to follow the 1600-calorie menu plan, as it is nutritionally balanced, and burn calories through activity. If you wish to eat less than 1600 calories, use our meal plan but consult a Registered Dietitian or other nutrition professional for adjustments.

Another way to add calories is to have a glass of milk. One cup (250 mL) of 1% milk adds about 100 calories, along with vitamin D, calcium, protein, potassium and many other nutrients. This will help you meet the three servings of dairy products recommended by MyPlate and Canada's Food Guide (for adults over 50). Our menu provides two servings each day.

> If you are overweight, aim for a 5% to 10% weight loss. For example, a 200-pound (90 kg) person would lose 10 to 20 pounds (4.5 to 9 kg).

Do I Need Any Supplements?

For certain nutrients, and at certain times in your life, you may not be able to get the amount you need from the bounty of nature alone. While our menus are very nutritious, we remind readers that:

- Women capable of becoming pregnant should take 400 micrograms (mcg) of folic acid (also called folate) daily.

- Vegetarians and adults 50 years and older should eat foods that are fortified with vitamin B_{12} or take a supplement (see box, page 76).

- Calcium and vitamin D may be difficult to obtain in adequate amounts. See page 28 to determine your needs and learn what foods are sources of these nutrients.

These are general guidelines only. Ask your health care provider whether you should be taking any other supplements.

Calcium and Vitamin D: Are You Getting Enough?

Calcium and vitamin D are already well known for their importance in bone health, but recent research suggests they may also reduce the risk of chronic diseases such as cancer, cardiovascular disease, metabolic syndrome and type 2 diabetes (and vitamin D may also play a role in preventing type 1 diabetes). Calcium is found naturally in quite a few foods, and some foods are fortified with it. Vitamin D is less common in the diet, so it has been added to milk for almost 100 years. Despite this, it can sometimes be difficult to get enough calcium and vitamin D. We have included the charts opposite to help you find your requirements and learn what food sources will help you meet your needs.

If you are consuming milk and/or milk alternatives, it is reasonably easy to meet your calcium needs. That's because a typical healthy diet provides about 300 to 400 milligrams of calcium, and consuming two servings from the dairy or milk and alternatives group (cheese, yogurt, fortified soy milk) adds another 600 milligrams. This amount meets the needs of a woman up to age 50 or a man up to age 70. In keeping with our whole foods message, always try to get calcium from your diet. Our daily menus provide an average of 1100 milligrams. If you do need to supplement, use the smallest amount you can. Keep in mind that calcium is better absorbed in smaller doses, so take smaller amounts throughout the day rather than one or two large doses (for example, 250 milligrams taken twice a day will be better absorbed than one dose of 500 milligrams).

Vitamin D can be a bit more tricky to obtain. Historically, the sun was our main source of vitamin D. Even brief sun exposure creates many thousands of international units (IUs) in our skin. With today's concerns about skin cancer, we may spend very little time outdoors, and when we are outside, we wear sunscreen and keep covered up. Our vitamin D synthesis is limited.

Another problem is that vitamin D occurs naturally in very few foods. This has led manufacturers to fortify milk, soy milk and certain juices, yogurts, cheeses and cereals. If you think there is a shortfall in your vitamin D intake, and you are not inclined to be outdoors, supplements can be very useful. Vitamin D is very safe, so you *can* take more than the RDA. In fact, you may need to supplement with 1000 to 2000 IU of vitamin D per day if you:

- spend little time outdoors, use sunscreen, or wear clothing that covers most of the skin;

Did You Know?

Most North Americans spend 90% of their time indoors.

Calcium and Vitamin D Daily Requirements

	Age	Calcium (mg)*	Vitamin D (IU)*
Women	19–50	1000	600
	50+	1200	800
Men	19–70	1000	600
	70+	1200	800

* Recommended Dietary Allowance (RDA)

Food Sources of Calcium and Vitamin D

Food	Serving size	Calcium (mg)	Vitamin D (IU)
Cheese (18% M.F.)	2 oz (60 g)	542	7
Cottage cheese (1% M.F.)	½ cup (125 mL)	73	0
Kefir	¾ cup (175 g)	187	0
Milk (1% M.F.)	1 cup (250 mL)	322	102
Milk powder, skim	4 tbsp (60 mL)	302	103
Soy milk, fortified with calcium and vitamin D	1 cup (250 mL)	321	87
Yogurt (1% M.F.)	¾ cup (175 g)	332	0
Beans, chickpeas (garbanzo beans), red kidney, black	¾ cup (175 mL)	50–60	0
Beans, white	¾ cup (175 mL)	141	0
Eggs	2 large	50	56
Salmon, canned with bones	½ cup (125 mL)	190	580
Sardines, canned with bones	½ cup (125 mL)	300	46

- have dark skin;
- are over 50 (aging reduces the synthesis of vitamin D in the skin); and/or
- are overweight (fat cells store vitamin D, making it less available to the body).

In most of North America, supplementing with vitamin D is a particularly good idea during the fall and winter months. Not only are the sun's rays weak during a northern winter, but people are bundled up against the cold.

Vitamin D comes in two forms: D_2 (ergocalciferol) and D_3 (cholecalciferol). Both forms are used, but D_3 may be more effective. Ask your health care provider which type and what dose are right for you.

Did You Know?

Unless fortified with calcium and vitamins A and D, rice milk and almond milk are not suitable alternatives to milk and soy milk.

How to Read a Food Label

Food packaging has a lot of work to do. It has to tell you the name of the food, it has to list the ingredients, and it has to display the Nutrition Facts table. It might provide cooking instructions and a recipe. It might also make a nutrition claim, such as "reduced in calories" or "cholesterol-free." As a consumer, this means a lot of work for you, too. Reading all the package information and comparing brands makes for long shopping trips!

These tips will help you focus on what's important.

What NOT to Focus On

Nutrition Claims and Health Claims

Don't focus on health and nutrition claims. Some very healthy foods do not make any claims on their packages, yet they are worth buying. Read the Nutrition Facts table instead.

Nutrition claims are statements such as "source of fiber," "cholesterol-free" or "light." An example of a health claim is "a healthy diet low in saturated and trans fat may reduce the risk of heart disease." These bold claims, while approved by governing bodies such the United States Food and Drug Administration and Health Canada, are general statements that may only distract you from what is really important. For example, just because a soup claims to be "sodium reduced," that doesn't mean it is actually low in sodium. Even reduced-sodium soups can contain almost *half* your daily limit. You'll get better information from the Nutrition Facts table, which will tell you exactly how much sodium is in each serving.

% Daily Value (% DV)

Although the Nutrition Facts table contains a lot of useful information, % DV is something you can skip over. These figures are designed to help consumers find foods that contain less total fat, saturated fat and sodium, and foods that provide fiber, vitamin A, vitamin C, calcium and iron. The trouble is, the % DV is a generality that doesn't apply to everybody (or even most people). For example, the % DV for fiber is based on a goal of 25 grams per day. This is, indeed, your fiber requirement if you are a woman between the ages of 19 and 50 (see page 49). But if you're a man, or a woman over 50, the percentages are misleading. Let's say a particular food contains

5 grams of fiber. That would be listed as 20% DV. But a man aged 19 to 50 requires 38 grams of fiber per day, so he is not getting 20% of his fiber from that product.

A better plan is to learn what your personal daily requirements are for fiber, and what your daily limits are for total fat, saturated fat and sodium, then compare your needs to the amounts of each nutrient listed in grams or milligrams on the Nutrition Facts table. As for calcium, vitamin A and vitamin C, which have *only* % DV listed on the table, eat a balanced diet and you should do fine. The vitamins are covered if you eat plenty of vegetables and fruit, and two servings of dairy or soy products will provide a substantial amount of your calcium (as seen on page 29). Iron needs can be more individual, so if you have concerns about your iron intake, speak to your doctor or dietitian.

What TO Focus On

The Ingredients List

This is a list of what the product is made of, starting with the ingredient that is present in the highest amount and ending with the one that is present in the smallest amount. Know what main ingredient you're looking for in a product, then choose accordingly. Here are some specific examples:

- *For bread, cereal, crackers, pasta or rice:* The first ingredient should be a whole grain (whole-grain wheat, whole-grain oats, whole-grain brown rice, etc.). See the FAQ on page 61 for more information.

- *For canned or frozen fruit or fruit juice:* The first ingredient should be fruit, not sugar (believe it or not, there are many fruit imposters that are more sugar than fruit).

- *For yogurt:* The first ingredient should be milk or "milk ingredients," not sugar.

- *For margarine:* The first ingredient should be a liquid vegetable oil such as soy, canola or sunflower oil. Avoid margarines that list partially hydrogenated oils as the first ingredient.

> These days, grocery stores can be very large. Wear comfy shoes and don't shop on an empty stomach. If you plan on reading labels, you will need a little more time. Don't forget to bring your reading glasses!

The Nutrition Facts Table

The Nutrition Facts table is a feature that must be included on almost every packaged food sold in North America. Nutritionists, government agencies and food manufacturers debated for a long time before they settled on which nutrients to list on the Nutrition Facts table. With 50 vitamins and minerals and thousands of phytochemicals to choose from, this was no easy task. In the end, they decided the Nutrition Facts table must list the macronutrients (fat, carbohydrate and protein) and a few micronutrients (sodium, calcium, iron and vitamins A and C).

Within the macronutrients, some subheadings are provided. Under "Total Fat" ("Fat" in Canada), two specific types of fat, saturated fat and trans fat, are also listed. These are a portion of the total fat, not in addition to it (as suggested by the small indent in front of them). These fats are listed because we need to eat less of them. Foods that are primarily fat, such as margarine, may also list amounts of monounsaturated and polyunsaturated fat. Under "Total Carbohydrate" ("Carbohydrate" in Canada), two specific types of carb, dietary fiber and sugars, are also listed. These are a portion of the total carb and not in addition to it. Some tables have even more information, such as other types of fat (polyunsaturated omega-3s and -6s) or carbohydrate (sugar alcohols and types of fiber), or additional micronutrients.

American Table

Nutrition Facts

Serving Size 1 cup (228 g)

Amount Per Serving

Calories 250   **Calories** from Fat 110

	% Daily Value
Total Fat 12 g	**18%**
Saturated Fat 3 g	**15%**
Trans Fat 3 g	
Cholesterol 30 mg	**10%**
Sodium 470 mg	**20%**
Total Carbohydrate 31 g	**10%**
Dietary Fiber 0 g	**0%**
Sugars 5 g	
Protein 5 g	

Vitamin A 4%	•	Calcium 20%
Vitamin C 2%	•	Iron 4%

* Percent Daily Values are based on a 2,000 calorie diet. Your Daily Values may be higher or lower depending on your calorie needs.

		Calories	2,000	2,500
Total Fat	Less than		65 g	80 g
Sat Fat	Less than		20 g	25 g
Cholesterol	Less than		300 mg	300 mg
Sodium	Less than		2,400 mg	2,400 mg
Total Carbohydrate			300 g	375 g
Dietary Fiber			25 g	30 g

Canadian Table

Nutrition Facts

Per 250 mL (228 g)

Amount	% Daily Value
Calories 250	
Fat 12 g	18%
Saturated 3 g + Trans 3 g	15%
Cholesterol 30 mg	
Sodium 470 mg	20%
Carbohydrate 31 g	10%
Fibre 0 g	0%
Sugars 5 g	
Protein 5 g	

Vitamin A	4%	Vitamin C	20%
Calcium	2%	Iron	4%

These tables are not as daunting as they seem. Read on to understand each part of the Nutrition Facts table.

Serving Size

All nutrition information is for the serving size stated (per 1 cup/250 mL or 228 grams in the examples opposite). If you eat more or less of the food, you are getting more or less of the nutrients. For example, if you eat 2 cups (500 mL) or 456 grams of this food, you will be getting 62 grams of carbohydrate; 1/2 cup (125 mL) or 114 grams of the food would provide 16 grams of carbohydrate.

Calories

If you are counting calories, this information is important. And it will come in handy if you want to make up your own menus rather than following ours. Let's say you want to buy a frozen meal to take to work for lunch. Our lunches provide around 550 calories. If you find one at that level, you are on the right track. Or perhaps you are looking for another snack option. Our snacks provide 100 or 200 calories. You will find many commercial snack items that fall into that range.

Total Fat

To reduce unwanted calories, keep your daily fat intake to around 30% of your daily calories. One gram of fat has 9 calories, so:

- If you eat 1600 calories per day, no more than 480 calories should come from fat. This translates to 53 grams of fat.

Did You Know?

Foods without packaging, such as fresh produce and foods you scoop from bulk bins, will not have any nutrition information. That's okay. There are a few ways you can learn what you need to know:
- Look up the foods online.
- Buy the bulk food, but read the Nutrition Facts on a very similar packaged food.
- Browse through this book for a variety of nutrition information.

- If you eat 1800 calories per day, no more than 540 calories should come from fat. This translates to 60 grams of fat.
- If you eat 2000 calories per day, no more than 600 calories should come from fat. This translates to 66 grams of fat.

Saturated and Trans Fat

Keep trans fat to a minimum, preferably less than 2 grams per day. To promote heart health, limit your intake of saturated fat to a maximum of 7% of your daily calories. This means:

- If you eat 1600 calories per day, no more than 112 calories should come from saturated fat. This translates to 12 grams of saturated fat.
- If you eat 1800 calories per day, no more than 126 calories should come from saturated fat. This translates to 14 grams of saturated fat.
- If you eat 2000 calories per day, no more than 140 calories should come from saturated fat. This translates to 16 grams of saturated fat.

In the 1600-calorie example, the total daily fat intake is 53 grams. Of that, no more than 12 grams should be from saturated fat. If you follow these guidelines, the majority of the fat you eat will be the healthy unsaturated form.

Cholesterol

If you have high blood cholesterol (see page 70), keep dietary cholesterol to a maximum of 200 milligrams per day. Otherwise, 300 milligrams is an acceptable daily amount.

Sodium

Try to eat a maximum of 1500 milligrams per day. Minimally processed, natural foods, such as fresh or frozen vegetables and fruits, milk, yogurt, meat, fish, poultry, dried legumes, drained and rinsed canned legumes, rice, pasta and flour, have 0 to 150 milligrams of sodium per serving, so a whole foods approach is an excellent way to keep your sodium down. For more information on reducing sodium, see Step 6 (page 81).

To promote heart health, limit your intake of saturated fat to a maximum of 7% of your daily calories.

If you have high LDL cholesterol, limit saturated fat, trans fat and cholesterol. Read the Nutrition Facts label to find foods low in saturated fat (consider your 12-gram daily budget), trans fat (maximum 0.5 grams per serving) and cholesterol (maximum 200 milligrams per day).

Total Carbohydrate and Fiber

Subtract the amount of fiber from the amount of total carbohydrate to learn the amount of available carbohydrate (see sidebar, page 46, for more information). We recommend up to 75 grams of available carbohydrate per meal, with a maximum of 30 grams per snack.

Sugar

You've probably heard a lot of "rules" about sugar. We try not to focus too much on sugar, because carb counting and eating whole foods should protect you from excess. In any case, the Nutrition Facts table does not make the distinction between added sugars and naturally occurring sugars. This may lead you to mistakenly avoid healthy foods (such as fruit and milk), or to consume foods that are low in sugar but overly high in other carbohydrates (such as bagels).

If a fresh apple had a label, you would see that almost all the carbohydrate is from sugar: there is 15 grams of total carbohydrate per apple, of which 2 grams is fiber and 13 grams is sugar. This is typical of most fruits, but there's no need to avoid fruit because each serving contains the equivalent of about 3 teaspoons (15 mL) of sugar. That much sugar is really not excessive, plus you're getting the benefit of fruit's many nutrients (as opposed to the "empty calories" of most products made with added sugar). You do need to avoid *large* servings of fruit and fruit juice. But it's likely you would do so anyway, as the total carb would be too high to fit into your budget.

Did You Know?

A bagel can have up to 60 grams of carbohydrate, but most bagels have less than 5 grams of sugar. Don't fix on the low sugar value and think a bagel is a good choice. It uses up a carb budget very fast!

Did You Know?

If you drink juice, make sure it is "100% juice, no sugar added," or you will be paying for more sugar than juice.

Choose Breakfast Cereal Wisely

There are many, many cereal choices today. The best choices will be tasty, high in fiber and not too high in sugar. How high is too high? Here's a suggestion. Eat cereals that have 5 grams of sugar or less. This is an easy-to-remember figure that is equal to about 1 teaspoon (5 mL) of sugar (1 teaspoon actually holds 4 grams). If the cereal has dried fruit in it, aim for 10 grams of sugar or less. If you want fiber, look for a cereal with 5 grams or more, or mix a high-fiber cereal with a low-fiber one.

FAQ

Q: Healthy eating costs more. How can I afford it?

A. Depending on where you live, healthy eating can indeed cost more. People who live in remote areas, or in neighborhoods without many grocery stores, will agree that good food is expensive. It can be very tempting to buy fast food instead; it appears to be a bargain. In truth, empty calories will cost you dearly in more ways than one.

If you are really having trouble affording food, see if you qualify for an income supplement. In some states and provinces, people with diabetes and prediabetes get a small allowance. It is worth looking into. You can also stretch your healthy food dollars with these tips:

- Plan your menus so you buy what you need and don't forget to use what you purchased.
- Read flyers to find good deals.
- Shop from a list and avoid impulse buys.
- Use coupons only for things you actually want to buy. Don't buy something just because you have a coupon for it.
- Shop the perimeter of the store, where the fresh produce, bakery, meat and dairy counters are found. The inner aisles, which hold all the prepared foods, are where money can quickly fly out of your pocket.
- Choose store or no-name brands rather than national brands.
- Only buy in bulk if you know you will be able to use the food up before it expires. Consider splitting bulk purchases with friends or family.
- Purchase bricks of cheese rather than grated, and whole fruits and vegetables rather than chopped. Buy whole chickens if you are handy with a knife. The more a food has been prepared in advance, the more expensive it is, so save the money and do the work of grating and chopping yourself.
- Buy the ingredients for homemade cookies and muffins: they cost much less than purchased baked goods, and they're very easy to make from scratch.
- Be careful not to waste your purchases. Keep track of the "use by" dates and plan your meals accordingly.
- Serve smaller portions of meat (one-quarter of the plate is plenty).
- If you cook more than you can eat at one meal, refrigerate or freeze the leftovers for an easy option another day.
- See if your city or town has a food recovery program or low-cost grocery. These shops sell food at bargain prices because it is close to expiry or has slightly damaged packaging.

Milk is another example. Milk has 12 grams of carbohydrate per 1 cup (250 mL), all of which is from sugar. Again, 3 teaspoons (15 mL) of sugar is not that much, considering the other great nutrients milk provides. Avoid drinking *too much* milk, however, as that can raise your blood glucose and lead to weight gain. Sticking to your total carbohydrate budget for each meal will help keep your milk portions sensible.

Protein

If you are looking for a high-protein cereal, energy bar, prepared/frozen meal or protein powder, keep in mind that 7 grams of protein is equal to the amount of protein in 1 ounce (30 g) of meat. A high-protein snack should therefore have at least 7 grams of protein (and no more than 30 grams of carbohydrate). A prepared meal should have at least 14 grams of protein. A protein powder (to stir into cereal or a smoothie) should have at least 7 grams of protein per serving. If there is carbohydrate in the powder, remember to count it.

Use Food Labels to Choose Wisely

It takes time to understand what's really in our food, but it is time well invested. Use the information on food labels to find foods that are higher in fiber and lower in sodium, saturated fat and trans fat. Choose them for your meals and snacks.

It takes time to understand what's really in our food, but it is time well invested.

Food labeling — especially the ingredient list and the Nutrition Facts table — is an indispensable tool for choosing well. Take a few minutes to compare products. When you pick the healthier option, it's good for you *and* more bang for your grocery buck.

Chapter 3

A 10-Step Approach to Preventing and Managing Diabetes

> **You really can** have a positive impact on your health, even one step at a time.

Welcome to an exciting opportunity to improve your health. Our 10-step plan is a carefully organized guide to nutrition, activity, stress management and sleep. Each step gives you specific directions and provides the rationale and research so you can see the value in it. The steps are designed to help prevent and manage diabetes, but will also help with other health conditions, such as high blood pressure, high cholesterol and obesity. Do not feel you have to do all the steps at once; start with the one you feel you will be most successful with, then build from there. If you need help implementing the steps, SMART goal setting (see page 135) will guide you.

You really can have a positive impact on your health, even one step at a time. Viewing the body as a whole helps us realize that doing good in one area has direct results in another. What if you started sleeping better? That would translate into more energy and perhaps ready you for more activity. What if you developed some healthy stress management techniques? That could result in lower blood glucose readings. If blood pressure is your main concern, reduce your sodium and up your vegetables and fruit. You may find you lose weight as well.

Good health is a journey, not a destination. Don't expect yourself to be perfect as you adapt to a new lifestyle. Give yourself plenty of praise for the good you do, and don't waste time feeling bad when you get off track. Tomorrow is another day and another opportunity. Take it!

Step 1: Eat Three Meals a Day, Spread 4 to 6 Hours Apart

Running late, George skipped breakfast. He was busy at work, so he missed his coffee breaks and just had time to grab a quick sandwich at lunch. By supper he was starved! A big meal left him too full to do much except relax in front of the TV. A few evening snacks crept in (those commercials are so effective!), and then it was time for bed. The next morning, he wasn't very hungry, so he passed on breakfast again.

What's wrong with this picture? Everything!

Let's start at the beginning. Skipping breakfast is one of the most common mistakes people make. By skipping breakfast, George lost out on an important opportunity to give his body energy, putting it into a semi-starvation state, which can contribute to weight gain. With nothing for breakfast and only a sandwich for lunch, he likely wasn't able to get the full number of recommended servings from each food group for the day. He didn't take time to enjoy his food at lunch. He allowed himself to get overly hungry and ate too much at supper. He ate unhealthy snacks despite having a large meal. He may have experienced low, then high, blood glucose. He was unable to take advantage of the second meal effect (see box, page 40). Overall, he probably didn't feel very well. His final mistake was to skip breakfast the next day!

People all over the globe eat three or more times per day for a reason: humans thrive on this meal pattern! By eating regularly, we're less likely to eat too much at any meal, and every meal is an opportunity to include foods from each food group. For people with diabetes, regular meals prevent lows and highs.

The timing of meals is also important. Long gaps between meals can make you very hungry and may contribute to low blood glucose. Start with breakfast, then try to eat a meal every four to six hours after that.

> Eating is a pleasure. Why not do it often?

> Measure your blood glucose before a meal and two hours after to understand how food affects you. See page 126 for information on blood glucose self-testing.

If you eat a proper meal in the morning, your blood glucose, blood fats and insulin levels will be favorable after that meal, and also after the next one!

Have Three Squares a Day

A "square meal" is an old-fashioned term for a satisfying meal. Make meals satisfying by eating foods from all of the food groups. This is also known as a balanced meal. You will find many examples of balanced meals in this book, and you can create your own by combining at least three of the food groups at each meal. For example, if you have a turkey sandwich on whole-grain bread, a glass of milk and an apple for lunch, you've created a balanced meal with a meat, a grain, a dairy product and a fruit.

FAQ

Q. I don't like eating breakfast. What can I do?

A. Start small. You don't have to have a balanced meal. Think of quick and tasty items from any of the food groups:

- a slice of whole-grain toast, a whole-grain English muffin or a homemade muffin;
- a banana, an apple, half a grapefruit or $\frac{1}{2}$ cup (125 mL) orange juice;
- a boiled egg or a handful of nuts;
- a single-serving container of yogurt or a slice of cheese.

Have something from one or two of the groups. There. You are now a breakfast eater! Eventually, aim for at least three of the food groups.

Also, be sure not to eat too much for supper or your bedtime snack. Waking up hungry will inspire you to eat!

What About Snacks?

While three daily meals is the minimum number of times to eat, having between-meal snacks or six smaller meals can also work well. There are no hard and fast rules, but the following tips might help you determine which pattern is better for you.

Try eating three meals:

- If you only need 1600 to 1700 calories in a day (see chart, page 26). When you don't need to eat a lot of food, it might be difficult to break down your requirements into many meals and snacks. Each meal becomes very small and may not be satisfying.

- If you have a tendency to choose less healthy snacks. If snacking might get you into trouble, it's better to concentrate on three healthy meals

- If you are not used to eating regularly.

- If you have difficulty controlling portions once you start eating.

- If work or other commitments interfere with frequent meal breaks.

Try eating four or more times:

- If you need 1800 calories or more in a day. The more you eat at one time, the higher your blood glucose will be. Protect yourself by being careful not to overeat. Try to stick to 45 to 75 grams of carb at each meal (see Step 2, page 44). If you are still hungry, eat more vegetables at the meal and plan to have a snack in two to three hours.

- If you get full easily. If your stomach can't hold very much, plan for smaller meals and more frequent snacks.

- If you have plenty of opportunities to eat. Eating five or six times a day requires a flexible schedule.

Snacks help you stay fueled from meal to meal, especially that long stretch between lunch to dinner. Have a mid-afternoon snack so you don't come home ravenous.

Did You Know?

If you are testing your blood glucose before a meal, make sure your last snack was at least 2½ hours before; otherwise, the result may be elevated.

The Value of the Family Meal

Families come in many different sizes and shapes, but these days most of them have something in common: they are time-stressed, with adults handling jobs and commutes and children involved in after-school activities. So often,

Feeding yourself and your children well *today* is diabetes prevention in action.

what should be the dinner hour is the "running to baseball/soccer/hockey/ballet/swimming" hour! In some cases, family members rarely or never eat together.

New research provides strong encouragement to eat as a family, showing that children and teens who eat with adults not only eat more nutritiously, consuming more vegetables and fruit and drinking more milk, but also have a healthier weight and relationship with food (and fewer instances of eating disorders); engage less often in risky behaviors such as smoking, drinking or taking drugs; do better academically; have improved communication skills; and are more likely to share their "trials and tribulations" with their caregivers.

If there is diabetes in your family, eating healthfully becomes even more important. Diabetes is passed from generation to generation, but good eating habits can reduce this risk. Every person is the sum of inherited parts from two parents. Beyond the way we look, our very health, present and future, is affected by our parents. But having an inherited tendency toward high blood pressure, diabetes or obesity does not mean this condition is inevitable for you or your family. Putting the right ingredients into the body can alter the future. Feeding yourself and your children well *today* is diabetes prevention in action.

Mini Gardeners

Consider growing some vegetables at home. Even a small tomato plant on the windowsill can inspire kids to eat better — especially if they helped with planting and watering.

Mini Chefs

Let children help prepare dinner. Young kids can wash vegetables and separate broccoli into "trees." Older kids can peel, cut and mash (or "smash") the potatoes.

FAQ

Q. My family doesn't like my "healthy" food, but I don't want to cook two meals. How can I make everyone happy?

A. Good things take time, so give your family a chance to get on board rather than coming home one day and throwing out all the foods that don't fit into your new lifestyle! Start by making less healthy meals better. Add frozen vegetables to canned soup or add a higher-fiber cereal to a lower-fiber one. Make pizza at home, so you can use lower-fat mozzarella and more vegetables as toppings. Use lean or extra-lean ground beef to make hamburgers and serve them on whole-grain buns. Make your own chicken strips and fries with our recipes (pages 274 and 337). Always pack a vegetable in lunch bags and serve one or two types at dinner. If you eat at a fast-food restaurant, have a side salad rather than fries or onion rings, or buy one order for everyone to share. Have milk instead of soda, and a single burger rather than a double (hint: no supersizing!).

Buy a variety of healthy cookbooks or borrow them from the library. Choose those with lots of inspiring pictures. Let the kids help with food preparation. See if your local community college has diabetes-friendly or heart-smart cooking courses for adults and children.

As you try new foods, not everything will be a winner. But don't give up. Children tend to dislike new things but often come around after a few attempts. You may still need to compromise. Fortunately, it is easy to buy two kinds of milk or two kinds of cereal. And buying a variety of vegetables and fruits means everyone gets their favorite sometimes.

Reduce the amount of junk food you keep in the house. You can even stop buying it completely. Go out for treats on special occasions instead.

Value yourself as an individual and as a family member. Your health is vital. Furthermore, chances are very high that members of your family, especially your children, are at an increased risk for diabetes. So ask yourself: Is it really okay to put them in danger just because change can be difficult? Is it okay to risk your own health? We didn't think so.

Tips for success:

- It may be difficult to eat together every night, but commit to several nights each week. Try hard to stick to the schedule. On nights when some family members are missing, the remainder can still eat together. Even two people make a family!

- If you can't make dinner work at all, try sharing another meal. For example, if one parent consistently misses the family dinner, let the children eat their bedtime snack with that parent's (late) dinner.

It has been said, "Meals eaten alone lack the condiment of company." If you're single, here are some ways to bring more people to your table:

- Join a community kitchen. Not only do you cook and eat with a group, but you usually get to bring home meals for the week.

- See if your local community center or faith-based organization has any regular meal events. If you are a senior, these may also include a movie, a speaker or another attraction. A nominal fee may be required.

- Invite a friend or two over, or take turns at each other's homes. You might even expand this to a weekly cooking club. Cook together or have potluck. Try different ethnic cuisines for variety.

- During the meal, make sure everyone gets a chance to talk. Ask about each person's day, and discuss school, work or current events. Dinner table conversation gives you a chance to monitor your kids' friends, their progress in school and other challenges or successes they are experiencing.

- Keep the conversation positive. Never use mealtimes to dish out punishment or air grievances.

- Turn the TV off, and keep cell phones and other devices away from the dinner table.

- Involve your children in meal planning, preparation and cleanup.

The Bottom Line

Regular meals are the key to optimal nutrition, a positive relationship with food and good glucose control. Start each day by eating breakfast, then spread your meals four to six hours apart. Add between-meal snacks if needed. Eat meals with family or friends as often as possible.

Step 2: Limit Carbohydrate to 45 to 75 Grams per Meal

Most of what we eat, in North America and around the world, is carbohydrate. Whenever you have a bowl of cereal and milk, a sandwich and a piece of fruit, or a plate of spaghetti, you are eating carbohydrate. Because our diet contains many carbohydrate-containing foods, carbohydrate is considered a macronutrient, along with protein and fat (see page 23).

Our bodies break carbohydrate down into glucose. That's right: many of the foods you eat eventually increase your blood glucose levels. But that's no reason to avoid all carbs. Instead, it's important to learn to eat the right amount.

There are three main types of carbohydrate:

- *Sugar* is found in fruit, milk, table sugar, honey and sweet treats (candies, pies, cake, soft drinks). It is considered a "simple" carbohydrate because sugar is made of single units or very short chains of glucose and other small compounds.

- *Starch* is found in bread, rice, oatmeal, pasta, potatoes and flour. It is considered a "complex" carbohydrate because it is made of long chains of glucose.

- *Fiber* is found in fruit, vegetables, nuts, legumes and wholesome starchy foods. It is also a complex carb, but humans do not digest fiber into glucose because it is made of very long and intricate chains of glucose.

As you can see in the chart below, each of the food groups provides carbohydrate.

> **Many of the** foods you eat eventually increase your blood glucose levels. But that's no reason to avoid all carbs. Instead, it's important to learn to eat the right amount.

Where to Find Carbohydrate

MyPlate	Canada's Food Guide	Type of Carb
Grains	Grain Products	• Starch and fiber (in breads, cereals, pasta and rice) • Added sugar (in sweetened cereals, breads and muffins)
Vegetables Fruits	Vegetables and Fruit	• Natural sugar and fiber • Added sugar (in sweetened juices)
Dairy	Milk and Alternatives	• Natural sugar (in milk, soy milk and yogurt) • Added sugar (in sweetened milk, soy milk and yogurt)
Protein	Meat and Alternatives	• Starch and fiber (in legumes and nuts)

Counting Carbs

Because much of what we eat is carbohydrate, and because carbohydrate becomes glucose in your blood, it is very important to eat the right amount. The more carbohydrate you eat, the higher your blood glucose can rise, so we suggest a range of 45 to 75 grams of carbohydrate for meals and 15 to 30 grams for snacks. Our daily menus (see page 148) provide exactly that! But when you're designing a meal yourself, you'll need to count carbs, using simple addition to help you figure out how much carbohydrate you are eating.

Many basic foods — a piece of fruit, a slice of bread, 1 cup (250 mL) of milk — contain about 15 grams of available

> Enjoy seven servings of vegetables and fruit a day.

Did You Know?

Because fiber does not raise blood glucose, as sugars and starches do, you can subtract fiber from total carbohydrate. This leaves the available carbohydrate (also known as "net carb") — the amount of carbohydrate that will actually affect your blood glucose level. Our daily menus contain about 210 grams of total carbohydrate, 30 grams of fiber and 180 grams of available carbohydrate. Breakfast provides about 45 grams, lunch provides about 60 grams and dinner provides about 75 grams of available carbohydrate.

carbohydrate (see "Did You Know," at left), so it's fairly easy to build a meal that contains 45 to 75 grams. For example, you could have a sandwich with two slices of bread (30 grams), a piece of fruit (15 grams) and a glass of milk (15 grams), for a total of 60 grams. When you're assembling your dinner plate, you can limit your portion of starch to 30 to 45 grams by keeping it to one-quarter of the plate, with your protein choice on another quarter and vegetables occupying fully half the plate. Add a glass of milk and a fruit for dessert, and you're at 60 to 75 grams of carbs for the meal.

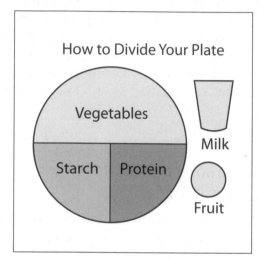

How to Divide Your Plate

Here are some examples of foods that contain 15 grams of available carbohydrate:

- 1 slice of bread
- ½ English muffin
- ½ pita
- ¾ cup (175 mL) cold cereal
- ¾ cup (175 mL) cooked oatmeal
- ½ cup (125 mL) cooked pasta
- ½ cup (125 mL) mashed potato
- ⅓ cup (75 mL) cooked rice
- 1 medium apple or orange
- 1 small banana
- 1 small grapefruit
- 15 cherries
- 2 cups (500 mL) strawberries
- 1 cup (250 mL) blueberries
- 1 cup (250 mL) chopped melon

If You Need More Calories

We have designed our menus to provide a maximum of 1600 calories and 45 to 75 grams of available carbohydrate per meal. As discussed on page 26, you can add snacks if you need more food. For example, add three 200-calorie snacks if you need 2200 calories. If you require even more than that, you will have to eat larger meals. This may increase your carbohydrate to 90 grams or more, and will, of course, increase your fat, saturated fat and sodium intake as well. See how this affects your appetite, weight, glucose control and overall sense of well-being. If you have questions or concerns, speak to a Registered Dietitian, your physician or another qualified health professional.

Did You Know?

You will probably find that balanced meals and healthy snacks use up your carb budget quite easily. If you want a treat, however, keep in mind that artificially sweetened foods (see page 56) have fewer carbs, as do treats made with less sugar. We have given you several recipes to try. There are also many bars, cookies and portioned snacks that are between 15 and 30 grams of carb (and 100 to 200 calories). These fun foods add variety to your menu. For more ideas, see our snack lists on pages 162–164.

- 1 cup (250 mL) milk, buttermilk or soy milk
- ¾ cup (175 mL) plain yogurt
- ½ cup (125 mL) evaporated milk or sweetened soy milk
- ½ cup (125 mL) yogurt beverage or ice cream
- 3 gingersnap cookies
- 1 granola bar (2 oz/56 g)
- 3 cups (750 mL) popcorn
- 10 potato chips
- 1 tbsp (15 mL) sugar, syrup, honey or jam

Source: Adapted from *Beyond the Basics*, Canadian Diabetes Association.

Using the Nutrition Facts Table

Did You Know?

You can also find carb information in smartphone apps, nutrient composition books, restaurant brochures, computer software and on the Internet.

Most packaged foods include a Nutrition Facts table, where you can find the amount of total carbohydrate, sugar and fiber provided by that food (see page 31 for more information on the Nutrition Facts table). It is very important to note the serving size, which may be given as a number of pieces (for crackers, cookies or bread), as a weight (in ounces or grams) or as a volume (in fluid ounces, cups or milliliters). The nutrition information on the table is specific to that serving size. If you eat more or less, you are eating more or fewer grams of carbohydrate.

Look at some of the packages in your pantry. A store-bought muffin can have 45 grams of carbohydrate, a bagel 60 grams and a cinnamon bun 80 grams! You might be surprised to find that potato chips have 25 grams of carbohydrate in just 15 chips. Who ever ate only 15 chips?

Many restaurants and fast-food chains now provide nutrition information on their websites or menu boards. They are to be applauded for this. It is an eye-opener, however, to discover a typical fast-food meal, with a burger, large fries and a milkshake, can provide over 200 grams of carbohydrate. Other surprises: a pancake breakfast has over 100 grams, and a large sub with a can of cola has 90 grams. Ice cream treats range from a reasonable 25 grams (for a small cone) to a whopping 130 grams (for a large chocolate sundae served in a waffle bowl). It seems the sky's the limit for carbs. But studies show having access to nutrition information is starting to make consumers choose more sensibly.

Fiber Facts

As mentioned earlier, fiber's intricate structure is resistant to our digestive juices, so we don't break it down into glucose. Therefore, higher-fiber foods raise blood glucose less. And because fiber-rich foods are chewy, they slow down our rate of eating, helping us feel full after less food. High-fiber foods also tend to be whole foods. An apple, for example, provides 2 grams of fiber, while apple juice has none. The apple will raise blood glucose less, yet is more filling.

The highest-fiber breads have 5 grams of fiber per slice, and 15 grams of total carbohydrate.

There are several types of fiber, but many people are familiar with the terms "soluble" and "insoluble." Generally speaking, soluble fiber slows the digestion of food, which stops your blood glucose from spiking while keeping you feeling full. It also reduces the absorption of cholesterol from your food. Soluble fiber is found in oats, barley, apples, strawberries, citrus fruits, legumes, okra, eggplant and psyllium-enriched cereals. Insoluble fiber (which used to be called "roughage") performs lower in the digestive tract. Bran is the best example. The fiber in bran (found in whole-grain breads, cereals and pastas) attracts water to the stool, making it softer, bulkier and easier to pass.

You do not need a specific proportion of soluble fiber versus insoluble fiber in your diet. Instead, eat a variety of high-fiber foods to enjoy all the benefits of both types.

How Much Fiber Do I Need?

Most people eat between 11 and 14 grams of fiber each day. But how much do we really need?

Daily Fiber Requirements

	Age	Fiber*
Women	19–50	25 g
	51+	21 g
Men	19–50	38 g
	51+	30 g

*Acceptable Intake (AI)

Meanwhile, research suggests that people with diabetes can benefit from eating up to 50 grams of fiber per day!

Our menus deliver 30 grams of fiber in the 1600-calorie level, by using whole foods such as vegetables and fruit (with their skins), nuts, seeds, legumes and whole-grain products. Some recipes receive an extra fiber punch through the addition of oat bran, wheat bran, hemp or chia.

Look at the chart on page 50 to estimate how much fiber you are eating now. If following our menus will mean an increase for you, plan to increase slowly, as it can take time for the body to adjust to a higher-fiber menu. For example, keep eating your usual bread or cereal until you are comfortable with the rest of the menu. You may also want to drink more fluid, because high-fiber foods are processed better when accompanied by liquid.

Increase your fiber intake slowly, as it can take time for your body to adjust to a higher-fiber menu.

Higher-fiber foods raise blood glucose less. And because fiber-rich foods are chewy, they slow down our rate of eating, helping us feel full after less food.

Did You Know?

Whole grains have three edible parts: the bran (which provides fiber), the endosperm (with starch) and the germ (with fat, vitamins and minerals). Wheat is the most familiar grain; others include corn, rice, oats, rye and barley. Expand your horizons to include a variety of whole grains in your diet. Studies show whole grains are associated with improved insulin sensitivity, lower LDL cholesterol and triglycerides (see page 72) and a reduced risk of obesity, diabetes and hypertension.

To add fiber, nutrients, texture and taste, our recipes use whole wheat flour, wheat germ, old-fashioned (large-flake) oats and oat bran, among other high-fiber ingredients.

Sources of Fiber

Food	Fiber (g)	Total Carbohydrate (g)
Grains		
1 slice whole-grain bread, $\frac{1}{2}$ whole-grain pita or $\frac{1}{4}$ stone-ground bagel $\frac{1}{2}$ cup (125 mL) cooked whole wheat pasta $\frac{3}{4}$ cup (175 mL) oat bran or $\frac{1}{2}$ cup (125 mL) corn bran or shredded wheat cereal	2 or more	15
1 slice white bread, $\frac{1}{2}$ white pita or $\frac{1}{4}$ white bagel $\frac{1}{2}$ cup (125 mL) cooked white pasta or $\frac{1}{3}$ cup (75 mL) cooked rice $\frac{3}{4}$ cup (175 mL) cream of wheat cereal, $\frac{2}{3}$ cup (150 mL) toasted O or crisped rice cereal or $\frac{1}{2}$ cup (125 mL) corn flakes	up to 2	15
Fruits		
4 apricots 1 large peach or nectarine, or 1 medium apple, orange or pear 2 cups (500 mL) blackberries, raspberries or strawberries 1 cup (250 mL) blueberries or cubed papaya	2 or more	15
2 plums 1 small banana or grapefruit $\frac{1}{2}$ mango 1 cup (250 mL) grapes or cubed cantaloupe $\frac{1}{2}$ cup (125 mL) applesauce or fruit cocktail	1 to 2	15
Legumes and Vegetables		
$\frac{1}{2}$ cup (125 mL) cooked legumes (lentils, kidney beans, pinto beans)	5 or more	15
1 cup (250 mL) Brussels sprouts	6	5 or less
1 cup (250 mL) corn kernels, peas or chopped beets, carrots, parsnips or mixed vegetables (carrots, corn, green beans, lima beans, peas) $\frac{1}{2}$ cup (125 mL) lima beans	2 or more	15
6 spears asparagus 1 cup (250 mL) shredded cabbage, lettuce or spinach $\frac{1}{2}$ cup (125 mL) chopped broccoli, cauliflower, celery, green beans, tomatoes or zucchini	1 to 2	5 or less

How to Fit in Fiber

It may sound challenging to eat 25 to 38 grams of fiber each day, but it is actually fairly easy. This menu shows you how:

Meal	Food	Fiber (g)
Breakfast	1 Morning Glory Muffin (page 348)	4
	¼ cup (60 mL) cottage cheese	0
	½ cup (125 mL) diced honeydew melon	1
	1 serving Mocha Latte (page 182)	2
Lunch	2 Chickpea Patties with Tahini Parsley Sauce (page 306)	5
	½ whole wheat pita (7 inches/18 cm)	2
	2 cups (500 mL) tossed salad with dressing	2
	1 cup (250 mL) blueberries	3
	⅓ cup (75 mL) nonfat plain Greek yogurt	0
Supper	1 serving Pork Stuffed with Apple and Bread Crumbs (page 260)	2
	1 serving Mushroom Barley Pilaf (page 313)	5
	1 serving Roasted Butternut Squash with Onion and Sage (page 334)	3
	½ cup (125 mL) steamed green beans topped with 1 tbsp (15 mL) toasted slivered almonds	2
	1 cup (250 mL) grapes	1
Total		**32**

Fiber, Available Carb and Hypoglycemia

People taking insulin or diabetes tablets may be at risk of hypoglycemia when they start eating more fiber or less available carbohydrate.

- *If you are matching insulin to carbohydrate intake:*
  Our daily menus provide about 45 grams of available carbohydrate for breakfast, 60 grams for lunch and 75 grams for dinner. If you want more specifics, look up each recipe to see exactly how much carbohydrate and fiber there is per serving. Subtract the fiber from the total carb, or you may end up taking more insulin than you need. This will cause hypoglycemia.

Consumer Beware: Media Hype and Health Claims

Some of you will remember the oat bran craze of the 1980s, which began when it was found that eating oat bran could lower blood cholesterol levels. Oat bran was added to everything, even unhealthy foods, in hopes of attracting consumers. Then, after all the hype, one study found oat bran less effective than previously shown, and oat bran's time in the spotlight ended.

This experience confused consumers and made many people mistrustful of nutrition advice. The media and marketers were to blame, as they overstated oat bran's effectiveness in an attempt to sell products. That's a shame, because oat bran, as a source of soluble fiber, was — and still is — a wholesome and effective way to reduce blood cholesterol levels. (Oat bran potato chips, not so much!)

Nowadays, it seems we hear of at least one nutrition "breakthrough" every day, on the Internet, on the radio or on TV. Our best advice? Don't believe everything you hear. Wait a long while before jumping on any bandwagons. Most are just a flash in the pan. The tried and true steps to good health — eating a variety of whole foods, including plenty of vegetables and fruit, exercising and getting enough sleep — will never go out of style.

> **The tried and true steps to good health — eating a variety of whole foods, including plenty of vegetables and fruit, exercising and getting enough sleep — will never go out of style.**

- *If you are taking a set dose of insulin at meals (with good glucose control):* Eating more fiber or less available carbohydrate than usual can reduce your blood glucose. Test yourself before and two hours after a meal to judge the effects. If you are experiencing hypoglycemia, ask your health care provider about reducing your insulin dose.

- *If your diabetes is well controlled on the diabetes tablets glyburide/glibenclamide (Diaßeta), gliclazide (Diamicron), glimepiride (Amaryl), glipizide (Glucotrol), repaglinide (Prandin, GlucoNorm) or nateglinide (Starlix):* Eating more fiber or less available carbohydrate than usual can reduce your blood glucose. Test yourself before and two hours after a meal to judge the effects. If you are experiencing hypoglycemia, ask your health care provider if you need to reduce or stop these tablets.

If you use insulin or the above diabetes medications, always carry glucose tablets. Treat hypoglycemia promptly. See page 130 for more information.

What About Sugar?

Most people enjoy the sweet taste of sugar, and sugar in moderation is safe. Even people with prediabetes and diabetes can consume sugar and sweet foods if they wish. As with many things, the key is how much.

One teaspoon (5 mL) of sugar has just 4 grams of carbohydrate, and a tablespoon (15 mL) of jam has about 15 grams. But consider this: a 12-ounce (355 mL) can of cola has a whopping 10 teaspoons (50 mL) of sugar — that's 40 grams of carbohydrate! This is a lot of carbohydrate, virtually an entire meal's worth. Most people are entirely unaware of the carb (and calorie) cost of beverages. We have devoted an entire step to this issue (see Step 7, page 88).

The chart below shows how added sugar translates into added calories and carbs.

Sugar can be enjoyed as part of a healthy diet. Understanding the carbohydrate "cost" of using sugar helps put it in perspective. A little is fine, a lot is not.

Added Sugar = Added Calories and Carbs

Iced tea, unsweetened
12 oz (355 mL)

Iced tea, sweetened
12 oz (355 mL)

0 calories	160 calories
0 g carb	40 g carb
0 g sugar	40 g sugar

Plain oatmeal
1/2 cup (125 mL)

Flavored oatmeal

80 calories	120 calories
20 g carb	30 g carb
1 g sugar	11 g sugar

Plain popcorn
3 cups (750 mL)

Caramel corn
3 cups (750 mL)

90 calories	480 calories
18 g carb	90 g carb
0 g sugar	60 g sugar

Q. Does eating sugar cause diabetes?

A. The short answer is no. The long answer is… maybe. Any food that contributes to extra body weight could be implicated as a cause of diabetes. When people carry extra weight, their insulin does not work well, and that sets the stage for diabetes.

Sugar by Any Other Name

For the most part, we have used real sugar, honey, pure maple syrup or molasses to sweeten recipes where needed. We have limited the portion and counted the carbs. Occasionally, we have instead called for artificial sweeteners to add sweetness without carbohydrate. All of this is to offer you variety while demonstrating that many foods can fit into a sensible menu. What we don't want is for you to think sugar is forbidden, or that one sugar is better than another. Just as fancy salts (kosher, Himalayan, sea salt) are all sources of sodium, sugars are sugars, and are apt to raise your blood glucose if you overdo it. For example, there has been a lot of debate about high-fructose corn syrup. Scientists have been questioning whether this sweetener is a particularly unhealthy type of sugar. Some feel it contributes more to obesity and heart disease than would be expected. Because of this concern, some beverage manufacturers are switching to using regular table sugar (sucrose). Does that make sugar-sweetened beverages more healthy? We hope you agree with us: no. Ten teaspoons of sugar, from any source, is a large amount of empty calories, and a terrible way to spend your carb budget!

Agave syrup (also known as agave nectar) is a new player on the sugar scene. Because it has a lower glycemic index than sugar (see Step 3, page 58), it may raise blood glucose less. Interestingly, 60% to 90% of agave syrup is fructose. If health concerns about fructose turn out to be legitimate, it would be wise to limit agave syrup, too. (Note: the major sugar in fruit is fructose, but we are not trying to imply that fruit is unhealthy. We are simply saying that *any* sugar that is eaten in excess, whether as milk, fruit or added sugar, is a problem.)

Did You Know?

People with diabetes were once told to avoid sweets entirely. However, you can enjoy them occasionally; the key is to monitor total carbs when eating dessert with your meal. Simply sub in a small portion of dessert in place of bread, pasta, rice or crackers with a similar amount of carbohydrate. Rather than selecting empty-calorie sweets, choose a dessert that is low in fat and contains fiber and other valuable nutrients.

FAQ

Q. Since I developed diabetes, I've been using all "brown" foods: whole-grain bread and flour, brown rice and multigrain pasta. Is brown sugar a good choice too?

A. Great job for eating more whole grains! But there are exceptions to every rule. Brown sugar is only brown because it contains molasses. And it is no better than white sugar when it comes to its effect on your blood glucose. Both white sugar and brown sugar have 4 grams of carbohydrate and 16 calories per teaspoon (5 mL).

Sugar Alcohols

Sugar alcohols are yet another player at the sweetener table. These are not alcohols in the usual sense — rather, the term refers to the sweetener's chemical structure. Sugar alcohols include maltitol, xylitol, sorbitol, mannitol and others with the "ol" ending (as opposed to sugars, which end in "ose"). Sugar alcohols are used to sweeten "no added sugar" candies or baked goods, sometimes in combination with other sugars or artificial sweeteners. You can also buy granulated xylitol to sweeten foods at home.

Did You Know?

If you are matching insulin to carb intake, it is wise to subtract sugar alcohols from the total carb, as you would fiber.

FAQ

Q. How can I handle my cravings for sweets?

A. First of all, make sure to eat three balanced meals a day. Eat your meals slowly. Drink plenty of fluids. Be sure you are getting enough sleep and managing your stress. Taking care of yourself will reduce your cravings. Having said that, it is okay to have a treat. Have a small portion and don't feel guilty about it. Share a portion if that will help you eat less. Enjoy your treat by eating it slowly and not sneaking it! Try to eat it during the day, so you have time to burn off the calories with some exercise. Why not walk or ride your bike to the ice cream store? You could also count the carb in your treat and reduce the rest of your carb for that meal. If a small portion of your favorite treat does not satisfy you, there may be issues that are interfering with your fullness signals. See Step 8 (page 92) for more information.

Did You Know?

Diet soft drinks have been the topic of several research studies. Scientists report that some people gain weight when consuming diet soft drinks. The theory is that the sweet taste creates a craving for more food and sweets. Diet soft drinks have also been linked to metabolic syndrome, a complex of high blood pressure, low HDL "good" cholesterol, high triglycerides (blood fats), weight gain around the middle and high blood glucose. It is not known why diet soft drinks have this effect.

Sugar alcohols raise blood glucose less than sugar and have fewer calories per gram because the body cannot fully digest them. But that poor absorption also makes them available to bacteria in your digestive system, which ferment the sweeteners, possibly leading to bloating, gas and diarrhea. Use sugar alcohols with care.

Are Artificial Sweeteners Safe?

Artificial sweeteners, also called sugar substitutes, are compounds that are intensely sweet, so only a tiny amount is needed to sweeten food and drinks. Compare a can of regular and diet cola. The regular cola contains about 160 calories and 40 grams of carbohydrate, all from sugar. The diet cola, made with artificial sweetener, contains about 0.1 gram of sweetener, resulting in a significant reduction in calories and carbohydrate (essentially to zero of each).

There are several artificial sweeteners approved for use in North America, with subtle differences depending upon which side of the border you live on.

Safety concerns have been raised about artificial sweeteners, and the Internet has been abuzz about aspartame in particular. Regardless, sweeteners appear to be safe for most people. Each sweetener has a safety limit, and very few people are likely to exceed it. Cyclamate and saccharin are not recommended in pregnancy, and aspartame is definitely not allowed for people with a rare condition called

Artificial Sweeteners

Sweetener	Approved in the U.S.	Approved in Canada
Acesulfame potassium	✓ in food and as a tabletop sweetener	✓ in food only
Aspartame	✓ in food and as a tabletop sweetener	✓ in food and as a tabletop sweetener
Cyclamate	not approved	✓ as a tabletop sweetener only
Saccharin	✓ in food and as a tabletop sweetener	✓ as a tabletop sweetener only
Sucralose	✓ in food and as a tabletop sweetener	✓ in food and as a tabletop sweetener

Note: Tabletop sweeteners are sachets, tablets or bulk product (granular or liquid form) you add to foods or drinks yourself. Each of the above sweeteners may also be marketed under a brand name, such as NutraSweet for aspartame or Splenda for sucralose.

phenylketonuria (PKU), as they cannot break down one of its components. For this reason, all products that contain aspartame carry a warning to people with PKU.

Despite the negative press, we believe the balance presently lies in sweeteners' favor. In other words, sugar substitutes are safe in moderation — and they really do help reduce calories and carbs. The table below lists various artificial sweeteners, their safety limits and the amount in a typical serving.

Safety Limits for Artificial Sweeteners

Sweetener	ADI*	Daily Allowance for a 155-lb (70 kg) Person	Amount per Serving (equal in sweetness to 2 tsp/5 mL of sugar)
Acesulfame potassium	15 mg/kg	1050 mg/day	50 mg
Aspartame	40 mg/kg	2800 mg/day	40 mg
Cyclamate	11 mg/kg	770 mg/day	250 mg
Saccharin	5 mg/kg	350 mg/day	40 mg
Sucralose	15 mg/kg**	630 mg/day	15 mg

* ADI stands for "acceptable daily intake," the amount a person can safely consume every day for a lifetime. It is calculated as an amount (in milligrams) that is safe per kilogram of body weight. With the exception of cyclamate, it is unlikely anyone would reach the ADI for an artificial sweetener, as most are used in very small amounts.
** In Canada, the ADI for sucralose is 9 mg/kg.

Stevia

Gradually growing in popularity in North America, this intensely sweet herb has been used in Central America, Japan and other Asian countries for years. Traditionally, stevia leaves were ground or boiled to make medicines and teas. In modern times, the sweet-tasting components (called steviol glycosides) are extracted and added to food and drinks, or sold as a tabletop sweetener.

Because stevia extract is so sweet, only a tiny amount is needed. This makes stevia similar to artificial sweeteners. Used in moderation, stevia should add no calories and should not cause blood glucose to rise. The ADI for steviol glycosides is 4 mg/kg.

Step 3: Choose Low- and Medium-GI Foods Most Often

As discussed in Step 2, when we eat, we digest carbohydrate into glucose, which makes our blood glucose level go up. Scientists can measure how fast blood glucose rises after we eat carb-containing foods, a measurement called the glycemic index (GI).

With the help of many, many volunteers, scientists have measured the glycemic index of thousands of foods. The volunteers are fed a set amount of a carb-containing food, then their blood glucose is monitored over a period of several hours. Foods that digest quickly cause glucose to rise quickly, which typically signals the pancreas to release a big burst of insulin, resulting in a quick drop in blood glucose levels. Foods that digest slowly raise blood glucose slowly and do not trigger a large burst of insulin, so the glucose level also decreases gradually.

After its effect on blood glucose is measured, each carb-containing food is assigned a number from 1 to 100, based on how quickly it raises blood glucose. For convenience, foods are then ranked as low-GI (55 or less), medium-GI (56–69) or high-GI (70 or more). As you might have guessed, high-GI foods raise blood glucose quickly, low-GI foods raise it slowly and medium-GI foods have a moderate effect.

Low- and medium-GI foods are associated with many health benefits.

Low- and medium-GI foods:

- reduce the risk of type 2 diabetes;
- help manage diabetes;
- help with weight control by keeping people full longer;
- lower blood cholesterol levels; and
- reduce the risk of heart disease.

Many countries around the world are recommending that people eat lower-GI foods as often as possible. In Australia, for example, the glycemic index is listed on food packages, making it easy to find lower-GI choices. (You can even look up specific foods at the University of Sydney's GI website: http://glycemicindex.com). In the United States and Canada, the glycemic index is not yet included on food labels, so we've provided the chart on page 60, which shows the glycemic index of some common foods. If you are used to eating a particular high-GI food, look in the medium-GI and low-GI columns to see if you might enjoy a similar food in its place. Most of the information in the chart is about starchy foods, because starch usually contributes the most carbohydrate at a given meal. This means you can make the biggest improvement by changing your starch choices.

Note that foods without carbohydrate do not have a glycemic index, so they don't appear on the chart. These include fats, most protein foods and most vegetables. (Vegetables have carbohydrate, but most of it is in the form of fiber, leaving only a small amount of available carbohydrate.) Fruits do raise blood glucose, and some have a higher glycemic index than others, but this should not be a problem if you are eating portion sizes that fit into your carb targets (a fist-sized piece of fruit provides about 15 g of carbohydrate).

If your diabetes is well controlled with medication (see page 129), you should experience lower blood glucose levels when you start eating low-GI foods. If this results in hypoglycemia, talk to your health care provider. You may need a change or reduction in your diabetes medication.

But what if your diabetes is not in good control and you usually have high blood glucose levels? If you have had diabetes for a long time, you will lack the insulin supply to handle high-GI foods. You won't crash after meals; instead, you will have lasting high blood glucose. In this case, eating low-GI foods becomes a new tool to reduce your blood glucose. You may also need to adjust other aspects of your

---

SOUND BITE

What a nice surprise! I found that eating a bowl of steel-cut oats kept me full longer than when I ate a large white bagel. With the oatmeal, I was full until lunch, so I didn't fall for the doughnuts when they were served at the morning staff meeting. Now I am eating a more nutritious breakfast, and my glucose levels aren't spiking and crashing anymore!
— Beverley, 47

Did You Know?

Many processed foods have a high glycemic index. As people around the world eat more processed foods, the glycemic index of the world's diet is increasing. This is not good, as lower-GI foods help prevent and manage disease, while high-GI foods contribute to health problems.

The Glycemic Index of Common Foods

Low-GI	Medium-GI	High-GI
Sweet potatoes, taro, yams, plantain, cassava	New potatoes	Russet potatoes, french fries, mashed potatoes
Converted (parboiled) rice	Brown rice, basmati rice	White rice
Breads and buns made from heavy mixed grains, pumpernickel or stone-ground flours	Rye or whole wheat bread, pita bread or roti (chapati), corn tortillas or taco shells	White bread, bagel, Kaiser roll or baguette
All Bran/All Bran Buds	Puffed wheat, cream of wheat, Grape Nuts	Corn flakes, bran flakes, crisped rice cereal, puffed rice, toasted O cereal
Oat bran, large-flake or steel-cut oats	Quick oats (oatmeal)	Instant oats
Barley, quinoa, buckwheat, bulgur, pasta, noodles	Couscous, rice noodles, kernel corn	Millet
Legumes	Popcorn, rye crispbreads, Melba toast	Pretzels, soda crackers

Did You Know?

While not actually grains, quinoa and buckwheat are low-GI seeds that are eaten as grains. They are very nutritious.

management, including medication, activity and stress control, but don't overlook the potential that is on the end of your spoon.

Do-It-Yourself GI Testing

If you test your own blood glucose, you can test the glycemic index of your meals. Check your blood glucose before a meal, then again two hours afterward to see how high it went. Compare meals with low- and high-GI carbohydrates, keeping the carb portions similar — use 1 cup (250 mL) of brown rice instead of white rice, or have two slices of whole-grain bread instead of white bread. You'll soon see that your blood glucose goes up less when you eat lower-GI foods, and that you feel more content after eating a low-GI meal.

FAQ

Q. What is the difference between "whole grain" and "whole wheat"?

A. A whole grain is exactly that: the entire grain, or kernel. The kernel consists of three parts: the fiber-rich bran, the germ (a source of healthy fat) and the starchy endosperm. Whole grains usually have a low glycemic index, as they are harder to digest. This is especially true if the grain is intact, as with corn, pot barley, steel-cut oats, wheat berries, wild rice and sprouted grains, or is less processed, as with large-flake (old-fashioned) rolled oats, brown rice and whole-grain flour.

In the United States, whole wheat flour is made from the whole grain. In Canada, however, whole wheat flour is missing a portion of the germ. Canadian consumers need to make sure they are buying whole-grain flour and bread. For more information, visit www.wholegrainscouncil.org.

Did You Know?

Pastas are generally low- or medium-GI, but can become high-GI if overcooked. Cook pasta until "al dente," which means it is tender to the bite but is not soft or overcooked. For extra vitamins, minerals and fiber, try whole-grain or whole wheat pastas.

Glycemic Variability

The creation of the glycemic index was a real breakthrough, adding the concept of carb *quality* to carb *quantity*. Now we can count carbs *and* choose those that give us a sense of fullness and satisfaction, rather than those that cause our blood glucose to spike then drop fast, leaving us hungry again.

Today, researchers use the term "glycemic variability" to describe the ups and downs of blood glucose levels. Eating lower-GI foods can help reduce your glycemic variability. Creating a "flatter" glucose profile — a gradual rise and fall of blood glucose levels — is the goal everyone should be aiming for.

Did You Know?

Legumes are truly a superfood. They are high in protein and fiber, but low on the glycemic index (and your grocery bill). Lentils, chickpeas, kidney beans, white peas and edamame are just a few of the many options. Buy them dried, canned or frozen and enjoy them regularly.

Did You Know?

Starchy foods usually make the biggest contribution to your blood glucose levels, so it's important to choose low-GI types. Here are some other ways you can help your blood glucose:

- Dress your salads with vinegar or lemon juice. Acid slows digestion, making your blood glucose rise more slowly.
- Balance your meal with healthy fat and lean protein.
- Keep your starch portion to about a quarter of your plate.
- Eat slowly and savor your food.

How to reduce your glycemic variability:

- Try to have one low- or medium-GI food at each meal.
- Balance your meals by eating protein and healthy fats as well as carbohydrate.
- Include more legumes (lentils, chickpeas, kidney beans and navy beans) in your meals — they're a low-GI, high-fiber, low-fat protein option.
- Add vinegar to your recipes, or include a salad with a vinegar dressing as part of your meal. Vinegar slows digestion, effectively lowering the glycemic index of the entire meal.

Sometimes You Need to Spike!

Although we recommend choosing low-GI carbs on a regular basis, sometimes you need to raise your blood glucose quickly. If your blood glucose is low — 70 mg/dL (3.9 mmol/L) or less — the best treatment is pure glucose. Pure glucose has a glycemic index of 100, so it raises your blood glucose very fast. If you take medication or insulin to lower your blood glucose, always keep glucose tablets handy. Take the equivalent of 15 to 20 grams of carbohydrate. Eat a small snack after that if your next meal is an hour or more away. (For more information on treating hypoglycemia, see page 130.)

The Bottom Line

One of the most important steps you can take toward preventing or managing diabetes is to choose low- and medium-GI carbohydrates. Enjoy whole grains, legumes, fruit and vegetables for fiber, vitamins, minerals, great taste *and* a healthy effect on your blood glucose.

Step 4: Choose Healthy Fats

There is no macronutrient more misunderstood or maligned than fat. Many of us think of fat as greasy and unhealthy, all the while yearning for juicy burgers and fries. We wonder why the French can eat butter and still have low rates of heart disease. We ask why the Mediterranean diet, high in olive oil, is considered beneficial. As confusing as it all is, our understanding of fat is increasing. We are gradually learning *which* fats to choose and *how much* we can safely eat.

Fats, also known as lipids, are important components of our bodies and our diet. In the body, fat is a source of energy, usually one that is "stored for a rainy day." You can find that fat on your buttocks, thighs and belly. Stored fat also cushions our organs and helps keep us warm. On a microscopic level, fats have a key role as structural agents in our cell walls.

Fat is found in most foods. Even foods we think of as fat-free may actually have a small amount. Fat is essential in our diet because it provides certain nutrients, such as vitamins A, D and E, and helps us absorb them, too. Fat adds flavor, aroma and richness to food and helps us feel full. Unfortunately, fat can also contribute to weight gain, high blood cholesterol and insulin resistance.

Choosing the best fats begins with two terms: "saturated" and "unsaturated." These fats are different in their appearance, taste and how they affect our health. Saturated fats have a chemical structure that makes them firm or solid at room temperature. Unsaturated fats are liquid at room temperature. All fats contain a mixture of saturates and unsaturates. Fats that contain mainly saturates will be solid; these include butter, hard (stick) margarine, shortening and the fat in meat. Fats that contain mainly unsaturates will be liquid or easy to spread, even right out of the fridge; vegetable oil, olive oil and soft (tub) margarine are some examples.

Although eating a variety of foods creates the most enjoyment, research suggests we should eat less saturated fat and choose soft margarine and oils (with the exception of coconut, palm kernel and palm oil, which are not true oils, as they are solid at room temperature). As you can see in the chart on page 64, oils and soft margarine are very high in unsaturates, the healthier choice.

As you can see in the chart on page 64

Did You Know?

"Fat" is the catch-all word for fats and oils, but what really is the difference? "Fat" properly refers to solid fat, such as butter and lard, while "oil" refers to liquid fat, such as olive oil and sunflower oil. Of course, there are exceptions to every rule. Coconut oil is solid at room temperature unless you live in the tropics, where the high temperature melts it.

Did You Know?

Fats are made of two major components: fatty acids and glycerol. Fatty acids are attached to a glycerol backbone and may be bound alone (monoglycerides), in pairs (diglycerides) or in groups of three (triglycerides). The fats we eat and the fats stored in our bodies are mainly triglycerides.

Saturates and Unsaturates in Common Fats and Oils

Type of Fat or Oil	Amount of Saturates (%)	Amount of Unsaturates (%)
Coconut oil	91	9
Palm kernel oil	86	14
Butter	65	35
Shortening*	60	40
Beef fat (tallow)	58	42
Hard (stick) margarine*	56	44
Lard	43	57
Peanut oil	19	81
Soy oil	15	85
Soft (tub) margarine	16	84
Corn oil	14	86
Olive oil	10	90
Walnut oil	10	90
Safflower oil	8	92

* The saturated fat component also includes trans fat (see page 71).

Did You Know?

All fats contain a lot of calories — about 9 calories per gram or 40 calories per teaspoon (5 mL). Limiting fat helps control calories. However, we do need some fat. Eat healthy (unsaturated) fats, in reasonable portions, to get the benefits of fat without excess calories.

When Fat Is Your Friend

Unsaturated fats are healthy to eat and versatile to use. There are two main types of unsaturates: monounsaturates and polyunsaturates. These terms describe the structure of unsaturated fat more specifically. This structure may not be important to us as consumers, but knowing the terms will help you seek out foods that contain each type, so you can enjoy the taste and health benefits of both.

Within these categories is another layer of detail, as there are several types of mono- and polyunsaturated fats. Omega-3s and omega-6s are two important types of polyunsaturates.

Cardiovascular Disease: Public Enemy Number 1

"Cardiovascular disease" is the term used to describe diseases of the heart and arteries (blood vessels). It is the leading cause of death and illness in people with prediabetes and diabetes. While a number of things can go wrong, very common problems are claudication, angina, heart attack and stroke. In these situations, blood flow has been slowed or blocked by atherosclerosis (hardening of the arteries). In claudication, the blood flow is restricted in the lower limbs, causing pain in the calves when walking. Angina is a type of chest pain caused by restricted blood flow in the vessels leading to the heart. A heart attack results when the blood flow is completely blocked and part of the heart muscle dies. This can be fatal. A stroke happens when blood flow to the brain is stopped. Strokes can cause death or serious disability. High LDL ("bad") cholesterol, hypertension (high blood pressure), high blood glucose, smoking and obesity are the main contributors to atherosclerosis. It is impossible to overstate the importance of preventing or managing cardiovascular disease. Healthy eating, including eating the right kind of fat, is a key player in the fight.

It is impossible to overstate the importance of preventing or managing cardiovascular disease. Healthy eating, including eating the right kind of fat, is a key player in the fight.

Omega-3s

Omega-3 fats are good for the heart, joints, brain, eyes and nerves. They are found in walnuts, flax seeds, hemp and chia (and their oils), and in fatty fish (salmon, herring, mackerel, anchovies, sardines, sablefish (black cod), trout and some tuna). Omega-3 from plants is called alpha-linolenic acid (ALA). Fish provide two key types of omega-3: eicosapentaenoic acid (EPA) and docosahexaenoic acid (DHA).

ALA is essential for normal growth and development. The Acceptable Intake (AI) is 1100 milligrams per day for women and 1600 milligrams for men (see page 23 for a definition of Acceptable Intake). While EPA and DHA are not essential fats, some experts suggest people should consume about 250 to 500 milligrams of EPA and DHA (combined) per day.

Did You Know?

It is not worthwhile to "micromanage" your diet by trying to eat exact amounts of specific fatty acids. After all, we eat food, not fatty acids and glycerol. Eat foods such as fish, olives, nuts, seeds and their oils, and you will get the right types of fats.

Where to Find Unsaturated Fats

Type of Fat	Found In
Monounsaturated fat	• Avocados and avocado oil • Canola oil* • Peanuts and peanut oil • Olives and olive oil
Polyunsaturated fat	• Almonds and almond oil • Canola oil* • Cashews and cashew oil • Chia seeds and chia seed oil* • Corn and corn oil • Grapeseed oil • Fish and fish oil* • Flax seeds and flaxseed oil* • Hazelnuts and hazelnut oil • Hemp seeds and hempseed oil* • Safflower oil • Sesame seeds and sesame oil • Soybeans and soy oil* • Sunflower seeds and sunflower oil • Walnuts and walnut oil*

* Also contains omega-3 polyunsaturated fats.

Did You Know?

If you eat whole flax, hemp or chia seeds, you will get the benefit of fiber, but if you grind the seeds first, you will also absorb the omega-3-rich oils.

The Mediterranean Diet

People in Greece, Italy and Spain have low rates of heart disease and cancer. Their traditional eating pattern, now called the Mediterranean diet, is based on fish, legumes, nuts, vegetables, fruit and whole grains. The main fat used is olive oil. Researchers suggest that this monounsaturated fat is part of what makes the diet healthful. They also eat a lesser amount of saturated fat (from meat and dairy) than many North Americans, obtaining only about 8% of their calories from saturated fat — consistent with a cholesterol-lowering diet.

Interest in the Mediterranean diet is high, and nowadays many people have olive oil in their kitchens. This is a good choice, especially if hard fats (butter and lard) were the mainstays before. We use extra virgin olive oil in many of our recipes. If you want the health benefits of monounsaturated fat without the taste of olive oil, canola oil is a great option. Or make a blend of extra virgin olive oil and canola oil.

Good Sources of Omega-3 Fats

ALA	Walnuts, 1 oz (30 g)	2600 mg
	Flax seeds, 1 tbsp (15 mL)	2400 mg
	Chia seeds, 1 tbsp (15 mL)	1900 mg
	Canola oil, 2 tsp (10 mL)	865 mg
	Hemp seeds, 1 tbsp (15 mL)	830 mg
	Soy oil, 2 tsp (10 mL)	600 mg
	Canola oil margarine, 2 tsp (10 g)	600 mg
	Whole-grain bread, 1 slice	500 mg
	Tofu (firm), 5 oz (150 g)	480 mg
EPA and DHA (combined)*	Salmon, 3½ oz (100 g)	2000 mg
	Herring, 3½ oz (100 g)	2000 mg
	Sablefish (black cod), 3½ oz (100 g)	1700 mg
	Sardines, 3½ oz (100 g)	1400 mg
	Mackerel, 3½ oz (100 g)	1200 mg
	Anchovies, 3½ oz (100 g)	900 mg
	Rainbow trout (farmed), 3½ oz (100 g)	800 mg

* With the exception of rainbow trout, all information is for wild fish.

It is easy to meet your requirement for ALA. Simply having two slices of whole-grain bread with 2 tsp (10 mL) of canola oil margarine will give you 1600 milligrams. A small handful of walnuts is 2600 milligrams. A serving of flax seeds is 2400 milligrams. Add them to cereal or a smoothie (grind them first to release the oils).

When it comes to EPA and DHA, if you eat fatty fish twice weekly, your intake will average out to 250 to 500 milligrams a day. For people who don't like fish, or who don't eat it often, manufacturers are adding these fats to various foods to help consumers increase their intake. If you think you cannot eat enough of these fats, or if your doctor has recommended a larger amount of EPA/DHA, read labels on fish oil capsules to find the amount you need.

> **Did You Know?**
> If you are a vegetarian, you can still consume "fish oils." Just cut out the middle man! Fish are only high in EPA/DHA because they eat algae. Algae-based vegetarian-friendly oils are available.

Omega-6s

Omega-6 fats are also thought to be beneficial for heart health. They are found in just about every type of vegetable oil, including canola, soy, sunflower, safflower, peanut and corn oils, and soft margarines made from these oils. As they

Safe, Sustainable Seafood

Fish is tasty, versatile and quick to prepare. Some fish are also an excellent source of omega-3 fats. Unfortunately, fish can be high in mercury, dioxins and PCBs, toxic compounds they consume due to our polluted environment. Furthermore, many of the fish we enjoy have been victims of their taste and versatility — they are being fished to extinction. That is why you do not see tuna as a recommended omega-3–rich fish.

The fish listed in the chart on page 67 contain fewer contaminants and are more likely to be fished or farmed in a sustainable manner. If you want to learn more, the following organizations have excellent websites with up-to-date information on sustainable seafood options: the Marine Stewardship Council (www.msc.org); Monterey Bay Aquarium Seafood Watch (www.seafoodwatch.org); and SeaChoice (www.seachoice.org). You may also want to check with local authorities for what's safe in your nearby lakes and rivers.

Did You Know?

The omega-3 fat alpha-linolenic acid (ALA) and the omega-6 fat linoleic acid (LA) are essential fats. We must get them from our diet, as they are required for normal growth and development. This makes them similar to vitamins. Indeed, when they were initially discovered, essential fats were called vitamin F.

are so common, it should be easy to get enough if you are eating a balanced diet. The Acceptable Intake is 12 grams per day for women and 17 grams for men. A small handful ($1/4$ cup/60 mL) of walnuts or sunflower seeds provides about 10 grams. Even though these nuts and seeds are high in fat, that small portion has less than 200 calories. Eat them "out of hand" or add them to a salad or yogurt.

There has been some research suggesting North Americans eat too much omega-6 fat and not enough omega-3. This imbalance is theorized to increase inflammation and diseases resulting from it. We do not know whether further research will bear this out. Meanwhile, a safe and reasonable approach is to use a variety of fats and not too much of any one fat. Our menus are low in fats of all kinds, while calling for several different types of fish, oils, nuts, seeds and whole grains.

When Fat Is Your Foe

While certain unsaturated fats are essential for health, this is not the case for saturated fats, as the body can synthesize them from other foods we eat. Cholesterol is another compound the body can make on its own, so it is not essential to eat cholesterol-containing foods. Of course we can eat these compounds safely, but some people eat too much. Trans fats are another thing altogether. These man-made fats are to be avoided as much as possible (see page 71). In fact, a diet low in saturated fat and cholesterol, and very low in trans fat, is recommended to reduce the risk of cardiovascular disease.

Reduce Saturated Fat

Our recipes use reduced-fat dairy products, lean meat and skinless poultry, so they are low in saturated fat. We have also taken care to ensure that our daily menus provide a maximum of 7% of calories from saturated fat (a maximum of 12 grams per 1600 calories). To reduce saturated fat when cooking your own recipes, eating prepared foods or eating out, avoid:

- fatty cuts of meat, such as ribs, prime rib, bacon and the skin on poultry;
- mixed meat products such as sausage, bologna, pepperoni and salami;
- high-fat dairy products, such as whole milk, cream and cheese;
- baked goods that use shortening, beef tallow, lard or hard margarine; and
- deep-fried foods (because shortening or palm oil may be used to deep-fry; these foods may also contain trans fat).

Did You Know?

A good way to reduce saturated fat is to cook meat and poultry in a way that allows the fat to drip out. Try baking, poaching, roasting or steaming instead of frying.

Did You Know?

Fat cells are able to sense and tell the difference between different types of fatty acids. When saturated fatty acids reach the fat cell wall, they trigger enzymes that interfere with insulin action.

The French Paradox?

French cooking is famous for its rich sauces, butter and cheese, yet French people have lower rates of heart disease than Americans. How can that be? Scientists have analyzed the French diet and realized there's no paradox at all. While French food can definitely be high in fat, French people eat small portions, as well as less sugar and little or no soda pop. They eat very little trans fat, as they avoid fried snack foods. Furthermore, they are committed to savoring their meals (see "Mindful Eating" in Step 8, page 98), which promotes a healthy weight.

FAQ

Q. Can I deep-fry in cholesterol-free oil?

A. All vegetable oils are cholesterol-free. The problem is that deep-frying immerses the food in hot fat. Foods that contain carbohydrate, such as potatoes (for chips or fries), flour (for batters, doughnuts or fritters) or crumbs, soak up the oil like a sponge, adding a lot of fat and calories to the food. Commercially fried foods may also have trans fat, as the high temperature of the oil, and the fact that it is used repeatedly, can damage the oil and create trans fat, even if a trans fat–free oil was initially used. Don't forget, high-temperature cooking methods also create AGEs (see pages 15 and 266).

It is suggested that people with diabetes or cardiovascular disease limit their dietary cholesterol to 200 milligrams per day.

Limit Dietary Cholesterol

Like fat, cholesterol is found in our diet and in our bodies. In our diet, cholesterol is found in animal foods, such as meat, poultry, fish, seafood, eggs and dairy products. In our bodies, cholesterol is found in high amounts in the brain and spinal cord, and is needed to produce many compounds, from digestive juices to vitamin D. More proof of cholesterol's importance is its high level in breast milk.

And yet too much cholesterol is a risk factor for cardiovascular disease. Why is this? Cholesterol is a waxy substance that needs to be "packaged" to be transported through the blood. How you package cholesterol is determined by your genes and your lifestyle, and that packaging can be "good" or "bad." "Good" cholesterol is packaged with high-density lipoprotein (HDL). HDL cholesterol does not build up to unhealthy levels in the arteries. "Bad" cholesterol is packaged with low-density lipoprotein (LDL). Cholesterol in an LDL wrapper can contribute to fatty plaques, or build-ups, in the arteries. When these plaques accumulate on blood vessel walls, blood flow can be slowed. When plaques accumulate enough to stop blood flow, a heart attack or stroke is the result.

Most of our cholesterol is made by our own bodies. The diet usually contributes only about 20% to our cholesterol content. Regardless, it is suggested that people with diabetes or cardiovascular disease limit their dietary cholesterol to 200 milligrams per day. (If you have neither condition, and your blood cholesterol is normal, 300 milligrams is allowed.) This means eating appropriate portions of meat, fish and poultry, limiting egg yolks to two per week, and eating liver,

FAQ

Q. Can I eat "good" cholesterol?

A. No. Dietary cholesterol is neither bad nor good. How your body packages cholesterol is what makes it bad or good. To make more "good" cholesterol packages, be active and eat healthy fats. If you smoke, quit. Lose weight if you need to. Know also that how you package cholesterol is very much genetically determined. Sometimes, despite your efforts, you will have too much "bad" and not enough "good" cholesterol. You may need medications to meet your targets.

Phytosterols

Plants create cholesterol-like compounds called phytosterols (or phytostanols) that may actually help lower cholesterol in our bodies by partially blocking the absorption of dietary cholesterol. Vegetables and fruit, nuts and whole grains provide phytosterols, but in an amount so small it is not likely to make a difference. Therefore, food manufacturers are now adding phytosterols to margarine, yogurt, juice and other foods. Phytosterol supplements are also available, with a daily dose of 2 to 3 grams.

Phytosterol supplements and fortified foods may contribute to a modest reduction in your LDL cholesterol level, but the jury is still out regarding the long-term risks and benefits. Check with your doctor before using these products.

> **Our daily menus** provide a maximum of 200 milligrams of cholesterol.

liver pâté and other organ meats (kidneys, brains) on rare occasions only. Our daily menus provide a maximum of 200 milligrams of cholesterol.

Avoid Trans Fat

About 100 years ago, hydrogenation was invented. This chemical process turned liquid oil into solid fat (in other words, it turned unsaturated fat into saturated fat) and led to the creation of shortening and margarine. Food makers found shortening very useful in bakery and fried products, and taught consumers how to cook and bake with it. As hydrogenated fats became more common, however, it was suspected that they might be harmful. Research has since shown that the process of hydrogenation creates a type of fat called trans fat, which raises LDL cholesterol while *lowering* HDL cholesterol, increasing the risk of cardiovascular disease.

Did You Know?

Moderate alcohol intake is defined as two drinks per day for a man (or a maximum of 14 drinks per week) and one drink per day for a woman (or a maximum of nine drinks per week). For more information about alcohol, see page 90.

Achieving Your Target "Lipid Profile"

Eating more unsaturated fat and less saturated fat, trans fat and cholesterol can help lower your LDL ("bad") cholesterol and raise your HDL ("good") cholesterol. This supports a blood lipid profile that reduces your risk of cardiovascular disease. But that's not all you can do. More fiber, especially soluble types (see Step 2, page 48), can help lower LDL cholesterol. Exercise and weight loss raise HDL cholesterol, as does quitting smoking. Moderate alcohol intake can also raise HDL cholesterol. In discussion with your doctor, give these lifestyle changes three to six months to make a difference. Then, if you are not meeting your goals, you may need medication. Some people simply make too much bad cholesterol (thanks to their genes), and lifestyle is not sufficient to correct this.

You may also be dealing with high triglycerides. We store body fat as triglycerides and also have triglycerides circulating in our blood. High blood triglycerides may be a risk factor for cardiovascular disease. If your triglycerides are high — you guessed it — eat well, be active and lose weight if you are overweight. Cutting out alcohol and sweets is also recommended. Discuss your lipid profile with your physician to understand your personal goals.

Women who are past menopause and/or over 50 and men over 40 should have their lipids measured every one to three years. Adults of any age should have their lipids measured every one to two years if they have diabetes, high blood pressure, obesity or cardiovascular disease. A lipid profile is usually measured after a 12-hour fast (that is, no food overnight). Ask your physician how often you should have your lipids measured.

Trans fat is found in some commercially prepared foods, such as bakery items, fried foods, crackers and snack foods. Shortening and hard (stick) margarines can also be high in trans fat.

Health officials around the world have recognized the hazards of trans fat and are now advising consumers to avoid it. For this reason, Nutrition Facts tables must list trans fat. To avoid trans fat, read the Nutrition Facts on the foods you buy. They should have 0 grams of trans fat, or as little as possible. When reading the ingredient list, avoid hydrogenated and partially hydrogenated oils. This is becoming easier, as food manufacturers are gradually switching to trans-free fats. Many margarines now use a non-hydrogenation process that retains a large amount of unsaturated fat, avoids trans production and creates a product that is still firm enough for baking and spreading.

Enjoy Healthy Fats

You don't need a chemistry degree to know that healthy fats are delicious. Oils, nuts, seeds and fatty fish add flavor to food and flexibility in cooking. When you shop, buy small amounts of unsaturated fats and oils (to keep them fresh) and try new flavors:

- *Extra virgin olive oil:* Use in cooking, salad dressings, dips and spreads.
- *Sesame and peanut oil:* Use in Asian cooking.
- *Canola, grapeseed and soy oil:* Use these mild-tasting oils for baking and general cooking.
- *Specialty oils:* Use walnut oil, almond oil, hazelnut oil or avocado oil for salad dressings, dips and sauces. These are expensive, but a little goes a long way.
- *Non-hydrogenated margarine:* Spread on toast and sandwiches, or use for baking.

To learn more about various types of oils and their culinary uses, see page 242.

We use a variety of fats in our recipes, emphasizing liquid and soft fats whenever possible. Because fats add a lot of calories, we keep the portions down, usually to a couple of teaspoons (10 mL) at most. You will not miss the fat, as we use seasonings and spices to make meals delicious! Occasionally, we use butter. Although butter contains both saturates and cholesterol, sometimes its flavor just can't be beat. Again, the portions are reasonable. We use some higher-fat ingredients,

Did You Know?

We call for extra virgin olive oil in many of our recipes because it's the highest quality and has undergone the least amount of processing, thus maintaining the oil's natural flavor and health benefits. Regular olive oil has been refined, often with the use of chemical solvents to extract the oil. Light olive oil is also a refined oil. It is not lighter in calories, only lighter in flavor. If you prefer a mild-flavored olive oil, mix canola oil with extra virgin olive oil instead.

> Having small portions of high-fat foods allows you to enjoy flavor and variety without consuming too many calories.

such as nuts and fatty fish, but eating a sensible amount allows you to benefit from the healthy fats without consuming too many calories.

The Bottom Line

Eat nutritious fats, such as oils, nuts, seeds and fatty fish. Limit saturated fat and cholesterol by choosing lean meats and lower-fat dairy products. Avoid trans fat.

Step 5: Eat Low-Fat Protein at Every Meal

Did You Know?

As we age, our muscles tend to become smaller. This is not helpful for glucose control, as muscles are powerful glucose-burning factories! Eating more protein as we age can reduce muscle loss.

Protein is a macronutrient that is found in many foods. It is most concentrated in animal sources such as meat, fish, poultry, eggs and milk products, and in plant sources such as legumes, tofu and nuts. When we eat these foods, our digestive system breaks the protein down into tiny building blocks called amino acids. Our bodies then reassemble amino acids into skin, muscles, blood cells, antibodies and much more.

You may already know that protein is an important part of the diet, but it has special benefits for people with diabetes and prediabetes. For one thing, protein foods tend to be filling, a bonus for people who are watching their weight. Some protein-rich foods, such as beans and lentils, are a great source of cholesterol-lowering soluble fiber. Nuts and nut butters provide protein, fiber and healthy fat, and are a versatile part of meals and snacks.

Of special interest is how protein protects our muscles. As we age, our muscles tend to become smaller. This is a normal change for the body, but one that is *not* helpful for glucose control. Muscles are powerful glucose-burning factories! Some scientists suggest we need more protein as we age to reduce muscle loss. For weight-loss dieters, making sure to eat a certain amount of protein even while cutting back on calories can protect their muscles.

For all these reasons, we have built protein into every meal and provided some protein-rich snacks. We have used a variety of animal and plant sources. The chart on page 75 lists some of the protein-rich foods you will see in our menus. Other foods, such as whole grains, vegetables and fruits, contribute a few grams of protein per serving. Legumes, nuts, yogurt and milk contain carbohydrate as well as protein. We have counted the carbohydrate into our menu plans.

Protein-Rich Foods

Food	Serving Size	Protein (g)
Lean meat, fish or poultry	3½ oz (100 g)	25 (on average)
Tofu, firm	¾ cup (175 mL)	17
Cheddar cheese (18% M.F.)	2 oz (60 g)	16
Yogurt, Greek-style	¾ cup (175 g)	16
Cottage cheese (1% M.F.)	½ cup (125 mL)	15
Legumes	¾ cup (175 mL)	12
Eggs	2 large	12
Veggie patty/soy burger	2 oz (55 g)	10
Egg whites	3 large	10
Yogurt	¾ cup (175 g)	9
Milk (1% M.F.)	1 cup (250 mL)	9
Peanut butter	2 tbsp (30 mL)	8
Kefir (nonfat)	¾ cup (175 g)	6
Nuts and seeds	¼ cup (60 mL)	6
Soy milk	1 cup (250 mL)	4

Source: Canadian Nutrient File (version 2007b), supplemented with information from the USDA National Nutrient Database for Standard Reference (Release 21).

What About Fat?

Many foods that contain protein also contain fat. We advise you to use lower-fat protein foods for several reasons. One is that fat is high in calories. Too much fat of any kind will add too many calories to food (although we do use nuts in our recipes and menus, we limit the portion size). Another is that some proteins contain saturated fat. As discussed in Step 4, saturated fat contributes to insulin resistance and can raise LDL ("bad") cholesterol.

Fortunately, with so many lower-fat options, there is no need to consume unhealthy fats. You will be pleasantly surprised to learn even red meat can be low in fat and saturated fat. Of course, all of our recipes meet strict

Did You Know?

If you have been used to eating higher-fat foods, you may think less fat means less flavor. Try our recipes and menus — we bet you will forget you are eating less fat!

guidelines (discussed on page 138) and explain exactly how to shop and cook for success!

You can limit fat in general and saturated fat in particular with some label-reading savvy. For example, most dairy products list a percentage of milk fat (% M.F.) on the package. The lower the percentage, the lower the amount of fat. Choose the lowest % M.F. you can for milk, yogurt and cheese. For meats, look for a fat percentage or for the words "lean" or "extra-lean." The words "round" (as in eye of round, bottom round, etc.), "rump" and "loin" (as in sirloin or tenderloin) also indicate lower-fat cuts. Pork tenderloin is almost as low in fat as chicken breast.

To reduce fat even further, always cut off any fat around the edges of meat and discard fat that cooks out of the meat.

Chicken and turkey are generally low in fat if you don't eat the skin. Also be sure to avoid battered and deep-fried poultry. Batters mean deep-frying, and deep-fried foods are high in fat. For that reason, steer clear of fish in batter, too.

A Vegetarian Diet Is High in Protein

It is a myth that vegetarians struggle to get enough protein. Vegetarians who use milk and eggs have those options, but even vegans (who avoid all animal products) get plenty of protein from legumes, tofu, soy milk (and soy cheese and yogurt), nuts and nut butters. Many whole grains also contribute protein. Our protein-rich vegetarian recipes, such as Soba Noodles with Tofu and Greens (page 295) and Curried Lentils with Vegetables (page 302), provide over 15 grams of protein per serving — and are so delicious even meat-lovers won't miss the meat!

Vegan diets are also cholesterol-free and are usually low in saturated fat (they can still be high in total fat and calories if many nuts and oils are used). Nutrients that may be of concern are iron and vitamin B_{12}. Good vegetable sources of iron are legumes, especially soybeans and lentils, and dark green leafy vegetables, such as spinach and Swiss chard. Vegans are advised to take a B_{12} supplement and/or choose foods fortified with this vitamin. The recommended dietary allowance for B_{12} is 2.4 micrograms (mcg or µg) for adults.

Animal proteins are also a source of cholesterol. Cholesterol we eat, called dietary cholesterol, can cause our blood cholesterol to rise. With some exceptions, meat, whether high in fat or very lean, has around 25 milligrams of cholesterol per ounce (30 g). Most of us need to limit dietary cholesterol to 200 to 300 milligrams per day. See Step 4 (page 70) for more information on cholesterol.

The chart on page 78 illustrates how choosing lean proteins saves calories, fat and saturated fat. Note also how cholesterol is quite stable across the cuts of meat, meaning a larger serving of meat may still be low in fat, but can provide excessive cholesterol.

The Healthy Plate

An easy way to make sure you are eating appropriate proportions of protein, starch and vegetables is to picture them fitting into quadrants on your plate. As seen in the illustration below, vegetables should take up a full half of the plate, while protein and starch each get one-quarter.

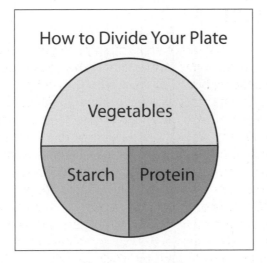

How to Divide Your Plate

For some people, a quarter of the plate may seem like a very small amount of protein. This is not surprising, as North Americans have become used to eating very large servings. Double and even triple hamburgers, foot-long hot dogs, "hungry man" portions and sandwiches stacked with meat and cheese teach us this is the norm. It's not. If you wish to eat a little more, that's okay if you can handle the extra calories, as well as the additional cholesterol and saturated fat (in animal proteins) or extra carbohydrate (in plant sources).

Greek yogurt and kefir are dairy products that may be new to you. Greek yogurt is very thick and very high in protein. We have used it often in our menus. Kefir is particularly high in probiotics and has a thinner consistency. It is pourable like milk and is often used as a drink, on cereal or in smoothies. It has the same amount of carbohydrate, protein and calcium as milk, but does not contain vitamin D unless fortified. Because yogurt and kefir are fermented, people with lactose intolerance may still be able to enjoy them.

Higher-Fat vs. Lower-Fat Options

Food	Serving Size	
Milk, 3.25% M.F.	1 cup (250 mL)	
Milk, 1% M.F.	1 cup (250 mL)	
Cheddar cheese, 30% M.F.	2 oz (60 g)	
Cheddar cheese, 18% M.F.	2 oz (60 g)	
Beef, rib-eye steak	3½ oz (100 g) cooked	
Beef, eye of round roast	3½ oz (100 g) cooked	
Ground beef, regular	3½ oz (100 g) cooked	
Ground beef, extra-lean	3½ oz (100 g) cooked	
Pork, back ribs	3½ oz (100 g) cooked	
Pork, shoulder blade roast	3½ oz (100 g) cooked	
Pork, tenderloin	3½ oz (100 g) cooked	
Chicken thighs, with skin	3½ oz (100 g) cooked	
Chicken thighs, skinless	3½ oz (100 g) cooked	
Chicken breast, skinless	3½ oz (100 g) cooked	
Fish in batter	3½ oz (100 g) cooked	
Crispy Almond Baked Fish (page 280)	1 serving	
Eggs	2 large	
Egg whites	3 large	

Source: Canadian Nutrient File (version 2007b), supplemented with information from the USDA National Nutrient Database for Standard Reference (Release 21).

Protein — It's Not Just for Dinner!

> Have a minimum of 15 grams of protein at each meal.

The body builds muscle better when you provide it with three smaller amounts of protein over the course of a day instead of one or two large servings. Many people eat too little protein at breakfast and lunch. If you only have toast or cold cereal for breakfast and a light sandwich with fruit for lunch, you're not having enough protein at these meals.

How to add protein at breakfast:

- Eat cottage cheese and fruit with your toast.
- Add low-carb protein powder to cereal or a smoothie.

Calories	Protein (g)	Total Fat (g)	Saturated Fat (g)	Cholesterol (mg)
157	8	8	6	26
108	9	3	1	13
242	15	20	13	62
170	16	11	7	34
248	30	14	6	69
172	33	3	1	65
324	29	22	9	84
219	31	9	4	81
365	28	27	11	113
228	27	13	4	95
144	28	3	1	70
244	20	18	4	76
166	24	7	2	75
149	30	2	1	75
197	17	12	3	53
170	24	6	1	60
153	12	11	3	385
48	10	0	0	0

- Spread 2 tbsp (30 mL) of nut butter on your toast and drink a full cup (250 mL) of milk.
- Make a quick microwave "scramble" of one egg and two egg whites, mixed with salsa and grated cheese. Stuff the mixture into a whole-grain wrap or pita for breakfast on the go. See our recipe on page 177.

How to add protein at lunch:

- Have 2 ounces (60 g) of meat, fish or poultry in your sandwich, not just one skinny slice. See our Combo Sandwiches chart on page 158.
- Add ½ cup (125 mL) of legumes to your salad. See our Combo Salads chart on page 160.
- Eat Greek yogurt for dessert.

Did You Know?

The promise of protein is in the serving size. Eat enough to help your body build muscle and help you feel full, but not so much that you consume unwanted calories or raise your blood cholesterol level.

FAQ

Q. My family is acting like the "diabetes police," always telling me I can't eat this or that! How can I get them to back off?

A. Tell your family you appreciate their concern but you are an adult and can make your own decisions. Suggest constructive ways they can support you, such as letting you have a say about what foods are brought into the home. If you shouldn't be eating junk food, chances are neither should the rest of the family. If you want a treat, prove you are sensible by not eating a huge portion. It would also be helpful if your loved ones attended a diabetes education program. They would learn that moderation is key, and that no foods are always "off-limits." Have a frank discussion with the diabetes police. Tell them you will do your best to take care of yourself, but you won't always be perfect. Ultimately, nagging and being nagged helps no one.

How to make your evening protein portion seem larger:

Eat slowly by putting your fork down between bites. Relax and breathe.

- Thinly slice your meat, then "fan" it (as you would hold playing cards).
- Stretch your protein with vegetables and legumes, as in a stew or chili.
- Cut meat or chicken into strips to stir-fry with vegetables and noodles.
- Add oatmeal, oat bran or vegetables to meatloaf (try our recipe on page 252).
- Use a smaller plate so your portion will cover more of it.
- Eat slowly, chew well and savor your meal.

The Bottom Line

Protein foods are filling, are good for your muscles and can be a source of fiber. Choose proteins that are low in saturated fat, and keep an eye on portion sizes. Eat protein at every meal.

Step 6: Aim to Limit Sodium to 1500 Milligrams per Day

According to the World Health Organization, high blood pressure (also called hypertension) is the leading cause of death around the world. Even tobacco kills fewer people. By some estimates, 40% of the world's people have high blood pressure. This epidemic is in bad company with the epidemic of diabetes, and it's no wonder: diabetes and high blood pressure have many of the same risk factors.

As with diabetes, some of the risk factors for high blood pressure cannot be avoided or controlled, but there are many modifiable risk factors, and a key one is reducing the amount of sodium in the diet.

> **Did You Know?**
>
> People who use medications to lower their blood pressure will see better results if they also eat a lower-sodium diet.

Why Is Blood Pressure Important?

High blood pressure and high blood glucose often go hand in hand. High blood pressure is a risk factor for diabetes, and *most* people with diabetes eventually develop high blood pressure. This unfortunate relationship is due to several factors. High blood glucose damages small blood vessels called

> Our menus provide a maximum of 1500 milligrams of sodium in 1600 calories. If you are eating more food, it only makes sense that you will be eating more sodium. Keep sodium intake reasonable by adding calories with unprocessed grains, unsalted nuts, fruits, milk and lean proteins.

Risk Factors for High Blood Pressure

- family history
- increasing age
- ethnicity (especially people of African descent)
- obesity
- stress
- sedentary lifestyle
- unhealthy diet, including excess sodium
- smoking
- excess alcohol

Your Blood Pressure: How Do You Measure Up?

Category	Systolic		Diastolic
Optimal	<120	and/or	<80
Normal	<130	and/or	<85
High-normal	130–139	and/or	85–89
Stage 1 (mild) hypertension	140–159	and/or	90–99
Stage 2 (moderate to severe) hypertension	≥ 160	and/or	≥ 100–109
Isolated systolic hypertension (ISH)	≥ 140	and	<90

Source: National Heart, Lung, and Blood Institute, *The Seventh Report of the Joint National Committee on Prevention, Detection, Evaluation, and Treatment of High Blood Pressure*, 2004.

Facts About Blood Pressure

An average heart beats around *100,000 times a day*. With each beat, the heart pushes blood around the entire body, using the force of the heart's pumping action to get it there. How much force the heart uses can be estimated by measuring blood pressure, as indeed, the blood is under pressure or force from that powerful pump.

In each heartbeat there are two main actions: squeezing and releasing. When the heart squeezes, the blood is sent on its way. Blood courses through large, small and tiny tubes, called arteries and arterioles, like water through a pipe. When the heart releases, the blood flows back to the heart, but more gently. Your physician measures your blood flow at the brachial artery on your arm to estimate the high force (systolic) value and at rest (diastolic) value. Blood pressure is measured in millimeters of mercury (mmHg), with the systolic value on top of the diastolic, such as 120/80.

Did You Know?

Most people do not eat enough potassium-rich foods, which can help lower blood pressure. Some especially high sources of potassium are oranges, bananas, sweet potatoes, squash, avocados, dark green leafy vegetables, beans and lentils, milk and yogurt, wheat bran and wheat germ.

capillaries. Damage to capillaries in the kidneys affects the regulation of blood pressure. High blood pressure can damage the insulin-secreting cells of the pancreas. In addition, diabetes increases the total amount of fluid in the body. This raises blood pressure, as more fluid has to fit in a limited amount of space. The body can only adapt so far.

These factors contribute to a vicious circle that can worsen both diseases. Furthermore, both diseases can lead to stroke, heart attack, kidney disease, erectile dysfunction and other problems.

Fortunately, many of the steps you take to prevent or manage diabetes are also good for your blood pressure. A healthy lifestyle is always the first step. Know what your blood pressure is and what it should be. If you cannot reach your target through lifestyle changes, you may also need medications that lower blood pressure.

Many of the steps you take to prevent or manage diabetes are also good for your blood pressure.

See How Salt Piles Up

Diet and lifestyle play a major role in high blood pressure, and a particular culprit is sodium. North American and European people eat large, large amounts of sodium, contributing to a very high prevalence of high blood pressure. Sodium is consumed as salt and is also an ingredient in many food additives, such as monosodium glutamate. Sodium raises blood pressure by attracting fluid into the blood vessels. The higher volume of fluid puts extra pressure on the vessel walls, making it harder for the heart to pump blood around the body. The heart also has to pump a higher volume of fluid, so it works harder than is ideal.

Governments around the world are encouraging people to eat less sodium and are developing targets for their citizens. Despite some improvements, most people still eat vastly more

Did You Know?

Sodium and salt are not exactly the same thing. Sodium is one of two ingredients in salt — sodium and chloride — which is why salt is also known as sodium chloride. To reduce sodium, it is important to reduce sodium chloride, as well as other sodium-containing compounds.

Make the DASH to Good Health!

Those of you with high blood pressure may have heard of the DASH diet. DASH stands for Dietary Approaches to Stop Hypertension. This diet is proven to reduce blood pressure by an average of 5 mmHg systolic and 2 to 3 mmHg diastolic. The DASH diet is based on whole grains, low-fat dairy, lean proteins, nuts and plenty of vegetables and fruit. It is not only low in sodium (1500 to 2300 milligrams per day), but is also high in nutrients that lower blood pressure: calcium, potassium, magnesium and vitamin D. If you are already following the DASH diet, our menus fit in with its overall goals. Enjoy our tasty recipes and lower your blood pressure too.

Because most of the sodium we eat is in processed foods, cooking at home using unprocessed foods is the first step to reducing sodium.

sodium than they need. Compare the amount of sodium needed for health versus what North American adults (ages 19 and 50) typically consume:

- Acceptable Intake (basic requirement): 1500 mg
- Tolerable Upper Intake Level (maximum safe limit): 2300 mg
- Typical North American intake: 3400 mg

In North America, 75% of sodium intake comes from salt and other sodium compounds added to processed and fast foods. Only a small percentage comes from salt (and sodium compounds, like baking powder) added at home (15%) and from sodium found naturally in foods (10%).

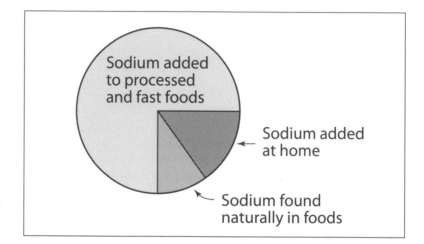

Did You Know?

It takes time to transition to a low-sodium diet. Start with one of these strategies:

- Switch to lower-sodium processed foods, such as soups, sauces and crackers.
- Cook with less salt and enjoy herbs and spices instead.
- Take the salt shaker off the table.
- At a restaurant, ask that no salt or MSG be added to your meal.

Shake the Salt Habit

Because most of the sodium we eat is in processed foods, cooking at home using unprocessed foods such as lean meats, poultry, fish and fresh vegetables and fruits is the first step to reducing sodium. Take a second step by cooking with less salt, using smaller amounts of sodium-spiked sauces and reading labels on ingredients you are using.

When you create the delectable low-sodium dishes in this book, you'll note that the recipes are packed with flavor even as they help you aim for 1500 milligrams of sodium per day. If you wish to further reduce your sodium intake, ask your health care provider for guidance.

Higher-Sodium vs. Lower-Sodium Options

Good Choices		Foods to Avoid	
Food	Sodium	Food	Sodium
Cucumber	1	Pickle	573
Baked potato	5	French fries, salted	555
Rice, brown	2	Rice, instant, with seasoning	840
Hot cereal	5	Hot cereal, instant	265
Chicken breast	51	Chicken strips	955
Chicken Noodle Soup (page 207)	160	Canned chicken noodle soup	920
Old-Fashioned Beef Stew (page 248)	230	Canned beef stew	875
Hamburger, homemade	457	Hamburger, fast-food chain	765

Shopping the Low-Sodium Way

When shopping, be ready to scrutinize ingredient lists and Nutrition Facts tables. Despite the gradual introduction of some lower-sodium foods into the marketplace, many items are still extremely high. If the ingredient list includes salt, monosodium glutamate, disodium phosphate or sodium nitrate (or nitrite), the amount of sodium on the Nutrition Facts is likely to be high. Baking powder and baking soda also contain sodium (as sodium bicarbonate), so baked goods may be high. Even for us, creating lower-sodium baked products for this book presented a challenge!

Buy these unprocessed foods as much as possible:

- fresh and frozen meats, poultry, fish and seafood (but beware of fresh meats and poultry packed in a brine solution or a seasoning mixture)
- fresh and frozen fruits and vegetables (without any added sauces or seasonings)
- dried beans, peas and legumes
- whole grains, such as barley, brown rice, wild rice, quinoa, oats and popcorn (but avoid all packaged products with added seasonings)

Did You Know?

Whole-grain breads, cereals and crackers are a mainstay of the grains food group, but they are often extremely high in sodium. Look for lower-sodium choices whenever possible.

Avoid or limit:

- processed meats and deli meats, such as cold cuts, bacon and sausages
- smoked, salted and brined meat, fish and seafood
- condiments such as pickles, ketchup, relish, chutney, mustard, soy sauce and teriyaki sauce
- prepared and restaurant-style foods sold in supermarkets, such as fresh and frozen meals, pizza, battered chicken and fish, pot pies, party appetizers, dips, cooked vegetables, salads, baked goods and desserts (if you do need to eat a prepared/frozen meal on occasion, choose the lowest-sodium one you can)

Cooking the Low-Sodium Way

Cook from scratch as often as you can so you know exactly what is going into your food. Stock your pantry and refrigerator with the right ingredients. These sodium-savvy tips will help you get maximum flavor with minimum sodium:

- Refrain from adding salt when cooking, as it just disappears into the food. Instead, season with a small amount of salt, if needed, at the end of cooking. (And remove the salt shaker from the dining table.)

Did You Know?

Managing high blood pressure requires a holistic approach. Diet is key, but so is stress management, sleep, activity and avoidance of smoking. Use your healthy, balanced lifestyle to reduce your blood pressure and you will need less medication.

Potassium-Based Salt Substitutes

When shopping, you may come across salt substitutes that contain potassium instead of sodium. Most people don't get enough potassium in their diet, and this important nutrient can offer protection from high blood pressure and stroke. However, potassium may pose a health risk for those with kidney disease, so do not add a potassium-based salt substitute to your diet without first consulting your health care provider.

Ultimately, salt substitutes don't really resolve our craving for salt. Get used to eating less salty-tasting food instead.

FAQ

Q. Can I use sea salt instead of regular salt?

A. It's just wishful thinking to believe that one type of salt is better than another when it comes to sodium. All salts have about the same amount of sodium per teaspoon (5 mL). Whether you choose plain old table salt, kosher salt, pickling salt or sea salt, use less.

- Keep your pepper mill handy and perk up dishes with lots of freshly ground black pepper — it contains antioxidants and potassium, and aids in digestion!

- Rely on spices and fresh and dried herbs to generously flavor your foods in place of salt. In addition to flavor, herbs provide an array of health-promoting vitamins, minerals and phytochemicals, and spices have antibacterial, antioxidant and anti-inflammatory properties.

- Add tang with citrus — both the juice and the aromatic zest of lemons, limes and oranges — to season a wide variety of dishes, from soups to desserts.

- Enhance the natural flavor of foods with vinegar instead of salt. Try balsamic vinegar, unprocessed natural rice vinegar, white or red wine vinegar, and fruit-flavored vinegars.

- Baking powder and baking soda contain a lot of sodium (1 tsp/5 mL of baking soda has over 1000 milligrams). When baking, omit salt from your recipes or add just a small amount — no more than 1/4 tsp (1 mL) in a recipe.

> ## SOUND BITE
>
> *Since I started eating lower-sodium foods, regular foods seem overly salty. I can't believe I used to enjoy them!*
>
> *— Fred, 60*

The Bottom Line

The more sodium you eat, the higher your blood pressure will be. Follow our menus to aim for a sodium intake of 1500 milligrams per day.

Step 7: Choose Low-Carb, Low-Calorie Beverages

As if selecting healthy foods wasn't challenging enough, there are now thousands of beverages to choose from. Any typical grocery store has a mile-long beverage aisle and an array of choices in the refrigerated section. Coffee shops serve endless combinations of coffees, teas and smoothies, and even gas stations sell soft drinks and energy drinks. The choices are indeed amazing, and the serving sizes can be as well!

Few people realize how high in calories, fat and carbohydrate many beverages are. Even a simple juice box, containing 6.8 ounces (200 mL) of unsweetened apple juice, has 100 calories and 20 grams of carbohydrate. Since the carb is in the form of sugar, and since 4 grams of sugar is equal to 1 teaspoon (5 mL), this is the same as 5 teaspoons (25 mL) of sugar! A typical 12-ounce (355 mL) sugar-sweetened beverage has 10 teaspoons (50 mL), and a 24-ounce (710 mL) fountain drink has 20 teaspoons (100 mL)! Beverages that also contain fat, such as milkshakes and special coffees, have even more calories — they're really a meal in a glass.

Did You Know?

Elderly people may not feel thirsty and may need to make an effort to drink enough. People with heart or kidney failure, on the other hand, may need to consume less liquid than the general recommendations and should consult their health care provider for advice.

Sugar-Sweetened Beverages

The term "sugar-sweetened beverages" includes an immense range of products, called "soda," "pop," "soft drinks," "cola," "sport beverages," "fruit drinks" or "flavored water," in both carbonated and non-carbonated formats. Whatever the beverage, use the Nutrition Facts table to see how much sugar you are actually drinking. Always be aware that the amount of sugar is based on a certain serving size, such as 1 cup (250 mL), but the actual can or bottle may be much larger! Do the math to determine how much sugar is in *your* serving.

Make Your Own Low-Carb Drinks

- Try club soda with a twist of lime or lemon, or a splash of your favorite juice.
- Make ice cubes with juice and add a couple to water or club soda.
- Place a few pieces of fruit, vegetable and/or fresh herbs in cold water and chill in the fridge for a few hours or overnight. Yummy combinations are strawberry-kiwi, cucumber-mint and mango-orange.
- Steep herbal or black tea, then cool. Garnish with a fresh mint leaf.
- When you need a lift, pour hot coffee over ice and add a little milk or cream.

Choose beverages that contain 0 to 1 gram of carbohydrates. The exceptions are milk and milk alternatives, which provide protein, calcium, potassium and vitamins A and D, with only about 12 grams of carbohydrate per cup (250 mL).

To protect your blood glucose and avoid unnecessary calories, choose beverages that are close to 0 grams of carbohydrate and 10 calories or less per serving. These include coffee and tea (you can add a small amount of sugar, honey or sweetener and a splash of milk if you like), water, diet soft drinks and low-calorie fruit drinks. Milk and soy beverages are the exceptions to the rule. They are higher in calories and carbohydrate but provide important protein, vitamins and minerals. We have included these healthy drinks in our daily menus.

How Many Glasses a Day?

Many of us have heard the recommendation to drink 8 cups (2 L) of water a day. Scientists have recently reviewed the evidence and found that while 8 cups of liquid is about right for a woman, and 10 cups (2.5 L) for a man, not all of the liquid must be water. Coffee, tea, milk, soup and other liquids count toward the daily total. The same scientists note that the guidelines are just guidelines, and fluid needs are very individual. People who are exercising, working physically hard or spending time in the heat may need more. Others may need less.

Did You Know?

Lattes, cappuccinos, mistos and café con leches are a great way to add milk products to your diet. Stick with servings that are close to 1 cup (250 mL), as this counts as just 12 to 15 grams of carb. Likewise, you can have iced coffee, as long as it is coffee with about 1 cup of milk. It is the jumbo-sized sweetened drinks, including slushy types, that are simply over the top. These do not fit into a carb-controlled way of eating.

FAQ

Q. I love fruit juice. The label says it has "no added sugar." Can I drink as much as I want?

A. No. Fruit juice may have no added sugar, but it is high in naturally occurring sugars. Portion control is very important. A half-cup (125 mL) of fruit juice has at least 15 grams of carbohydrate — some have much more. Read the Nutrition Facts table to see how much carbohydrate is in your favorite juice.

Think Before You Drink

Use this chart to become sip-savvy. Remember: 1 teaspoon (5 mL) holds about 5 grams of sugar or fat. Divide the total grams by five to see how many teaspoons of sugar or fat a beverage contains.

Beverage	Serving Size	Calories	Carb (g)	Fat (g)
Unsweetened apple juice	6.8-oz (200 mL) juice box	110	25	0
Fruit drink, regular	6.8-oz (200 mL) juice box	82	21	0
Fruit drink, low-calorie	1 cup (250 mL)	40	10	0
Iced tea, sweetened	12-oz (355 mL) can	120	33	0
Energy drink	20-oz (591 mL) bottle	150	38	0
Milk, 2% M.F.	1 cup (250 mL)	129	12	5
Milk, 1% M.F.	1 cup (250 mL)	108	13	3
Chocolate milk, 2% M.F.	1 cup (250 mL)	203	32	5
Soy beverage, unsweetened	1 cup (250 mL)	110	12	4
Soy beverage, chocolate	1 cup (250 mL)	170	28	4
Soft drink, can	12-oz (355 mL) can	160	40	0
Soft drink, fountain	21 oz or 730 mL	292	73	0
Diet soft drink	12-oz (355 mL) can	0	0	0
Milkshake, chocolate	12 oz (355 mL)	560	89	18
Coffee or tea, black	10 oz (300 mL)	0	0	0
Coffee with 2 tbsp (30 mL) cream and 2 tsp (10 mL) sugar	10 oz (300 mL)	105	11	6
Mocha Latte (page 182)	10 oz (300 mL)	110	17	2
Mocha latte, store-bought	10 oz (300 mL)	300	45	10

Your thirst is *usually* a good guide to how much liquid you need. By all means, if you enjoy drinking 8 cups of water daily, continue to do so. If you have been having trouble getting it all in, you will be happy to know you can count your morning java. Be sure to drink liquid throughout the day, as even mild dehydration can interfere with concentration and bring on headaches and fatigue.

Cheers! Or Cheers?

You may have heard that drinking alcohol in moderation is good for the heart. Indeed, there may be health benefits. If you choose to drink alcohol, here are some tips for doing so safely:

- Set a limit for yourself and stick to it.
- Plan non-drinking days so you don't become dependent upon alcohol.
- Consume alcohol with food and drink slowly — no more than two drinks in three hours.
- Have one non-alcoholic drink for every alcoholic one.
- If you take diabetes medication or insulin, do not drink on an empty stomach. This increases the chance of hypoglycemia. Also, be aware of the possibility of hypoglycemia many hours after drinking. This occurs because the liver is unable to release emergency sugar into the body while it is busy processing the alcohol.
- If you take medication of any kind — even over-the-counter or herbal types — ask your doctor or pharmacist whether alcohol is safe to use.

> Moderate alcohol consumption can be healthy, but if you don't drink, there's no need to start! If you do drink, enjoy a maximum of one drink per day if you're a woman or two drinks per day if you're a man. Be ready to find a way to burn off the extra calories in alcohol, as we have not built them into our menus.

What Counts as a Drink?

Beverage	Calories	Carb (g)	Notes
1½-oz (43 mL) serving of 40% distilled alcohol (rye, gin, rum, etc.)	98	0	Use low-carb mix.
5-oz (142 mL) glass of 12% alcohol dry wine	127	4	Sweet wines have more calories and carbohydrate.
12-oz (341 mL) bottle of 5% alcohol beer or cider	147	12	Light beers (4%) have 100 calories and 6 g of carb.
12-oz (341 mL) wine cooler	180	20	Make your own low-cal, low-carb cooler by combining dry wine with sparkling water or club soda.

Our daily menus do not account for the calories in alcohol. If you would like to drink, you will need to find a way to burn the approximately 100 to 150 calories in every drink or you may gain weight. You can find charts in books or online that show how many calories can be burned through exercise.

The Bottom Line

Don't let liquid calories trip up your healthy lifestyle. Choose beverages that are close to 0 grams of carbohydrate and 10 calories or less per serving. If you drink alcohol, enjoy it within safe limits.

Step 8: If You Are Overweight, Lose 5% to 10% of Your Weight

North Americans spend more than $30 billion dollars *per year* on products and programs to help them lose weight. Unfortunately, about 60% of North Americans are still overweight or obese. And many people who lose weight regain it after time. These facts are discouraging. It *is* possible to lose weight and keep it off, however.

Deciding whether to try to lose weight is your choice. You may have already tried various diets and lost and regained lots of weight. For some people, the very thought of dieting is stressful. If this is you, don't burden yourself. Focus on a healthy lifestyle instead. You owe it to yourself to eat properly and exercise regularly. In fact, some research shows no increased risk of cardiovascular disease or death among obese individuals who are physically fit. Follow the principles in this book and prepare the tasty recipes to support your overall well-being.

If you *would* like to try to lose weight, we are talking about losing 5% to 10% of your body weight. This is the same as losing 10 to 20 pounds (4.5 to 9 kg) if you weigh 200 pounds (90 kg). This amount helps reduce the risk of type 2 diabetes. By the end of the Finnish Diabetes Prevention Study (see page 16), people had lost 7% of their weight. If you already have diabetes, this small weight loss helps manage it.

Here's another piece of good news (which you have probably heard before): it took time to gain the weight, and it will take time to lose it. Losing 1 to 2 pounds (0.5 to 1 kg) per week, or even less, is considered a sensible approach and carries a lower risk of gaining the weight back.

The National Weight Control Registry is a database of over 10,000 people who have maintained a weight loss of 30 pounds (13.5 kg) or more for at least a year. People report a variety of methods to achieve this goal, but there are some key similarities. Most people follow a low-fat diet and:

- 90% exercise for about an hour per day.
- 78% eat breakfast every day.
- 75% weigh themselves at least once a week.
- 62% watch less than 10 hours of TV per week.

These findings make sense and add support to the importance of eating breakfast and being active.

> A weight loss of 5% to 10% can substantially improve insulin sensitivity, glucose control, blood pressure and lipids.

New Words for New Problems

Coined by the World Health Organization, "globesity," a blend of the words "global" and "obesity," describes the extent of overweight and obesity around the world. Of about 7 billion people on the planet, 1 billion or more are estimated to be overweight or obese. This means, for the first time in history, people with excess weight exceed those with malnutrition. This is a serious threat to the health of nations, as obesity sets the stage for diabetes, high blood pressure, arthritis, sleep apnea, polycystic ovarian syndrome, cardiovascular disease and stroke, gallbladder disease, depression and some cancers.

While excess weight is the result of more calories in than calories out, the factors that contribute to this are many. Increasing urbanization, with a change from traditional to Western diets (sometimes called "coca-colonization"), more stress, less sleep, less exercise and possibly even exposure to environmental chemicals all play a role. No matter the cause, a calorie imbalance can lead to weight gain, which in turn causes insulin resistance and diabetes. Another new word, "diabesity," is born.

A special threat exists for developing nations, as people of Asian and African descent are more susceptible to the effects of obesity than their Western counterparts. BMI and waist circumference measures that are safe for Caucasian people put others into the "at risk" category (see page 94 for more information).

No matter where diabetes is found, it takes personal and public efforts to manage it. Experts are calling on governments to help citizens by making healthy food more affordable and creating more opportunities for exercise. This has resulted in a new term we really like: "active transportation." It refers to initiatives that help people commute with less reliance on vehicles.

What Is BMI?

BMI stands for "body mass index," an estimate of body fat based on a calculation of weight and height. Knowing your BMI can help you decide if you need to lose weight and, if so, how much. Use the table below to learn your BMI. For example, Linda is a 5-foot 5-inch (65-inch/165 cm), 156-pound (71 kg) woman. Her BMI is 26. Here's how BMI results are classified:

Underweight	18.4 or less
Normal	18.5–24.9
Overweight	25.0–29.9
Obese	30.0 or more

This puts Linda into the overweight category. To get down to a normal BMI, she needs to lose 12 pounds (5.5 kg), or about 8% of her body weight.

Here is another example: Manny is 5-foot 9-inches (69 inches/173 cm) and 190 pounds (86 kg). His BMI is 28. If he loses 5% of his weight (almost 10 pounds or 4.3 kg) his BMI will drop to 26.6. This will reduce his risk of diabetes,

BODY MASS INDEX TABLE

BMI	19	20	21	22	23	24	25	26	27	28	29	30	31	32	33	34	35	36
Height (inches)	Body Weight (pounds)																	
	NORMAL						OVERWEIGHT					OBESE						
58	91	96	100	105	110	115	119	124	129	134	138	143	148	153	158	162	167	172
59	94	99	104	109	114	119	124	128	133	138	143	148	153	158	163	168	173	178
60	97	102	107	112	118	123	128	133	138	143	148	153	158	163	168	174	179	184
61	100	106	111	116	122	127	132	137	143	148	153	158	164	169	174	180	185	190
62	104	109	115	120	126	131	136	142	147	153	158	164	169	175	180	186	191	196
63	107	113	118	124	130	135	141	146	152	158	163	169	175	180	186	191	197	203
64	110	116	122	128	134	140	145	151	157	163	169	174	180	186	192	197	204	209
65	114	120	126	132	138	144	150	156	162	168	174	180	186	192	198	204	210	216
66	118	124	130	136	142	148	155	161	167	173	179	186	192	198	204	210	216	223
67	121	127	134	140	146	153	159	166	172	178	185	191	198	204	211	217	223	230
68	125	131	138	144	151	158	164	171	177	184	190	197	203	210	216	223	230	236
69	128	135	142	149	155	162	169	176	182	189	196	203	209	216	223	230	236	243
70	132	139	146	153	160	167	174	181	188	195	202	209	216	222	229	236	243	250
71	136	143	150	157	165	172	179	186	193	200	208	215	222	229	236	243	250	257
72	140	147	154	162	169	177	184	191	199	206	213	221	228	235	242	250	258	265
73	144	151	159	166	174	182	189	197	204	212	219	227	235	242	250	257	265	272
74	148	155	163	171	179	186	194	202	210	218	225	233	241	249	256	264	272	280
75	152	160	168	176	184	192	200	208	216	224	232	240	248	256	264	272	279	287
76	156	164	172	180	189	197	205	213	221	230	238	246	254	263	271	279	287	295

Source: Adapted with permission from *Clinical Guidelines on the Identification, Evaluation, and Treatment of Overweight and Obesity in Adults: The Evidence Report.*

even though he has not achieved a normal BMI. (If he wishes to lose more weight, that is always an option.)

BMI is not a reliable tool for everyone. For example, it cannot be used by pregnant women or bodybuilders, as these individuals are heavy without being overweight. There are also different charts for children.

In addition, the above classifications are not suitable for all ethnic groups. Asian people, for example, may be overweight at a BMI of 23 and obese at a BMI of 25. There are several theories about why this is. One well-known theory is that of the "thrifty gene." In the past, some peoples had to live on few calories, or to survive on few calories between more abundant times. They developed the ability to endure even during famine. No one was overweight; indeed, they were very slim. Today, their descendants live in a world of plenty but are not adapted to it. They may gain weight very easily and be less healthy at BMI values that are safe for Caucasians.

There is growing interest in defining BMI for different ethnic groups, but until that goal has been accomplished, non-Caucasians may find it more helpful to look at other measures of health.

> **BMI is not** a reliable tool for pregnant women or bodybuilders, as these individuals are heavy without being overweight.

BODY MASS INDEX TABLE																		
BMI	37	38	39	40	41	42	43	44	45	46	47	48	49	50	51	52	53	54
Height (inches)	Body Weight (pounds)																	
	OBESE			EXTREME OBESITY														
58	177	181	186	191	196	201	205	210	215	220	224	229	234	239	244	248	253	258
59	183	188	193	198	203	208	212	217	222	227	232	237	242	247	252	257	262	267
60	189	194	199	204	209	215	220	225	230	235	240	245	250	255	261	266	271	276
61	195	201	206	211	217	222	227	232	238	243	248	254	259	264	269	275	280	285
62	202	207	213	218	224	229	235	240	246	251	256	262	267	273	278	284	289	295
63	208	214	220	225	231	237	242	248	254	259	265	270	278	282	287	293	299	304
64	215	221	227	232	238	244	250	256	262	267	273	279	285	291	296	302	308	314
65	222	228	234	240	246	252	258	264	270	276	282	288	294	300	306	312	318	324
66	229	235	241	247	253	260	266	272	278	284	291	297	303	309	315	322	328	334
67	236	242	249	255	261	268	274	280	287	293	299	306	312	319	325	331	338	344
68	243	249	256	262	269	276	282	289	295	302	308	315	322	328	335	341	348	354
69	250	257	263	270	277	284	291	297	304	311	318	324	331	338	345	351	358	365
70	257	264	271	278	285	292	299	306	313	320	327	334	341	348	355	362	369	376
71	265	272	279	286	293	301	308	315	322	329	338	343	351	358	365	372	379	386
72	272	279	287	294	302	309	316	324	331	338	346	353	361	368	375	383	390	397
73	280	288	295	302	310	318	325	333	340	348	355	363	371	378	386	393	401	408
74	287	295	303	311	319	326	334	342	350	358	365	373	381	389	396	404	412	420
75	295	303	311	319	327	335	343	351	359	367	375	383	391	399	407	415	423	431
76	304	312	320	328	336	344	353	361	369	377	385	394	402	410	418	426	435	443

Waist Circumference

Waist circumference is the distance around one's waist, measured at the level of the belly button (navel). Among the Caucasian population in the United States and Canada, a waist circumference of more than 40 inches (102 cm) for men and 35 inches (88 cm) for women is considered a risk factor for diabetes, high blood pressure and cardiovascular disease. Scientists are still defining exact goals for other races; as with BMI, it is likely that some groups need to have smaller waists.

The Value of Traditional Foods

In keeping with the idea that different races have different body types is the suggestion that certain groups may be better adapted to eating certain foods. Consider the case of the Pima, a group of Native Americans living in Arizona. For centuries, the people worked the land, growing corn, beans, squash and other nutritious low-fat, high-fiber foods. They also did a great deal of physical activity, as is typical of a farming lifestyle. Diabetes was unknown in these times. As European settlers moved in, the landscape changed and the Pima were unable to grow their traditional foods. They came to rely on supplements from the government — foods such as lard, white flour and sugar. Today, the Pima have the highest prevalence of diabetes in the world. Up to 50% of the population is affected. They also have extremely high rates of the complications of diabetes, including eye, kidney and heart disease. The Pima understand that the rapid change in their diet and activity level has contributed to their poor health. They are working with researchers to try to understand how to reverse or delay diabetes through a return to a more traditional lifestyle.

Emotions and Food

Many people use food to make them feel better in times of stress and unhappiness. This is understandable but can interfere greatly with weight loss. Failure to lose weight can, in turn, result in attempts to "crash diet," which can only be sustained for so long. Intense deprivation and hunger often result in binge eating, leading to weight gain, more guilt and a poor self-image. Others feel guilty when they eat "forbidden" foods, believing that certain things should never be eaten and doing so means "I've blown it, so I might as well forget my diet." These folks also use inflexible words like "always," "never," "should" and "must." These are just some of the mind traps people encounter when their intake is ruled by their emotions rather than their hunger and fullness cues. If you struggle with emotional eating, support is available. Some options are Overeaters Anonymous, Weight Watchers, friends, family, or your dietitian, physician or counselor. See Step 10 (page 112) for suggestions on more beneficial ways to deal with stress. Emotional eating is a tough bond to break, but it is possible. You deserve freedom!

SOUND BITE

It's funny. I never had any issues with food when I was a kid. When I was a teenager, however, I watched a TV show where the character had a heartbreak, so she ate a whole chocolate cake. At that very moment, I said to myself, What a great idea! And food became my comfort from that day on.
— *Margaret, 57*

Stuffing Down Your Feelings

One of the most troubling ways of coping with stress is overeating. It is troubling because eating should be a pleasure, one that is enjoyed throughout life, and because eating is something we can't quit. Everyone has to find a healthy relationship with food or face a daily struggle. Some struggles escalate into eating disorders, which cross the spectrum from severe dieting (anorexia nervosa) to binge eating, sometimes with vomiting (bulimia nervosa). These extremes are life-threatening and require urgent professional help. In the middle are people who have guilty feelings about food, have a poor body image and engage in chronic negative self-talk. Although food seems like the issue in these tough situations, it is actually only the symptom of a bigger issue. If you can identify with any of these problems, counseling and support are needed to get at the root of "what's eating you."

Mindful Eating

To learn more about mindful eating, visit these websites:
- Am I Hungry?: www.amihungry.com
- Intuitive Eating: www.intuitiveeating.org

Mindful eating techniques take practice but, once mastered, will help you each and every time you eat, throughout your life.

Wouldn't it be great if there was a way to enjoy food more while eating the right amount for your body? Mindful eating can help. Mindful eating is a technique that maximizes your connection with food. It has also been called a meditation or a concentration. Whatever term is used, it is ultimately a *focus* you bring to the table that allows you to really experience the taste, smell and texture of food, and be aware of *how* you are eating.

These are the basic steps:

1. As much as possible, remove all distractions during your meal or snack time. Turn off the TV, put away the newspaper or smartphone, and certainly don't eat while driving.

2. Sit down and take a deep breath. Relax.

3. Take a bite of your meal, then set your cutlery down on the plate.

4. Chew slowly, concentrating on how the food tastes, smells and feels in your mouth.

   Chew until the food is smooth or liquid before swallowing.

5. Pause before taking your next bite. Simply wait, sip a beverage or use your napkin.

Repeat the steps several times. If you become distracted or your thoughts wander while you are eating, resume your focus. As you eat, ask yourself if you are full. You can rank your fullness on a scale from 1 to 10, where 1 is still very hungry and 10 is overly stuffed. Keep eating until you are a 7 or 8. If you have not finished what's on your plate, wrap up the leftovers for another time. Then congratulate yourself for taking the steps that will help you listen to your stomach!

Another tool for mindful eating is the food journal. In our world of plenty, it is easy for calories to sneak in. Keeping a food journal helps you realize what you are really eating. Also, having to write down what you eat will make you more mindful of whether you really wanted that food or ate it "just because it was there." Write down everything you eat and drink, on weekdays and weekends. You will find a sample food journal on page 370, which you can photocopy or use as a template for creating your own. Look for unnecessary calories you can cut out of your diet.

Mindful eating techniques take practice but, once mastered, will help you each and every time you eat, throughout your life.

Eating Mindfully in a Mindless Society

We live in a fast-paced society that can interfere with our intention to eat mindfully. Many of us eat takeout while driving, eat at our desks or eat larger portions because they seem economical. And food is so easily available, we may eat even when we are not hungry. Have you ever bought snack food at the service station because it seemed like a good deal?

Our environment is a powerful force in eating mindfully — or mindlessly! Take your mindful eating techniques one step further by creating a mindful eating environment wherever you are.

At home:

- Set the table attractively and use smaller plates or bowls. If eating soup, use a teaspoon instead of a tablespoon.

- Always serve yourself a portion, rather than eating straight out of the bag.

- Eat at only one or two designated eating places, such as the kitchen or dining room table.

- Don't eat on your feet! That is, don't nibble while you're preparing food or clearing away leftovers. Don't stand munching in front of the cupboards or over the sink.

- Cook only what you need for a meal so you are not tempted to overeat. If you prefer to cook larger batches, place a portion on your plate, then store the leftovers promptly.

- Plate meals at the stove, rather than placing serving dishes on the table. But to help you eat more vegetables, do bring the veggies to the table!

- Brush your teeth or chew sugar-free gum after meals.

When dining out:

- Decline the basket of bread, rolls or tortilla chips.

- Order first so you are not influenced by other diners at the table.

- Share an entrée or skip the entrée and order an appetizer and a salad.

- Make sure your meal includes a salad or vegetable. Order a side of vegetables if none come with your meal.

- Ask for sauces and gravies on the side, and do not use the whole portion.

Researcher and author Brian Wansink has observed some very amusing human eating behavior. He invented the bottomless soup bowl (it sneakily fills up from the bottom, using a hidden tank), and found that people just kept on eating. With this and other experiments, Dr. Wansink has shown how easy it is to overeat, whereas using the right size plates and glasses helps protect us from mindless eating. Check out his entertaining and informative website: www. mindlesseating.org.

SOUND BITE

It is liberating to know I can have whatever I want, once in a while. I make sure to really be present when I am eating a treat, to enjoy it to the fullest!
— *Pindy, 47*

Advertising is a powerful force in your food choices — both the type and the amount of food. Skillful marketers spend billions of dollars to entice you to eat. This would be great if they were promoting vegetables and fruits, but they're not. On some television channels, there is a food ad every five minutes. Next time you watch the tube, make a list of which foods were advertised, then ask yourself if these ads affect your purchases and portion sizes.

- Visualize how much you are going to eat off your plate before you begin eating.
- Consider asking for half of your portion to be packed up and brought out with the bill.
- Share your dessert or have a bite or two of someone else's.

At a cocktail party:

- Help the hostess by passing out drinks and canapés. This is also a fun way to mingle.
- Don't stand by the chips.
- Take one plate and fill it up, rather than grazing all night.
- Don't eat items that don't thrill you. Leave them on your plate.
- Alternate alcoholic beverages with sparkling water or diet soda.

Remember, it not just *what* you eat, but also *how* you eat. Mindful eating will help you get the most enjoyment and satisfaction out of your food.

Foster a Positive Self-Image

So many people are plagued by negative thoughts about their body, to the point that they are unable to recognize the other wonderful qualities they possess. All of their goodness is erased in their minds by their "lack of willpower" or "failure" to lose weight. How sad that they cannot appreciate themselves! If you are unkind to yourself, try to replace your negative thoughts with positive ones. You have many marvelous qualities. Make a list of them if you need to. Or ask good friends to help "pump you up" by telling you things they like about you. Your friends see strengths in you that you never would have realized on your own. If you see good in yourself, you are more likely to *feel* good about yourself. And feeling good will motivate you to take healthy steps.

Step 9: Aim for 30 Minutes of Exercise a Day

The human body was designed to move. Unfortunately, our modern world has just about made physical activity obsolete. Consider the example of Dorothy. She works from home as a writer, so she sits for long periods. She does much of her shopping online and, since she doesn't like to cook, often orders meals in. At night she watches TV, then goes to bed. Her son, a young adult in university, drives to school, sits in class all day, does homework in the evenings, then relaxes with computer games. In their lives, sitting is pervasive and activity virtually nonexistent.

This family is not unusual. The average North American is quite sedentary. Recent surveys have found that few people meet even basic fitness targets. Lack of time, fatigue and habit are some of the reasons. But there are many reasons to exercise. Which ones inspire you?

Exercise can:

- build muscle
- increase cardiovascular fitness
- reduce body fat
- improve your overall sense of well-being
- increase motivation for other good health habits
- reduce insulin resistance
- reduce blood pressure
- increase HDL ("good") cholesterol
- improve the immune system

When was the last time you did something fun? Exercise can be a way to reconnect with "play." Get a few friends or family members together for a game of tag, street hockey, hoops or catch. The latest in outdoor activity is geocaching, a treasure-hunting game that uses GPS. Geocaching will get you exploring!

Did You Know?

Over 2,000 years ago, Hippocrates said, "That which if used develops, and that which if not used wastes away." Today we say, "Use it or lose it!"

- reduce the risk of some cancers
- reduce the risk of osteoporosis
- reduce the risk of stroke
- *help prevent or manage diabetes*

If you are already physically active, you are enjoying these benefits. If you are not, imagine how your body will thank you when you start. There are unlimited ways to be active. For diabetes prevention, studies have shown that walking or jogging for 30 minutes, five times a week, is effective. New research shows that everyone can benefit from strength training and stretching, too.

A Terrific Trio

There are three main types of exercise: cardio, strength training and flexibility.

- *Cardio* is activity that increases your heart rate: brisk walking, jogging, aerobics, water aerobics (Aquasize), pole walking, hiking, cycling, dancing, swimming, Zumba, martial arts, downhill or cross-country skiing, tennis and other racket sports, wheeling quickly.
- *Strength training* is activity that builds muscle: lifting hand weights, barbells or kettlebells; using resistance bands, tubing or weight machines; circuit training; doing Pilates; doing core exercises on an exercise ball.
- *Flexibility* is activity that lengthens muscles and provides relaxation: yoga, stretching, tai chi.

Many of these exercises provide both strength training and cardio at the same time. For example, most aerobics classes have a strength component, and Aquasize builds muscle as you move your limbs against the resistance of the water. At home, gardening and heavy housework will build your muscles while making you breathe a little faster. If you move quickly between sets of weights, your heart rate will go up. This is exactly how circuit training works.

Mix up your physical activity by doing a variety of cardio, strength and stretching exercises. Inspiration is everywhere! Try a new fitness or dance class, go for a swim or follow a workout video at home. Vary your route when you walk. Try interval training, which can be as simple as adding bursts of speed walking to your usual pace (start with 30-second bouts and work up).

Start with Your Heart

Almost anyone can walk. Walking is a natural, easy way to start a fitness program. It is safe and inexpensive, and you don't need to go anywhere special to do it. A pair of comfortable sneakers or walking shoes is all you need. Biking is also a good way to ease into fitness. Perhaps you have an old stationary

I Don't Have Time to Exercise!

If there never seems to be enough time in your day for a trip to the gym, here is something NEAT for you! NEAT stands for non-exercise activity thermogenesis. "Non-exercise activity" sounds like a contradiction in terms, but it is activity that is not "exercise" per se. And "thermogenesis" is a fancy word for burning calories. The "non-exercise" part we can all relate to, but how do you burn calories doing nothing? Here's how:

- Sit up straight instead of slouching.
- Pump or bounce your foot on the ground when you are sitting — otherwise known as fidgeting!
- Stand instead of sitting whenever you can. Stand up straight. Try standing on one foot for brief periods of time.
- Raise and lower yourself on the balls of your feet or pace instead of standing in one spot.
- Sit on an exercise ball for part of your work day or while watching TV (use caution if you have balance or back problems). Once you feel stable, you can add gentle bouncing while you sit.
- Avoid long periods of sitting. Stretch or walk around at least once per hour. (Hint: drink plenty of water so you will need to use the restroom!)

These small changes increase the calories you burn and improve your health. Studies have shown that leaner people perform more NEAT than obese ones, burning up to 350 more calories per day!

Here are some more sneaky ways to add activity to your day:

- Rather than pile things at the bottom of the stairs to take one big load, make several trips — in other words, be inefficient! This also works with grocery bags. Make several trips into the house instead of bringing five bags in at once.
- Do bicep curls with your grocery bags.
- Get off the bus one stop earlier.
- Use a treadmill or stationary bike in front of the TV.
- Dance around the house.
- Close your office door and do a bit of stretching.
- Have "walking meetings" with colleagues.
- Walk the golf course.

bike in your house. Walking and biking provide a cardio-type workout, as they raise your heart rate. This means your heart is beating faster, and you may begin to sweat.

Whatever you decide to do, start with short sessions. Five to 10 minutes is enough. Include a warm-up and a cool-down. Warm-ups prepare the body for exercise, while cool-downs gradually return your heart rate to normal. If you are walking, this could mean a slow stroll to warm up, a brisk walk for five to seven minutes, then a slow walk to cool down. When you get

Check out your town's walking and cycling paths. Pack some water and a small snack and see where your feet take you.

The 10,000-Step Challenge

A pedometer is a small, inexpensive device that counts your daily steps. Wear one to see how many step you take in a day. A widely recommended goal is 10,000 steps. If you are a mail carrier, you are easily achieving this! The rest of us, not so much. Whatever your personal goal, sneak in steps by parking your car a little farther from the door, take the stairs instead of the elevator, walk over to your colleague instead of sending an email or take a walk on your lunch break.

home, do a few stretches to make your entire body feel more limber. If you are using a stationary bike, use a slower pedaling speed as your warm-up and cool-down. Pick up the pace in the middle part of your ride. If you are lifting weights, start with a brief walk to warm up, then stretch after your workout.

Always include a warm-up and cool-down, but gradually lengthen the time you are exercising briskly. Eventually, aim for 30 minutes. If you find you cannot do 30 minutes at once, do smaller bouts two or three times a day.

Pick Your Pace

If it's safe for you to do so, aim for a moderate to intense pace for your cardio exercise. There are different ways to estimate how hard you are working. The "talk test" is a simple measure of effort. It works like this:

- If you are able to talk while exercising, you are probably working out at a moderate level.
- If you are able to sing, you are working out at a level that is too easy.
- If you are unable to say more than a few words without pausing for breath, you are working out at an intense level.

Another way to gauge your effort is the "scale of perceived exertion." The next time you exercise, rate your effort on a scale from 1 to 10, where 1 is the easiest and 10 is extremely difficult. This would make 5 "moderate" and 7 to 8 "intense." Work out at a pace where you are comfortable but still making an effort. Listen to your body. Exercise should make you feel refreshed, not exhausted. If you have questions, talk to your health care provider or a fitness professional.

Strengthening More Than Your Muscles

Looking for the fountain of youth? It just might be strength training. Strong muscles fight back at age-related decline. Strength training builds not only muscle, but also strong bones and mental fitness, and these support confidence, vitality and independence.

There are myriad ways to strengthen your muscles. Dumbbells and barbells are commonly used, but resistance bands, kettlebells, medicine balls, exercise machines and even soup cans are all effective. You can also simply use your own body weight (see box, below).

Strength training builds muscle because it is *repetitive*. If you are raking leaves, you are doing a back-and-forth motion over and over. This repetition works the back and shoulder muscles. In the gym, you lift weights to mimic exercise you don't get in everyday life. Repeating the motion challenges

Build physical activity into your daily life. Whether it is parking a little farther away from the door or taking a flight of stairs instead of the elevator, small things really add up!

Using Your Body Weight to Strengthen Your Muscles

You can exercise without any equipment at all. If you want to strengthen your muscles but don't feel ready for weights or resistance bands, start with these simple exercises:

- Stand or sit with your arms held straight out from your shoulders. Hold them in place until they are tired. This works your shoulder muscles (deltoids). As you get stronger, you can repeatedly lift and lower your arms a few inches or rotate them in a small circle.
- From a standing position, lower yourself into a sturdy chair. Stand up and sit down until your thigh muscles (quadriceps) are tired. (Hint: don't use your arms to help you out of the chair.)
- Lie on a mat or carpet and cross your arms over your chest. Bend your knees and keep your feet flat on the floor. Lift your head and shoulders off the floor, being very careful *not* to pull on your head or bend your neck. Hold for a count of "one Mississippi." Return to the starting position. Repeat until your abdominal muscles are fatigued. As you build strength, hold for up to three seconds.
- Standing up, place your hands shoulder-width apart on the wall in front of you. Slowly bend your arms to bring your body closer to the wall. Slowly push yourself back to a standing position. As you build strength, you can try doing pushups on the floor, either from your knees or your toes.

Aging causes a natural and normal decline in our body muscle, making us smaller and weaker. But muscle loss may also contribute to increased insulin resistance, loss of balance, reduced bone density and loss of independence. The exciting flipside is that even elderly people can increase their muscle strength. Keeping your muscles strong, through a combination of strength training and adequate protein intake, will benefit much more than your biceps!

the muscle and makes it grow. Each time you lift a weight, or pull down on a bar, it's called a "rep" (short for repetition). Doing several reps in a row until your muscles are tired is called a "set." Doing the right number of reps, with the correct weight, creates that perfect combination of increasing strength without causing undue muscle soreness.

If this sounds difficult, it really isn't. There are many videos (free in the public library or on the Internet) that demonstrate basic motions. Most gyms and community centers have staff to orient you to the hand weights (also called free weights) and exercise machines. Choose a weight you can lift 8 to 12 times. By the twelfth time, the muscle you are working should be tired. This is how you complete one set. The goal is two or three sets of each exercise per session. You will need different weights (lighter or heavier) depending on which muscle you are exercising.

If weights are intimidating, a resistance band or tube weighs almost nothing. Instead of lifting it, you stretch it. If you buy a resistance band, it should come with a user guide, or you can look online for instructions.

Stretching and Range of Motion

Have you ever watched older adults performing tai chi in the park? They look so serene. There is a reason for that serenity: the exercise they're doing is about much more than just moving their limbs in pleasing ways; they are also improving their balance, flexibility and *awareness* (see "Where Did I Put My Zen?" on page 114).

Tai chi and yoga — and even stretching exercises on your bedroom carpet — increase flexibility, the third component of a full fitness program. All of these exercises involve stretching. Stretching is when you extend your limbs away from your trunk and hold the position to lengthen the muscles. You instinctively stretch when getting out of bed or after a long ride in the car. Stretching should feel wonderful. (Just watch your cat or dog do it!)

Another component of flexibility is range of motion. You can improve your range of motion by moving your arms and legs around in their sockets, bending your torso from side to side and circling your wrists and ankles. These exercises increase flexibility at the joints.

Flexibility exercises also promote an inner quiet as you relax into, then hold the stretch. What a wonderful change from the "to do" list we usually run in our heads!

Include a warm-up and a cool-down with every exercise session.

Every Move Is a Good Move

If you have trouble standing, or want to exercise while seated, you can:

- Ride a stationary bike.
- Sit on an exercise ball instead of a desk chair.
- Use hand weights or resistance bands (hint: try sitting on an exercise ball for more of a challenge).
- Stretch or do yoga (there are many seated or kneeling yoga poses).
- Use an ergometer (a pedal machine you place on the floor to exercise your legs or place on a table to exercise your arms).
- Work out on a rowing machine.

Reduce the burden on your beta cells by helping your insulin work better. Lose weight if you are overweight and get active.

As with any exercise, it is important to stretch properly. Ask a fitness professional, consult current exercise books or look online for stretching suggestions.

Keep an Exercise Journal

It is very motivating to record your activity. Find a prominent place to log what you are doing. Simply putting a "star" on your calendar can be a start. Aim for three stars a week, then five, then try for daily exercise, alternating between cardio and strength workouts. You might use different-colored stars for the different types of exercise you do. If you are detail-oriented, record how far you walked or what muscles you exercised. Many people who lift weights keep a log to remind them which muscles to work on and how much weight to use.

Did You Know?

There are fitness apps and podcasts available for your smartphone, iPod or tablet. These remarkable tools teach you how to exercise, motivate you and even play your favorite tunes.

Exercise Precautions

People with diabetes need to take a few precautions when exercising:

- Wear comfy shoes and socks. Examine your feet after exercise for any redness, blisters or broken skin. If you have nerve damage and/or poor circulation, these small injuries could become more serious. Keep an eye on them and consult your health care provider promptly if they do not heal.

- If you take diabetes medications, watch for hypoglycemia. Test your blood glucose before and after the exercise, and again several hours later. Always have glucose tablets, juice or regular soda pop (not diet) available. If you are experiencing hypoglycemia more often than usual, you may need to reduce the dose of your diabetes pills or insulin (see page 130 for more information on hypoglycemia).

- If you have heart disease and have been sedentary, you may need to have an exercise electrocardiogram (ECG) before starting any exercise more strenuous than walking.

- If you have diabetic retinopathy, ask your health care provider if you need to avoid certain types of activity. Very strenuous or jarring exercises may be unsafe, because they can raise your blood pressure excessively. These may include martial arts, court sports, hockey, sprinting, diving and very heavy weight-lifting.

The Bottom Line

Exercise is a gift to yourself. Enjoy a variety of cardio and strength activities most days of the week. Add some stretching whenever you can to improve flexibility and mindfulness.

Step 10: Get 7 to 9 Hours of Sleep and Safeguard Your Mental Health

It is very exciting to think that something as natural and good as sleep is a new weapon in the fight against diabetes. More and more evidence shows sleep is essential for glucose and weight control, and lack of sleep may be a risk factor for weight gain and type 2 diabetes. There are many reasons why people don't get enough sleep. Stress, anxiety and depression are some of the factors. Everyone has to deal with negative emotions but, if prolonged, they can contribute to a vicious circle of poor glucose control and a less healthy lifestyle. Caring for one's mental health and getting enough sleep are important health measures for everyone, and doubly important for people who are managing their blood glucose.

The Importance of Sleep

Sleep has two important elements: duration and quality. Sleep that is too short and/or of poor quality is associated with obesity, glucose intolerance in people without diabetes and poorer glucose control in those with diabetes.

Sleep and obesity:

- Many studies have found a significant association between obesity and getting less than seven hours of sleep per night.

- A study of 80,000 nurses found that the slimmest women (as measured by BMI) slept between seven and eight hours per night.

Sleep and the risk of developing diabetes:

- A study of healthy, middle-aged Japanese men without diabetes (and without a family history of diabetes) found that those who slept less than five hours a night were more likely to develop diabetes than those who slept seven hours or more. The men who developed diabetes were also more likely to report poor quality of sleep, such as awakening during the night. This study concluded that both quality *and* quantity of sleep were important.

- In population studies (studies of large groups of people), Caucasian and Hispanic people who slept five hours or less per night, or more than nine hours per night, had an increased risk of developing type 2. People who slept seven to eight hours had normal glucose and insulin levels.

- In a study of Americans who already had prediabetes, those who slept less than six hours most nights of the week were almost five times more likely to develop diabetes than people who slept six to eight hours.

Poor sleep is a side effect of a busy, stressful lifestyle, and millions of people are struggling. This topic is so important it makes our top 10 list of diabetes prevention strategies.

Sleep and people with diabetes:

- In a study lasting six nights, people with diabetes who slept poorly had 82% worse insulin resistance than people who slept soundly.

- African-Americans with diabetes had a higher hemoglobin A1c (see page 13) if they reported less than adequate sleep or sleep of lower quality.

Poor sleep is considered a behavioral risk factor for diabetes — meaning it is a lifestyle issue that can be managed or corrected.

Sleep, Weight and Diabetes

Many of us are too busy to eat well or exercise, and now we may add poor sleep as another hazard of our demanding lifestyle. Researchers are still looking into exactly why lack of sleep is harmful, but there are several theories. For example, how much we eat is partly determined by hormones. These chemical messengers tell us when we are hungry and when we are full. After inadequate sleep, levels of leptin (which makes us feel full) are lower and levels of ghrelin (which makes us feel hungry) are increased. In addition, the more hours we are awake, the more opportunity we have to eat — and it's not salad we are eating. In fact, sleep-deprived people snack more, eat fewer servings of vegetables and are more likely to

Obstructive Sleep Apnea

Snoring, restless sleep, morning headaches, daytime drowsiness, forgetfulness, irritability, depression — these are the signs of obstructive sleep apnea (OSA). While sleep should be a time of relaxation and restoration, people with OSA sleep fitfully, fighting for breath all night long. OSA occurs when the soft tissue in the back of the throat relaxes during sleep, causing a blockage of the airway. OSA obviously reduces the quality of sleep, but it also is a risk factor for cardiovascular disease, stroke, diabetes, hypertension and accidents.

Men, women, children and the elderly can have sleep apnea, but it is more common in smokers and in people who are overweight.

There are various treatments, and successful management of OSA can be life-changing! Lifestyle treatments include losing weight, quitting smoking and avoiding alcohol. Sleeping in a recliner or on one's side helps keep airways open. Some people have surgery to adjust their airways and others use oral appliances. Also effective is the continuous positive air pressure (CPAP) machine.

If you think you may have OSA, don't hesitate to seek diagnosis and treatment.

have irregular meals. Poor sleep can also raise levels of cortisol, one of the "fight or flight" hormones. Cortisol is released into the body when we need extra energy (from glucose) during times of stress. Chronically elevated cortisol may also lead to weight gain around the waist. Finally, if we are tired, exercise is the last thing on our minds. Our "get up and go" has "got up and went."

The good news is that poor sleep is considered a behavioral risk factor for diabetes — meaning it is a lifestyle issue that can be managed or corrected. Researchers believe better sleep could be a new tool for diabetes control.

Everyone is different, but most adults need between seven and nine hours of sleep each night. Perhaps you are able to get by on less, but what if you truly got enough sleep? Imagine waking up refreshed and energetic *before* the alarm rings! Maybe it is just a dream, but it's certainly one worth pursuing. Invest in sleep and enjoy many health dividends.

Getting a Good Night's Sleep

There are many simple lifestyle changes you can make that may help you fall asleep more easily and stay asleep through the night.

- Develop a restful bedtime routine. This could include taking a short stroll or doing some stretching or relaxation exercises, having a small snack or a glass of milk, doing some light reading or taking a warm bath or shower. Avoid activities that might be stimulating (intense exercise) or upsetting (like paying bills). And avoid large meals, caffeine and alcohol at night.

- Make your bedroom cool, dark and tidy. Remove clutter, piles of paper and that overflowing laundry basket. Try not to have a television or home office in the bedroom, as these can distract you from going to bed on time. Reserve the bedroom for sleep and intimacy.

- If you can't sleep after about 20 minutes, get out of bed and do something quiet for a short while. Go back to bed when you feel tired. If you need to nap the next day, keep it to 10 to 15 minutes. Longer naps may interfere with your sleep that night.

- Get up and go to bed at the same time every day, even on weekends.

Get the one-eyed monster out of your bedroom — and out of your child's. A great deal of research shows TV viewing is contributing to our sleepless society.

- If you regularly have trouble falling asleep, or staying asleep, talk to your doctor or pharmacist. Perhaps you are taking medications that affect your sleep, or perhaps it might be worthwhile to take a sleep aid for a short time.

Taking Care of Your Mental Health

Our mind is not separate from our body, and the way we feel has a major impact on our health. This mind-body connection is fascinating and one we can use to our advantage. Putting the right ingredients into your body, such as nutritious food, exercise and rest, makes your brain healthy. Thinking positive, surrounding yourself with supportive people and contributing to society makes your body healthy. Envisioning yourself as a "whole" will help you see the immediate and long-term value in self-care.

Reducing Your Stress

Stress is a normal part of life. It can be positive or negative. Positive stress, such as preparing for a holiday or starting a new job, can be energizing and make us more productive. Negative stress, such as financial or family troubles, can make us angry or depressed. If a negative situation goes on too long, it can be exhausting. At a minimum, stress can interfere with sleep. Worse, it can raise blood glucose levels, increase inflammation and perhaps increase weight.

There are many sources of stress in our lives. Some come and go, and some plague us for years. Stress often arises because of a situation we can't control: an accident, an unexpected deadline or other change at work, illness, personality conflicts — the list goes on. But sometimes we cause our own stress, whether it's through perfectionism, procrastination, an inability to accept help, trying to be everything to everyone or a tendency to overreact.

Pinpoint your most troublesome sources of stress by keeping a diary of the regular stressors in your life. Record which ones bother you the most and how you respond to them. If you keep a daily log, hopefully you will begin to see patterns, which may point to particular people or events. You may also learn whether your coping strategies are useful or counterproductive. Many coping strategies — overeating, smoking, using drugs or alcohol — just add new problems.

The Four A's

Because stress is unavoidable, everyone needs to develop useful coping strategies. Experts recommend an approach based on the four A's — avoid, alter, adapt, accept.

- *Avoid the stressor:* Stay away from or minimize the time you spend in a stressful place or with a person who upsets you. Learn to say "no" to unrealistic demands, from others and from yourself.

- *Alter the stressor:* See if you can change the situation. Take a support person with you, or meet in a location that makes you feel more comfortable.

- *Adapt to the stressor:* Consider whether you can change your behavior around the stressful person or place. Perhaps a different communication style would help. Practice what you want to say. Try deep breathing before going into a stressful situation. And always, before you blow up, count to 10. That will give you time to look at the big picture. Ask yourself if the situation is really worth getting upset about.

Don't Sweat the Small Stuff

Before you get really upset about something, ask yourself: Will this still be important in five minutes? Five hours? Five months? Five years? Most of the things that make us angry are really only minor annoyances.

Where Did I Put My Zen?

Zen is a type of Buddhism that seeks enlightenment (awareness) through meditation and self-contemplation. In popular usage, it has come to mean a state of relaxation, especially one you might experience after being pampered.

If your lifestyle doesn't include regular trips to the spa (and whose does?), you can still find inner quiet through meditation. In as little as five to 10 minutes a day, regular meditation can reduce fear, worry, depression and pain while creating a sense of calm, acceptance and balance. This calmness and acceptance can enable you to improve your relationship with yourself and others, which in turn can reduce stress and conflict. Meditation can also complement therapies for other health conditions you may have.

The simplest way to begin is to sit comfortably. Lying on the floor also works well. The next step is more challenging. Try to empty your mind. Shut down your running to-do list. Stop replaying unpleasant conversations. Some people find thinking about "nothing" very difficult. Still your mind by focusing on your breathing. Pay attention to the sensation of the inhale and the exhale. Or you could create your own mantra, a pleasing word or phrase that you repeat slowly during your meditation. Focusing on your mantra keeps you from thinking about other things and allows you to relax.

Like other parts of a healthy lifestyle, meditation works better if you do it regularly. Give yourself time for stillness amid the daily hubbub.

- *Accept the stressor:* Stressful people, places and events are sometimes here to stay. Think about how you can support yourself through these situations. Try not to be angry about things you can't change. Share your feelings with a close friend, a family member or a counselor. Take time to reflect on all the things you are grateful for, including your own positive qualities.

Dealing with Anxiety

If you are experiencing anxiety because of diabetes or any other reason, voice your concerns to your health care provider.

Life is hectic enough without adding a chronic disease to the mix, and diabetes is a pretty challenging condition. On a day-to-day basis, you need to take medication, check your blood glucose and pay attention to your diet and other aspects of your lifestyle. Several times a year you must visit your doctor and have lab work done. You try to stay within your glucose, cholesterol and blood pressure targets, but sometimes you just can't. Despite this, you have a positive attitude, and you take good care of yourself most of the time. Your doctor says you are doing well overall. But sometimes it all seems too much. You wonder if you will develop the long-term complications of diabetes. Diabetes is also pretty expensive. What will happen when you retire and your company drug plan expires?

The diagnosis of diabetes can certainly add a lot of worry to your life, and chronic anxiety may be the result. Many diabetes education programs now screen their clients for anxiety and have a mental health specialist on staff. You can also expect your doctor to ask how you are coping. These proactive measures can stop anxiety from taking hold. If you are experiencing anxiety because of diabetes or any other reason, voice your concerns to your health care provider.

Coping with Depression

Diabetes can sometimes have an unwanted associate: depression. These two conditions reinforce each other, and either can lead to the other. If you have diabetes, you may find yourself stressed or saddened about the time-consuming tasks related to self-management, or you may be upset that there is no cure. If you are suffering from depression, you may find it too challenging to follow a healthy lifestyle, which will interfere with good glucose control.

Diabetes can affect sexual health, so expect your doctor to ask how you are doing. If he doesn't and you have concerns, don't be shy. High blood glucose, hypertension and atherosclerosis can interfere with normal function, as can stress and depression. Support is available through counseling and medication, and good control of your diabetes and overall health will help you get back to normal.

Chronic Disease Self-Management Workshops

When you are managing a chronic illness, it is easy to feel like no one understands what you are going through. The acclaimed chronic disease workshops developed at Stanford University will show you that you are not alone. These workshops, offered all around the United States and Canada, consist of six sessions of two and a half hours each. The sessions are facilitated by laypeople, at least one of whom has a chronic illness. People just like you attend for support, education and help with problem-solving. Each participant receives a workbook and, over the six sessions, learns about:

- communicating effectively with family, friends and health professionals;
- techniques to deal with problems such as frustration, fatigue, pain and isolation;
- exercises for maintaining and improving strength, flexibility and endurance;
- use of medications and how to evaluate new treatments;
- a healthy lifestyle; and
- specific information about common chronic conditions (asthma and other lung diseases, heart disease and diabetes).

The workshops help increase your motivation and confidence to manage whatever heath challenge, or challenges, you may have. It is a terrific complement to the care and information you receive from your health care providers. Programs are offered worldwide. Check this web page for one in your area: http://patienteducation.stanford.edu/organ/cdsites.html#top.

Either way, depression should be taken seriously. Watch for signs and symptoms of depression, such as loss of interest in normal activities, feelings of sadness or hopelessness, or unexplained physical problems like back pain or headaches. If you think you might be depressed, seek help right away. Your doctor or diabetes educator can refer you to a mental health professional, who will help you get to the root of your depression with the goal or managing or even defeating it.

Depression is often the result of faulty brain chemistry, which can be corrected with medication. Cognitive behavioral therapy (CBT) can also be an effective treatment. CBT encompasses a number of different techniques that, in essence, help you change how you think about something. A new way of thinking can lead to new, more positive behavior. For example, if you are depressed, it is easy to think that *everything* is going badly or things will *never* get better. You may magnify the bad things in your life and minimize or ignore the good. CBT's various techniques — goal-setting, relaxation exercises, mindfulness (meditation), replacing negative thoughts with positive ones — may help get you back on the right track.

> **If you think you might be depressed, seek help right away.**

Am I Depressed or Do I Just Have the Blues?

Everyone feels down sometimes, but depression is something else. Take this short test. If you answer "Yes" to any of these questions, you may be depressed. Talk to your health care provider right away.

1. Do you have difficulty sleeping or sleep too much?
2. Do you eat too much or too little?
3. Do you feel things will never get better?
4. Do you find yourself not enjoying the things you used to?
5. Do you feel drained and exhausted all the time?
6. Do you have trouble concentrating and making decisions?
7. Are you easily annoyed? Do you have a short fuse and feel angry?
8. Do you have body pain (headaches, stomach aches, muscle stiffness or back pain) not related to any particular illness?
9. Are you acting recklessly, such as abusing alcohol, driving dangerously or gambling to excess?
10. Do you hate yourself?
11. Are you contemplating suicide? In this case, *seek help immediately!*

Group therapy and chronic disease self-management workshops (see box, page 115) can also be very helpful because you learn you are not alone in your struggle. You'll be able to share experiences with others like you, learn practical solutions to everyday challenges, brainstorm healthy coping strategies and support one another.

Regular exercise is also effective. You may not feel like doing anything when you're depressed, but getting out of the house for some fresh air is amazingly restorative.

(see box, page 115)

Did You Know?

Cognitive behavioral therapy (CBT) uses the mind-body connection to help you manage stress and depression, sleep better and enjoy your food more. It can also help you focus and set priorities for your health goals. CBT uses many techniques, but one of the best is eliminating negative self-talk. When you have negative thoughts about yourself, you are less likely to invest in your health. Let CBT help you turn that around! You can find information about CBT at the library or on the Internet, or ask your health care provider.

Healthy Mind in a Healthy Body

Supporting your physical health will also bolster your mental health. Eat well, exercise regularly and get enough sleep. Do things you enjoy: reading a book, solving a crossword puzzle, taking a walk, calling a friend. Jot down a list of activities that make you feel good, and do something nice for yourself every day. When you need a break:

- Play with a pet (borrow one if necessary!).
- Work in your garden.
- Do something creative.
- Listen to music — or make your own.
- Relax with a hot drink.
- Exercise.
- Have a massage or pedicure.
- Write a letter or write in your journal.
- Arrange photos in an album.
- Meditate.

   Most of all, laugh every day.

The Bottom Line

A healthy lifestyle means attending to your body *and* your mind. Take care of your mental health by managing stress during the day and getting quality sleep at night. If you think you may be experiencing anxiety or depression, discuss your concerns with your health care provider.

Chapter 4

Other Aspects of Diabetes Care

The American and Canadian national diabetes associations have exceptional websites. Visit www. diabetes.org or www.diabetes.ca for information about everything diabetes, including recipes, online support groups, local and national events and so much more.

You have many roles in life. These roles change as jobs change, as your children grow and as you grow. If you care about your health, you will always be trying to fulfill the role of savvy shopper, sound sleeper, exercise enthusiast and so on. Here is a new role for you: "glucose manager." Maybe you didn't expect this job, but with the help of your family, friends and health care providers, you will be managing your glucose, blood pressure, lipids and more.

To do so, you will need to call on "self-efficacy." This means having the confidence to change, even a little at a time, by recognizing your ability to learn, plan and do — and redo, if the first result wasn't what you wanted. Self-efficacy isn't something you can buy, unfortunately. It is something you develop with time and maturity. Just as a child needs to crawl, then walk before he can run, having successful experiences builds the belief "I can do it." Goal-setting can help you define, then achieve what you want to do.

Of course, to succeed, you first need to know what is required of you. We hope the 10 steps gave you concrete reasons for following a healthy lifestyle and explained how to do so. We hope the menus and recipes that follow in Part 2 will become part of your regular eating habits. But there is more to learn. In this chapter, we discuss some other aspects of your care. Whether you have prediabetes or type 2, ongoing monitoring will tell you how you are doing. We describe what, why and how often various tests need to be done, and the targets for those tests. For those with diabetes, we introduce you to your health care team and some of the services they will provide. This chapter also has information on blood glucose self-testing and diabetes medicines you may use now or in the future. Finally, we offer some advice on goal-setting, to help you achieve your goals, one step at a time.

The important thing to know is, when it comes to health, you are never finished. It takes time and effort every day. We

Striving for Synergy

Synergy happens when two or more units work together to achieve more than would be expected from their individual contributions, creating a wonderful and effective whole. It can be seen in everything from bee hives to ballets. Your body is in synergy when it is working well. (It can feel like it is in a vicious circle when it is not.)

While no one is perfect — or even needs to be — you can help your body achieve synergy by putting the key ingredients in reach: food, fitness, stress management, sleep and, as necessary, medications. Whatever good you do in one area will have positive effects in another. Take sleep, for example. A good night's sleep will give you energy for work and play, and will support your overall mental health. It can make your relationships, your job performance and even your blood glucose better. Synergy is not just healthy parts; it's your body and mind in harmony and wellness.

> Here's another example of the mind-body connection: Keeping your blood glucose under control protects your brain from cognitive decline and dementia.

encourage you to view this as an opportunity, not a bore, and put your knowledge to good use. Imagine yourself healthier next year than you are today!

If You Have Prediabetes

A diagnosis of prediabetes is an opportunity to understand your risk factors and take stock of your lifestyle. Appreciating the risk factors you can and can't control will help you home in on the most important strategies for preventing diabetes. These strategies are often also helpful for other common health issues, such as high blood pressure or high cholesterol, so expect to have better health all around! Each day presents an opportunity to improve. Having prediabetes is not a negative, it is a window on the future — a future you can change for the better!

Have your glucose checked regularly, yearly at minimum. This could be done by a fasting test, but a two-hour, 75-gram glucose tolerance test will yield more information. Your doctor may opt for a hemoglobin A1c test instead. (See page 13 for more information on these tests.) You can also check your own blood glucose (see page 126), but this is not generally required.

> **Having prediabetes is** not a **negative, it is a window on the future — a future you can change for the better!**

If you do monitor your glucose levels, ideally you will be in the normal range as much as possible. This means:

- *Fasting (overnight) or before eating:* 72–108 mg/dL (4.0–6.0 mmol/L)
- *Two hours after eating:* 90–144 mg/dL (5.0–8.0 mmol/L)

Limiting your carbohydrate intake, eating low-GI carbs and exercising after meals will help you meet your after-meal target. If you find your fasting glucose creeping up over time, a small bedtime snack (try one of our 100-calorie options) can sometimes lead to lower glucose levels in the morning. Another strategy is to take metformin at bedtime, but this would, of course, be in consultation with your physician. She may already have you on metformin or acarbose anyway, as these medications are approved for diabetes prevention. You will also need medications for high cholesterol or high blood pressure if you are not meeting your targets by lifestyle alone. Make sure these conditions are monitored regularly — usually yearly for cholesterol and several times a year for blood pressure. Know your targets and keep track of the results. Be an informed partner in your health.

If You Have Diabetes

Have you ever heard the saying "You don't know what you don't know"? Well, this saying really applies to diabetes. Here is another one, this one by the famous diabetes physician Elliott P. Joslin, who said, "The diabetic who knows the most lives the longest." Consider these statements your invitation to learn all you can about your condition. After all, information is power. Here's how to get informed:

- Stay abreast of improvements and changes to diabetes management. Visit a diabetes education program (or center) at least every two to three years if your diabetes is in control, and more often if it is not.
- Check your blood glucose often enough to know where you stand. Know your goals for glucose and hemoglobin A1c. Know what to do if your glucose is too high or too low.
- If you take diabetes medications and/or insulin, understand what your medications do and when to take them.

Did You Know?

You can estimate your risk for diabetes and other conditions using a "risk engine," a series of questions that results in a score. Check out:

- The American Diabetes Association's Type 2 Diabetes Risk Test and My Health Advisor: www.diabetes. org (search on "diabetes risk test" or "my health advisor").
- The American Heart Association's Heart Attack Risk Assessment: www.heart. org (search on "heart attack risk assessment").
- The Public Health Agency of Canada's Canadian Diabetes Risk Questionnaire: www.publichealth. gc.ca (search on "canrisk").

- Check your feet every day for redness, blisters or injuries of any kind. Make sure your doctor or another professional checks your feet at least yearly.

- Schedule regular appointments to measure your blood cholesterol, blood pressure, kidney function and eye, heart and nerve health. Understand your targets and keep track of your results.

- Develop a good working relationship with your team, and learn all you can. Think about how to apply your knowledge; after all, *you* are the expert in your life. SMART goal-setting (see page 135) can help you turn information into action.

We realize that taking care of your health requires commitment. You may be feeling overwhelmed or stressed, but take it one day at a time. Nobody is perfect, but everyone can find a way to live with diabetes. It is important to feel that you are in control. Talk to your health care team about any concerns you have. Think positive: you can live a long and healthy life.

> For convenience, we often use the word "doctor" to describe the individual who provides most of your care. However, your primary care may be provided by a nurse practitioner or physician assistant. Many other people will also help you with diabetes management, and their roles may have some crossover.

The World's First Diabetes Specialist

Elliott P. Joslin (1869–1962) dedicated his life to studying diabetes. Although the condition was rare at the turn of the 20th century, it was becoming, in his words, a "silent epidemic" by the 1940s. He treated many thousands of people with diabetes, using diet, exercise and insulin to help them have the best glucose control possible. Not everyone agreed that controlling glucose was important, however, and debate on this topic raged over the decades. The Diabetes Control and Complications Trial — a landmark study conducted by the U.S. National Institute of Diabetes and Digestive and Kidney Diseases — proved in 1993 that Joslin's approach to diabetes management was correct. Unfortunately, he died long before his theory was validated. To honor Dr. Joslin's foresight, buttons were produced for Joslin Clinic patients and staff that read, "I told you so."

Know Your ABCs — and Your U

Diabetes is a numbers game, but the initialism ABC will make it easier to remember your key health targets.

- *A = A1c.* Hemoglobin A1c is a three-month "average" of your blood glucose values. The target is 7% or less. Have this test done twice a year if you're usually on target, or up to four times a year if you're usually over 7%. (Note: for some people, a higher or lower target will be set. Be sure you know your personal A1c target.)

- *B = Blood pressure.* For most people, the target is less than 130/80. Your blood pressure should be measured at least quarterly. Some people check their own blood pressure at home, or at the drugstore, as this removes the chance of "white coat syndrome" (raised blood pressure due to feeling nervous in the doctor's office).

- *C = Cholesterol.* LDL cholesterol, to be exact. For most people, the target is 77 mg/dL (2.0 mmol/L) or less. In the United States, high-risk patients are advised to aim for less than 70 mg/dL. LDL cholesterol and other lipids (HDL cholesterol, triglycerides) should be measured every one to two years.

All people with diabetes should have their kidney health measured every year.

In addition to your ABCs, there is your U, or urine test. Urine (and blood) tests help measure your kidney health. Simply stated, kidneys filter and clean the blood, keeping important compounds (like protein) in the body and allowing waste products (like creatinine) to be excreted in the urine. Uncontrolled diabetes and high blood pressure can cause kidney damage.

The first sign of kidney damage is the presence of very small amounts of protein in the urine. This condition is known as "microalbuminuria" (*micro* means "small," *albumin* is a type of protein and *uria* means "in the urine"). Microalbuminuria is a warning that the kidneys are at risk and tighter control of glucose, blood pressure and even lipid levels may be necessary. Many people start on blood pressure medications when microalbuminuria is detected, and some use these pills as a preventative measure.

Urine protein can be measured in a variety of ways. One common method is a test called albumin-creatinine ratio (ACR). The normal reading for this test is 2.0 mg/mmol or less. Urine albumin alone can also be measured, although this test may not be quite as accurate. The normal amount of urine albumin is less than 30 micrograms per milligram of creatinine. Another important measure of kidney health is called eGFR, short for "estimated glomerular filtration rate." By measuring how much creatinine you have in your blood, the laboratory can estimate how well your kidneys are cleaning your blood. If only a little creatinine is found, it means your kidneys are working well. This translates into a high eGFR. In fact, this test is reported as a percent, so the higher the better.

All people with diabetes should have their kidney health measured every year. Because type 2 diabetes can be unnoticed or undiagnosed for years, people with this condition should also have their kidneys checked at diagnosis. As type 1 does not go undiagnosed, people with this condition can wait five years before their first test. Ask your health care provider how your kidney health is being monitored and how you are faring.

Did You Know?

Approximately one quarter of people with diabetes are undiagnosed.

Your Diabetes Team

As a person with diabetes, you need knowledge, practical skills and, sometimes, emotional support and encouragement. Although you are the most important person on your health care team, there are a variety of other people who are there to help you.

Health Professionals

The professional players on your team include (but are not limited to): a primary care provider (such as a family physician or nurse practitioner), a diabetes specialist (internist or endocrinologist), a nurse, a dietitian, a pharmacist and a psychologist, counselor or social worker.

People with diabetes are very lucky to have a team of professionals to work with. From primary care providers to specialists, and paramedicals such as dietitians and physiotherapists, all contribute their own expertise to your well-being.

CDEs and BC-ADMs

Some members of your health care team may have the designation Certified Diabetes Educator (CDE). This means they have a well-rounded knowledge about diabetes, have extensive hands-on experience and have passed a national exam. They maintain their certification by keeping up to date. You may also be fortunate to work with a Board-Certified Advanced Diabetes Manager (BC-ADM). This certification is awarded to those with graduate degrees and hands-on experience, and who have passed the advanced certification exam. As the name implies, BC-ADMs have specialized skills in a variety of diabetes issues.

An eye-healthy diet includes foods rich in lutein, zeaxanthin, vitamins C and E, zinc and omega-3s. Where do you find these special compounds? In everyday food, of course:

- Lutein and zeaxanthin: dark green and orange vegetables, egg yolks
- Vitamin C: citrus fruits, strawberries, kiwis, tomatoes, bell peppers, leafy greens
- Vitamin E: nuts, seeds, vegetable oils, eggs
- Zinc: meat, fish, seafood, nuts, whole grains
- Omega-3s: fatty fish

These health professionals provide a wide variety of services, and there can be overlap between them. For example, it could be a doctor, nurse, nurse practitioner or pharmacist who teaches you how to take insulin. And while a dietitian is primarily a food and nutrition expert, he will also help you troubleshoot ups and downs in your blood glucose. Meet with each member of your team to see what services he can offer you.

Other key players:

- *Eye specialist:* Schedule regular appointments (every year or two) with an optometrist or ophthalmologist to have your eyes examined for signs of diabetic eye disease. If you need treatment for eye disease, you will see an ophthalmologist.
- *Dentist:* See your dentist every six months (or as necessary) to keep your teeth and gums healthy.
- *Exercise physiologist or physiotherapist:* This specialist can create a customized exercise plan for you, whether you are well or are rehabilitating after an injury.
- *Podiatrist or chiropodist:* In case of foot problems arising from diabetes or other conditions, your podiatrist will help you care for your feet and give you tips and tools (such as orthotics) to prevent future issues.

Healthy Feet

It has been said, "My feet are ugly and they stink, but I don't want to get rid of them." I am sure you feel the same way! It is a tragedy that people with diabetes still experience serious foot problems and even amputation. Your feet are at risk if you are experiencing poor circulation (from atherosclerosis) and nerve damage (from long-term hyperglycemia.) You can protect your feet in three ways:

1. Think synergy. Anything you do to help meet your glucose, blood pressure and lipid targets is good for your feet. After all, your feet cannot be healthy if your circulation and nerves are not healthy.
2. Look at your feet every day. Watch for blisters, reddened areas, broken skin, dry and cracked areas or calluses. Watch for swelling or any changes to the shape of your feet. Report any problems to your health care provider immediately. Also have a qualified professional examine your feet at least once a year, to check your circulation, your sensation and the overall health of your skin.
3. Wear supportive shoes and socks that are not too tight… then take those feet for a walk! Exercise is great for your circulation and your blood glucose.

For more information, attend a diabetes education program or visit www.diabetes.org or www.diabetes.ca.

Your Friends and Family

People who care about you want to help, but there can be a fine line between helping and nagging. Think of *specific* ways they can help. If you need time to go for a walk, ask for it. If you want to keep higher-fiber bread or lower-fat milk in the house, say so. If you want a smaller portion of starch and a larger portion of vegetables, show your loved one the "healthy plate" on page 46 or serve your own meal. Ask your friends not to smoke around you. And speak up if your loved ones are not being helpful. Be honest about how they make you feel, and tell them you appreciate their concern and will ask for information when you need it. Taking good care of yourself will also alleviate their worries!

Diabetes Education Programs

All diabetes education programs are different, but in general they use a variety of team members — at minimum a nurse and a dietitian — to provide information, skills training and support. Programs are usually delivered in a group format, but there is often one-to-one counseling as well. Some programs offer education only, while others have personnel who can write prescriptions, adjust your medication and guide you day by day to excellent diabetes control. If you attend a diabetes education program, you will learn:

- the facts about diabetes, such as how it is diagnosed and treated;
- how to eat healthfully while honoring your food preferences and culture;
- how diabetes medications work and how to use them effectively;
- how to manage stress and emotions;
- the value of physical activity and how to fit it into your life;
- how to monitor your blood glucose and what to do if results are too high or low;
- how to meet your health targets (glucose, lipids, blood pressure, etc.);
- how to protect your feet and examine them for problems; and
- how to manage your diabetes, developing personal strategies for your lifestyle.

Did You Know?

All adults should have regular eye exams to look for problems such as cataracts, glaucoma and age-related macular degeneration. People with diabetes must be even more diligent, as they are also at risk for diabetic retinopathy — damage to the retina caused by high blood glucose. It is preventable and treatable if caught early. Because type 2 diabetes often goes undiagnosed, diabetic retinopathy may be brewing undetected. All type 2s should have a thorough eye exam when they are diagnosed. If all is well, annual or biannual exams are usually sufficient.

Blood Glucose Self-Testing

To ensure your blood glucose meter is reading correctly, compare your fingertip reading against your fasting blood glucose (done at the lab) once a year.

There have been many wonderful developments in diabetes management. The discovery of insulin was, of course, the most important, but we can appreciate the smaller victories, such as oral medication and the ability to self-test blood glucose. Also called self-monitoring of blood glucose (SMBG), this procedure takes "real time" data from your fingertips — data you can use to manage your diabetes effectively. The test involves a meter, test strips, a lancing device and lancets. The lancet is placed in the lancing device, creating a tool that can be used to obtain a very small drop of blood. The test strip goes into the meter, the blood drop goes onto the strip and presto, your blood glucose is displayed on a small screen. SMBG is, for many people with diabetes, simply indispensable. Other people with diabetes may need to test rarely or not at all.

How Often to Test

Each person is different. For people whose diabetes is very stable, testing a few times a week may be adequate. People who are adjusting their medication on a frequent basis may need to test several times a day. Some people do not need to test at all, but should make sure their physician is monitoring them (this would likely be done with a hemoglobin A1c test). If you are performing SMBG, create a testing pattern that yields the right amount of information for you. Here are some suggestions to help you decide how often to check:

Check less often if:

- Your blood glucose levels are usually in the target range.
- Your hemoglobin A1c is in the target range.
- You adjust your diabetes medication rarely or not at all.
- You keep a regular schedule.

Check more often if:

- You are working with your health care team to correct high and/or low blood glucose values.
- You are adjusting your own medications to correct high and/or low glucose values. This includes people who use an insulin pump or multiple daily injections to adjust for larger or smaller meals, or to correct high/low readings before meals.
- Your schedule varies, with frequent changes to your exercise and eating habits (as might be the case if you do shift work, for example).

- You are ill or otherwise not following your regular lifestyle, as when traveling.

- You are using a new medication for diabetes or any other condition, especially if it could raise or lower your glucose level or change your appetite. Always ask your physician or pharmacist if a change to medication might affect your blood glucose.

- You are starting a new or more strenuous exercise, or if you are exercising less than usual.

- You are experiencing new or increased stress.

Record the results in a notebook or logbook, or use a meter that can download data into a computer. Most meters are able to do this, and they come with software that can create charts and other reports. There are also glucose logging apps for your phone or tablet. Whatever meter you use, and whether you go paper or digital, use the results to inform yourself. Take action if your glucose levels are not where you want them.

Blood Glucose Targets

Although everyone with diabetes is an individual, these are the blood glucose targets for most adults:

- *Fasting (overnight) or before eating:* 72–108 mg/dL (4.0–6.0 mmol/L) if it can be achieved safely; otherwise, 72–126 mg/dL (4.0-7.0 mmol/L).

- *Two hours after eating:* 90–144 mg/dL (5.0–8.0 mmol/L) if it can be achieved safely; otherwise, 90–180 mg/dL (5.0–10.0 mmol/L).

Developing a Testing Pattern

Self-monitoring of blood glucose in and of itself will not improve your diabetes control. Instead, you test to *learn* something — either your lifestyle/medication regimen is working or it isn't.

Before you start SMBG, think about what you want to know. Would you simply like to get an overview of your glucose levels? If so, one option is to test once a day, before a meal or your bedtime snack. In this case, you are aiming for a "before eating" target. The first day, test before breakfast; the next, before lunch; and so on. On the fifth day, you'll be back to testing before breakfast. (See the sample logbook page on page 128.) By rotating through the different times, you'll gain information about your glucose levels over the course of the day, rather than just first thing in the morning, for example. If

Self-monitoring of blood glucose in and of itself will not improve your diabetes control. Instead, you test to learn something — either your lifestyle/ medication regimen is working or it isn't.

testing every day seems too intensive for you, try a few times a week. Just be sure to pick a different testing time than the one you did last.

Sample Logbook Page

Date	Before Breakfast	Before Lunch	Before Dinner	Before Bedtime	Comments
Nov 2	106*				
Nov 3		130			
Nov 4			77		
Nov 5				157	Didn't walk after dinner
Nov 6	117				

* mg/dL

Reduce your blood glucose after meals by choosing low-GI carbohydrates and doing some exercise after you eat.

If you want to learn how high your glucose goes after meals, try testing both before *and* two hours after eating. You can rotate through the different meals or, if you are particularly interested in a specific meal, stick to that meal for several days in a row. In this case, you are comparing your results to the targets for before and after eating. You will soon discover what foods work best for you. If you are active after a meal, you will notice your glucose level is lower. (Note: it is difficult to get your after-meal glucose on target if you were high *before* the meal. Work with your team to ensure your before-meal tests are on target before you start testing after meals.)

Sample Logbook Page

Date	Before Breakfast	Two Hours After Breakfast	Before Lunch	Two Hours After Lunch	Before Dinner	Two Hours After Dinner	Comments
Nov 2	6.5*	9.3					
Nov 3			5.2	8.6			
Nov 4					7.4	14.1	Ate fast food
Nov 5	5.5	6.9					

* mmol/L

In addition to these common testing times, you could check your glucose any time you don't feel well. If your glucose turns out to be normal, you can look for other explanations.

Testing for Insulin Adjustments

If you have type 2 diabetes and are starting on insulin, chances are you will begin with a nighttime dose of a long-acting insulin called N (or NPH). This insulin works all night so you can wake up with a desirable blood glucose level in the morning. Your doctor will start you on a small dose that you will gradually increase until your fasting glucose is on target. Thus, you will want to test your blood glucose first thing in the morning. You might also want to try the occasional test around 3 a.m., because N taken at dinner may peak in the middle of the night, causing blood glucose to drop too low. If you are becoming hypoglycemic at night, this can be prevented by having a bedtime snack, reducing the dose of insulin or taking the insulin later in the evening (closer to bedtime). As always, work with your team to reach your glucose targets safely.

If you are taking N twice a day (morning and night), you will want to test your blood glucose twice, just before each injection. The morning glucose test will tell you if the nighttime dose of N was suitable. Testing before dinner will tell you if the morning dose was suitable.

If you take short-acting insulin at meals, you may be testing before and after *each* meal. This pattern is very intensive, but it allows you to see how well the insulin is covering the carbohydrates in your meal.

There are other patterns to consider, each affected by your status and goals. Talk to your diabetes team for ideas.

Did You Know?

Self-monitoring of blood glucose is a terrific tool if used correctly. If you understand why you are testing, you will be able to determine the right pattern for you. Keep in mind that SMBG is expensive and a little painful, so make every test count.

Instead of N, you might use even longer-acting insulins called detemir or glargine. These are discussed on page 134.

Oral Medications for Diabetes

There are quite a few medications for type 2 diabetes. Each falls into a type, or "class," of drugs, and each class lowers glucose in a different way. Many people with diabetes will start on one class of drug, then add another if need be. Sometimes, a small dose of two classes of medication works better than a larger dose of one kind, as the problem is approached from two different directions. Two smaller doses may also mean fewer side effects.

Medications can be taken orally (by mouth) or by injection. Below is a list of common oral medications.

Sometimes, a small dose of two classes of medication works better than a larger dose of one kind.

Sulfonylureas

The main job of sulfonylureas is to help your pancreas make more insulin. This class of drugs includes glyburide/

glibenclamide (Diaßeta), gliclazide (Diamicron), glimepiride (Amaryl) and glipizide (Glucotrol). Some sulfonylureas work all day, so you take them only once a day — usually before breakfast. Others you take twice a day, typically before breakfast and before supper. Because these drugs actively lower your blood glucose, they can cause hypoglycemia. Know how to prevent, recognize and treat hypoglycemia if using sulfonylureas. Weight gain can also be a side effect, perhaps

Healthier but Hypoglycemic?

A healthy lifestyle can lower blood glucose. This is a great success, and the whole point of this book! But if you are frequently experiencing hypoglycemia — blood glucose of 70 mg/dL (3.9 mmol/L) or less — your diabetes medication may need to be reduced or stopped.*

WATCH for the early symptoms:
- trembling/shakiness
- sweating
- feeling anxious
- feeling hungry and/or nauseous
- tingling in the lips or fingers

TEST your blood glucose to verify it is low. If it is:

TAKE (one of):
- 15 grams of glucose tablets (read the package to determine how many tablets to take)
- ¾ cup (175 mL) of juice or a regular soft drink (not diet)
- 6 Life Savers
- 1 tbsp (15 mL) of honey
- 1 tbsp (15 mL) of sugar, dissolved in water

WAIT 15 minutes and test your glucose again. If it is still low, take another portion of one of the above fast-acting sugars. Repeat as necessary until your glucose has returned to normal. Then have a snack that will carry you to your next meal.

TELL your health care provider. Document all episodes of hypoglycemia in your logbook. See if there are any patterns.

Hypoglycemia can be very serious. If not treated right away, blood glucose can drop to dangerous levels, causing confusion, blurry vision, slurred speech and even loss of consciousness. *If you think you are low but are unable to test, treat as if you **are** low.*

* Insulin, glyburide/glibenclamide (Diaßeta), glipizide (Glucotrol), gliclazide (Diamicron), glimepiride (Amaryl), repaglinide (Prandin, GlucoNorm) and nateglinide (Starlix) lower glucose levels and may need to be reduced or stopped if you are experiencing hypoglycemia. Other drugs (see page 131) rarely cause hypoglycemia on their own.

related to hypoglycemia — frequent low blood glucose will have you eating extra carbohydrates (hence calories) to get your blood glucose levels back up. It is very important to take the smallest dose necessary to avoid undue hypoglycemia and weight gain. It is also important to eat meals on time, and possibly have a snack before exercising, if taking these medications.

Biguanides

Biguanides reduce insulin restistance and prevent your liver from releasing too much glucose into the blood. This can reduce the amount of insulin your body needs to make. Metformin (also sold under the brand name Glucophage) does not cause hypoglycemia or weight gain. Metformin is typically taken two to three times a day with meals. There is also a once-daily (extended-release) version of metformin. The main side effects of metformin are an upset stomach (possibly with diarrhea) and a metallic taste in the mouth. Starting on a low dose and gradually increasing can help reduce these side effects. It is also important to take metformin with food.

Alpha-Glucosidase Inhibitors

Sold under the names acarbose (Precose, Prandase or Glucobay) and miglitol (Glyset), alpha-glucosidase inhibitors block the enzymes that digest the starches you eat. This action causes a slower and lower rise of blood glucose throughout the day, but mainly right after meals. Because these drugs slow your digestion of starches, they can cause gas, bloating and diarrhea. Taking a small dose, with the first bite of food, reduces these effects, and your body adapts over time. This class of drug does not cause hypoglycemia or weight gain.

Dipeptidyl Peptidase-4 Inhibitors (DPP-4 Inhibitors)

The DPP-4 inhibitors sitagliptin (Januvia), saxagliptin (Onglyza), vildagliptin (Galvus) and linagliptin (Tradjenta) are once-a-day pills that help lower blood glucose by increasing insulin when blood glucose is high, especially after you eat, and by reducing the amount of glucose released by your liver. Possible side effects include flu-like symptoms, such as a stuffy or runny nose, sore throat and headache. They do not cause hypoglycemia or weight gain, however. These drugs are relatively new to the market, so long-term safety is not known.

Did You Know?

Although alpha-glucosidase inhibitors do not cause hypoglycemia on their own, they may be taken with drugs that do. If you become hypoglycemic while using an alpha-glucosidase inhibitor, you must treat the low with glucose tablets, 1 tbsp (15 mL) of honey or 1 cup (250 mL) of milk.

Meglitinides

These drugs, sold under the names repaglinide (Prandin, GlucoNorm) and nateglinide (Starlix), are similar to sulfonylureas in that they cause your pancreas to release insulin. They are taken right before meals as they work fast and do not linger as long as sulfonylureas do. Regardless, they can cause hypoglycemia — and if you are not eating, *do not* take a dose. Weight gain is another possible side effect.

Thiazolidinediones (TZDs)

Pioglitazone (Actos) and rosiglitazone (Avandia) help make your liver, muscles and fat cells more sensitive to insulin. Pioglitazone is usually taken once a day, while rosiglitazone is taken either once or twice a day, with or without food. They do not cause hypoglycemia, but side effects may include weight gain, anemia and swelling in the legs or ankles. They may also increase the risk of fracture and heart failure. In addition, it is important for your doctor to check your liver enzyme levels regularly. Because of these side effects, TZDs are not recommended for diabetes prevention, even though they were successfully used in a prevention study called the DREAM Trial.

Injectable Medications for Diabetes

People with type 2 make insulin, but it is either not effective or not in adequate supply, or both. The oral medications discussed above counteract these problems, and as long as the pancreas remains able to make insulin, blood glucose is controllable. If the pancreas makes too little insulin, as may happen over time, the pills become ineffective. Insulin is the next step to restoring glucose control.

People with type 2 diabetes may also make fewer incretins. Incretins help lower glucose by several mechanisms, and incretin-like compounds (called mimetics) are a new tool in diabetes management. Insulin and incretin mimetics may be used alone or in combination with oral medications.

Insulin and incretins are hormones, which, chemically speaking, are similar to proteins. If they were to be taken in pill form, they would enter the digestive system and be destroyed. So they are instead injected with an extremely short, thin needle into a fatty part of the body and are gradually absorbed. People who use injectable medications can administer them themselves. The abdomen (belly) is often a good spot to use, but some people prefer areas on their arms, legs or buttocks.

If you need to take insulin or an incretin mimetic, you will be taught how to do so safely and effectively.

Insulin

When the pancreas is working well, it secretes a small amount of insulin all day long and sends out extra insulin whenever a meal or snack is eaten. People who take insulin by injection are trying to copy this pattern. Injected insulin thus comes in two main types: long-acting (or basal) and mealtime (or bolus). Long-acting insulins are taken once or twice a day and, as the name suggests, have a long action time. They are designed to copy the slow and steady trickle the pancreas would normally release, and some last as long as 24 hours. Mealtime insulins are taken just before eating, and the dose may be adjusted for larger or smaller portions. Some people take this type of insulin at each meal, while others take a dose only at their largest meal. Finally, there are premixed insulins, which are a combination of long-acting and mealtime insulins. Within these main types are some sub-categories, as well as different brands.

If you are not meeting your blood glucose targets despite taking pills and managing your lifestyle as well you can, consider starting insulin. Some people add insulin to pills (for example, adding nighttime insulin to daytime pills) or stop taking pills altogether and use insulin alone. Approximately

> **Did You Know?**
>
> Before 1922, type 1 diabetes was a fatal disease. Then one of the biggest breakthroughs in medicine occurred. Dr. Frederick Banting, medical student Charles Best and biochemist Bertram Collip discovered and purified insulin in a University of Toronto laboratory. People with type 1 could now manage their condition and live for many years. Today, insulin remains essential in type 1 and is also commonly used in type 2.

Psychological Insulin Resistance

This is not the same as the insulin resistance described on page 10. With psychological insulin resistance, the person with diabetes has his mind made up: "I'm not going on the needle!" This can become an unfortunate struggle between the person and his physician, and it can cause unhealthy delays in reaching glucose targets. Psychological insulin resistance is more common if the person:

- has no idea insulin injections are a common treatment for type 2 diabetes;
- has been made to feel bad that his glucose is off target ("You didn't follow advice, and now you have to use insulin") or has had insulin used as a threat ("If you don't get your blood sugar down, you are going on insulin");
- is afraid of needles and doesn't know today's needles are truly tiny; or
- is under the mistaken impression that insulin will make him less healthy, or that it has unmanageable side effects.

Don't let psychological insulin resistance stop you from achieving your health goals. Learning all about insulin will help you be successful.

Types of Insulin and Their Brand Names

Type of Insulin	Onset	Peak	Duration	How It's Used
Mealtime (Bolus) Insulins				
Rapid-Acting				
Aspart (NovoLog; NovoRapid)	10–15 minutes	60–90 minutes	3–5 hours	Rapid-acting insulin is convenient because it is taken just before eating.
Glulisine (Apidra)	10–15 minutes	60–90 minutes	3–5 hours	
Lispro (Humalog)	10–15 minutes	60–120 minutes	3–5 hours	
Short-Acting				
Humulin R; Novolin ge Toronto; Novolin R	30 minutes	2–3 hours	6–7 hours	Short-acting insulin takes time to be absorbed so must be taken about 30 minutes before the meal.
Long-Acting (Basal) Insulins				
Intermediate-Acting				
Humulin N; Novolin ge NPH; Novolin N	1–3 hours	5–8 hours	Up to 18 hours	Intermediate-acting insulin covers insulin needs for about half the day or overnight.
Long-Acting				
Detemir (Levemir)	90 minutes	6–8 hours	16–24 hours	Long-acting insulin covers insulin needs for about one full day.
Glargine (Lantus)	90 minutes	No peak time; insulin is delivered at a steady level	Up to 24 hours	
Premixed Insulins*				
Humalog Mix 75/25	Each type has a unique profile. Discuss your needs with your health care team.			These products are generally taken twice a day, before breakfast and dinner.
Humalog Mix 50				
Humulin 70/30				
Novolin ge 70/30				
Novolin ge 60/40				
Novolin ge 50/50				
NovoLog 70/30 (NovoMix 30 in Canada)				

* Premixed insulins are a combination of specific proportions of intermediate-acting and short- or rapid-acting insulin in one vial or cartridge. The numbers following the brand name indicate the percentage of each type of insulin. In Canada, the numbers are reversed (e.g., Humulin 30/70 instead of 70/30).

40% of people with type 2 take insulin, and the number might be higher but for "psychological insulin resistance" (see box, page 133). If you decide insulin is a good fit for you, take time to learn all about it — how it works, how to inject it, how to store it and so on. As always, knowledge is the first step to success.

Incretin Mimetics

Incretins are hormones we make when we eat. These natural compounds tell us when we are full, and they help the pancreas make and release insulin. People with diabetes may not make enough incretins, or they may be broken down by the body's enzymes too rapidly to be effective, but incretins are now available as medications. The incretins in these medications are not exactly like our naturally occurring ones, so they do not break down as quickly. But they are very similar, which is why they are called mimetics (as in "mimics"). Exenatide (Byetta, Bydureon) and liraglutide (Victoza) are both versions of the natural glucagon-like peptide-1 (GLP-1). These compounds are taken once or twice daily (Bydureon requires just once weekly dosing). Side effects include nausea, headache and a reduced appetite. Some people lose weight while on incretin mimetics.

> **Did You Know?**
>
> Two new classes of medication are related to the incretin system: incretin mimetics are injected substitutes for the missing natural compounds; DPP-4 inhibitors are pills that inhibit the enzymes that break down incretins.

Congratulations! You have come to the end of Part 1. You have reviewed the facts about diabetes and learned about nutrition and the 10 steps. We hope you will embrace this information with enthusiasm and confidence. When you are ready to try something new, here is your SMART strategy.

Setting Goals the SMART Way

When tackling a new project, it can be challenging to know where to start. Lifestyle changes are no exception. Try this SMART strategy for any goal you want to achieve. SMART stands for:

- Specific
- Measurable
- Achievable
- Relevant
- Time-oriented

Plan for Success with SMART Goal Setting

My specific goal is:

I will measure my progress by:

I think my goal is achievable because:

My goal is relevant because:

I have considered when and how long this will take:

Diabetes has not been left behind by social media. Online communities offer support, information and the benefit of connecting with someone who may know exactly how you feel. Blogs, Twitter, YouTube and Facebook provide thousands of opportunities to learn and connect.

Being time-oriented helps you commit to a time frame. This is much more useful than a "someday" approach.

Specific means the goal you have in mind is clear. Think carefully about what your goal is. Rather than say, "I want to get more exercise," say, "I will walk on my lunch break." This specific goal spells out what type of exercise you will do and when you will do it. To be even more precise, you could add, "I will walk on my lunch break three times a week."

Measurable means you will be able to monitor your progress. If walking on your lunch break is your goal, plan to keep an exercise diary or put stars on your calendar to mark the days you walked. If your goal is to walk a certain distance, log that as well. Measuring progress helps you stay on track and can show you if things are getting in your way, so you can plan a different approach to meeting your goal.

Achievable means setting your sights on goals you know you can accomplish. Focus on "quick wins" rather than goals that will require more effort than you can put in right now.

Relevant means you are choosing goals that matter. Any step you take for your health matters, so good for you!

Being *time-oriented* will help you gear up for the change you are about to make. For example, if you are going to start walking on your lunch break, you need to plan *when* you will start. If it is next week, you will need to remember to bring your walking shoes and to plan your route so that you are able to complete your walk in the time you have (and still fit in time to eat!)

If your health has been on the back burner for a while, or if you knew a change was necessary but didn't know where to start, take a moment to think about what will give you most bang for your buck. Then plan your next moves the SMART way.

Part 2

Recipes and Menus for Diabetes Prevention and Management

Introduction to the Menus and Recipes

Nutrition has been a hot topic for many years, and it seems it's still as controversial as ever. With so much information coming at you from all directions, some of it contradictory, it can be truly difficult to know what to eat. It is important to let common sense rule, and we have also used our personal and professional experiences and scientific research to guide us. The 10-step plan is the result of this work. But we didn't stop there. Our ultimate goal is to turn nutrition information into food you can eat and enjoy.

We have developed 28 days of menus from our collection of over 150 recipes. These menus are based on Dietary Guidelines for Americans (and MyPlate) and Eating Well with Canada's Food Guide. This means they emphasize vegetables and fruit, lower-fat dairy foods, lean meat and alternatives (such as legumes) and whole-grain starchy carbohydrates. These healthy choices are the ingredients for each recipe, which has then been carefully developed, tested and retested. We hope you will enjoy making the recipes and will also try adding your own spin with what you have on hand. With many of the recipes, we've provided suggested variations that will not greatly change the nutritional profile.

The Nutrients in Our Menus and Recipes

We had very specific goals in mind when we created the recipes and menus. Taste was always number one, but as you know from reading the 10 steps, calories, carbohydrate, fat and so on were also vital. Each menu delivers three meals that fit into the steps by providing (on average):

- 1600 calories;
- 210 grams of total carbohydrate;
- 30 grams of fiber;

- 45 grams of fat (with no more than 12 grams of saturated fat and minimal trans fat);
- less than 200 milligrams of cholesterol;
- 90 grams of protein; and
- less than 1500 milligrams of sodium.

As a percent of calories, this is about 53% carbohydrate, 22% protein and 25% fat. Fat is the highest-calorie macronutrient, at 9 calories per gram (compared to 4 calories per gram in carbohydrate and protein). Keeping the fat low allowed us to put more calories toward carbs and protein, which translates into bigger portions on your plate!

Our healthy, balanced daily menus provide two servings of milk and alternatives, two to three servings of meat and alternatives (the equivalent of 6 ounces/175 grams), seven servings of vegetables and fruits and five to six servings of starchy carbohydrates (grains, potatoes, bread, etc.).

The menus were created after the nutrient content of each recipe was analyzed. You will find the nutrient analysis in a table in the bottom left corner of each recipe. This table looks similar to a Nutrition Facts table, but, as it does not provide the exact same information, we have called it "Nutrition info" instead. This detailed information is helpful if you want to know the specifics for any of the macronutrients (for example, if you are carefully matching insulin to carbohydrate), or for fiber, cholesterol or sodium. (Remember, if you are counting grams of available carbohydrate, make sure to subtract the fiber from the total carbohydrate listed.)

If you're not sure how many calories you should be eating each day, see "How Much Should I Eat?" on page 26.

Remember, if you are counting grams of available carbohydrate, make sure to subtract the fiber from the total carbohydrate listed.

A Menu for Living

There are many different ways to reduce calories. From low fat, high carb to higher fat and lower carb, *all* diets work if they reduce calories. How do you choose? We have tried to reflect the best of the various meal strategies, while keeping consistent with food guides for the United States and Canada. We have translated a moderate amount of carbohydrate, protein and fat into plenty of vegetables, fruit and whole grains, rounded out by lean animal and vegetable proteins and healthy oils. We insist on three balanced meals and satisfying portions. We offer between-meal snacks to boost nutrition and fullness. This is not a "diet"; this is a plan for life.

Our nutrition info does not include % DV, as these values do not apply to all of our readers and could be misleading. But we know our menus are high in vitamin A and C because of the abundance of vegetables and fruit. In addition, the menus provide an average of 1100 milligrams of calcium per day, thanks to dairy and other calcium-rich foods (legumes, green leafy vegetables, whole grains), while meat and alternatives, whole grains and dark leafy greens contribute 12 milligrams of iron.

Desserts in Our 1600-Calorie Menu Plans

People with diabetes were once told to avoid sweets entirely. However, you can enjoy them occasionally; the key is to monitor total carbs when eating dessert with your meal. Simply sub in a small portion of dessert in place of bread, pasta, rice or crackers with a similar amount of carbohydrate (in our menus we've done the figuring for you). Rather than selecting empty-calorie sweets, choose a dessert that is low in fat and contains fiber and other valuable nutrients. Many of the desserts included in our menus provide a good dose of calcium. Others are high in fiber, and many also contain fruit. The bottom line: everything in moderation!

About the Nutrition Info

Food Intelligence (Toronto, Ontario) performed computer-assisted nutrient calculations for the recipes and menus, using Genesis R&D SQL (ESHA Research). The primary database was the Canadian Nutrient File (version 2010), supplemented with information from the USDA National Nutrient Database for Standard Reference (Releases 21 to 25) and other sources. Food Intelligence also assigned Food Choices to the recipe servings.

Recipes were evaluated as follows:

- Nutrient calculations were based on common household weights and measures (cup, tsp, lb, etc.) unless a metric package would typically be purchased and a specified portion of it used in the recipe.

- Optional ingredients and unspecified amounts of ingredients were not included in the calculations.
- Where there is a choice of ingredients, the first one listed was used in the calculation.

About the Food Choices

Food Choices assignments were based on the CDA food choice values in the table below. Available carbohydrate is total carbohydrate minus fiber. Low-fat (1%) milk and fat-free yogurt were used in the recipes and menus.

Food Choice Values

Food Choice	Available Carbohydrate	Protein	Fat
Carbohydrate			
Grains and Starches	15 g	3 g	0 g
Fruits	15 g	1 g	0 g
Milk and Alternatives *Low-Fat* *Fat-Free*	 15 g 15 g	 8 g 8 g	 2.5 g 0 g
Other Choices	15 g	variable	variable
Vegetables	<5 g (most) Not usually counted in Carbohydrate Choices	2 g	0 g
Meat and Alternatives	0 g	7 g	3–5 g
Fats	0 g	0 g	5 g

Adapted from: Canadian Diabetes Association, Beyond the Basics: Meal Planning for Healthy Eating, Diabetes Prevention and Management. December 20, 2005, Version 2.

Food Choices have been assigned to each recipe and appear at the bottom left-hand corner of each recipe page. Average Food Choices for the meals in the menus (pages 148–155) appear in the table below.

Average Food Choices Per Meal

Meal	Carbohydrate	Meat and Alternatives	Fats
Breakfast	3	$\frac{1}{2}$	1
Lunch	4	2	$1\frac{1}{2}$
Dinner	4	3	2

Incorporating Our Recipes into Your Routine

Note to readers who use the American Dietetic Association and American Diabetes Association's *Choose Your Foods: Exchange Lists for Diabetes:* The values for ADA Exchanges and CDA Food Choices are very similar. However, the ADA system "counts" more of the fiber and more of the vegetables. This results in more Carbohydrate Exchanges per day in the ADA system — roughly 13, compared with 11 CDA Food Choices.

When you review the menus, please don't think we expect you to cook every single dish we have included in our four weeks of meal plans. We all have busy lives with family, jobs and other interests. We understand it may be intimidating at first, depending on your cooking experience, to prepare recipes from scratch instead of relying on convenient packaged foods or perhaps eating out for many of your meals, which you may have become accustomed to as part of your weekly routine.

The recipes in this book will help you put a new healthy approach to eating into everyday practice. If you have been relying on prepared foods from supermarkets or eating out often, you may find it a big change at first. While these prepared meals may look and taste appetizing and wholesome, the extra-large portions are often loaded with calories, fat and sodium, and can hamper your efforts to prevent or manage diabetes. Start with small steps: try a new recipe or two each week, beginning with those that are familiar and appealing, then gradually becoming more adventurous. You can also use our recipes as templates — especially when it comes to portion size and reduced fat and sodium — to help you modify family favorites or create your own new recipes.

Creating Your Own Weekly Menus

Here's a summary of what we've included in the weekly menus, for you to use as a template for building your own menus.

Planning a Nutritionally Balanced Weekly Menu

Food Options	How Often to Eat
Breakfast	
Grain-based cereals such as oatmeal, porridge and muesli; commercial cereals; whole-grain breads and muffins	3 or more times per week
Egg or egg white dish	1 to 2 times per week
French toast or pancakes	1 to 2 times per week
Lunch	
Legume-, grain- or vegetable-based soups served with ½ sandwich or whole-grain crackers and bean spread	2 to 3 times per week
Salad (see chart, page 160; include salmon and/or tuna once per week each)	1 to 2 times per week
Sandwich (see chart, page 158; include salmon and/or tuna once per week each)	1 to 2 times per week
Legume and/or grain dish, or chili (leftovers from the night before make great lunches)	1 to 2 times per week
Dinner	
Whole grains, pasta, beans or tofu	1 to 2 times per week
Beef, pork or lamb	1 to 2 times per week
Chicken or turkey	1 to 2 times per week
Salmon or trout	1 time per week
Other fish (cod, halibut, sole)	1 time per week
Fruit	
Refer to our list of suggestions on page 156	2 to 3 servings per day: 1 at breakfast, 1 at lunch and/or 1 at dinner (or save fruit for a snack)
Vegetables	
Choose from a wide array of vegetables and eat out of hand or as part of a soup, salad, sandwich, casserole, side dish or snack	4 servings or more per day: 2 at lunch; 2 at dinner
Dairy (Milk and Alternatives)	
Low-fat (1%) milk, plain soy milk, low-fat or nonfat yogurt (plain or artificially sweetened fruit-flavored)	2 servings per day: 1 at breakfast; 1 at lunch or dinner, or as a snack

Low-Sodium Cooking

In Step 6 (page 81), we outlined why it's so important to reduce sodium in your diet, especially if you have diabetes or prediabetes. Major health organizations are advising people with high blood pressure, heart disease, diabetes or prediabetes to limit their sodium intake to 1500 milligrams a day. North Americans typically consume 3400 milligrams of sodium each day, so meeting the recommendations requires reducing sodium intake by at least half.

This may at first seem like a daunting task. Our best advice is to make changes gradually, following the suggestions we gave you in Step 6. It takes time for your taste buds to adjust if they're accustomed to saltier foods — but adjust they will! And there are many things you can do to maximize flavor in low-sodium recipes. Here are some of the techniques we used when creating the recipes in this book:

- We incorporated a variety of flavor-boosting ingredients and seasonings, such as garlic, ginger, citrus juice and zest, tangy vinegars, fresh and dried herbs, and spices such as freshly ground black pepper and cinnamon.

- We didn't shy away from high-sodium condiments such as mustard, soy sauce or hoisin sauce, but we chose lower-sodium versions whenever possible and used less.

- We sometimes used a small amount of sugar — granulated sugar, brown sugar, honey or maple syrup — as a seasoning. We found that, by adding a little bit of sugar to recipes with citrus juice or vinegar to create a pleasing sweet-sour effect, we could rely less on sodium.

- We eliminated salt in our baked goods, except for the occasional recipe where a bit of salt balanced the flavors. Baking powder and baking soda are essential ingredients in baking, but are also high in sodium, so we reduced the quantities whenever possible (with denser ingredients, such as whole wheat flour or oat bran, however, you often need a bit of extra leavening to achieve a light texture).

- We also eliminated deli and processed meats, such as bacon, ham and cold cuts, from our menus. Our lunch menus recommend using home-roasted beef, chicken or turkey, poached chicken, turkey or salmon, or choose no-salt-added canned salmon or tuna, if available, for sandwiches and salads.

The main stumbling block we encountered when putting together the 28 days of menus came from commercial high-fiber whole-grain cereals and bread products, which are surprisingly high in sodium. It's nearly impossible to get anywhere close to the 1500-milligram mark if you aren't careful about your choice of breakfast cereals, whole-grain breads, pitas and wraps. While the selection of lower-sodium products in supermarkets is expanding, the options are currently limited when it comes to lower-sodium bread. We encourage you to contact bread manufacturers in your area to ask if they make lower-sodium bread products and, if so, where you can buy them. This will also help make them aware of consumer demand for these products.

> The greatest sources of sodium in our diets are packaged and processed foods.

FAQ

Q. I love Chinese food. Can I still eat it?

A. One of the pleasures of living in a multicultural society is enjoying foods from around the world. This does not have to change when you get diabetes; in fact, many ethnic foods are very healthy, as they rely on smaller portions of meat and lots of vegetables. The following chart lists the best choices from a variety of international cuisines. Some of these choices are higher in fat or sodium than is ideal, but sometimes we have to make compromises to "live in the real world." As always, use mindful eating techniques to eat the portion that is right for you, and if a meal is in high in calories and sodium, try to balance your intake throughout the rest of the day.

Type of Food	Best Choices
Chinese*	Stir-fried vegetables, chow mein and other dishes that are primarily vegetables; soup, including wonton soup, egg drop soup and congee; mixed dishes such as beef and broccoli, kung pao chicken and moo goo gai pan; steamed items such as beef balls, chicken wraps and shrimp dumplings. Ask for brown, red or black rice, and in general, for foods that are poached (*jum*), roasted (*kow*) or cooked in vegetable stock. Order with less sauce to reduce sodium, fat and sugar, and request "no MSG." Use very little soy sauce at the table, even if it is reduced-sodium.
Japanese*	Starters such as edamame, cucumber salad (sunomono) or green salad; sushi (ask for brown rice); main courses such as shabu-shabu, sukiyaki, grilled salmon and black cod, yakitori and teriyaki beef and chicken (ask for less sauce). Udon soups with vegetables and chicken are also a filling, low-fat meal, but the portion of noodles may be large.

* Use chopsticks at Asian restaurants to slow your rate of eating.

continued

Type of Food	Best Choices
Mexican	Meals made with soft tacos, black beans or pinto beans, chicken or fish (such as fajitas and fish tacos). Order your taco salad on a plate rather than in the large, deep-fried tortilla. Avoid sour cream, but use a small portion of guacamole. Salsa and pico de gallo are healthy, low-fat condiments. Order food cooked *fresco* to reduce fat. Portions can be large, so plan to share or take home leftovers.
Italian	Pasta with tomato sauce (marinara, primavera, clam sauce, bolognese); pasta e fagioli (pasta and beans); antipasti with vegetables; tomato, basil and bocconcini salad; roasted meat, chicken or fish; thin-crust pizza; minestrone; marinated mussels and calamari (not deep-fried).
Greek	Greek salad; hummus, tzatziki or baba ghanoush with pita; dolmades; main courses such as chicken, beef or shrimp souvlaki, stifado stew or fish with steamed vegetables. Main dishes may come with rice and roasted potatoes, so watch your portions, especially if you had pita to start.
Indian	Roti or chapati (bread); *dhal* (lentils or other pulses); basmati or brown rice; *dahi* (yogurt) or raita (yogurt sauce), lassi (yogurt drink); *sabzi* (avoid potato, aka *aloo*); chicken tikka, *saag* (spinach or kale); tandoori dishes.

How to Make the Most of Your Shopping Trip

Even after you've established a routine, keep an eye out for new products, as food manufacturers are constantly introducing healthier options.

1. Decide on the menu for the upcoming week. Include breakfasts and meals you intend to take to work, as well as snacks. If you have time or can double a recipe, plan to cook extras to store in the freezer, for easy meals another week.

2. Make a grocery list. Scan your pantry and refrigerator and jot down missing staples. Review the recipes you plan to make, and add to the list any ingredients you don't have on hand. Organize your shopping list according to the supermarket layout, grouping items such as fresh meats, dairy, produce and canned goods together, so you won't have to backtrack.

3. Go shopping at the right time. You're likely to purchase more than you intend if you shop when you're hungry. Also, try not to shop when you're tired or not in the mood. Shopping is a weekly necessity, so make it as pleasant and enjoyable as possible.

4. Give yourself enough time to make healthy choices. Initially, you'll need to read food labels to learn which products have the lowest amount of fat, sugar and sodium. But even after you've established a routine, keep an eye out for new products, as food manufacturers are constantly introducing healthier options.

5. Make shopping a family event. Food selection is an important life skill that goes hand in hand with cooking, so include your spouse and children so they too can learn how to make wise food choices.

Time-Saving Kitchen Strategies

1. Wash loose lettuce, salad greens and fresh herbs as soon as you get home from the supermarket. Fill a sink with cold water, swish the leaves around and scoop them into a salad spinner to dry. Wrap the leaves in a clean, dry kitchen towel or paper towels, place in a plastic bag and refrigerate.

2. Peel a week's worth of onions and store them in a plastic bag in the refrigerator. Not only will you save time prepping onions for recipes, but the cold temperature will help minimize tears when you chop the onions.

3. Keep bags of raw chopped onions, bell peppers and hot peppers in the freezer to add to soups, casseroles and stews. They can be frozen for up to two months.

4. Separate a head of garlic into cloves and remove the skins. Place in an airtight container in the refrigerator and use within a week.

5. To get a head start on another meal, cook extra rice, pasta and grains. Pack in airtight containers and store in the refrigerator for up to three days.

6. Double a recipe and freeze the extras for another meal. Use masking tape and a permanent marker to label and date all freezer foods. Take stock of frozen foods often, so you can use them up while they're still at their peak.

7. Batch-cook on weekends so you can rely on the refrigerator or freezer for speedy weeknight meals.

8. Don't let leftovers become costly throwaways. Place them in airtight containers, label and date. Store them on a designated shelf in the refrigerator so everyone in the family knows where to find them.

> Cooked soups, stews and casseroles can be stored safely for two to three days in an airtight container in the refrigerator.

1600-Calorie Daily Menu Plans

Week 1

	Monday	Tuesday	Wednesday	
Breakfast	Breakfast Oat Pudding* 1 fruit choice**	Breakfast Fruit Smoothie* Spiced Applesauce Flax Muffin*	Swiss Muesli* 1 nut or seed choice†	
Lunch	Hearty Minestrone* 2 whole-grain Melba toasts ½ whole wheat pita (7 inches/18 cm), spread with 2 tsp (10 mL) light mayonnaise and 1 tsp (5 mL) Dijon mustard, and filled with 2 oz (60 g) lean roast beef, ½ cup (125 mL) shredded lettuce and ½ tomato, sliced ¾ cup (175 mL) nonfat plain yogurt 1 fruit choice**	Combo sandwich with chicken (see page 158) ¾ cup (175 mL) nonfat plain yogurt or artificially sweetened fruit-flavored yogurt 1 fruit choice**	Chicken Noodle Soup* Lentil Tapenade* 1 cup (250 mL) vegetable dippers (baby carrots, cauliflower florets and celery sticks) 1 oz (30 g) lower-fat (<20% M.F.) Cheddar cheese 2 whole-grain crispbreads (see footnote, page 158) 1 fruit choice**	
Dinner	Turkey Bulgur Meatloaf* 4 small new potatoes (3½ oz/100 g) with 1 tbsp (15 mL) light sour cream Orange Broccoli with Red Pepper* Bumbleberry Oat Crisp*	Mediterranean Cod* Quinoa with Sautéed Spinach* topped with 1 tbsp (15 mL) chopped toasted hazelnuts ½ cup (125 mL) steamed carrot strips ½ cup (125 mL) steamed green peas Gingered Fresh Fruit Compote* 1 cup (250 mL) 1% milk	Baked Sesame Tofu* 2 servings Ginger Brown Basmati Rice* Steamed Baby Bok Choy* 1 cup (250 mL) 1% milk Oatmeal Chocolate Chip Cookie*	

* The recipe is in the book; unless otherwise indicated, the amount is 1 serving.

** A list of fruit choices appears on page 156.

Thursday	Friday	Saturday	Sunday
¼ cup (60 mL) low-fat (2% M.F.) cottage cheese ½ cup (125 mL) cubed honeydew melon Morning Glory Muffin* Mocha Latte*	Cinnamon Oats and Barley Porridge* 1 fruit choice**	Asparagus Mushroom Frittata* 1 slice toasted 7-grain bread with 2 tsp (10 mL) no-sugar-added fruit spread 1 fruit choice** ¾ cup (175 mL) nonfat plain yogurt	Blueberry Pancakes for One*
Chickpea Patties with Tahini Parsley Sauce* ½ whole wheat pita (7 inches/18 cm) 2 cups (500 mL) tossed salad with vegetables†† 2 tbsp (30 mL) Italian Balsamic Dressing* (variation, page 240) ⅓ cup (75 mL) nonfat plain Greek yogurt 1 fruit choice**	Combo salad with salmon (see page 160) 1 cup (250 mL) 1% milk 1 nut or seed choice† 1 fruit choice**	Old-Fashioned Split Pea Soup* Creamy Spinach Dip* 8 Pita Crisps* (2 servings) 1 cup (250 mL) raw vegetable dippers (red bell pepper, celery and cucumber) 1 cup (250 mL) 1% milk 1 fruit choice**	Harvest Vegetable Barley Soup* Ratatouille Pita Pizza* 1 cup (250 mL) 1% milk 1 fruit choice**
Stuffed Pork with Apples and Bread Crumbs* Mushroom Barley Pilaf* Roasted Butternut Squash with Onion and Sage* ½ cup (125 mL) steamed green beans topped with 1 tbsp (15 mL) toasted slivered almonds 1 fruit choice**	Moroccan-Spiced Carrot Soup* Curried Lentils with Vegetables* ⅓ cup (75 mL) nonfat plain Greek yogurt topped with Apple Slices with Dried Cranberries* and 1 tbsp (15 mL) chopped toasted walnuts	Salmon with Maple Balsamic Glaze and Ginger Mango Salsa* Wild and Brown Rice Pilaf* Green Bean and Plum Tomato Salad* 1 fruit choice**	Pan-Seared Beef with Red Wine* Fork-Mashed New Potatoes with Fresh Herbs* Roasted Asparagus* 2 cups (500 mL) tossed salad with vegetables†† 2 tbsp (30 mL) Classic Salad Dressing* Peach Cherry Gingerbread Cobbler* 1 cup (250 mL) 1% milk

† A list of nut and seed choices appears on page 157.

†† For 2 cups (500 mL) tossed salad with vegetables, see the vegetable choices on page 161 for suggestions.

Week 2			
	Monday	**Tuesday**	**Wednesday**
Breakfast	Multigrain Granola and Fruit Parfait*	Hot Oat Bran and Flax Porridge* 1 fruit choice**	Scrambled Egg Burrito* ¾ cup (175 mL) nonfat plain yogurt or artificially sweetened fruit-flavored yogurt 1 fruit choice**
Lunch	Corn and Red Pepper Chowder* 3 mini whole-grain pitas (1 oz/30 g), spread with 1 tbsp (15 mL) light mayonnaise and filled with 2 oz (60 g) diced roast chicken, 2 lettuce leaves and ½ tomato, sliced 1 cup (250 mL) 1% milk 1 fruit choice**	Combo sandwich with tuna (see page 158) 2 nut or seed choices† 1 cup (250 mL) 1% milk 1 fruit choice**	Whole-Grain Bulgur and Citrus Salad* 2 whole-grain crispbreads (see footnote, page 158) 2 tbsp (30 mL) unsalted peanut butter 1 cup (250 mL) 1% milk
Dinner	Grilled Salmon and Romaine Salad* Whole-Grain Buttermilk Biscuit* ¾ cup (175 mL) nonfat plain yogurt or artificially sweetened fruit-flavored yogurt Oatmeal Chocolate Chip Cookie* 1 fruit choice**	Chicken Shepherd's Pie* 2 cups (500 mL) tossed salad with vegetables†† 2 tbsp (30 mL) Buttermilk Herb Dressing* Banana Bran Bread*	Old-Fashioned Beef Stew* 2 cups (500 mL) tossed salad with vegetables†† 2 tbsp (30 mL) Sesame Ginger Dressing* Granola Spice Cake* 1 fruit choice**

* The recipe is in the book; unless otherwise indicated, the amount is 1 serving.

** A list of fruit choices appears on page 156.

Thursday	Friday	Saturday	Sunday
Breakfast Fruit Smoothie* 1 toasted whole-grain English muffin 2 tbsp (30 mL) light (5% M.F.) ricotta cheese	Hot Whole-Grain Cereal* 1 fruit choice**	Ratatouille Omelet* ½ toasted whole-grain English Muffin with 2 tsp (10 mL) no-sugar-added fruit spread ¾ cup (175 mL) nonfat plain yogurt 1 fruit choice**	Baked Cinnamon French Toast with Strawberries*
Combo salad with salmon (see page 160) ¾ cup (175 mL) nonfat plain yogurt or artificially sweetened fruit-flavored yogurt 1 fruit choice**	Chili Tofu Vegetable Wrap* ⅓ cup (75 mL) nonfat plain Greek yogurt 1 nut or seed choice† 1 fruit choice**	Terrific Chili* Cheese Cornbread* 1 cup (250 mL) 1% milk 2 nut or seed choices† 1 fruit choice**	Moroccan-Spiced Carrot Soup* ½ cup (60 mL) light water-packed tuna with 1 tbsp (15 mL) light mayonnaise 3 whole-grain crispbreads (see footnote, page 158) 1 cup (250 mL) 1% milk 1 nut or seed choice† 1 fruit choice**
Pork Stir-Fry with Bell Peppers and Spicy Peanut Sauce* ½ cup (125 mL) steamed sugar snap peas 1 cup (250 mL) 1% milk Pumpkin Spice Custard*	Tilapia with Lemon Caper Sauce* Wild and Brown Rice Pilaf* Cherry Tomato and Zucchini Sauté* 1 cup (250 mL) 1% milk 1 fruit choice**	Grilled Lamb Chops with Rosemary Mustard Baste* Quinoa Tabbouleh* ½ cup (125 mL) steamed frozen corn Grilled Vegetable Salad* Lemon Mango Sorbet* 1 cup (250 mL) mixed fresh or frozen berries	*Roasted Vegetable Lasagna* 2 cups (500 mL) tossed salad with vegetables†† 2 tbsp (30 mL) Italian Balsamic Dressing* (variation, page 240) Creamy Chocolate Banana Pudding*

† A list of nut and seed choices appears on page 157.

†† For 2 cups (500 mL) tossed salad with vegetables, see the vegetable choices on page 161 for suggestions.

Week 3			
	Monday	**Tuesday**	**Wednesday**
Breakfast	Breakfast Fruit Smoothie* Blueberry Oat Bran Muffin*	1 shredded wheat biscuit with ½ cup (125 mL) 1% milk and ¼ cup (60 mL) sliced banana Buttermilk Bran Muffin* 1 oz (30 g) lower-fat (<20% M.F.) Cheddar cheese	Breakfast Oat Pudding* 1 fruit choice**
Lunch	Combo sandwich with chicken (see page 158) ¾ cup (175 mL) nonfat plain yogurt or artificially sweetened fruit-flavored yogurt 1 fruit choice**	Leek, Potato and Kale Soup* Wrap made with 1 whole wheat flour tortilla (7 inches/18 cm), 1½ tsp (7 mL) light mayonnaise, 2 oz (60 g) diced roast turkey, ½ cup (125 mL) shredded lettuce and ½ tomato, diced 1 cup (250 mL) 1% milk Hazelnut and Dried Cranberry Biscotti* 1 fruit choice**	1 Greek Chicken Pita with Tzatziki* ⅓ cup (75 mL) nonfat plain Greek yogurt Hazelnut and Dried Cranberry Biscotti* 1 fruit choice**
Dinner	Sweet-and-Sour Pineapple Meatballs* 1 cup (250 mL) cooked whole wheat spaghetti 2 cups (500 mL) tossed salad with vegetables†† 2 tbsp (30 mL) Classic Salad Dressing* 1 fruit choice**	Chili Black Bean Dip* 4 Pita Crisps* Crispy Almond Baked Fish* ⅔ cup (150 mL) cooked quinoa Ratatouille* 1 fruit choice**	Baked Sesame Tofu* Middle Eastern Couscous with Chickpeas* Kale and Pear Salad with Warmed Shallot Dressing* Vanilla Pudding*

* The recipe is in the book; unless otherwise indicated, the amount is 1 serving.

** A list of fruit choices appears on page 156.

Thursday	Friday	Saturday	Sunday
Multigrain Granola and Fruit Parfait*	Hot Oat Bran and Flax Porridge* 1 fruit choice**	Oatmeal Cottage Cheese Pancakes* 1 fruit choice**	1 toasted whole-grain English muffin, spread with 1 tbsp (15 mL) light mayonnaise and layered with Western Omelet* and 2 slices tomato Mocha Latte* Hazelnut and Dried Cranberry Biscotti*
Harvest Vegetable Barley Soup* Tuna Cheddar Melt* 1 cup (250 mL) 1% milk 1 fruit choice**	Combo salad with salmon (see page 160) ¾ cup (175 mL) nonfat plain yogurt or artificially sweetened fruit-flavored yogurt 1 nut or seed choice† 1 fruit choice**	Mushroom Lentil Soup* 2 whole-grain crispbreads (see footnote, page 158) 1 oz (30 g) soft goat's cheese (plain or with herbs) ½ celery stalk 3 baby carrots ¾ cup (175 mL) nonfat plain yogurt 2 nut or seed choices† 1 fruit choice**	Whole-Grain Orzo Pasta Salad with Creamy Basil Pesto* 2 whole-grain crispbreads (see footnote, page 158) 1 tbsp (15 mL) almond butter ¾ cup (175 mL) nonfat plain yogurt or artificially sweetened fruit-flavored yogurt 1 fruit choice**
Chicken Stir-Fry with Rice Noodles and Vegetables* Orange Pumpkin Loaf* 2 nut and seed choices† 1 fruit choice**	Jamaican Jerk Pork with Pineapple Pepper Salsa* Jamaican Rice and Peas* ½ cup (125 mL) steamed broccoli and ½ cup (125 mL) steamed red bell pepper strips Lemon Mango Sorbet*	Pan-Roasted Trout with Fresh Tomato Basil Sauce* Wild and Brown Rice Pilaf* Steamed Sugar Snap Peas with Ginger* Blueberry Lemon Upside-Down Cake*	Thyme-Roasted Chicken* Parmesan Two-Potato Bake* Braised Brussels Sprouts* Spinach Salad with Carrots and Mushrooms* Gingered Fresh Fruit Compote*

† A list of nut and seed choices appears on page 157.

†† For 2 cups (500 mL) tossed salad with vegetables, see the vegetable choices on page 161 for suggestions.

Week 4			
	Monday	**Tuesday**	**Wednesday**
Breakfast	Cinnamon Oats and Barley Porridge* 1 oz (30 g) lower-fat (<20% M.F.) Cheddar cheese 1 fruit choice**	1 toasted whole-grain English muffin, spread with 2 tbsp (30 mL) unsalted peanut butter 1 fruit choice**	¾ cup (175 mL) bran flakes cereal with 1 cup (250 mL) 1% milk and 1 small banana, sliced 1 boiled egg
Lunch	Combo sandwich with chicken (see page 158) 1 cup (250 mL) 1% milk 1 nut or seed choice† 1 fruit choice**	Combo salad with beef (see page 160) 1 cup (250 mL) 1% milk 1 fruit choice**	Salmon Broccoli Chowder* ½ whole wheat pita (7 inches/18 cm), spread with White Bean Spread* and filled with ¼ cup (60 mL) diced red bell pepper and 6 cucumber slices 1 cup (250 mL) 1% milk 1 fruit choice**
Dinner	Shrimp and Vegetable Salad with Sesame Ginger Dressing* Granola Spice Cake* 1 fruit choice**	Salmon Cakes with Tartar Sauce* Warm Barley Salad with Roasted Beets and Greens* 1 fruit choice**	*Turkey Scaloppini with Mushrooms* ⅔ cup (150 mL) cooked long-grain brown rice Steamed Vegetables with Toasted Almonds* ¾ cup (175 mL) nonfat plain or artificially sweetened fruit-flavored yogurt 1 nut or seed choice† 1 fruit choice**

* The recipe is in the book; unless otherwise indicated, the amount is 1 serving.

** A list of fruit choices appears on page 156.

Thursday	Friday	Saturday	Sunday
Scrambled Tofu Burrito* (variation, page 177) ¾ cup (175 mL) nonfat plain or artificially sweetened fruit-flavored yogurt 1 fruit choice**	Hot Whole-Grain Cereal* 1 fruit choice**	Breakfast Oat Pudding* 1 fruit choice**	Baked Cinnamon French Toast with Strawberries* Mocha Latte*
White Bean and Wheat Berry Salad* 1 whole-grain crispbread (see footnote, page 158) Ricotta Herb Spread* ¾ cup (175 mL) nonfat plain yogurt or artificially sweetened fruit-flavored yogurt 1 nut or seed choice† 1 fruit choice**	Hearty Minestrone* 1 whole wheat pita (7 inches/18 cm), spread with ¼ cup (60 mL) Tzatziki* (page 199) and filled with 2 oz (60 g) sliced roasted turkey, 1 cup (250 mL) shredded lettuce, 6 slices cucumber and ½ tomato, sliced 1 nut or seed choice† 1 fruit choice**	Grilled Portobello Mushroom Burger with Goat Cheese* 2 cups (500 mL) tossed salad with vegetables†† 2 tbsp (30 mL) Classic Salad Dressing* 1 cup (250 mL) 1% milk 1 fruit choice**	Chickpea Patties with Tahini Parsley Sauce* 2 cups (500 mL) tossed salad with vegetables†† 2 tbsp (30 mL) Sesame Ginger Dressing* ¾ cup (175 mL) nonfat plain yogurt or artificially sweetened fruit-flavored yogurt 1 fruit choice**
Creamy Tuna Pasta Bake* 2 cups (500 mL) tossed salad with vegetables†† 2 tbsp (30 mL) Classic Salad Dressing* Oatmeal Chocolate Chip Cookie* 1 fruit choice**	Pork Chops with Honey and Thyme* Sweet Potato Oven Fries* Sweet and Spicy Cabbage* Oatmeal Chocolate Chip Cookie* 1 cup (250 mL) 1% milk	Tandoori Chicken with Cucumber Mint Raita* Edamame and Corn Sauté* ⅓ cup (75 mL) cooked brown basmati rice Creamy Chocolate Banana Pudding*	Sunday Roast Beef with Wine Gravy* Creamy Mashed Potatoes with Cauliflower* Roasted Root Vegetables with Rosemary* 1 cup (250 mL) 1% milk 1 fruit choice**

† A list of nut and seed choices appears on page 157.

†† For 2 cups (500 mL) tossed salad with vegetables, see the vegetable choices on page 161 for suggestions.

Fruit Choices

The following fruits each qualify as "1 fruit choice," as called for in the menus (pages 148 to 155). This is equal to approximately 15 grams of available carbohydrate. Vary your selections from meal to meal and from day to day so you can enjoy the health benefits of a wide array of fruits. Fruit juices are not included here because whole fruit is a healthier option, providing fiber and other valuable nutrients, such as antioxidants, in the skin and pulp. The juice equivalent of 1 serving of whole fruit is $\frac{1}{2}$ cup (125 mL). It is very easy to drink more than this, increasing the overall amount of carbohydrates you consume. In addition, because it's a thirst quencher, you might drink juice quickly, which can spike your blood glucose level.

Fruit	Serving Size
Fresh Fruit	
Apple	1 medium
Apricots	4 medium
Asian pears	2 small
Banana	1 small or $\frac{1}{2}$ large
Berries	
Blackberries, boysenberries, cranberries, gooseberries, raspberries, strawberries	2 cups (500 mL) whole
Blueberries, currants, Saskatoon berries	1 cup (250 mL) whole
Cherries	15 cherries, 1 cup (250 mL) with pits or $\frac{3}{4}$ cup (175 mL) pitted
Citrus fruits	
Clementines	2 medium
Grapefruit (all colors)	1 small or 1 cup (250 mL) sections
Orange	1 medium or 1 cup (250 mL) sections
Pomelo (shaddock)	1 cup (250 mL) sections
Tangerines	2 medium
Ugli fruit	$1\frac{1}{2}$ medium
Dates	2 medium
Figs	2 small
Grapes, Concord	1 cup (250 mL)
Grapes, red or green	15 grapes or $\frac{1}{2}$ cup (125 mL)
Guavas	3 medium
Kiwifruit	2 medium
Kumquats	8 medium
Lychees	10 lychees
Mango	$\frac{1}{2}$ medium or $\frac{1}{2}$ cup (125 mL) chopped
Melons: cantaloupe, casaba, honeydew, watermelon	1 cup (250 mL) chopped

Fruit	Serving Size
Fresh Fruit	
Nectarine	1 large or 1 cup (250 mL) chopped
Papaya	1 small or 1 cup (250 mL) chopped
Peach	1 large or 1 cup (250 mL) chopped
Pear	1 medium or 1 cup (250 mL) chopped
Persimmon (kaki; Sharon fruit)	1 medium
Pineapple	2 slices or ¾ cup (175 mL) chopped
Plums	2 medium
Prickly pears	2 medium or 1½ cups (375 mL) chopped
Star fruit (carambola)	3 medium or 3 cups (750 mL) sliced
Canned Fruit	
Applesauce, unsweetened	½ cup (125 mL)
Apricots, packed in light syrup	½ cup (125 mL)
Cherries, packed in light syrup	½ cup (125 mL)
Fruit cocktail, packed in light syrup	½ cup (125 mL)
Mandarin oranges, packed in light syrup	¾ cup (175 mL)
Peaches, packed in light syrup	½ cup (125 mL)
Pears, packed in light syrup	½ cup (125 mL)
Pineapple rings, packed in juice	2 slices or ½ cup (125 mL)

Adapted from: Canadian Diabetes Association, "Fruits," in *Beyond the Basics: Meal Planning for Healthy Eating, Diabetes Prevention and Management*, December 20, 2005, Version 2.

Nut and Seed Choices

The serving size is 1 tbsp (15 mL) for all nuts and seeds. This portion equals 1 Fat Choice and approximately 50 calories.

Nuts	Seeds
Almonds	Chia seeds
Brazil nuts	Flax seeds and flaxseed meal
Cashews	Hemp seeds
Hazelnuts	Pumpkin seeds (raw or roasted pepitas, unsalted)
Macadamia nuts	Sesame seeds
Peanuts	Sunflower seeds (raw or roasted, unsalted)
Pecans	
Pine nuts	
Pistachios	
Walnuts	

Combo Sandwiches

Have lunches become routine? Team nutritious sandwich options with intriguing breads and crisp greens to create your own personalized meal-worthy sandwiches, then pair them with crunchy vegetables. Not only are these tasty combos easy to assemble, but they score high points in terms of taste and appeal when tucked into bagged lunches for school or office. Here are some suggestions and portion sizes to get you on your way.

Meat and Alternatives Choices (choose 2)	Carbohydrate Choices (Grains and Starches) (choose 2)
1 oz (30 g) sliced roasted or poached chicken or turkey; lean roast beef, flank or sirloin steak; or roasted lean pork loin or tenderloin	1 thin slice whole-grain, whole wheat or pumpernickel bread (30 g)
1/4 cup (60 mL) drained canned water-packed light tuna or salmon (preferably with no salt added)	1 whole wheat or whole-grain flour tortilla (7 inches/18 cm)
1 oz (30 g) cooked shellfish, such as shrimp, Alaska king crab or lobster	1/2 whole wheat or whole-grain pita (7 inches/18 cm)
1 oz (30 g) sliced lower-fat cheese (less than 20% M.F.), such as Cheddar, Swiss, Gouda or soft goat cheese	1/2 small bagel (30 g)
1/4 cup (60 mL) low-fat cottage cheese or light ricotta cheese	1/2 whole-grain roll, Kaiser bun or thin whole-grain burger bun (30 g)
1 sliced hard-cooked egg or 2 sliced hard-cooked egg whites	1/2 whole wheat or whole-grain English muffin
1/3 cup (75 mL) Lentil Tapenade (page 186), White Bean Spread (page 187) or hummus	2 whole-grain crispbreads*
1/2 cup (125 mL) cooked lentils, red or white kidney beans, black beans or chickpeas (if canned, choose no added salt or drain and rinse well)	3 thin dark rye crispbreads*

* Crispbreads are Scandinavian crackers often made with whole-grain rye and seeds. They are high in fiber and low in fat and sodium. Two whole-grain crispbreads (20 grams total), such as Wasa or Ryvita, are 1 Carbohydrate Choice. Three thin dark rye crispbreads (20 g total), such Finn Crisp, are 1 Carbohydrate Choice.

Deli meats are very high in sodium, so cook and slice your own meats at home. Whole-grain bread slices can weigh as much as 45 to 50 grams per slice, versus 30 grams for traditional whole wheat sandwich bread slices. Bagels and buns may also be oversized. Look for the weight in the Nutrition Facts table and adjust accordingly. For example, 2 slices of dense whole-grain bread (45 g each) or 1 bagel or large whole-grain roll (45 g) counts as 3 Carbohydrate Choices, not 2.

Vegetable Choices (choose 2)	Fat Choices (choose 1)	Extras (choose 1)
1 cup (250 mL) salad greens, such as leaf lettuce, romaine, Boston lettuce, spinach, arugula, watercress, mixed baby greens, chicory, curly or Belgian endive, kale, shredded red or green cabbage, coleslaw mix (no dressing), broccoli slaw mix (no dressing) or fresh herbs (basil, parsley, cilantro, chives, mint, etc.)	1 tbsp (15 mL) light mayonnaise	2 tbsp (30 mL) Classic Tomato Salsa (page 189)
1 cup (250 mL) raw vegetables, such as tomato slices, cherry tomatoes, cucumber slices, onion slices, celery sticks, pepper strips, fennel strips, kohlrabi wedges, jicama strips, broccoli florets and stems or cauliflower florets (to enjoy alongside your sandwich)	1 tsp (5 mL) non-hydrogenated margarine	2 tbsp (30 mL) Cucumber Mint Raita (page 271), Cucumber Dill Sauce (page 283) or Tzatziki (page 199)
1 medium carrot, cut into sticks, or 5 baby carrots (to enjoy alongside your sandwich)	1 tsp (5 mL) butter	1 tbsp (15 mL) ketchup**
½ cup (125 mL) grilled or cooked vegetables: bell peppers, zucchini, summer squash, eggplant, onions or asparagus	2 tbsp (30 mL) light cream cheese	2 tsp (10 mL) barbecue sauce**
½ cup (125 mL) steamed greens, such as rapini, spinach, kale, Swiss chard, mustard greens or collard greens	2 tbsp (30 mL) light (3% to 5% M.F.) sour cream	1 tsp (5 mL) Dijon, honey Dijon or grainy mustard**
	2 tbsp (30 mL) Classic Salad Dressing or variation Italian Balsamic Dressing (page 240)	1 tsp (5 mL) mango chutney
	2 tbsp (30 mL) Sesame Ginger Dressing (page 244)	
	⅙ avocado, mashed	

** Condiments such as ketchup, mustard and commercial salsa contain a generous amount of sodium, so use them sparingly or choose other low-sodium spreads instead.

Combo Salads

Create your own meal-size salad with what you have on hand in the fridge — it's a delicious and economical way to take advantage of leftovers. Select your protein, carbohydrates such as grains, pasta or rice, and your choice of crunchy vegetables and toss with your choice of dressing. In addition to the dressing options given below, any amount of lemon juice, lime juice or vinegar, such as balsamic or cider, can be used. If desired, your carbohydrate choices can be bread, pita or crispbreads to serve alongside the salad.

Meat and Alternatives Choices (choose 2)	Carbohydrate Choices (Grains and Starches) (choose 2)	
1 oz (30 g) sliced or diced roasted or poached chicken or turkey; lean roast beef, flank or sirloin steak; or roasted lean pork loin or tenderloin	1/2 cup (125 mL) cooked pot barley, bulgur, buckwheat, fresh or frozen corn kernels, couscous, pasta (white, whole wheat, Kamut, spelt, etc.), oat groats or wheat berries	
1/4 cup (60 mL) drained canned water-packed light tuna or salmon (preferably with no salt added)	1/3 cup (75 mL) cooked millet, quinoa, rice (white or brown), Kamut or spelt berries	
1 oz (30 g) cooked shellfish, such as shrimp, Alaska king crab or lobster	2 whole-grain crispbreads or 3 thin dark rye crispbreads*	
1 oz (30 g) shredded or diced lower-fat cheese (less than 20% M.F.), such as Cheddar, Swiss, Gouda or soft goat cheese	1 thin slice whole-grain, whole wheat or pumpernickel bread (30 g)	
1/4 cup (60 mL) low-fat cottage cheese or light ricotta cheese	1/2 small bagel (30 g); whole-grain roll, Kaiser bun or thin whole-grain burger bun (30 g); or 1/2 whole wheat or whole-grain English muffin	
1 sliced hard-cooked egg or 2 diced hard-cooked egg whites	1 whole wheat or whole-grain flour tortilla (7 inches/18 cm)	
1/2 cup (125 mL) cooked lentils, red or white kidney beans, black beans or chickpeas (if canned, choose no added salt or drain and rinse well)	1/2 whole wheat or whole-grain pita (7 inches/18 cm)	

* Crispbreads are Scandinavian crackers often made with whole-grain rye and seeds. They are high in fiber and low in fat and sodium. Two whole-grain crispbreads (20 grams total), such as Wasa or Ryvita, are 1 Carbohydrate Choice. Three thin dark rye crispbreads (20 g total), such Finn Crisp, are 1 Carbohydrate Choice.

Deli meats are very high in sodium, so cook and slice your own meats at home. Whole-grain bread slices can weigh as much as 45 to 50 grams per slice, versus 30 grams for traditional whole wheat sandwich bread slices. Bagels and buns may also be oversized. Look for the weight in the Nutrition Facts table and adjust accordingly. For example, 2 slices of dense whole-grain bread (45 g each) or 1 bagel or large whole-grain roll (45 g) counts as 3 Carbohydrate Choices, not 2.

Vegetable Choices (choose 2)	Fat Choices (choose 1)	Extras (choose 1)
1 cup (250 mL) salad greens, such as leaf lettuce, romaine, Boston lettuce, spinach, arugula, watercress, mixed baby greens, chicory, curly or Belgian endive, kale, shredded red or green cabbage, coleslaw mix (no dressing), broccoli slaw mix (no dressing) or fresh herbs (basil, parsley, cilantro, chives, mint, etc.)	¼ cup (60 mL) Buttermilk Herb Dressing (page 241)	2 tbsp (30 mL) Classic Tomato Salsa (page 189)
1 cup (250 mL) raw vegetables, such as tomato slices, cherry tomatoes, cucumber slices, onion slices, chopped celery, bell pepper strips, diced fennel, shredded or diced kohlrabi, shredded or diced jicama, broccoli florets and stems or cauliflower florets	2 tbsp (30 mL) Classic Salad Dressing or variation Italian Balsamic Dressing (page 240)	2 tbsp (30 mL) Cucumber Mint Raita (page 271), Cucumber Dill Sauce (page 283) or Tzatziki (page 199)
½ cup (125 mL) grated carrots or 5 baby carrots	2 tbsp (30 mL) Sesame Ginger Dressing (page 244)	1 tsp (5 mL) Dijon, honey Dijon or grainy mustard
½ cup (125 mL) grilled or cooked vegetables, such as string beans, bell peppers, zucchini, summer squash, eggplant, onions or asparagus	2 tbsp (30 mL) store-bought low-fat salad dressing	1 tsp (5 mL) mango chutney
½ cup (125 mL) steamed greens, such as rapini, spinach, kale, Swiss chard, mustard greens or collard greens	1 tsp (5 mL) extra virgin olive oil, canola oil or vegetable oil of your choice	

100-Calorie Snacks

Snack	Available Carbohydrate (g)*
1 medium pear	21
1 small banana	21
4 dried apricots and 6 cherry tomatoes	19
Snack Mix: 1/3 cup (75 mL) dry unsweetened miniature shredded wheat, 2 tsp (10 mL) unsalted roasted sunflower seeds and 1 tbsp (15 mL) dried cranberries	18
1/2 cup (125 mL) nonfat plain or artificially sweetened fruit-flavored yogurt topped with 1/4 cup (60 mL) fresh or thawed frozen blueberries and 1 tbsp (15 mL) Multigrain Granola with Walnuts and Dried Fruit (page 172)	18
2 kiwifruit	17
Blueberry Smoothie: 1/2 cup (125 mL) frozen blueberries puréed with 1/3 cup (75 mL) nonfat plain or artificially sweetened vanilla-flavored yogurt and 1/3 cup (75 mL) 1% milk (makes about 1 cup/250 mL)	17
1/4 cup (60 mL) Chili Black Bean Dip (page 188) with 4 Pita Crisps (page 193) and 8 cucumber slices	16
1 serving Mocha Latte (page 182)	15
3 cups (750 mL) air-popped popcorn (unseasoned)	15
3 tbsp (45 mL) White Bean Spread (page 187) with 6 baby carrots and 6 celery sticks	14
1/2 sliced apple with 1 1/2 tsp (7 mL) unsalted peanut butter or almond butter	14
15 grapes	13
1 cup (250 mL) cut-up raw vegetables and 1/4 cup (60 mL) Cucumber Dill Sauce (page 283)	13
1 tbsp (15 mL) unsalted roasted sunflower seeds and 2 tbsp (15 mL) dried cranberries	13
1/2 toasted whole-grain English muffin spread with 2 tbsp (30 mL) low-fat (2% M.F.) cottage cheese and topped with 2 tomato slices and chopped fresh basil (or sprinkled with dried basil)	13
Fruit and Yogurt Parfait: 1/2 cup (125 mL) diced fresh fruit (such as kiwi and peaches) with 1/3 cup (75 mL) nonfat plain or artificially sweetened fruit-flavored yogurt, topped with 1 tbsp (15 mL) sliced toasted almonds	12

Snack	Available Carbohydrate (g)*
1 Shrimp and Vegetable Spring Roll (page 196)	11
1/2 cup (125 mL) chopped fresh pineapple or fresh peach slices with 1/4 cup (60 mL) low-fat (2% M.F.) cottage cheese	11
4 Whole-Grain Crostini (page 194), spread with 2 tbsp (30 mL) light (5% M.F.) ricotta cheese and topped with 1 tbsp (15 mL) chopped sun-dried tomatoes (if oil-packed, rinse well and pat dry) and chopped fresh basil (or sprinkled with dried basil)	11
4 Whole-Grain Crostini (page 194) topped with 1/4 cup (60 mL) Tomato Avocado Salsa (page 190) or Classic Tomato Salsa (page 189)	10
1 celery stalk stuffed with 2 tbsp (30 mL) light (5% M.F.) ricotta cheese and topped with 1 tbsp (15 mL) raisins and 2 tsp (10 mL) unsalted roasted sunflower seeds	10
1/3 cup (75 mL) nonfat plain Greek yogurt topped with 3/4 cup (175 mL) sliced strawberries and 1 tsp (5 mL) hemp or chia seeds	10
2 whole wheat Melba toasts, spread with 1/4 cup (60 mL) low-fat (2% M.F.) cottage cheese and topped with 4 thin tomato or cucumber slices and freshly ground black pepper	9
1 whole-grain crispbread (see footnote, page 160), spread with 2 tbsp (30 mL) Sardine Spread (page 192)	9
1 cup (250 mL) broccoli and cauliflower florets with 2 tbsp (30 mL) Buttermilk Herb Dressing (page 241) or store-bought low-fat salad dressing	9
1/3 cup (75 mL) shelled edamame (frozen soybeans blanched in boiling water for 1 minute)	4
3 tbsp (45 mL) toasted unsalted soy nuts	3
2 tbsp (30 mL) unsalted roasted sunflower seeds or green pumpkin seeds (pepitas) or unsalted chopped walnuts or cashews	2

* Available carbohydrate is total carbohydrate minus fiber.

200-Calorie Snacks

Snack	Available Carbohydrate (g)
¾ cup (175 mL) nonfat plain or artificially sweetened fruit-flavored yogurt topped with ½ cup (125 mL) low-fat, low-sugar whole-grain cereal (such as bran flakes) and ½ sliced small banana	34
1 mandarin orange and 1 slice Orange Pumpkin Loaf (page 341)	32
Pita Roll-Up: ½ whole wheat pita round, spread with ⅓ cup (75 mL) White Bean Spread (page 187), with ½ red bell pepper, cut into long, thin strips, placed along bottom edge; roll up and slice into 1-inch (2.5 cm) pieces	31
Strawberry Shortcake: 1 Whole-Grain Buttermilk Biscuit (page 342), spread with a mixture of ¼ cup (60 mL) nonfat plain Greek yogurt and 1 tsp (5 mL) liquid honey, and topped with ½ cup (125 mL) sliced strawberries	31
1 Blueberry Oat Bran Muffin (page 346) and ½ cup (125 mL) 1% milk	30
¾ cup (175 mL) cooked whole wheat pasta with ⅓ cup (75 mL) Tomato Pasta Sauce (page 298) and 1 tbsp (15 mL) freshly grated Parmesan cheese	29
½ cup (125 mL) low-fat, low-sugar whole-grain cereal with ½ cup (125 mL) 1% milk and ¾ cup (175 mL) sliced strawberries	29
¼ cup (60 mL) canned drained water-packed light tuna mixed with 1 tbsp (15 mL) light mayonnaise and 2 tbsp (30 mL) minced celery, spread on 3 whole-grain crispbreads (see footnote, page 160) and topped with 6 thin cucumber slices	27
1 Morning Glory Muffin (page 348)	27
½ cup (125 mL) nonfat plain yogurt topped with ¾ cup (175 mL) fresh or thawed frozen raspberries and 3 tbsp (45 mL) Multigrain Granola with Walnuts and Dried Fruit (page 172)	26
1 Granola Power Bar (page 350) and ½ cup (125 mL) nonfat plain or artificially sweetened fruit-flavored yogurt	25
½ whole-grain bagel, spread with ¼ avocado, mashed, and topped with 3 thin tomato slices and chopped fresh cilantro	23
½ thin whole wheat bun topped with ¼ cup (60 mL) Classic Tomato Salsa (page 189) and ¼ cup (60 mL) shredded part-skim mozzarella cheese, broiled until cheese is melted	22
1 Ratatouille Pita Pizza (page 195)	21
8 low-fat whole-grain crackers (25 g total) with 1 oz (30 g) sliced lower-fat (<20% M.F.) Swiss cheese	17

Breakfast and Brunch

Good health starts at breakfast. Eating breakfast helps manage your blood glucose, blood fats and insulin levels. But don't stop there. Eat three meals a day, spaced four to six hours apart. Regular meals help prevent low and high glucose, and balanced meals (with at least three of the four food groups) give you a variety of nutrients.

Hot Whole-Grain Cereal

Start your day off right with this nourishing hot cereal that takes no time to cook on your stovetop or in your microwave.

Tip

Microwave Method: Place cereal, milk and water in a 4-cup (1 L) glass measuring cup or heatproof bowl and microwave on High, stirring once, for 3 to 4 minutes or until mixture comes to a boil and thickens. Continue with step 2.

½ cup	Whole-Grain Cereal Mix (see recipe, opposite)	125 mL
¾ cup	low-fat (1%) milk or plain soy milk	175 mL
¼ cup	water	60 mL
	Stevia extract or artificial sweetener (optional)	

1. In a small saucepan, combine cereal, milk and water. Bring to a boil over medium-high heat. Reduce heat and simmer, stirring, for 2 to 3 minutes or until thickened. Remove from heat.

2. Let stand for 1 minute to thicken. Sweeten with stevia or artificial sweetener to taste, if desired.

Nutrition Tip

If you're not a breakfast eater, start small and have something from one or two of the food groups. Some options include a slice of whole-grain toast, a whole-grain English muffin or a homemade muffin; a banana, an apple, half a grapefruit or ½ cup (125 mL) orange juice; a boiled egg or a handful of nuts; a single-serving container of yogurt or a slice of cheese.

Nutrition info per serving

Calories	298
Carbohydrate	45 g
Fiber	6 g
Protein	16 g
Fat	8 g
Saturated fat	2 g
Cholesterol	9 mg
Sodium	85 mg

Food Choices
2½ Carbohydrate
1 Fat

Whole-Grain Cereal Mix

Supermarkets and bulk food stores sell whole-grain cereal mixes, such as 5- and 7-grain, but it's more economical to make your own, especially if you already have most of the ingredients on hand.

Tips

Any combination of rolled grains, such as oats, rye, Kamut or spelt flakes, can be used to make up the 3 cups (750 mL) called for in this recipe.

Several of the ingredients in this mix contain natural oils that can go rancid over time; for longer storage, refrigerate or freeze it.

2 cups	large-flake (old-fashioned) rolled oats	500 mL
1 cup	barley, rye or wheat flakes	250 mL
1/2 cup	oat bran or natural wheat bran	125 mL
1/2 cup	wheat germ	125 mL
3 tbsp	toasted unsalted sunflower seeds	45 mL
3 tbsp	hemp seeds or chia seeds	45 mL
2 tsp	ground cinnamon	10 mL

1. In a large bowl, combine oats, barley flakes, oat bran, wheat germ, sunflower seeds, hemp seeds and cinnamon. Store in an airtight container in a cool, dry place for up to 3 weeks, or refrigerate or freeze for up to 3 months.

Nutrition Tip

At breakfast, enjoy a variety of whole-grain cereals often. Whole grains are low-GI foods that help reduce your blood glucose levels, reduce your risk of developing type 2 diabetes and heart disease, manage your weight and lower your blood cholesterol levels.

Nutrition info per 1/2 cup (125 mL)

Calories	222
Carbohydrate	36 g
Fiber	6 g
Protein	9 g
Fat	6 g
Saturated fat	1 g
Cholesterol	0 mg
Sodium	4 mg

Food Choices
2 Carbohydrate
1 Fat

Breakfast Oat Pudding

Makes 4 servings

Reminiscent of rice pudding, this wholesome porridge made with steel-cut oats is ideal for breakfast, served hot or cold, or as a snack or dessert.

- - - - - - - - - - - - - - - -

Tips

If making ahead or preparing extras for another morning's breakfast, stir in additional milk or water when reheating porridge, to give it a creamy consistency.

To serve as a snack or dessert, spoon $1/2$ cup (125 mL) pudding into a bowl, thin with water or milk, and top with $1/2$ cup (125 mL) fresh berries.

$3^{1}/_{2}$ cups	low-fat (1%) milk or plain soy milk, divided	875 mL
1 cup	water	250 mL
1 cup	steel-cut oats	250 mL
3 tbsp	ground flax seeds (flaxseed meal)	45 mL
2 tbsp	toasted unsalted sunflower seeds, chia seeds or hemp seeds	30 mL
1 tsp	ground cinnamon	5 mL
	Stevia extract or artificial sweetener (optional)	

1. In a large saucepan, bring 3 cups (750 mL) of the milk and water to a boil over medium-high heat. Stir in oats. Reduce heat to low, cover, leaving lid ajar, and simmer, stirring occasionally and removing any milk scum as it forms, for 20 minutes or until thickened. Remove from heat.

2. Stir in remaining milk, flax seeds, sunflower seeds and cinnamon. Sweeten with stevia to taste, if desired. Serve either hot or cold. Pudding thickens as it cools. Add more milk or water to thin to desired consistency.

Microwave Method

Makes 2 servings (halve the ingredients to prevent spill-over). In a large 8-cup (2 L) glass measuring cup, combine $1^{1}/_{2}$ cups (375 mL) milk, $1/2$ cup (125 mL) water and $1/2$ cup (125 mL) steel-cut oats. Microwave on High for 5 minutes or until boiling. Microwave on Medium (50%) for 13 to 15 minutes or until thickened. Continue with step 2, adding the remaining $1/4$ cup (60 mL) milk, flax seeds, sunflower seeds and cinnamon.

Nutrition info per 1 cup (250 mL)

Calories	305
Carbohydrate	41 g
Fiber	7 g
Protein	15 g
Fat	10 g
Saturated fat	2 g
Cholesterol	11 mg
Sodium	99 mg

Food Choices
2 Carbohydrate
1 Fat

Cinnamon Oats and Barley Porridge

Here's a creamy whole-grain cereal with the double benefit of oats and barley to reduce cholesterol. Cook extra barley ahead and have it handy in the fridge or freezer as a time-saver when preparing this wholesome breakfast.

Tip

Porridge thickens as it cools. If making ahead or preparing extras for another morning's breakfast, stir in additional milk or water when reheating porridge, to give it a creamy consistency.

1/3 cup	large-flake (old-fashioned) rolled oats	75 mL
1 1/2 cups	low-fat (1%) milk or plain soy milk	375 mL
3/4 cup	cooked pot barley (see page 318)	175 mL
2 tbsp	ground flax seeds (flaxseed meal)	30 mL
1/2 tsp	ground cinnamon	2 mL
	Stevia extract or artificial sweetener (optional)	

1. In a medium saucepan, combine oats and milk. Bring to a boil over medium-high heat. Reduce heat and simmer, stirring often, for 3 minutes or until thickened.

2. Stir in barley and flax seeds; cook for 2 minutes or until heated through and creamy. Remove from heat and stir in cinnamon and stevia to taste, if desired. Let stand for 2 minutes to thicken slightly.

Nutrition Tip

Fruit in its whole form is a healthier option than juice, as the skin and pulp provide fiber and other valuable nutrients, such as antioxidants. The juice equivalent of 1 serving of whole fruit is 1/2 cup (125 mL). It is very easy to drink more juice than this, thus increasing the overall amount of carbohydrates consumed. As juice is so readily digested, it can also cause a spike in blood glucose levels.

Nutrition info per 1 cup (250 mL)	
Calories	254
Carbohydrate	39 g
Fiber	8 g
Protein	11 g
Fat	7 g
Saturated fat	2 g
Cholesterol	9 mg
Sodium	86 mg

Food Choices
2 Carbohydrate
1 Fat

Hot Oat Bran and Flax Porridge

If you're not fond of oatmeal made with quick-cooking rolled oats, try this deliciously creamy porridge instead. It has a sweet oats flavor and smooth texture, takes no time to prepare — and it's nourishing, too!

Tips

Ground flax seeds (flaxseed meal), hemp seeds and chia seeds contain oil, so store them in airtight containers in the refrigerator or freezer.

Microwave Method: Combine milk and bran in a 4-cup (1 L) glass measuring cup or heatproof bowl and microwave on High, stirring once, for 3 minutes or until mixture comes to a boil and thickens. Continue with step 2.

1/3 cup	oat bran	75 mL
1 cup	low-fat (1%) milk or plain soy milk	250 mL
1 tbsp	ground flax seeds (flaxseed meal)	15 mL
1 tbsp	dried cranberries	15 mL
1 tbsp	toasted unsalted sunflower seeds	15 mL
1/4 tsp	ground cinnamon	1 mL

1. In a small saucepan, combine oat bran and milk. Bring to a boil over medium-high heat. Reduce heat and simmer, stirring, for 1 to 2 minutes or until thickened. Remove from heat.

2. Stir in flax seeds, cranberries and sunflower seeds; sprinkle with cinnamon. Serve immediately.

Nutrition Tip

Our balanced breakfasts provide 3 Carbohydrate Choices, 1/2 Meat & Alternatives Choice and 1 Fat Choice. The whole grains and milk in this recipe supply a significant amount of protein (17 grams), so there is no need to add a Meat & Alternatives Choice.

Nutrition info per serving

Calories	290
Carbohydrate	44 g
Fiber	7 g
Protein	17 g
Fat	11 g
Saturated fat	3 g
Cholesterol	12 mg
Sodium	112 mg

Food Choices
2 Carbohydrate
1 1/2 Fat

Swiss Muesli

Muesli is a creamy cold porridge that combines uncooked grains, yogurt, fresh and dried fruits, nuts and seeds. This version is often called Swiss or Bircher Muesli, as it was first developed in the early 1900s by Dr. Bircher, a Swiss physician. This refreshing complete breakfast is a great way to get your daily dose of morning grains, fruit and dairy.

Tip

Any combination of berries can used, such as blueberries, raspberries and strawberries. Or combine berries with other fruits, such as grapes, pitted cherries, chopped peaches or plums — whatever is in season and on hand.

1	small apple	1
2 tsp	freshly squeezed lemon juice	10 mL
2/3 cup	large-flake (old-fashioned) rolled oats	150 mL
2 tbsp	dried cranberries, raisins, chopped apricots or dates	30 mL
3/4 cup	low-fat (1%) milk or plain soy milk	175 mL
2/3 cup	nonfat plain Greek yogurt	150 mL
1 cup	fresh or thawed frozen berries (see tip, at left)	250 mL
2 tbsp	chopped toasted hazelnuts, hemp seeds or chia seeds	30 mL

1. Using the large holes of a box grater, grate apple into a bowl or storage container. Add lemon juice and toss to coat. Stir in oats, cranberries and milk. Cover and refrigerate for at least 4 hours or preferably overnight to allow grains to soften. (The soaked grains can be refrigerated for up to 2 days.)

2. To serve, stir yogurt into grain mixture and ladle into bowls. Top with berries and sprinkle with hazelnuts.

Nutrition Tip

Count 1/3 cup (75 mL) nonfat plain Greek yogurt as 1 Meat & Alternatives Choice. Greek yogurt has a similar protein content to cottage cheese, but has the advantage of being much lower in sodium. It makes a great protein alternative for breakfast, in place of an egg or lower-fat cheese.

Nutrition info per 1¼ cups (300 mL)

Calories	337
Carbohydrate	53 g
Fiber	8 g
Protein	17 g
Fat	8 g
Saturated fat	1 g
Cholesterol	5 mg
Sodium	74 mg

Food Choices
3 Carbohydrate
1 Meat & Alternatives
1 Fat

Multigrain Granola with Walnuts and Dried Fruit

Makes about 6 cups (1.5 L)

Make your own granola for a delicious, healthy breakfast or snack that doesn't have the refined sugar and fats of more expensive commercial products. Vary the granola according to what grains, dried fruits and nuts you have on hand.

- - - - - - - - - - - - - - -

Tip

Store in an airtight container or glass jar in a cool, dry place for up to 3 weeks or in the freezer for up to 2 months.

- **Preheat oven to 325°F (160°F)**
- **2 rimmed baking sheets**

2 cups	large-flake (old-fashioned) rolled oats	500 mL
1 cup	spelt flakes	250 mL
1 cup	Kamut or rye flakes	250 mL
1 cup	natural wheat bran	250 mL
1/2 cup	chopped walnuts, slivered almonds or toasted skinned hazelnuts	125 mL
1/4 cup	unsalted raw sunflower seeds	60 mL
1/3 cup	liquid honey	75 mL
1/3 cup	water	75 mL
2 tsp	vanilla extract	10 mL
1/2 cup	raisins, dried cranberries, chopped dried apricots or currants, or a combination	125 mL

1. In a large bowl, combine oats, spelt flakes, Kamut flakes, wheat bran, walnuts and sunflower seeds.

2. In a small saucepan, heat honey and water over medium heat until hot. Stir in vanilla. Drizzle over oat mixture and toss until evenly coated. Spread on baking sheets.

3. Bake in preheated oven for 25 to 30 minutes, stirring occasionally and rotating baking sheets, until grains are golden and toasted. Remove from oven and stir in raisins. Let cool.

Nutrition info per 1/2 cup (125 mL)

Calories	218
Carbohydrate	38 g
Fiber	6 g
Protein	7 g
Fat	6 g
Saturated fat	1 g
Cholesterol	0 mg
Sodium	4 mg

Food Choices
2 Carbohydrate
1 Fat

Nutrition Tip

Nuts are very nutritious, containing protein, vitamins, minerals and fiber, along with heart-healthy mono- and polyunsaturated fats. They are high in calories, though, so keep your portion size small. Include nuts (without salt!) in your diet often.

Multigrain Granola and Fruit Parfait

One of the best convenience foods to appear in supermarkets is the vast selection of frozen fruit — ideal for this easy-to-assemble breakfast.

Tips

Use a variety of fruits, including berries, grapes, blueberries, melon, mango and apples.

To defrost frozen fruit, place in a heatproof bowl. Microwave on High for 30 to 40 seconds or just until fruit loses its ice crystals but is not fully defrosted (to prevent it from losing its juices).

1 cup	fresh or thawed frozen berries or a combination of fruits	250 mL
⅓ cup	nonfat plain Greek yogurt	75 mL
½ cup	Multigrain Granola with Walnuts and Dried Fruit (page 172)	150 mL

1. In a parfait dish or a bowl, layer half each of the fruit, yogurt and granola. Repeat layers and serve immediately. (The parfait can be made the night before and refrigerated, but the granola mixture will soften.)

Nutrition Tip

When buying commercial cereals, there are so many choices. Which one is the most nutritious? Choose a cereal made with whole grains and refer to the Nutrition Facts table. There should be at least 5 grams of fiber per serving and no more than 5 grams of sugar (or up to 10 grams if it contains dried fruit).

Nutrition info per serving

Calories	315
Carbohydrate	55 g
Fiber	7 g
Protein	15 g
Fat	7 g
Saturated fat	1 g
Cholesterol	0 mg
Sodium	35 mg

Food Choices
3 Carbohydrate
1 Meat & Alternatives
1 Fat

Oatmeal Cottage Cheese Pancakes

These delicious and nutritious pancakes provide your family with the energy and nutrients they need to do their best at school, work and play! No need to add syrup, as the pancakes have a touch of sweetness added — just add sliced fresh fruit, such as bananas, mango and melon.

Tip

Place pancakes on a baking sheet in a warm 200°F (100°C) oven, loosely covered with a dry kitchen towel, to keep them warm and prevent them from drying out until serving time.

Nutrition info per 4 pancakes

Calories	244
Carbohydrate	31 g
Fiber	4 g
Protein	14 g
Fat	8 g
Saturated fat	2 g
Cholesterol	52 mg
Sodium	324 mg

Food Choices

2 Carbohydrate
1 Meat & Alternatives
1 Fat

- Food processor
- Griddle or large nonstick skillet

1 cup	large-flake (old-fashioned) rolled oats	250 mL
1/3 cup	whole wheat flour	75 mL
1 tbsp	granulated sugar	15 mL
1 1/2 tsp	baking powder	7 mL
1	large egg	1
3/4 cup	low-fat (2%) creamed cottage cheese	175 mL
3/4 cup	low-fat (1%) milk or plain soy milk	175 mL
1 tsp	grated lemon zest	5 mL
1 tbsp	canola oil	15 mL

1. In food processor, process oats, flour, sugar, baking powder, egg, cottage cheese, milk and lemon zest until combined. Transfer to a bowl.

2. Heat griddle or skillet over medium heat. Lightly brush with some of the oil.

3. For each pancake, spread 2 tbsp (30 mL) batter into a 3-inch (7.5 cm) round on griddle. Cook for 1 to 2 minutes or until surface of pancake bubbles and bottom is golden brown. Flip over and cook for up to 1 minute or until bottom is golden. Keep warm. Brush griddle lightly with oil for each new batch of pancakes.

Nutrition Tip

Several no-sugar-added syrups are available. Be sure to check nutrition labels, as carbohydrate and calories vary depending on the sweeteners used.

Blueberry Pancakes for One

This recipe can serve as either breakfast or brunch. For additional servings, double or triple the recipe.

- - - - - - - - - - - - - - - -

Tip

There is no need to thaw the blueberries before sprinkling them over the batter. If you prefer to thaw the blueberries used as a topping, defrost them in the microwave until no ice crystals remain.

2	large egg whites	2
1/4 cup	low-fat (1%) milk or plain soy milk	60 mL
1/4 cup	whole wheat flour	60 mL
2 tbsp	natural wheat bran	30 mL
1 tsp	granulated sugar	5 mL
1/2 tsp	baking powder	2 mL
1 tsp	canola oil	5 mL
3/4 cup	frozen blueberries (divided)	175 mL
1/4 cup	nonfat plain or artificially sweetened fruit-flavored yogurt	60 mL

1. In a bowl, whisk together egg whites and milk. Whisk in flour, wheat bran, sugar and baking powder until smooth. Let stand for 1 minute to thicken.

2. Heat a large nonstick skillet over medium heat and brush with oil. Spoon batter into skillet to make 3 pancakes. Sprinkle with half of the blueberries. Cook for 2 to 3 minutes or until bubbles appear on top surface. Flip over and cook for 1 to 2 minutes or until bottoms are golden.

3. Arrange pancakes on a plate and top with yogurt and the remaining blueberries. Serve immediately.

> ## Variation
> Instead of blueberries, use 1/2 thinly sliced banana to top the batter.

Nutrition info per 3 pancakes

Calories	337
Carbohydrate	56 g
Fiber	9 g
Protein	19 g
Fat	6 g
Saturated fat	1 g
Cholesterol	5 mg
Sodium	354 mg

Food Choices
3 Carbohydrate
1 Meat & Alternatives
1 Fat

Baked Cinnamon French Toast with Strawberries

Instead of frying French toast in butter or oil, here's an easy baked version that does away with added fat and is just as delicious.

- - - - - - - - - - - - - - -

Tip

When shopping for whole-grain bread, read the label. It should list a whole grain, such as whole wheat (in the U.S.), whole-grain wheat (in Canada) or whole oats, as the first ingredient.

- Preheat oven to 400°F (200°C)
- Baking sheet, lined with parchment paper

1	large egg	1
2	large egg whites	2
½ cup	low-fat (1%) milk	125 mL
3 tsp	granulated sugar, divided	15 mL
1 tsp	vanilla extract	5 mL
½ tsp	ground cinnamon	2 mL
4	slices 7- or 12-grain bread (each 50 g; see nutrition tip, page 200)	4
2 tbsp	sliced almonds	30 mL
1 cup	nonfat strawberry-flavored Greek yogurt, divided	250 mL
4 cups	sliced strawberries	1 L

1. In a shallow bowl, whisk together egg, egg whites, milk, 1 tsp (5 mL) of the sugar and vanilla.

2. In a small bowl, combine the remaining sugar and cinnamon. Set aside.

3. Dip both sides of bread slices in egg mixture and let soak until very moist. Arrange 2 inches (5 cm) apart on prepared baking sheet. Sprinkle evenly with almonds.

4. Bake in preheated oven for 20 to 25 minutes or until bread slices are slightly puffed and tops are golden. Cut bread on the diagonal into half-slices.

5. Arrange two half-slices on each plate and sprinkle lightly with cinnamon sugar. Top each with ¼ cup (60 mL) Greek yogurt and 1 cup (250 mL) strawberries. Serve immediately.

Nutrition info per 2 half-slices

Calories	323
Carbohydrate	51 g
Fiber	8 g
Protein	18 g
Fat	6 g
Saturated fat	1 g
Cholesterol	53 mg
Sodium	300 mg

Food Choices

3 Carbohydrate
1 Meat & Alternatives
1 Fat

Scrambled Egg Burritos

Here's a tasty sandwich that's great for breakfast or lunch on the go.

- - - - - - - - - - - - - -

Tip

You can also serve the scrambled egg mixture on whole-grain toast and serve the salsa on the side. Omit the cheese, or add it to the scrambled egg mixture, if you wish.

● **Preheat oven to 350°F (180°C)**

2	7-inch (18 cm) whole wheat flour tortillas	2
2 tbsp	shredded lower-fat (<20% M.F.) Cheddar cheese	30 mL
2	large egg whites	2
1	large egg	1
	Freshly ground black pepper	
1 tsp	canola oil	5 mL
¼ cup	finely chopped red or green bell pepper	60 mL
1	large green onion, sliced	1
¼ cup	Classic Tomato Salsa (page 189)	60 mL

1. Place tortillas on a baking sheet and sprinkle with cheese. Bake in preheated oven for 5 minutes or until tortillas are warm and cheese is melted. (Or place tortillas, one at a time, on a plate lined with paper towels. Sprinkle with cheese and microwave on High for 20 to 25 seconds.)

2. Meanwhile, in a bowl, beat egg whites and egg. Season with pepper.

3. In a medium nonstick skillet, heat oil over medium heat. Stir-fry red pepper and green onion for 1 minute or until softened. Add eggs and cook, stirring, for about 1 minute or until set.

4. Spoon egg mixture along bottom third of tortillas. Top each with 2 tbsp (30 mL) salsa. Fold 1 inch (2.5 cm) of right and left sides of tortilla over filling and, starting from the bottom, roll up tortillas around filling. Serve immediately.

Nutrition info per burrito

Calories	221
Carbohydrate	23 g
Fiber	3 g
Protein	13 g
Fat	8 g
Saturated fat	2 g
Cholesterol	97 mg
Sodium	423 mg

Food Choices
1 Carbohydrate
1 Meat & Alternatives
1 Fat

Variation

Scrambled Tofu Burritos: Omit the egg whites and egg, and substitute ⅔ cup (150 mL) crumbled firm tofu sprinkled with ground turmeric. Heat 2 tsp (10 mL) canola oil over medium-high heat and stir-fry tofu, peppers and green onion for 4 minutes. Continue with step 4.

Western Omelet

This omelet is delicious tucked between slices of whole wheat toast or a toasted English muffin spread with light mayonnaise, along with tomato slices, for a classic toasted Western sandwich.

- - - - - - - - - - - - - - -

Tip

Use the cooking method in this recipe to create a simple omelet with or without the vegetables. Serve with a toasted whole-grain English muffin.

2	large egg whites	2
1	large egg	1
1 tbsp	freshly grated Parmesan cheese	15 mL
	Freshly ground black pepper	
1 tsp	extra virgin olive oil	1 mL
2 tbsp	finely chopped green onion or cooking onion	30 mL
¼ cup	finely chopped green or red bell pepper	60 mL
¼ cup	chopped mushrooms	60 mL

1. In a bowl, whisk together egg whites, egg and Parmesan. Season with pepper.

2. In small nonstick skillet, heat oil over medium heat. Add green onion, green pepper and mushrooms; cook, stirring, for about 2 minutes or until softened.

3. Pour in egg mixture and stir briefly with a heatproof rubber spatula. Cook for about 1 minute, using spatula to lift cooked edges to allow uncooked egg to flow underneath, until underside is golden and top is set. Fold omelet in half and cut crosswise into 2 servings.

Nutrition info per serving

Calories	95
Carbohydrate	3 g
Fiber	1 g
Protein	8 g
Fat	6 g
Saturated fat	2 g
Cholesterol	96 mg
Sodium	134 mg

Food Choices
1 Meat & Alternatives
½ Fat

Nutrition Tip

If you have high LDL (low-density lipoprotein) cholesterol, keep dietary cholesterol to a maximum of 200 milligrams per day. Otherwise, 300 milligrams is an acceptable limit. Foods that contain cholesterol include eggs, meat, poultry, fish, cheese and higher-fat dairy products. It's easy to hit the daily limit by eating just one egg (which has about 200 milligrams of cholesterol). Consider replacing one whole egg with two egg whites instead.

Ratatouille Omelet

Makes 3 servings

Ratatouille makes a delicious topping for this open-faced omelet, but you can use other toppings, such as sautéed mushrooms, red peppers and green onions.

- - - - - - - - - - - - - -

Tips

To warm the ratatouille, place it in a heatproof bowl, cover and microwave on High for 45 to 60 seconds or until warm.

If you don't have an ovenproof skillet, wrap the handle in a double layer of foil before placing it under the broiler.

- **Preheat broiler, with rack set 4 inches (10 cm) from heat**
- **8- to 10-inch (20 to 25 cm) ovenproof nonstick skillet (see tip, at left)**

4	large egg whites	4
2	large eggs	2
⅛ tsp	salt	0.5 mL
	Freshly ground black pepper	
1½ tsp	canola or olive oil	7 mL
½ cup	Ratatouille (page 331), warmed	125 mL
¼ cup	shredded lower-fat (<20% M.F.) Cheddar or part-skim mozzarella cheese	60 mL

1. In a bowl, whisk together egg whites, eggs and salt. Season with pepper.

2. In skillet, heat oil over medium heat. Pour in egg mixture and stir briefly with a heatproof rubber spatula. Cook for about 1 minute, using spatula to lift cooked edges to allow uncooked egg to flow underneath, until underside is golden and top is almost set.

3. Spread ratatouille over omelet. Sprinkle with cheese. Place under preheated broiler for 2 to 3 minutes or until cheese is melted. Cut into thirds and serve.

Nutrition info per serving

Calories	133
Carbohydrate	3 g
Fiber	1 g
Protein	12 g
Fat	8 g
Saturated fat	2 g
Cholesterol	129 mg
Sodium	280 mg

Food Choices
1½ Meat & Alternatives
½ Fat

Nutrition Tip

We recommend using a nonstick skillet in our recipes, as it reduces the amount of fat needed in cooking. Flimsy nonstick skillets overheat quickly and often have an inferior coating that can break down over time. Today there are many good-quality nonstick pans to choose from, made with newer materials and heavier bottoms to better regulate the heat and safely cook foods. Consider investing in a new skillet and follow the manufacturer's directions on how to use it correctly.

Asparagus Mushroom Frittata

Makes 5 servings

Versatile mushrooms and asparagus star in this terrific dish that's perfect for a weekend brunch or an easy supper.

- - - - - - - - - - - - - - -

Tips

If you don't have an ovenproof skillet, wrap the handle in a double layer of foil before placing it under the broiler.

Use a variety of mushrooms, such as white, cremini, shiitake and oyster.

Instead of asparagus, substitute the same amount of small broccoli florets and finely chopped red bell pepper.

- **Preheat broiler, with rack set 4 inches (10 cm) from heat**
- **Large ovenproof skillet (see tip, at left)**

1 tbsp	extra virgin olive oil	15 mL
1	onion, finely chopped	1
2	cloves garlic, minced	2
2 cups	sliced assorted mushrooms (see tip, at left)	500 mL
2 cups	chopped asparagus (1-inch/2.5 cm pieces)	500 mL
½ tsp	dried herbes de Provence or Italian seasoning	2 mL
6	large egg whites	6
3	large eggs	3
¼ tsp	freshly ground black pepper	1 mL
⅛ tsp	salt	0.5 mL
½ cup	shredded Gruyère, Edam or Gouda cheese	125 mL

1. In a large skillet, heat oil over medium heat. Add onion, garlic, mushrooms, asparagus and herbes de Provence; cook, stirring often, for 5 minutes or until vegetables are softened.

2. In a large bowl, whisk together egg whites, eggs, pepper and salt. Add to vegetable mixture. Cook, stirring gently, for 1 minute or until eggs are just starting to set. Sprinkle with cheese. Reduce heat to medium-low and cover skillet with lid. Cook for 5 minutes or until bottom of frittata is golden and top is still not set.

3. Uncover and place skillet under broiler for about 3 minutes or until top of frittata is lightly browned and set. Cut into wedges and serve.

Nutrition info per serving

Calories	175
Carbohydrate	7 g
Fiber	2 g
Protein	14 g
Fat	10 g
Saturated fat	4 g
Cholesterol	126 mg
Sodium	215 mg

Food Choices
2 Meat & Alternatives
½ Fat

Breakfast Fruit Smoothie

Makes 1 serving

With today's selection of luscious frozen berries in supermarkets, it takes no time to whip up this fast and refreshing beverage for breakfast on the go or as a snack for an afternoon nutrition boost.

- - - - - - - - - - - - -

Tips

Both flax seeds and chia seeds are high in omega-3 fat and add a thick richness to this luscious shake.

Reduce the number of ice cubes if using frozen berries.

• Blender or food processor

¾ cup	fresh or frozen strawberries, raspberries, blueberries or blackberries, or a combination	175 mL
1 tbsp	ground flax seeds (flaxseed meal) or chia seeds	15 mL
¾ cup	low-fat (1%) milk or plain soy milk	175 mL
¼ cup	nonfat plain Greek yogurt	60 mL
4 to 5	ice cubes	4 to 5
	Stevia extract or artificial sweetener (optional)	

1. In blender, combine berries, flax seeds, milk, yogurt and ice cubes; purée until smooth. Sweeten with stevia to taste, if desired. Serve immediately.

Nutrition Tip

Instead of milk, try using kefir in your smoothies. Kefir is a fermented dairy product that is high in probiotics (bacteria that help your digestive system). It is pourable, like milk, and has the same amount of carbohydrate, protein and calcium as milk, but does not contain vitamin D unless fortified. Because kefir is fermented, people with lactose intolerance may be able to enjoy it.

Nutrition info per 1½ cups (375 mL)

Calories	201
Carbohydrate	26 g
Fiber	6 g
Protein	14 g
Fat	6 g
Saturated fat	2 g
Cholesterol	9 mg
Sodium	110 mg

Food Choices
1 Carbohydrate
1 Meat & Alternatives
½ Fat

Mocha Latte

Makes 2 servings

Here's an easy and inexpensive way to make a superb specialty coffee blended with cocoa without leaving home.

- - - - - - - - - - - - - - - -

Tips

Microwave Method:
In step 2, transfer the mixture to a 2-cup (500 mL) glass measuring cup and microwave on High for 2 to 2½ minutes or until piping hot but not boiling. Stir in vanilla and continue with step 3.

To warm the mugs, fill them with boiling water and let stand while making the latte.

- Blender
- Two 12-oz (375 mL) mugs, warmed

1½ cups	low-fat (1%) milk or plain soy milk	375 mL
2 tbsp	unsweetened cocoa powder	30 mL
2 tsp	granulated sugar (optional)	10 mL
½ tsp	vanilla extract	2 mL
1 cup	hot freshly brewed strong coffee (regular or decaffeinated)	250 mL
	Stevia extract or artificial sweetener (optional)	
	Long cinnamon sticks or ground cinnamon	

1. In blender, combine milk, cocoa powder and sugar (if using); purée until smooth and frothy.

2. Transfer milk mixture to a small saucepan. Heat over medium heat, stirring, until piping hot. Stir in vanilla.

3. Pour hot coffee into warmed mugs, dividing equally. Top with hot chocolate mixture. Adjust sweetness with stevia to taste, if desired. Add a cinnamon stick to each mug or sprinkle with cinnamon. Serve immediately.

Nutrition Tip

Chocolate comes from cacao beans, which are rich in antioxidants called flavanols, known for their heart-healthy effects. The darker the chocolate, the higher the cocoa content and amount of flavanols. Unsweetened cocoa powder is an especially high source. One tablespoon (15 mL) of unsweetened cocoa powder has about 20 calories, with 5 grams of carbohydrate and 2 grams of fiber.

Nutrition info per 1¼ cups (300 mL)

Calories	110
Carbohydrate	17 g
Fiber	2 g
Protein	7 g
Fat	2 g
Saturated fat	2 g
Cholesterol	9 mg
Sodium	84 mg

Food Choices
1 Carbohydrate

Snacks, Appetizers and Sandwiches

Creamy Spinach Dip

Serve this refreshing dip with a variety of vegetable dippers, such as carrots, bell pepper strips, cucumber, celery, broccoli, fennel and cauliflower.

- - - - - - - - - - - - - - -

Tips

Use as a dressing for pasta and potato salads, or as a spread for sandwiches and wraps.

The dip can be stored in an airtight container in the refrigerator for up to 5 days.

● **Food processor**

1	package (8 oz/250 g) fresh spinach	1
2	green onions, sliced	2
1	clove garlic, finely chopped	1
½ cup	crumbled light feta cheese (2 oz/60 g)	125 mL
2 tbsp	chopped fresh dill	30 mL
1 tsp	grated lemon zest	5 mL
¼ tsp	freshly ground black pepper	1 mL
1 cup	nonfat sour cream	250 mL
¼ cup	light mayonnaise	60 mL

1. Rinse spinach in cold water and drain. Place spinach, with moisture clinging to leaves, in a large saucepan. Cook over high heat, stirring, until just wilted. Transfer spinach to a colander and rinse with cold water until chilled. Squeeze out moisture by hand, then wrap in a clean, dry towel and squeeze out excess moisture.

2. In food processor, combine spinach, green onions, garlic, feta, dill, lemon zest and pepper. Process until very finely chopped. Add sour cream and mayonnaise; pulse just until combined.

3. Transfer to a serving bowl, cover and refrigerate for 2 hours, until chilled, before serving.

Nutrition info per ¼ cup (60 mL)	
Calories	67
Carbohydrate	7 g
Fiber	1 g
Protein	3 g
Fat	3 g
Saturated fat	1 g
Cholesterol	5 mg
Sodium	187 mg

Food Choices
½ Fat
1 Extra

Ricotta Herb Spread

Makes about 1½ cups (375 mL)

This creamy spread relies on nonfat Greek yogurt and zesty fresh herbs. Serve on Whole-Grain Crostini (page 194) or crisp breads, or as a dip with fresh vegetables.

Tips

Instead of the fresh basil or dill, you can use 1 tsp (5 mL) dried basil, dill or fines herbes.

This spread makes a great sandwich filling or spread in place of mayonnaise.

The spread can be stored in an airtight container in the refrigerator for up to 5 days.

1 cup	light ricotta cheese	250 mL
½ cup	nonfat plain Greek yogurt	125 mL
1 tbsp	honey-Dijon mustard	15 mL
1 tsp	freshly squeezed lemon juice	5 mL
⅛ tsp	salt	0.5 mL
¼ tsp	freshly ground black pepper	1 mL
2 tbsp	finely chopped fresh parsley	30 mL
2 tbsp	chopped fresh basil or dill	30 mL
2 tbsp	finely chopped fresh chives or minced green onions	30 mL

1. In a bowl, stir together ricotta, yogurt, mustard, lemon juice, salt and pepper. Stir in parsley, basil and chives. Cover and refrigerate for 2 hours, until chilled, before serving.

Nutrition Tip

With 7 grams of protein in a serving (1 Meat & Alternatives Choice), this low-fat spread packs a nutritional punch. Use it instead of sliced meats in sandwiches or on whole-grain crispbreads.

Nutrition info per ¼ cup (60 mL)

Calories	64
Carbohydrate	3 g
Fiber	0 g
Protein	7 g
Fat	2 g
Saturated fat	1 g
Cholesterol	6 mg
Sodium	144 mg

Food Choices
1 Meat & Alternatives

Lentil Tapenade

Spread tapenade on your favorite whole-grain crackers or crisps for a wholesome snack. This robust spread also makes a superb sandwich filling on crusty bread with roasted vegetables and assertive greens such as arugula.

- - - - - - - - - - - - - - - - - -

Tips

Cooked dried lentils (which don't require presoaking) are so much better, both in flavor and texture, than mushy canned lentils, which are also very high in sodium.

Always rinse brined foods, such as olives and capers, to remove excess salt.

The spread can be stored in an airtight container in the refrigerator for up to 5 days.

Nutrition info per ¼ cup (60 mL)	
Calories	105
Carbohydrate	13 g
Fiber	3 g
Protein	5 g
Fat	4 g
Saturated fat	1 g
Cholesterol	0 mg
Sodium	108 mg

Food Choices
½ Carbohydrate
½ Meat & Alternatives
1 Fat

● **Food processor**

3 cups	water	750 mL
½ cup	dried brown or green lentils, rinsed	125 mL
1	small bay leaf	1
1	clove garlic, coarsely chopped	1
⅓ cup	pitted kalamata olives, rinsed and coarsely chopped (about 12)	75 mL
1 tbsp	extra virgin olive oil	15 mL
¼ tsp	freshly ground black pepper	1 mL
¼ cup	chopped fresh parsley	60 mL
1 tsp	grated lemon zest	5 mL

1. In a medium saucepan, bring water to a boil over high heat. Add lentils and bay leaf. Reduce heat to medium-low, cover and simmer for 25 to 30 minutes or until lentils are tender. Drain and let cool to room temperature. Discard bay leaf.

2. In food processor, combine lentils, garlic, olives, olive oil and pepper; process until smooth. Add parsley and lemon zest; pulse until combined.

3. Transfer to a serving bowl, cover and refrigerate for 2 hours, until chilled, before serving.

Nutrition Tip

High-fiber foods, such as lentils and beans, slow the absorption of glucose and stabilize blood glucose levels. In addition, they provide protein and are low in fat. Enjoy five servings of legumes in dips, soups, salads and main dishes each week and take advantage of their many health benefits.

White Bean Spread

Serve this tasty, easy-to-make spread with pita crisps as an appetizer or snack. It also makes a great alternative to butter, margarine or mayonnaise as a spread for sandwiches and wraps.

- - - - - - - - - - - - - -

Tips

The spread can be stored in an airtight container in the refrigerator for up to 5 days.

You will need a 19-oz (540 mL) can of beans for this recipe. If you can't find no-salt-added beans, use regular canned beans and omit the salt from the recipe.

Nutrition info per ¹/₃ cup (75 mL)

Calories	111
Carbohydrate	18 g
Fiber	6 g
Protein	6 g
Fat	2 g
Saturated fat	0 g
Cholesterol	0 mg
Sodium	119 mg

Food Choices
¹/₂ Carbohydrate
1 Meat & Alternatives
¹/₂ Fat

- Food processor

2 tsp	extra virgin olive oil	10 mL
1	onion, chopped	1
2	cloves garlic, finely chopped	2
2 tsp	dried oregano	10 mL
¹/₄ tsp	hot pepper flakes (or to taste)	1 mL
1 tbsp	white or red wine vinegar	15 mL
2 cups	well-rinsed drained no-salt-added canned white kidney beans	500 mL
¹/₄ tsp	salt	1 mL

1. In a medium nonstick skillet, heat oil over medium heat. Add onion, garlic, oregano and hot pepper flakes; cook, stirring often, for 5 minutes or until onion is tender. Stir in vinegar and remove from heat. (Or, in a small casserole dish or heatproof glass bowl, combine onion, garlic, oregano and hot pepper flakes. Cover with a lid or plate and microwave on high for 3 minutes. Stir in vinegar.)

2. In food processor, combine onion mixture, beans and salt; purée until smooth.

3. Transfer to a serving bowl, cover and refrigerate for 2 hours, until chilled, before serving.

Variation

Hummus (Chickpea Spread): Replace the kidney beans with chickpeas, use ¹/₂ tsp (2 mL) ground cumin instead of the oregano, and replace the vinegar with 2 tbsp (30 mL) freshly squeezed lemon juice.

Chili Black Bean Dip

Makes about 2 cups (500 mL)

Making your own tasty bean dip couldn't be any easier. Just purée the ingredients in your food processor and it's ready — a bowl of wholesome goodness to serve with vegetables or use as a sandwich spread.

Tips

If you have a fresh jalapeño pepper on hand, mince it and add it to the dip, along with coarsely chopped fresh cilantro, if you have some handy.

The dip can be stored in an airtight container in the refrigerator for up to 5 days.

● **Food processor**

2 cups	well-rinsed drained canned black beans or red kidney beans	500 mL
1	clove garlic, chopped	1
1½ tsp	chili powder	7 mL
1 tsp	dried oregano	5 mL
Pinch	cayenne pepper (optional)	Pinch
⅔ cup	light (5%) sour cream	150 mL

1. In food processor, combine beans, garlic, chili powder, oregano and cayenne (if using); pulse until beans are partially mashed. Add sour cream and process until smooth. Transfer to a serving dish.

Variation

Chili Black Bean Dip with Tomato Avocado Salsa: For an attractive party appetizer, spread Chili Black Bean Dip in an 8- to 10-inch (20 to 25 cm) shallow dish. Top with Tomato Avocado Salsa (page 190) no more than 1 hour before serving. Serve with Pita Crisps (page 193).

Nutrition info per ¼ cup (60 mL)

Calories	72
Carbohydrate	12 g
Fiber	3 g
Protein	4 g
Fat	1 g
Saturated fat	1 g
Cholesterol	4 mg
Sodium	163 mg

Food Choices
½ Carbohydrate

Classic Tomato Salsa

Makes about 2¼ cups (550 mL)

Commercial brands of salsa are loaded with salt. Here's an easy-to-make lower-sodium version, using canned tomatoes and tomato paste, that's ready in no time. Use it in any recipe that calls for salsa.

- - - - - - - - - - - - - -

Tips

This recipe makes a medium-hot salsa. For a milder version, reduce the hot pepper flakes to a pinch.

You can use 1 to 2 minced seeded jalapeño peppers in place of the hot pepper flakes.

Pack the salsa into airtight containers and freeze for up to 1 month.

To further reduce the sodium in this recipe, use no-salt-added canned tomatoes.

Nutrition info per ¼ cup (60 mL)

Calories	38
Carbohydrate	9 g
Fiber	2 g
Protein	1 g
Fat	0 g
Saturated fat	0 g
Cholesterol	0 mg
Sodium	139 mg
Food Choices	
1 Extra	

1	can (28 oz/796 mL) whole tomatoes, with juice	1
1 tbsp	packed brown sugar	15 mL
½ tsp	dried oregano	2 mL
½ tsp	ground cumin	2 mL
¼ tsp	hot pepper flakes (or to taste)	1 mL
⅓ cup	cider vinegar	75 mL
⅓ cup	no-salt-added tomato paste	75 mL
1	small onion, finely chopped	1
1	green bell pepper, finely chopped	1
2	cloves garlic, minced	2
¼ cup	finely chopped fresh cilantro	60 mL

1. Place tomatoes in a sieve over a bowl and drain juice, gently pressing down on tomatoes to extract as much juice as possible. Dice tomatoes and set aside.

2. In a medium saucepan, combine brown sugar, oregano, cumin, hot pepper flakes, tomato juice, vinegar and tomato paste. Bring to a boil over high heat. Reduce heat to medium and boil gently, stirring often, for about 5 minutes or until reduced and thickened to the consistency of ketchup.

3. Stir in onion, green pepper and garlic; boil gently for 2 minutes or until vegetables are tender-crisp. Add diced tomatoes and cook, stirring, until mixture comes to a boil. Remove from heat and stir in cilantro. Let cool.

4. Transfer salsa into a jar or airtight container and refrigerate for up to 2 weeks.

Tomato Avocado Salsa

Makes about 2 cups (500 mL)

You'll love this quick, creative salsa. Spoon it over fish or chicken, or eat it as a snack, paired with Whole-Grain Crostini (page 194) or crisp breads.

Tip

Fresh cilantro (also called coriander) lasts only a few days in the fridge before it deteriorates, so buy it shortly before you intend to use it. Wash it well in water to remove any dirt, spin dry and wrap in paper towels. Store in a plastic bag in the fridge. Leave the roots on — they keep the leaves fresh.

2	tomatoes, seeded and diced	2
2	green onions, thinly sliced	2
1	Hass avocado, peeled and diced	1
1	jalapeño pepper, seeded and minced	1
1/3 cup	chopped fresh cilantro or parsley	75 mL
2 tsp	freshly squeezed lime juice	10 mL

1. In a bowl, combine tomatoes, green onions, avocado, jalapeño, cilantro and lime juice; toss well. Serve immediately or let stand for 1 hour before serving.

Nutrition Tip

Avocados are often avoided, as they contain a lot of fat and calories. But they are also packed with heart-friendly monounsaturated oil and other valuable nutrients, so enjoy them in moderation for their many health benefits.

Nutrition info per 1/4 cup (60 mL)

Calories	36
Carbohydrate	3 g
Fiber	2 g
Protein	1 g
Fat	3 g
Saturated fat	0 g
Cholesterol	0 mg
Sodium	4 mg

Food Choices
1/2 Fat

Pineapple Pepper Salsa

Makes about 2 cups (500 mL)

This delightfully fresh, tropical salsa has a slight kick, thanks to the jalapeño, and makes a fabulous side dish for chicken, pork or fish.

Tips

To avoid skin irritation, wear rubber gloves when handling jalapeño peppers.

Prepare this salsa no more than 1 hour ahead to prevent it from becoming watery; cover and refrigerate. Wait to stir in the cilantro and lime juice until you're ready to serve.

1 cup	diced fresh pineapple	250 mL
2	green onions, thinly sliced	2
1	small red bell pepper, diced	1
1	small jalapeño pepper, seeded and minced	1
1 tsp	grated gingerroot	5 mL
1/3 cup	coarsely chopped fresh cilantro	75 mL
2 tsp	freshly squeezed lime juice	10 mL

1. In a bowl, combine pineapple, green onions, red pepper, jalapeño and ginger. Stir in cilantro and lime juice.

Variation

Substitute other fresh fruit, such as diced mango, peaches or plums, for the pineapple.

Nutrition info per 1/3 cup (75 mL)

Calories	19
Carbohydrate	5 g
Fiber	1 g
Protein	0 g
Fat	0 g
Saturated fat	0 g
Cholesterol	0 mg
Sodium	2 mg

Food Choices
1 Extra

Sardine Spread

The next time you're wondering what to make for a simple appetizer or snack to serve with crostini, reach for a can of sardines — they are rich in omega-3 fats and good for your heart.

- - - - - - - - - - - - - - - -

Tip

Canned sardines are great to have on hand, as they can be easily mashed for lunchtime sandwich fillings and to make this delicious spread.

The spread can be stored in an airtight container in the refrigerator for up to 3 days.

- **Food processor**

1	can (4 oz/125 g) skinless boneless sardines, drained and patted dry	1
¼ cup	packed fresh parsley leaves	60 mL
¼ cup	roasted red bell pepper, rinsed and patted dry	60 mL
2 tbsp	light mayonnaise	30 mL
½ tsp	grated lemon zest	2 mL
1 tsp	freshly squeezed lemon juice	5 mL
¼ tsp	hot pepper sauce	1 mL
	Freshly ground black pepper	

1. In food processor, combine sardines, parsley, red pepper, mayonnaise, lemon zest, lemon juice and hot pepper sauce; process until smooth. Season to taste with black pepper.

2. Transfer to a serving bowl, cover and refrigerate for 2 hours, until chilled, before serving.

Nutrition Tip

Canned sardines are a convenient and economical way to get your omega-3s. They also contain vitamin D and selenium, and are a good source of calcium when you eat the bones. Enjoy them as a snack on Melba toast or as a sandwich filling. The healthiest choice is to buy canned sardines packed in water, with no salt added.

Nutrition info per 2 tbsp (30 mL)

Calories	53
Carbohydrate	1 g
Fiber	0 g
Protein	4 g
Fat	3 g
Saturated fat	1 g
Cholesterol	25 mg
Sodium	148 mg

Food Choices
½ Meat & Alternatives
½ Fat

Multigrain Granola and Fruit Parfait (page 173)

Green Bean and Plum Tomato Salad (page 226)

Caesar Salad (page 224)

Quinoa Tabbouleh (page 239)

Tomato Soup with Fresh Herbs (page 220)

Southwestern Pork Stew (page 264)

Old-Fashioned Slow Cooker
Beef Stew (page 248)

Curried Lentils with Vegetables (page 302)

Parmesan Chicken Strips (page 274)

Chicken Stir-Fry with Rice Noodles
and Vegetables (page 273)

Creamy Tuna Pasta Bake (page 300)

Pan-Roasted Trout with
Fresh Tomato Basil Sauce (page 289)

Salmon with Balsamic Maple Glaze and
Ginger Mango Salsa (page 285)

Steamed Vegetables with Toasted Almonds (page 330)

Morning Glory Muffins (page 348)

Lemon Cream with Fresh Berries (page 364)

Pita Crisps

Makes 48 pita crisps

Here's a lower-fat alternative to tortilla chips or snack crackers that's easy to make.

- - - - - - - - - - - - - - -

Tip

Pita crisps can be stored in an airtight container at room temperature for up to 1 day, or layered in a rigid container and frozen for up to 2 weeks.

- **Preheat oven to 350°F (180°C)**

| 3 | thin 7-inch (18 cm) whole wheat pitas | 3 |

1. Separate pitas horizontally into two rounds each. Cut each round into 8 wedges. Place in a single layer on two baking sheets.

2. Bake in preheated oven for 8 to 10 minutes or until crisp and lightly toasted. Let cool.

Nutrition Tip

When buying whole-grain crackers, look at the Nutrition Facts table. Based on a suggested portion size of 1 ounce (30 g) and approximately 100 calories, the crackers should have no more than 15 grams of carbohydrate, should be low in total fat (less than 3 grams), saturated fat (less than 1 gram) and sodium (less than 140 milligrams), and should have 2 or more grams of fiber. To make sure you are buying crackers that are nutritious, look at the ingredient list: whole-grain flours and seeds should be listed at the top.

Nutrition info per 4 pita crisps

Calories	43
Carbohydrate	9 g
Fiber	1 g
Protein	2 g
Fat	0 g
Saturated fat	0 g
Cholesterol	0 mg
Sodium	85 mg

Food Choices
½ Carbohydrate

Whole-Grain Crostini

Makes 48 slices

These easy bread toasts make a tasty substitute for packaged high-sodium crackers. Serve them with dips, spreads and salsa.

- - - - - - - - - - - - -

Tip

To give these toasts a delicious garlic flavor, cut a large garlic clove in half. Rub the warm toasts with a cut side of the garlic.

● **Preheat oven to 350°F (180°C)**

1	thin whole-grain baguette (about 18 inches/45 cm long and 2½-inches/6 cm in diameter)	1

1. Cut baguette into ⅓-inch (8 mm) thick slices. Arrange on baking sheets. Bake in preheated oven for 7 to 9 minutes or until bread is crisp and edges are toasted. Transfer bread slices to a wire rack to cool.

2. Serve warm or let cool completely, place in an airtight container and store at room temperature for up to 1 day or in the freezer for up to 1 month.

Nutrition Tip

People are often surprised by how little salt it takes to reach the recommended daily sodium limit. Keep in mind that every ¼ teaspoon (1 mL) of salt contributes 600 milligrams of sodium. The upper limit of sodium recommended for healthy individuals is 2300 milligrams, but there is a growing number of people who should limit their sodium to 1500 milligrams. Count yourself in this group if you are of African descent, age 51 or more, or have diabetes, high blood pressure or heart disease.

Nutrition info per 4 slices

Calories	64
Carbohydrate	10 g
Fiber	2 g
Protein	3 g
Fat	1 g
Saturated fat	0 g
Cholesterol	0 mg
Sodium	101 mg

Food Choices
½ Carbohydrate

Ratatouille Pita Pizzas

Makes 4 servings

Serve these pizza wedges as a quick and easy lunch or supper, along with a bowl of soup.

Tips

The pitas can be toasted in the oven ahead, but wait to spread them with ratatouille until just before baking or the pizzas can become soggy.

You can also heat the ratatouille in the microwave. Place it in a heatproof glass bowl and microwave on High for 1 minute.

Ratatouille Pita Pizzas can also be served as an appetizer. Cut each round into 8 pieces.

Nutrition info per pita pizza	
Calories	217
Carbohydrate	25 g
Fiber	4 g
Protein	12 g
Fat	9 g
Saturated fat	4 g
Cholesterol	19 mg
Sodium	335 mg

Food Choices
1 Carbohydrate
1 Meat & Alternatives
1 Fat

- **Preheat oven to 400°F (200°C)**

2	thin 7-inch (18 cm) whole wheat pitas	2
2 cups	Ratatouille (page 331)	500 mL
1 cup	shredded part-skim mozzarella cheese	250 mL

1. Separate each pita horizontally into two rounds. Place smooth side down in a single layer on two baking sheets. Bake in preheated oven for 5 to 7 minutes or until light golden and crisp.

2. Meanwhile, in a small saucepan, heat ratatouille over medium heat, stirring often, until warm.

3. Spread $\frac{1}{2}$ cup (125 mL) ratatouille over each pita half, spreading to edges. Sprinkle each round with $\frac{1}{4}$ cup (60 mL) mozzarella.

4. Bake for 5 to 7 minutes or until cheese is melted and pita edges are crisp and browned. Cut each round into 4 wedges. Serve immediately.

Nutrition Tip

You can enjoy the occasional slice or two of takeout pizza, just keep it to a few times a month. Choose a pizza made with thin whole-grain crust, lots of vegetables, such as fresh tomatoes, peppers, mushrooms and spinach, and lean meats such as roasted chicken. Skip the high-fat and high-sodium pepperoni and sausage. Request a light sprinkling of part-skim mozzarella or goat cheese — they're a healthier option than higher-fat cheeses.

Shrimp and Vegetable Spring Rolls

Rice paper wrappers make great covers for a variety of fillings, like this colorful salad combo with shrimp and peanut dressing. If you haven't worked with rice paper wrappers, it may initially require a bit of practice to assemble them — it's similar to rolling a wrap sandwich. Once the rice paper roll is softened in water, assemble and roll the wrapper before going on to the next one.

- - - - - - - - - - - - - -

Tip

Rice paper wrappers are sold in the specialty food section of most supermarkets or at Asian food shops.

Nutrition info per 2 rolls	
Calories	214
Carbohydrate	26 g
Fiber	4 g
Protein	18 g
Fat	5 g
Saturated fat	1 g
Cholesterol	111 mg
Sodium	387 mg

Food Choices
1 Carbohydrate
2 Meat & Alternatives

Peanut Dressing

1 tsp	packed brown sugar	5 mL
1 tbsp	unsalted smooth peanut butter	15 mL
1 tbsp	freshly squeezed lime juice	15 mL
2 tsp	reduced-sodium soy sauce	10 mL
1/4 tsp	Asian chili sauce	1 mL

Spring Rolls

1	small red bell pepper, cut into thin strips	1
1 cup	shredded napa cabbage or romaine lettuce	250 mL
1 cup	bean sprouts	250 mL
1/2 cup	shredded carrots	125 mL
2	green onions, sliced	2
4	8 1/2-inch (22 cm) round rice paper wrappers	4
4 oz	small cooked peeled shrimp	125 g
8	fresh cilantro stems with leaves	8

1. *Dressing:* In a small bowl, whisk together brown sugar, peanut butter, lime juice, soy sauce and chili sauce. Set aside.

2. *Spring Rolls:* In a bowl, combine red pepper, cabbage, bean sprouts, carrots and green onions; toss lightly.

3. Working with one rice paper wrapper at a time, dip the wrapper in a large, shallow bowl of cold water for about 10 seconds or until pliable. Place on a clean wooden board or dry work surface. Mound one-quarter of the salad mixture on the lower half of the wrapper, leaving a 1-inch (2.5 cm) edge all around. Top with shrimp and 2 cilantro stems with leaves. Pat down lightly. Drizzle with 2 tsp (10 mL) peanut dressing. Carefully fold in sides of wrapper, then, starting at the bottom, tightly roll up to enclose filling. Place on a plate.

Tips

To prevent the rolls from getting soggy, prepare them no more than 4 hours ahead of serving.

Prepare extra peanut dressing and keep it handy in the fridge for when you make these rolls another time. The sauce keeps well for several weeks in an airtight container in the refrigerator.

Soy sauce is a popular condiment and ingredient, but it is also high in sodium. Choose reduced-sodium soy sauce. Brands vary, but there is typically about 1000 milligrams of sodium in 1 tablespoon (15 mL) of regular soy sauce and 500 milligrams in the same amount of reduced-sodium soy sauce.

4. Repeat with the remaining rice papers and filling to make 3 more rolls. Serve immediately or cover rolls with plastic wrap and refrigerate for up to 4 hours. To serve, cut each roll on the diagonal into halves.

Nutrition Tip

Eating out for lunch can be challenge, especially if you are surrounded by fast-food places offering few healthy choices. A better idea is to bring lunch from home. Use our sandwich and salad charts on pages 158–161 to build a wholesome lunch with foods you enjoy, and take advantage of leftovers or whatever you might have in the fridge.

Greek Chicken Pitas with Tzatziki

Makes 4 servings

These tasty pitas beat out other sandwiches and burgers from fast-food restaurants hands down.

Tips

The chicken in its marinade can be covered and refrigerated for up to 24 hours.

You can also heat the pita halves in the microwave. Arrange them in a circle on a plate lined with a paper towel and cover with another sheet of paper towel. Microwave on High for 1 minute or until warm. Rearrange halfway through so bread heats evenly.

Nutrition info per pita

Calories	318
Carbohydrate	46 g
Fiber	8 g
Protein	23 g
Fat	6 g
Saturated fat	1 g
Cholesterol	33 mg
Sodium	422 mg

Food Choices
2 Carbohydrate
2 Meat & Alternatives
1 Fat

● **Preheat oven to 350°F (180°C)**

1	clove garlic, minced	1
1 tsp	dried oregano	5 mL
¼ tsp	freshly ground black pepper	1 mL
1 tbsp	freshly squeezed lemon juice	15 mL
8 oz	boneless skinless chicken breast (1 large), cut crosswise into very thin strips	250 g
1 tbsp	extra virgin olive oil	15 mL
1	large red or green bell pepper, cut into thin 2-inch (5 cm) long strips	1
1	small onion, thinly sliced	1
1 cup	sliced mushrooms	250 mL
4	thin 7-inch (18 cm) whole wheat pitas, halved to make pockets	4
½ cup	Tzatziki (see recipe, opposite)	125 mL
2	tomatoes, cut into thin wedges	2
2 cups	finely shredded romaine lettuce	500 mL

1. In a bowl, combine garlic, oregano, pepper and lemon juice. Add chicken and coat in marinade.

2. In a large nonstick skillet, heat oil over medium-high heat. Add chicken and cook, stirring, for 3 minutes or until no longer pink inside. Add red pepper, onion and mushrooms; cook, stirring, for 2 to 3 minutes or until vegetables are tender-crisp.

3. Wrap pita halves in foil and bake in preheated oven for 10 minutes to warm.

4. Spoon chicken mixture into pita pockets; top with a spoonful of tzatziki, tomato wedges and lettuce.

Tzatziki

Makes about 1 cup (250 mL)

With Greek yogurt readily available in supermarkets, it's a breeze to make this tangy, garlicky sauce. Greek yogurt is thick and creamy, with a high protein content, and has less carbohydrates than regular yogurt.

Tip

The tzatziki can be stored in an airtight container in the refrigerator for up to 5 days.

½ cup	grated English cucumber (unpeeled)	125 mL
1	clove garlic, minced	1
¾ cup	nonfat plain Greek yogurt	175 mL
1 tsp	freshly squeezed lemon juice	5 mL
⅛ tsp	salt	0.5 mL

1. Place cucumber in a sieve and squeeze out excess water. Wrap in paper towels or a clean kitchen towel and squeeze out excess moisture.

2. In a bowl, combine cucumber, garlic, yogurt, lemon juice and salt.

Nutrition Tip

Instead of traditional condiments such as mayonnaise, ketchup and relish, which are higher in calories, carbs, fat and sodium, rely on homemade sauces such as tzatziki to dress up your favorite sandwiches and burgers.

Nutrition info per 2 tbsp (30 mL) serving

Calories	15
Carbohydrate	2 g
Fiber	0 g
Protein	2 g
Fat	0 g
Saturated fat	0 g
Cholesterol	0 mg
Sodium	45 mg

Food Choices
1 Extra

Tuna Cheddar Melts

Makes 4 servings

Chances are you have canned tuna in your cupboard to whip up these simple, satisfying open-faced sandwiches that are always a popular choice for lunch or dinner.

- - - - - - - - - - - - -

Tips

Lower-fat Cheddar is just one of the growing number of light (reduced-fat) cheeses available. A cheese is categorized as light if it contains at least 25% less fat than the full-fat version. When shopping, look for cheeses with less than 20% M.F. (milk fat).

The tuna salad can be prepared up to 1 day ahead. Cover and refrigerate.

● Preheat broiler

1	can (6 oz/170 g) water-packed light tuna, drained and flaked	1
1	green onion, finely sliced	1
¼ cup	finely chopped celery	60 mL
3 tbsp	light mayonnaise	45 mL
1 tsp	freshly squeezed lemon juice	5 mL
4	slices whole-grain bread (each 40 g), lightly toasted	4
8	thin tomato slices	8
	Freshly ground black pepper	
4 oz	lower-fat (<20% M.F.) Cheddar cheese, thinly sliced or shredded	125 g

1. In a bowl, combine tuna, green onion, celery, mayonnaise and lemon juice.

2. Spread tuna mixture over bread slices. Place tomato slices on top and season with pepper. Top with cheese. Arrange on baking sheet.

3. Broil for about 3 minutes or until cheese is melted. Serve immediately.

Nutrition info per sandwich

Calories	262
Carbohydrate	21 g
Fiber	4 g
Protein	21 g
Fat	11 g
Saturated fat	4 g
Cholesterol	29 mg
Sodium	553 mg

Food Choices
1 Carbohydrate
2 Meat & Alternatives
1 Fat

Nutrition Tip

When buying bread, always check the Nutrition Facts table for the weight in grams of carbohydrate and fiber per slice. Determine the available (net) carbohydrate by subtracting the fiber from the total carbohydrate. One Carbohydrate Choice is 12 to 18 grams of available carbohydrate.

If your bread slices are heavier than suggested in a recipe, trim off part or all of the crust. If it's a bun or roll, remove some of the doughy center. Make bread crumbs from the trimmings and use them in other recipes.

Chili Tofu Vegetable Wraps

These vegetarian wraps are so tasty, you shouldn't have any trouble winning over meat eaters.

- - - - - - - - - - - - -

Tips

The tofu filling can be made ahead through step 2. Let cool, transfer to an airtight container and refrigerate for up to 2 days.

For bagged lunches, assemble the wraps in the morning and place in a storage container or wrap in plastic wrap. Enjoy cold, or unwrap and place on a plate lined with a paper towel. Microwave on High for 1 minute.

12 oz	firm tofu, cut into 1/2-inch (1 cm) cubes	375 g
1 1/2 tsp	chili powder	7 mL
1 tsp	dried oregano	5 mL
1 tbsp	canola oil	15 mL
1	onion, halved lengthwise, cut into thin wedge slices	1
1	clove garlic, minced	1
1	large green bell pepper, cut into thin 2-inch (5 cm) long strips	1
1 cup	cooked fresh or frozen corn kernels	250 mL
1 cup	Classic Tomato Salsa (page 189)	250 mL
1/2 cup	coarsely chopped fresh cilantro	125 mL
4	9-inch (23 cm) whole wheat flour tortillas	4

1. Place tofu in a bowl and toss with chili powder and oregano.

2. In a large nonstick skillet, heat oil over medium-high heat. Stir-fry tofu for 4 minutes or until golden on all sides. Add onion, garlic, green pepper and corn; stir-fry for 2 to 3 minutes or until vegetables are tender-crisp.

3. Transfer tofu mixture to a bowl and stir in salsa and cilantro.

4. Spoon tofu mixture along bottom half of each tortilla. Fold 1 inch (2.5 cm) of left and right sides of tortilla over filling and roll up. Cut on the diagonal into halves.

Nutrition info per wrap with 1 1/4 cups (300 mL) filling

Calories	348
Carbohydrate	51 g
Fiber	6 g
Protein	15 g
Fat	11 g
Saturated fat	2 g
Cholesterol	0 mg
Sodium	509 mg

Food Choices
2 Carbohydrate
1 Meat & Alternatives
1 Fat

Nutrition Tip

Like meat, tofu supplies protein, iron and zinc, and it is also a source of calcium and folate. In these wraps, we call for firm tofu, which is more concentrated in protein than softer tofu.

Grilled Portobello Mushroom Burgers with Goat Cheese

Makes 4 servings

Meaty portobello mushrooms team up with creamy goat cheese and arugula to make these juicy burgers.

- - - - - - - - - - - - - - -

Tip

Rinse all produce you are using in food preparation. (The exception is triple-washed "ready to use" salad greens, sold in sealed containers.) For mushrooms, rinse them in a strainer under cold water, then wrap them in a clean kitchen towel or paper towels to absorb excess moisture.

Nutrition info per burger	
Calories	305
Carbohydrate	42 g
Fiber	8 g
Protein	15 g
Fat	10 g
Saturated fat	5 g
Cholesterol	13 mg
Sodium	479 mg

Food Choices
2 Carbohydrate
1 Meat & Alternatives
1 Fat

- **Preheat greased barbecue grill or stovetop grill pan over medium-high heat**

1½ tsp	chopped fresh thyme (or ¾ tsp/3 mL dried)	7 mL
¼ tsp	freshly ground black pepper	1 mL
2 tbsp	balsamic vinegar	30 mL
1 tbsp	honey-Dijon mustard	15 mL
4	large portobello mushrooms (1 lb/500 g total)	4
4	thin whole-grain buns	4
2	tomatoes, thinly sliced	2
4 oz	soft goat cheese	125 g
2 cups	arugula or baby spinach leaves	500 mL

1. In a bowl, whisk together thyme, pepper, vinegar and mustard.

2. Remove stems from mushrooms and reserve for another use. Brush both sides of mushroom tops with marinade.

3. Place mushrooms on preheated grill and cook, turning once, for about 6 minutes or until softened. Transfer to a plate.

4. Meanwhile, lightly toast buns. Spread cut sides of buns with goat cheese. Layer a grilled mushroom, tomato slices and arugula on bottom halves of buns. Cover with top halves. Serve immediately.

Soups

Low-Sodium Chicken Stock

Here is how to make homemade chicken stock instead of relying on commercial liquid broths, cubes and powders, which are often loaded with salt. As an added bonus, you can use the poached chicken meat for soups, sandwiches and casseroles.

Tip

The stock can be stored in airtight containers in the freezer for up to 2 months.

3- to 4-lb	whole chicken (or chicken pieces, such as legs and breasts)	1.5 to 2 kg
12 cups	water	3 L
4	carrots, coarsely chopped	4
3	stalks celery, including leaves, coarsely chopped	3
2	large onions, coarsely chopped	2
2	bay leaves	2
1/4 cup	coarsely chopped parsley with stems	60 mL
1 tsp	dried thyme	5 mL
1 tsp	whole black peppercorns	5 mL

1. Place chicken in a stockpot and pour in water. Add carrots, celery, onions, bay leaves, parsley, thyme and pepper. Bring to a boil over high heat. Skim foam from top. Reduce heat to medium-low, cover and simmer for 45 minutes.

2. Remove from heat and transfer chicken to a bowl. Let cool slightly, then remove meat from bones. Place meat in an airtight container and refrigerate for up to 3 days.

3. Return bones to stock, cover and simmer for 1½ hours.

4. Strain stock through a fine sieve into a large bowl, discarding solids. Let cool, then cover and refrigerate until chilled. Remove fat layer.

Nutrition info per ½ cup (125 mL)	
Calories	18
Carbohydrate	0 g
Fiber	0 g
Protein	3 g
Fat	1 g
Saturated fat	0 g
Cholesterol	3 mg
Sodium	65 mg
Food Choices	
1 Extra	

Variation

Turkey Stock: Make stock the day after roasting a turkey. Follow recipe for Low-Sodium Chicken Stock as directed, using the bones from a cooked 12- to 14-lb (6 to 7 kg) turkey, cut into large pieces. Bring to a boil and skim as directed in step 1, then simmer, covered, for 2 hours. Proceed with step 4.

Low-Sodium Vegetable Stock

Flavorful stocks are the key to delicious soups and stews. This homemade vegetable stock is not only easy to make, but is tastier and more economical than store-bought versions.

Tips

Sautéing the vegetables before stirring in the water adds depth and flavor to the stock.

The stock can be stored in airtight containers in the freezer for up to 2 months.

1 tbsp	canola oil	15 mL
4	carrots, coarsely chopped	4
3	stalks celery, including leaves, coarsely chopped	3
2	large onions, coarsely chopped	2
8 oz	mushrooms, quartered	250 g
12 cups	water	3 L
2	bay leaves	2
1/4 cup	coarsely chopped parsley, with stems	60 mL
1 tsp	dried thyme	5 mL
1 tsp	whole black peppercorns	5 mL

1. In a stockpot, heat oil over medium-high heat. Add carrots, celery, onions and mushrooms; cook, stirring often, for 10 minutes or until lightly colored.

2. Stir in water, bay leaves, parsley, thyme and peppercorns. Increase heat to high and bring to a boil. Skim foam from top, if necessary. Reduce heat to medium-low, cover and simmer for 2 hours.

3. Strain stock through a fine sieve into a large bowl, discarding solids.

Nutrition Tip

If you don't have time to make your own stock, check the sodium content of store-bought broths and stocks and choose one with 140 milligrams of sodium or less per 1 cup (250 mL).

Nutrition info per 1/2 cup (125 mL)

Calories	10
Carbohydrate	2 g
Fiber	0 g
Protein	0 g
Fat	0 g
Saturated fat	0 g
Cholesterol	0 mg
Sodium	70 mg

Food Choices
1 Extra

Asian Beef Noodle Soup

This warming Vietnamese-style soup makes a wonderful dinner. Chock full of vegetables and flavor, it takes less than 10 minutes to cook, so it's perfect for those nights when you don't have a lot of time to fuss over dinner.

Tips

Prepare and measure all of the ingredients before you begin cooking, as the soup cooks very quickly.

Substitute angel hair pasta for rice noodles, if desired. Boil pasta in broth for 2 minutes in step 2.

12 oz	lean boneless tender beef steak (such as sirloin)	375 g
4 tsp	reduced-sodium soy sauce	20 mL
7 cups	low-sodium or no-salt-added ready-to-use beef broth	1.75 L
3	slices gingerroot, smashed with side of knife	3
3 oz	brown rice noodles, broken into 3-inch (7.5 cm) pieces (about 3 cups/750 mL)	90 g
2	carrots, shredded	2
2 cups	thinly sliced napa cabbage or bok choy	500 mL
2 cups	bean sprouts, rinsed	500 mL
1 tsp	toasted sesame oil	5 mL
1 tsp	Asian chili sauce	5 mL
3	green onions, sliced	3
1/3 cup	coarsely chopped fresh cilantro	75 mL

1. Slice beef across the grain into very thin strips. In a bowl, combine beef and soy sauce. Set aside.

2. In a large saucepan, bring broth and ginger to a boil over high heat. Add rice noodles and boil for 1 minute. Add beef, carrots and cabbage. Return to a boil; boil for 2 minutes.

3. Stir in bean sprouts, sesame oil and chili sauce. Cook for 1 minute or until just heated through.

4. Immediately ladle soup into warm bowls. Sprinkle with green onions and cilantro.

Nutrition info per 2 cups (500 mL)

Calories	272
Carbohydrate	29 g
Fiber	3 g
Protein	24 g
Fat	6 g
Saturated fat	2 g
Cholesterol	42 mg
Sodium	477 mg

Food Choices
1 Carbohydrate
2 Meat & Alternatives
1/2 Fat
1 Extra

Chicken Noodle Soup

A steaming bowl of this homemade chicken soup is the perfect remedy to banish the winter chills.

- - - - - - - - - - - - - -

Tips

Instead of cooked chicken, use 12 oz (375 g) raw boneless skinless chicken breast, cut into very thin strips or cubes, and cook until no longer pink inside.

As the soup stands, the noodles absorb the broth and soften. If making ahead or freezing the soup, leave the noodles out, cook them separately and add to soup only when reheating.

2	carrots, diced	2
2	stalks celery, finely diced	2
1	onion, finely chopped	1
6 cups	Low-Sodium Chicken Stock (page 204) or low-sodium or no-salt-added ready-to-use chicken broth	1.5 L
1½ cups	broad whole wheat egg noodles (2 oz/60 g)	375 mL
1½ cups	diced cooked chicken	375 mL
1 cup	diced zucchini	250 mL
1 cup	small cauliflower florets	250 mL
2 tbsp	chopped fresh dill or parsley	30 mL

1. In a stockpot, combine carrots, celery, onion and stock. Bring to a boil over high heat. Reduce heat to medium-low, cover and simmer for 20 minutes or until vegetables are tender.

2. Increase heat to high and return to a boil. Once boiling, add noodles, chicken, zucchini, cauliflower and dill. Reduce heat and boil gently for 8 to 10 minutes or until noodles and vegetables are tender.

3. Ladle soup into warm soup bowls.

Nutrition info per 1⅓ cups (325 mL)

Calories	163
Carbohydrate	13 g
Fiber	3 g
Protein	18 g
Fat	4 g
Saturated fat	1 g
Cholesterol	36 mg
Sodium	191 mg

Food Choices
½ Carbohydrate
1½ Meat & Alternatives
1 Extra

Nutrition Tip

Soups often contain a surprising amount of sodium. When making your favorite soup recipes using low-sodium stock, refrain from adding any salt and taste to see if you really need it once you are ready to serve. If you do, just add a small amount — ⅛ to ¼ tsp (0.5 to 1 mL) per 4 to 6 servings. A small sprinkle of salt added just before serving is often enough to balance the flavors.

Creole Fish Soup

The trademark ingredients of Creole cooking — onion, green pepper and celery — are combined in a fragrant tomato broth to create this luscious, hearty soup, brimming with fish and vegetables.

- - - - - - - - - - - - - - - -

Tips

Use any kind of fish, such as cod, sole, haddock or tilapia. If using frozen fish fillets, remove packaging and arrange fish on plate; microwave on High for 3 to 4 minutes or until partially defrosted. Cut fish into cubes and let stand for 15 minutes to finish defrosting.

When purchasing broth, be sure to check the sodium content and choose one with 140 mg or less per 1 cup (250 mL).

Nutrition info per 1½ cups (375 mL)	
Calories	156
Carbohydrate	17 g
Fiber	3 g
Protein	16 g
Fat	3 g
Saturated fat	0 g
Cholesterol	32 mg
Sodium	228 mg

Food Choices
½ Carbohydrate
2 Meat & Alternatives
½ Fat

1 tbsp	extra virgin olive oil	15 mL
2	stalks celery, diced	2
2	cloves garlic, minced	2
1	onion, finely chopped	1
1	large green bell pepper, finely chopped	1
1 tsp	paprika	5 mL
¾ tsp	dried thyme	3 mL
Pinch	cayenne pepper	Pinch
2	small zucchini or yellow summer squash, diced	2
1	can (14 oz/398 mL) diced tomatoes, with juice	1
1½ cups	diced peeled potatoes (2 medium)	375 mL
3 cups	Low-Sodium Vegetable Stock (page 205) or low-sodium or no-salt-added ready-to-use vegetable broth (approx.)	750 mL
1 lb	fresh or frozen skinless fish fillets (see tip, at left), cut into cubes	500 g
2	green onions, sliced	2

1. In a large saucepan, heat oil over medium heat. Add celery, garlic, onion, green pepper, paprika, thyme and cayenne; cook, stirring, for 3 minutes or until softened.

2. Stir in zucchini, tomatoes with juice, potatoes and stock; bring to a boil. Reduce heat to medium-low, cover and simmer for 15 minutes or until vegetables are tender.

3. Stir in fish and green onions; cover and simmer for 2 minutes or until fish is opaque and flakes easily when tested with a fork.

4. Ladle soup into warm bowls.

Salmon Broccoli Chowder

Today, fresh and frozen salmon are readily available in supermarkets and are a better choice when making soups and sandwiches than traditional canned salmon, which is much higher in sodium.

- - - - - - - - - - - - - - - -

Tips

When purchasing broth, be sure to check the sodium content and choose one with 140 mg or less per 1 cup (250 mL).

If you have only canned salmon on hand, substitute one 7½-oz (213 g) can sockeye salmon for the fresh. Drain juices from salmon. Discard any skin, flake salmon and mash the calcium-rich bones with a fork. Omit the salt from the recipe.

Nutrition info per 1 cup (250 mL)

Calories	206
Carbohydrate	20 g
Fiber	3 g
Protein	15 g
Fat	8 g
Saturated fat	2 g
Cholesterol	36 mg
Sodium	253 mg

Food Choices
1 Carbohydrate
1 Meat & Alternatives
1 Fat

2 tsp	canola oil	10 mL
2	stalks celery, diced	2
1	small onion, finely chopped	1
1½ cups	diced peeled sweet potatoes	375 mL
2½ cups	Low-Sodium Chicken Stock (page 204) or low-sodium or no-salt-added ready-to-use chicken broth	625 mL
1	large bay leaf	1
¼ cup	all-purpose flour	60 mL
2 cups	low-fat (1%) milk	500 mL
3 cups	small broccoli florets and chopped peeled stems	750 mL
8 oz	skinless salmon fillet, cut into cubes	250 g
2 tbsp	chopped fresh dill	30 mL
¼ tsp	salt	1 mL
¼ tsp	freshly ground black pepper	1 mL

1. In a stockpot, heat oil over medium heat. Add celery and onion; cook, stirring often, for 3 minutes or until softened.

2. Stir in sweet potatoes, stock and bay leaf; bring to a boil. Reduce heat to medium-low, cover and simmer for 8 minutes or until sweet potatoes are almost tender.

3. Meanwhile, place flour in a glass measuring cup or bowl. Gradually whisk in ⅓ cup (75 mL) of the milk to make a smooth paste; stir in remaining milk. Gradually stir into soup. Increase heat to medium-high and cook, stirring, until mixture comes to a boil and thickens slightly. Add broccoli and cook, uncovered, for 2 minutes or until bright green and still crisp.

4. Stir in salmon, dill, salt and pepper. Cook for 2 minutes or until salmon is opaque and flakes easily when tested with a fork. Discard bay leaf.

5. Ladle soup into warm bowls.

Mushroom Lentil Soup

Dried lentils are so fast and easy to cook — and healthy, too! Just bring the stock to a boil, add the lentils and vegetables, and you'll soon enjoy a homey aroma as the soup simmers on the stovetop. In about 40 minutes, you'll be ladling out bowlfuls of wholesome soup.

Tips

To save time, chop the mushrooms, carrots, celery and onion in batches in a food processor.

When purchasing broth, be sure to check the sodium content and choose one with 140 mg or less per 1 cup (250 mL).

8 oz	mushrooms, chopped	250 g
3	carrots, chopped	3
2	stalks celery, including leaves, chopped	2
1	large onion, chopped	1
2	cloves garlic, minced	2
1 cup	dried brown or green lentils, rinsed	250 mL
1 tsp	dried thyme or marjoram	5 mL
¼ tsp	freshly ground black pepper	1 mL
8 cups	Low-Sodium Chicken Stock (page 204) or low-sodium or no-salt-added ready-to-use chicken broth	2 L
¼ cup	chopped fresh dill or parsley	60 mL

1. In a stockpot, combine mushrooms, carrots, celery, onion, garlic, lentils, thyme, pepper and stock. Bring to a boil over high heat. Reduce heat to medium-low, cover and simmer for 35 to 40 minutes or until lentils are tender. Stir in dill.

2. Ladle soup into warm bowls.

Nutrition Tip

Soup has a lot to offer in the way of health benefits, especially when made with fiber-rich, low-fat vegetables, grains and legumes that are also low in sodium. We've included several wholesome soups in our 28 days of menus, as they are satisfying and fill you up with fewer calories — a big plus when you're managing your weight.

Nutrition info per 1⅓ cups (325 mL)

Calories	184
Carbohydrate	25 g
Fiber	6 g
Protein	16 g
Fat	3 g
Saturated fat	1 g
Cholesterol	33 mg
Sodium	200 mg

Food Choices
1 Carbohydrate
1 Meat & Alternatives
1 Extra

Old-Fashioned Split Pea Soup

Split pea soup is typically made with ham or salt pork, but this lower-sodium version relies on vegetables that are first sautéed to bring out their sweet flavor.

Tips

Leftover soup thickens when cool; when reheating, thin with water to desired consistency.

Slow Cooker Method: Complete step 1, then transfer sautéed vegetables to a 5-quart (5 L) or larger slow cooker. Add split peas and stock. Cover and cook on Low for 8 to 10 hours or on High for 4 to 5 hours, until split peas are tender. Continue with step 3.

Nutrition info per 1⅓ cups (325 mL)

Calories	178
Carbohydrate	24 g
Fiber	4 g
Protein	13 g
Fat	4 g
Saturated fat	1 g
Cholesterol	25 mg
Sodium	157 mg

Food Choices
1 Carbohydrate
1 Meat & Alternatives
½ Fat
1 Extra

1 tbsp	canola oil	15 mL
3	carrots, diced	3
3	cloves garlic, minced	3
2	stalks celery, including leaves, chopped	2
1	leek (white and light green parts only), chopped	1
1	large onion, chopped	1
2	bay leaves	2
2 tsp	dried marjoram	10 mL
½ tsp	freshly ground black pepper	2 mL
1¼ cups	dried green or yellow split peas, rinsed	300 mL
8 cups	Low-Sodium Chicken Stock (page 204) or low-sodium or no-salt-added ready-to-use chicken broth	2 L
¼ cup	chopped fresh parsley	60 mL

1. In a stockpot, heat oil over medium-high heat. Add carrots, garlic, celery, leek, onion, bay leaves, marjoram and pepper; cook, stirring often, for 8 minutes or until vegetables are softened and lightly colored (reduce heat to medium if vegetables are browning).

2. Stir in split peas and stock; bring to a boil over high heat. Reduce heat to medium-low, cover and simmer, stirring occasionally, for 1½ to 2 hours or until peas are tender. Discard bay leaves and stir in parsley.

3. Ladle into warm bowls.

Variation

Curried Split Pea Soup: Add 2 tsp (10 mL) curry powder and a generous pinch of cayenne pepper along with the marjoram. Garnish bowls of soup with chopped fresh cilantro instead of stirring in parsley.

Black Bean and Corn Soup

It's reassuring to know that, when you come home from work, you can just reach for convenient canned and frozen products and have dinner on the table in no time. Serve with Cheese Cornbread (page 344).

Tips

When purchasing broth, be sure to check the sodium content and choose one with 140 mg or less per 1 cup (250 mL).

Instead of canned black beans, try chickpeas, romano beans or white kidney beans.

1 tbsp	extra virgin olive oil	15 mL
1	onion, chopped	1
1	green bell pepper, finely chopped	1
2	cloves garlic, minced	2
1 tsp	dried oregano	5 mL
1 tsp	ground cumin	5 mL
Pinch	cayenne pepper	Pinch
4 cups	Low-Sodium Chicken or Vegetable Stock (page 204 or 205) or low-sodium or no-salt-added ready-to-use chicken or vegetable broth	1 L
1	can (14 oz/398 mL) diced tomatoes, with juice	1
1½ cups	rinsed drained no-salt-added canned black beans	375 mL
1 cup	frozen corn kernels	250 mL
¼ cup	chopped fresh cilantro or parsley	60 mL

1. In a large saucepan, heat oil over medium heat. Add onion, green pepper, garlic, oregano, cumin and cayenne; cook, stirring, for 5 minutes or until softened.

2. Stir in stock and tomatoes with juice; bring to a boil over high heat. Reduce heat to medium-low, cover and simmer, stirring occasionally, for 20 minutes.

3. Stir in beans and corn. Cover and simmer for 8 to 10 minutes or until piping hot.

4. Ladle soup into warm bowls and sprinkle with cilantro.

Nutrition info per 1¼ cups (300 mL)

Calories	145
Carbohydrate	21 g
Fiber	5 g
Protein	9 g
Fat	4 g
Saturated fat	1 g
Cholesterol	17 mg
Sodium	228 mg

Food Choices
1 Carbohydrate
½ Meat & Alternatives
½ Fat

Nutrition Tip

Canned products, such as tomatoes and beans, can contain hefty quantities of sodium. In response to consumer demand, there is now a wider assortment of reduced-sodium and no-salt-added products available in supermarkets. Keep an eye out for new products and read labels to select products with the lowest sodium.

Hearty Minestrone

Makes 12 servings

This recipe makes a large quantity so you can enjoy the leftovers a day or two later and freeze the rest to enjoy in the coming weeks.

- - - - - - - - - - - - - - -

Tips

Use other fresh or frozen vegetables — whatever you might have in your fridge or freezer — to create this nourishing soup. Suggestions include peas, corn, mushrooms, shredded cabbage and spinach. Add to soup in step 2.

To help reduce the sodium in the soup, replace the canned tomatoes with 3 large ripe tomatoes, peeled and chopped.

Nutrition info per 1½ cups (375 mL)

Calories	134
Carbohydrate	20 g
Fiber	3 g
Protein	8 g
Fat	3 g
Saturated fat	1 g
Cholesterol	17 mg
Sodium	249 mg

Food Choices
½ Carbohydrate
½ Fat
1 Extra

1 tbsp	extra virgin olive oil	15 mL
3	carrots, diced	3
2	onions, chopped	2
2	stalks celery, including leaves, chopped	2
4	cloves garlic, minced	4
1½ tsp	dried basil	7 mL
1 tsp	dried oregano or marjoram	5 mL
½ tsp	freshly ground black pepper	2 mL
1	can (14 oz/398 mL) diced tomatoes, with juice	1
2 cups	small cauliflower florets	500 mL
1½ cups	green beans, cut into 1-inch (2.5 cm) lengths	375 mL
8 cups	Low-Sodium Chicken or Vegetable Stock (page 204 or 205) or low-sodium or no-salt-added ready-to-use chicken or vegetable broth	2 L
2 cups	water	500 mL
1 cup	small pasta shapes (such as tubetti or shells)	250 mL
2 cups	well-rinsed drained canned chickpeas	500 mL
⅓ cup	chopped fresh parsley	75 mL

1. In a stockpot, heat oil over medium heat. Add carrots, onions, celery, garlic, basil, oregano and pepper; cook, stirring, for 5 minutes or until softened.

2. Stir in tomatoes with juice, cauliflower, beans, stock and water; bring to a boil over high heat. Reduce heat to medium-low, cover and simmer for 20 minutes or until vegetables are tender.

3. Stir in pasta, cover and simmer for 10 minutes, stirring occasionally, until pasta is just tender.

4. Stir in chickpeas and parsley; cook for 5 minutes or until heated through.

5. Ladle soup into warm bowls.

Harvest Vegetable Barley Soup

Makes 6 servings

Vary this hearty soup according to the vegetables you have on hand, such as small cauliflower and broccoli florets or a generous handful of chopped fresh spinach or kale.

Tips

When purchasing broth, be sure to check the sodium content and choose one with 140 mg or less per 1 cup (250 mL).

Rutabaga, a traditional winter vegetable, is also known as yellow turnip or swede.

8 cups	Low-Sodium Chicken or Vegetable Stock (page 204 or 205) or low-sodium or no-salt-added ready-to-use chicken or vegetable broth	2 L
3	cloves garlic, finely chopped	3
1	large onion, chopped	1
1½ cups	diced peeled rutabaga or kohlrabi	375 mL
½ cup	pot barley, rinsed	125 mL
1 tsp	dried oregano	5 mL
½ tsp	dried thyme or marjoram	2 mL
¼ tsp	freshly ground black pepper	1 mL
1½ cups	diced peeled sweet potatoes	375 mL
1½ cups	diced zucchini	375 mL
⅓ cup	chopped fresh parsley	75 mL

1. In a stockpot, bring stock to a boil over high heat. Add garlic, onion, rutabaga, barley, oregano, thyme and pepper; return to a boil. Reduce heat to medium-low, cover and simmer for 25 minutes.

2. Stir in sweet potatoes and zucchini; cover and simmer for 10 to 15 minutes or until barley and sweet potatoes are tender. Stir in parsley.

3. Ladle soup into warm bowls.

Nutrition Tip

Barley is one of the grains with the greatest health benefits. Its slow-release carbohydrates help keep blood glucose levels stable. As a low-GI grain, it contains both soluble and insoluble fiber and, like oat bran, it helps lower blood cholesterol levels.

Nutrition info per 1½ cups (375 mL)

Calories	156
Carbohydrate	25 g
Fiber	5 g
Protein	9 g
Fat	2 g
Saturated fat	1 g
Cholesterol	33 mg
Sodium	192 mg

Food Choices
1 Carbohydrate
½ Fat

Moroccan-Spiced Carrot Soup

Makes 6 servings

The combination of cinnamon and turmeric provides a pleasantly sweet accent to the carrots and sweet potato.

- - - - - - - - - - - - -

Tip

When purchasing broth, be sure to check the sodium content and choose one with 140 mg or less per 1 cup (250 mL).

• Blender, food processor or immersion blender

1 tbsp	canola oil	15 mL
2	onions, chopped	2
2	cloves garlic, finely chopped	2
1½ tsp	ground cumin	7 mL
1 tsp	ground turmeric	5 mL
1 tsp	ground cinnamon	5 mL
½ tsp	freshly ground black pepper	2 mL
3 cups	sliced carrots (4 to 5 medium)	750 mL
1½ cups	diced peeled sweet potato	375 mL
5 cups	Low-Sodium Chicken or Vegetable Stock (page 204 or 205) or low-sodium or no-salt-added ready-to-use chicken or vegetable broth	1.25 L
¼ tsp	salt	1 mL
¼ cup	chopped fresh chives or cilantro	60 mL

1. In a large saucepan, heat oil over medium heat. Add onions, garlic, cumin, turmeric, cinnamon and pepper; cook, stirring often, for 4 minutes or until onions are softened.

2. Stir in carrots, sweet potato and stock; bring to a boil over high heat. Reduce heat to medium-low, cover and simmer for 25 minutes or until vegetables are very tender. Let cool slightly.

3. Working in batches, transfer soup to blender (or use immersion blender in pan) and purée until smooth. Return to saucepan, if necessary, and stir in salt. Heat over medium heat, stirring often, until piping hot.

4. Ladle soup into warm bowls and sprinkle with chives.

Nutrition info per 1⅓ cups (325 mL)	
Calories	121
Carbohydrate	16 g
Fiber	4 g
Protein	6 g
Fat	4 g
Saturated fat	1 g
Cholesterol	21 mg
Sodium	255 mg

Food Choices
½ Carbohydrate
½ Fat

Corn and Red Pepper Chowder

Sweet young corn, tender leeks and bell pepper make a delicately flavored fall soup. Kernels cut from cobs of corn are ideal in this recipe. You will need about three cobs.

- - - - - - - - - - - - - - -

Tips

To clean leeks, trim off dark green tops. Cut leek down center almost to root end and slice crosswise, discarding root end. Rinse sliced leek in a sink full of cold water to remove any sand; scoop up leek and place in colander to drain, or use a salad spinner.

To cut kernels from the cob easily, stand the ears on end and use a sharp knife.

1 tbsp	canola oil	15 mL
2	leeks (white and light green parts only), finely chopped	2
½ tsp	dried thyme	2 mL
1½ cups	fresh or frozen corn kernels	375 mL
2½ cups	Low-Sodium Chicken Stock (page 204) or low-sodium or no-salt-added ready-to-use chicken broth	625 mL
1	large red bell pepper, finely chopped	1
3 tbsp	all-purpose flour	45 mL
2 cups	low-fat (1%) milk	500 mL
¼ tsp	salt	1 mL
	Freshly ground black pepper	
2 tbsp	chopped fresh chives or parsley	30 mL

1. In a large saucepan, heat oil over medium heat. Add leeks and thyme; cook, stirring often, for 4 minutes or until softened (do not let brown).

2. Stir in corn and stock; bring to a boil over high heat. Reduce heat to medium-low, cover and simmer for 5 minutes.

3. Stir in red pepper, cover and simmer for 5 minutes or until vegetables are tender.

4. Meanwhile, place flour in a glass measuring cup or bowl. Gradually whisk in ⅓ cup (75 mL) of the milk to make a smooth paste; stir in remaining milk. Gradually stir into soup. Increase heat to medium-high and cook, stirring, until mixture comes to a boil and thickens slightly. Season with salt and pepper to taste.

5. Ladle soup into warm bowls and sprinkle with chives.

Nutrition info per 1¼ cups (300 mL)	
Calories	136
Carbohydrate	20 g
Fiber	2 g
Protein	7 g
Fat	4 g
Saturated fat	1 g
Cholesterol	14 mg
Sodium	193 mg

Food Choices
1 Carbohydrate
½ Fat

Leek, Potato and Kale Soup

Kale is an often overlooked vegetable. That's a shame as, in terms of nutrition, it's one of the best buys in the produce department. Although it's available year-round, kale is often considered a winter vegetable.

Tips

To prepare kale, remove the stalks and, using a paring knife, trim off the center core of the leaves. Discard any discolored leaves. Rinse leaves in a sinkful of cold water to remove any dirt. Place in a colander to drain.

Instead of kale, try any kind of greens, including Swiss chard, beet greens, collard leaves or spinach.

1 tbsp	extra virgin olive oil	15 mL
2	carrots, diced	2
1	leek (white and light green parts only), chopped	1
1	onion, chopped	1
3	cloves garlic, minced	3
1 tsp	curry powder	5 mL
1 tsp	dried thyme	5 mL
½ tsp	freshly ground black pepper	2 mL
1½ cups	diced peeled potatoes	375 mL
5 cups	Low-Sodium Chicken Stock (page 204) or low-sodium or no-salt-added ready-to-use chicken broth	1.25 L
3 cups	finely shredded kale leaves	750 mL

1. In a large saucepan, heat oil over medium heat. Add carrots, leek, onion, garlic, curry powder, thyme and pepper; cook, stirring often, for 4 minutes or until vegetables are softened.

2. Stir in potatoes and stock; bring to a boil over high heat. Reduce heat to medium-low, cover and simmer for 20 minutes or until potatoes are tender.

3. Stir in kale, cover and simmer for 6 to 8 minutes or until just tender.

Nutrition info per 1⅓ cups (325 mL)

Calories	115
Carbohydrate	15 g
Fiber	2 g
Protein	6 g
Fat	4 g
Saturated fat	1 g
Cholesterol	21 mg
Sodium	148 mg

Food Choices
½ Carbohydrate
½ Fat

Nutrition Tip

Kale, along with other nutrient-rich dark green leafy vegetables such as spinach and rapini, is a good source of folate, as well as the vital antioxidant lutein. Lutein is important for people with diabetes, as it helps protect the eyes from cataracts and macular degeneration, a condition that can cause damage to the retinas.

Curried Squash and Apple Soup

Take advantage of economical squash, sold at farmers' markets in the fall. Steam or bake the squash, purée it, pack it into airtight containers and freeze for up to 3 months.

- - - - - - - - - - - - - - -

Tip

When purchasing broth, be sure to check the sodium content and choose one with 140 mg or less per 1 cup (250 mL).

Nutrition info per 1 cup (250 mL)

Calories	85
Carbohydrate	12 g
Fiber	3 g
Protein	4 g
Fat	3 g
Saturated fat	0 g
Cholesterol	3 mg
Sodium	171 mg

Food Choices
½ Carbohydrate
½ Fat

• **Blender, food processor or immersion blender**

1 tbsp	canola oil	15 mL
3	stalks celery, diced	3
1	large onion, chopped	1
3	cloves garlic, minced	3
1½ cups	diced peeled apples	375 mL
2 tbsp	minced gingerroot	30 mL
1 tbsp	curry powder	15 mL
1 tsp	ground cumin	5 mL
1 tsp	ground coriander	5 mL
Pinch	cayenne pepper	Pinch
2 cups	thick winter squash or pumpkin purée (see box, opposite)	500 mL
5 cups	Low-Sodium Chicken or Vegetable Stock (page 204 or 205) or low-sodium or no-salt-added ready-to-use chicken or vegetable broth	1.25 L
¼ tsp	salt	1 mL
¼ tsp	freshly ground black pepper	1 mL
⅓ cup	chopped fresh cilantro, parsley or chives	75 mL

1. In a large saucepan, heat oil over medium heat. Add celery, onion, garlic, apples, ginger, curry powder, cumin, coriander and cayenne; cook, stirring often, for 5 minutes or until vegetables are softened.

2. Stir in squash purée and stock; bring to a boil over high-heat. Reduce heat to medium-low, cover and simmer for 20 minutes or until vegetables are very tender. Let cool slightly.

3. Working in batches, transfer soup to blender (or use immersion blender in pan) and purée until smooth. Return to saucepan, if necessary, and stir in salt and pepper. Heat over medium heat, stirring often, until piping hot.

4. Ladle soup into warm bowls and sprinkle with cilantro.

Tips

There are many varieties of winter squash and pumpkin, and any of them can be turned into a thick purée to use as a base for this delicious soup.

Use the purée in a variety of recipes, including Curried Squash and Apple Soup (opposite), Orange Pumpkin Loaf (page 341) and Pumpkin Spice Custard (page 366).

Winter Squash or Pumpkin Purée

Cut squash into halves or quarters and remove seeds. For large pumpkins, cut into chunks. Place in a large casserole dish or roasting pan. Add 1 cup (250 mL) water. Cover and bake in a preheated 350°F (180°C) oven for 1 to $1\frac{1}{4}$ hours or until tender when pierced with a fork. (Or place squash in a large casserole dish with $\frac{1}{2}$ cup/125 mL water, cover and microwave on High for 15 to 25 minutes or until tender when tested with a knife in several places.) Cooking time will vary according to the amount and type of squash or pumpkin. Let cool. Scoop out pulp, discarding skin, and purée in a food processor or blender. If required, place purée in a fine-mesh strainer for several hours, stirring occasionally, to drain off excess moisture. The purée should be thick enough to mound on a spoon without dripping off. Save liquid to add to soups and broths.

Tomato Soup with Fresh Herbs

Makes 6 servings

The aromatic fresh herb topping adds a fresh burst of flavor to this always popular low-calorie soup. It relies on the convenience of canned tomatoes, so you can make it year-round.

- - - - - - - - - - - - - - - -

Tips

Use a rasp grater, such as a Microplane, to grate whole nutmeg. It has an incredible aroma and adds a more pronounced and exotic flavor to dishes than the ground nutmeg sold in the spice section.

Instead of fresh basil and chives, add 1 tsp (5 mL) dried basil in step 2, and ¼ cup (60 mL) chopped fresh parsley when serving.

Nutrition info per 1¼ cups (300 mL)	
Calories	104
Carbohydrate	14 g
Fiber	3 g
Protein	6 g
Fat	4 g
Saturated fat	1 g
Cholesterol	17 mg
Sodium	138 mg

Food Choices
½ Fat
1 Extra

- **Blender, food processor or immersion blender**

1 tbsp	extra virgin olive oil	15 mL
2	onions, chopped	2
2	carrots, chopped	2
1	stalk celery, including leaves, chopped	1
3	cloves garlic, finely chopped	3
1	can (28 oz/796 mL) diced no-salt-added tomatoes, with juice	1
4 cups	Low-Sodium Chicken or Vegetable Stock (page 204 or 205) or low-sodium or no-salt-added ready-to-use chicken or vegetable broth	1 L
⅓ cup	no-salt-added tomato paste	75 mL
¼ tsp	freshly ground black pepper	1 mL
¼ tsp	freshly grated nutmeg (see tip, at left)	1 mL
2 tbsp	chopped fresh basil	30 mL
2 tbsp	chopped fresh chives	30 mL

1. In a large saucepan, heat oil over medium heat. Add onions, carrots, celery and garlic; cook, stirring often, for 7 minutes, or until softened and lightly colored.

2. Stir in tomatoes with juice, stock and tomato paste; bring to a boil over high heat. Reduce heat to medium-low, cover and simmer for 25 minutes or until vegetables are tender. Let cool slightly.

3. Working in batches, transfer soup to blender (or use immersion blender in pan) and purée until smooth. Return to saucepan, if necessary, and stir in pepper and nutmeg. Heat over medium heat, stirring often, until piping hot.

4. Ladle soup into warm bowls and sprinkle with basil and chives.

Salads and Dressings

Shrimp and Vegetable Salad with Sesame Ginger Dressing

On hot summer days, this meal-in-one salad with its fresh, lively flavors of cilantro, basil, sesame and ginger fits the bill when you don't feel like cooking or barbecuing.

Tips

Replace the vermicelli with 6 oz (175 g) whole wheat angel hair pasta or spaghettini. In step 1, cook according to package directions, then cut into thirds.

The salad can be prepared through step 2, covered and refrigerated for up to 8 hours.

Nutrition info per 2 cups (500 mL)	
Calories	399
Carbohydrate	48 g
Fiber	7 g
Protein	31 g
Fat	9 g
Saturated fat	2 g
Cholesterol	201 mg
Sodium	453 mg

Food Choices
2 Carbohydrate
3 Meat & Alternatives
1 Fat

6 oz	brown rice vermicelli	175 g
1½ cups	halved trimmed snow peas	375 mL
2	carrots, peeled and cut into 2-inch (5 cm) long matchsticks	2
1	large red bell pepper, cut into thin 2-inch (5 cm) long strips	1
1 lb	cooked peeled medium shrimp, with tails on	500 g
4	green onions, thinly sliced	4
½ cup	coarsely chopped fresh cilantro	125 mL
¼ cup	chopped fresh mint or basil	60 mL
2 tbsp	toasted sesame seeds	30 mL
¾ cup	Sesame Ginger Dressing (page 244)	175 mL

1. Place vermicelli in a bowl and cover vermicelli with hot water; let stand for 3 minutes or until softened. Drain well. Using scissors, cut noodles into thirds. Place in a large bowl.

2. In a medium saucepan of boiling water, blanch snow peas for 30 seconds or until bright green and crisp. Rinse under cold water to chill. Drain well. Add to noodles, along with carrots and red pepper.

3. Add shrimp, green onions, cilantro and mint. Sprinkle with sesame seeds. Just before serving, pour Ginger Sesame Dressing over salad and toss well to coat.

Nutrition Tip

Shrimp is a lean source of protein. Although higher in cholesterol than some meats and poultry, it is low in total fat and saturated fat. Shrimp also contains omega-3 fats — a heart-healthy bonus.

Grilled Salmon and Romaine Salad

Grilled salmon on a bed of freshly tossed greens makes for an easy and delicious dinner. The dressing, made in the food processor, does double duty as a marinade for the salmon and a dressing for the salad.

- Preheat greased barbecue grill or stovetop grill pan to medium
- Food processor
- Four 8-inch (20 cm) bamboo skewers, soaked in water for 15 minutes

1	clove garlic, coarsely chopped	1
2 cups	lightly packed fresh parsley leaves	500 mL
1/4 tsp	salt	1 mL
1/4 tsp	freshly ground black pepper	1 mL
1 tsp	grated orange zest	5 mL
1/4 cup	freshly squeezed orange juice	60 mL
2 tbsp	extra virgin olive oil	30 mL
2 tbsp	red wine vinegar	30 mL
1 tbsp	Dijon mustard	15 mL
1 lb	skinless salmon fillet (in one piece)	500 g
8 cups	torn romaine lettuce	2 L
2 cups	halved cherry tomatoes	500 mL
1/2	English cucumber, halved lengthwise and sliced	1/2

1. In food processor, combine garlic, parsley, salt, pepper, orange juice, oil, vinegar and mustard; process, scraping down sides occasionally with a spatula, until parsley is very finely chopped. Transfer to a bowl and stir in orange zest.

2. Cut salmon lengthwise into 4 equal strips. Thread lengthwise onto skewers. Arrange skewers in a shallow dish and spread with 1/4 cup (60 mL) of the dressing. Let marinate at room temperature for 10 minutes, turning occasionally.

3. Place salmon on preheated grill and cook, turning once, for 5 to 6 minutes per side or until fish is opaque and flakes easily when tested with a fork. Let stand for 5 minutes.

4. Meanwhile, in a bowl, combine romaine, tomatoes and cucumber. Pour the remaining dressing over salad and toss to lightly coat.

5. Divide salad among plates and top with salmon.

Nutrition info per serving

Calories	342
Carbohydrate	14 g
Fiber	5 g
Protein	27 g
Fat	21 g
Saturated fat	4 g
Cholesterol	64 mg
Sodium	343 mg

Food Choices
3 Meat & Alternatives
1 Fat

Caesar Salad

The king of tossed salads was named after a Tijuana restaurateur by the name of Caesar Cardini. Here, mayonnaise gives this classic an even creamier texture than the original.

Tips

Make sure salad greens are washed and dried thoroughly, preferably in a salad spinner, for best results.

Homemade croutons make a definite flavor difference and also have much less salt than store-bought croutons.

● **Food processor**

2	canned anchovies, blotted dry	2
2	cloves garlic, coarsely chopped	2
1/4 tsp	freshly ground black pepper	1 mL
2 tbsp	extra virgin olive oil	30 mL
2 tbsp	light mayonnaise	30 mL
2 tbsp	freshly squeezed lemon juice	30 mL
2 tbsp	water	30 mL
1 tsp	Dijon mustard	5 mL
10 cups	torn romaine lettuce	2.5 L
3 cups	Garlic Croutons (see recipe, opposite)	750 mL
1/3 cup	shaved Parmesan cheese	75 mL

1. In food processor, combine anchovies, garlic, pepper, oil, mayonnaise, lemon juice, water and mustard; purée until smooth.

2. Arrange lettuce in a salad bowl. Drizzle with dressing and toss to lightly coat. Add croutons and sprinkle with Parmesan cheese. Toss again. Serve immediately.

Nutrition Tip

Salted and brined foods, such as anchovies, are very high in sodium, but you don't have to banish them completely from your kitchen. Instead, reduce the amount you use in your favorite recipes, such as Caesar salad. Use canned anchovies, not anchovy paste, which is much higher in sodium.

Nutrition info per 1 1/2 cups (375 mL)

Calories	160
Carbohydrate	15 g
Fiber	3 g
Protein	5 g
Fat	10 g
Saturated fat	2 g
Cholesterol	6 mg
Sodium	286 mg

Food Choices
1/2 Carbohydrate
2 Fat

Garlic Croutons

Your kitchen will be filled with the tantalizing aroma of roasting garlic when you're toasting these croutons in the oven.

Tips

The croutons can be stored in an airtight container at room temperature for up to 1 day or in the freezer for up to 2 weeks.

Add these crunchy croutons to tossed salads or sprinkle a few on top of puréed soups.

- **Preheat oven to 375°F (190°C)**
- **Rimmed baking sheet**

3 cups	cubed white or whole-grain French baguette (½-inch/1 cm cubes)	750 mL
1	large clove garlic, pressed or minced	1
2 tsp	extra virgin olive oil	10 mL
2 tsp	water	10 mL

1. Place bread cubes in a bowl. Combine garlic, oil and water; drizzle over bread cubes and toss to coat. Arrange in a single layer on baking sheet.

2. Toast in preheated oven for 10 minutes, stirring once, until golden. Let cool on pan on a wire rack.

Nutrition info per ⅓ cup (75 mL)

Calories	64
Carbohydrate	10 g
Fiber	0 g
Protein	2 g
Fat	2 g
Saturated fat	0 g
Cholesterol	0 mg
Sodium	113 mg

Food Choices
½ Carbohydrate
½ Fat

Green Bean and Plum Tomato Salad

Makes 6 servings

This vibrant, refreshing salad combines fresh plum tomatoes with tender green beans in a grainy mustard dressing.

- - - - - - - - - - - - - - - -

Tips

If preparing this dish ahead, keep the blanched green beans, tomatoes and dressing separate and toss just a few hours before serving to preserve the beans' vibrant green color. When tossed ahead, the beans turn an olive green when exposed to the acid-based dressing.

The mustardy dressing is also wonderful with other favorite vegetable and bean salad mixtures.

1 lb	green beans, ends trimmed	500 g
1 lb	small plum (Roma) tomatoes (about 6 to 8)	500 g
2	green onions, sliced	2
1	small clove garlic, minced	1
2 tbsp	extra virgin olive oil	30 mL
4 tsp	red wine vinegar	20 mL
1 tbsp	grainy or Dijon mustard	15 mL
½ tsp	granulated sugar	2 mL
¼ tsp	freshly ground black pepper	1 mL
¼ cup	chopped fresh parsley or dill	60 mL

1. In a medium saucepan of boiling water, cook beans for 3 minutes or until crisp and bright green. Drain and rinse under cold water to chill; drain well. Wrap in a clean, dry towel to absorb excess moisture.

2. Cut tomatoes in half lengthwise. Using a small spoon, scoop out center and seeds. Cut each piece lengthwise into quarters. Place in a serving bowl.

3. Just before serving, combine beans, tomatoes and green onions.

4. In a small bowl, whisk together garlic, oil, vinegar, mustard, sugar and pepper. Pour over salad and toss to coat. Sprinkle with parsley.

Nutrition info per 1 cup (250 mL)	
Calories	84
Carbohydrate	9 g
Fiber	3 g
Protein	2 g
Fat	5 g
Saturated fat	1 g
Cholesterol	0 mg
Sodium	47 mg
Food Choices 1 Fat	

Kale and Pear Salad with Warmed Shallot Dressing

Any assertive green, such as dandelion, curly endive or arugula, will work in this tasty salad. Or use more mellow leaves, such as Swiss chard, watercress, beet tops, spinach or romaine.

Tips

Baby kale leaves are a new addition to the prewashed packaged salads available in supermarkets. If unavailable, use regular bunched kale. Remove tough stems and center ribs, and finely shred the leaves.

To toast walnuts, place on a rimmed baking sheet in 350°F (180°C) oven for 8 to 10 minutes or until light golden and fragrant.

Nutrition info per 1½ cups (375 mL)	
Calories	108
Carbohydrate	14 g
Fiber	3 g
Protein	2 g
Fat	6 g
Saturated fat	1 g
Cholesterol	0 mg
Sodium	134 mg

Food Choices
½ Carbohydrate
1 Fat

8 cups	lightly packed baby kale leaves	2 L
2	small pears or apples, cut lengthwise into thin slices, then halved diagonally	2
¼ cup	minced shallots	60 mL
¼ tsp	salt	1 mL
¼ tsp	freshly ground black pepper	1 mL
2 tbsp	pomegranate, cider or other fruit vinegar	30 mL
2 tsp	grainy Dijon mustard	10 mL
2 tsp	liquid honey	10 mL
4 tsp	walnut, hazelnut or extra virgin olive oil	20 mL
3 tbsp	chopped toasted walnuts or hazelnuts	45 mL

1. Place kale in a salad bowl and top with pear slices.

2. In a small saucepan, combine shallots, salt, pepper, vinegar, mustard and honey. Bring to a boil over medium-low heat, whisking. Remove from heat and whisk in oil.

3. Pour dressing over salad and toss to coat. Sprinkle with walnuts. Serve immediately.

> **Variation**
> Replace one of the pears with ¼ cup (60 mL) fresh pomegranate seeds.

Greens with Grapefruit and Avocado

Arrange this ideal brunch salad on a large platter, or, if serving it as a starter at dinner, arrange it on individual salad plates. Assemble just before serving to prevent the greens from wilting.

Tips

Section grapefruit over a bowl to catch juices for the dressing.

If preparing fennel ahead, thinly slice it and place in ice water to prevent it from discoloring. Drain well and pat dry before adding to salad.

Store this dressing in a condiment squeeze bottle in the refrigerator for up to 1 week, for easy drizzling over your favorite salad.

Nutrition info per 1½ cups (375 mL)	
Calories	151
Carbohydrate	17 g
Fiber	5 g
Protein	3 g
Fat	9 g
Saturated fat	1 g
Cholesterol	2 mg
Sodium	115 mg

Food Choices
½ Carbohydrate
2 Fat

3 tbsp	light mayonnaise	45 mL
2 tbsp	freshly squeezed grapefruit juice	30 mL
4 tsp	avocado, almond or extra virgin olive oil	20 mL
4 tsp	white wine vinegar	20 mL
1 tbsp	honey-Dijon mustard	15 mL
¼ tsp	freshly ground black pepper	1 mL
1	small head Boston lettuce	1
2 cups	lightly packed watercress leaves or arugula	500 mL
1	small fennel bulb, top trimmed	1
2	grapefruit, peeled and sectioned	2
1	small avocado, sliced	1

1. In a small bowl, whisk together mayonnaise, grapefruit juice, oil, vinegar, mustard and pepper. Transfer to a squeeze bottle or jar.

2. Tear lettuce into bite-size pieces and arrange on a large serving platter. Top with an even layer of watercress.

3. Cut fennel lengthwise into quarters and remove core. Cut lengthwise into thin strips. Scatter over greens.

4. Drizzle dressing over salad. Top with grapefruit and avocado. Serve immediately.

Variation
Instead of grapefruit, use orange juice in the dressing and 3 sectioned oranges in the salad.

Spinach Salad with Carrots and Mushrooms

The tangy dressing, accented with cumin, nicely balances the sweetness of the raisins and carrots in this colorful salad that is easy to assemble.

- - - - - - - - - - - - - -

Tip

Assemble salad up to 4 hours ahead, cover and refrigerate. Add dressing and toss just before serving.

8 cups	loosely packed fresh baby spinach	2 L
1½ cups	sliced mushrooms	375 mL
1½ cups	shredded or matchstick carrots	375 mL
1	small red onion, thinly sliced	1
¼ cup	dark raisins or dried cranberries	60 mL
2 tbsp	unsalted roasted green pumpkin seeds (pepitas)	30 mL

Dressing

1	clove garlic, minced	1
¾ tsp	ground cumin	3 mL
¼ tsp	salt	1 mL
¼ tsp	freshly ground black pepper	1 mL
2 tbsp	pumpkin seed oil or extra virgin olive oil	30 mL
2 tbsp	red wine vinegar	30 mL
1 tbsp	liquid honey	15 mL
2 tsp	Dijon mustard	10 mL

1. In a serving bowl, layer one-third of the spinach, all of the mushrooms, another third of the spinach, all of the carrots, then the remaining spinach. Arrange onion, raisins and pumpkin seeds on top.

2. *Dressing:* In a small bowl, whisk together garlic, cumin, salt, pepper, oil, vinegar, honey and mustard.

3. Drizzle dressing over salad and toss to coat.

Variation

Use 1 tsp (5 mL) dried fines herbes instead of the cumin.

Nutrition info per 1½ cups (375 mL)	
Calories	105
Carbohydrate	14 g
Fiber	2 g
Protein	2 g
Fat	5 g
Saturated fat	1 g
Cholesterol	0 mg
Sodium	180 mg

Food Choices
½ Carbohydrate
1 Fat

Vegetable Garden Salad

Makes 4 servings

Here is a very simple salad that can be made with whatever vegetables you have on hand, such as carrots, celery, cauliflower and broccoli, as well as any specialty oil, such as walnut, almond or olive. Count on 1 cup (250 mL) vegetables per serving.

- - - - - - - - - - - - - -

Tips

Always rinse fresh fruits and vegetables under running tap water — including those with skins or rinds that are not eaten — to remove any dirt, pesticides or bacteria. Packaged produce labeled "ready-to-eat," "washed" or "triple washed" does not need to be rinsed.

Tossing the vegetables with dressing just before serving prevents them from getting waterlogged.

1	large yellow bell pepper, finely chopped	1
½	small sweet onion (such as Vidalia), thinly sliced	½
2 cups	cherry tomatoes, halved or quartered if large	500 mL
1 cup	diced English cucumber	250 mL
4 tsp	extra virgin olive oil or walnut oil	20 mL
4 tsp	sherry vinegar or red wine vinegar	20 mL
⅛ tsp	salt	0.5 mL
	Freshly ground black pepper	
¼ cup	coarsely chopped fresh parsley, basil or chives, or a combination	60 mL

1. In a serving bowl, combine yellow pepper, onion, tomatoes and cucumber.

2. In a small bowl, whisk together oil, vinegar, salt and pepper to taste.

3. Just before serving, pour dressing over vegetables, sprinkle with parsley and toss to coat.

Nutrition Tip

Instead of relying on salt, add a generous handful of chopped fresh herbs, such as parsley, cilantro, basil, chives or mint, to dips, salads, soups and other dishes to give them an aromatic flavor boost.

Nutrition info per 1 cup (250 mL)

Calories	88
Carbohydrate	10 g
Fiber	2 g
Protein	2 g
Fat	5 g
Saturated fat	1 g
Cholesterol	0 mg
Sodium	45 mg

Food Choices
1 Fat

Grilled Vegetable Salad

Makes 6 servings

This delectable grilled salad can be made with whatever vegetables you have on hand. Other suggestions include sliced baby eggplant, thickly sliced fennel or thick asparagus spears.

Tips

Soaking bamboo skewers in cold water for 15 minutes prevents them from burning when you're grilling the onions.

Grill extra vegetables and have them on hand to add to lunch sandwiches and grain, rice or pasta salads.

- Preheat greased barbecue grill or stovetop grill pan to medium
- Four 8-inch (20 cm) bamboo skewers, soaked in water for 15 minutes

1	Vidalia onion	1
1	red bell pepper	1
1	yellow bell pepper	1
3	small zucchini	3

Dressing

2	cloves garlic, minced	2
2 tsp	finely chopped fresh rosemary or thyme (or 1 tsp/5 mL dried Italian seasoning)	10 mL
½ tsp	freshly ground black pepper	2 mL
2 tbsp	extra virgin olive oil	30 mL
1 tbsp	balsamic vinegar	15 mL
1 tbsp	red wine vinegar	15 mL
1 tsp	Dijon mustard	5 mL

1. Slice onion crosswise into four rounds; insert skewers through slices to prevent them from falling apart when grilling. Cut peppers into quarters and remove ribs and seeds. Cut zucchini in half crosswise, then cut each piece in half lengthwise. Arrange vegetables on a baking sheet.

2. *Dressing:* In a small bowl, combine garlic, rosemary, pepper, oil, balsamic vinegar, red wine vinegar and mustard. Brush vegetables with dressing.

3. Place vegetables on grill and cook for 13 to 16 minutes, turning occasionally, until tender-crisp. Remove each vegetable from grill as it is done. Transfer to a serving platter. Serve warm or at room temperature.

Nutrition info per 1 cup (250 mL)	
Calories	72
Carbohydrate	7 g
Fiber	2 g
Protein	1 g
Fat	5 g
Saturated fat	1 g
Cholesterol	0 mg
Sodium	25 mg

Food Choices
1 Fat

Creamy Coleslaw

A family barbecue or picnic calls for a generous bowl of old-fashioned cabbage slaw with a creamy mayonnaise-mustard dressing.

Tips

Use a combination of green and red cabbage, if desired.

Instead of shredding the cabbage yourself, buy convenient bags of coleslaw, carrot or broccoli slaw mix, available in produce departments, and toss with the creamy dressing.

5	green onions, sliced	5
2	carrots, shredded	2
8 cups	finely shredded green cabbage	2 L
1/4 cup	chopped fresh parsley	60 mL
1/3 cup	light mayonnaise	75 mL
1/4 cup	nonfat plain Greek yogurt	60 mL
2 tbsp	liquid honey	30 mL
2 tbsp	cider vinegar	30 mL
1 tbsp	Dijon mustard	15 mL
1/4 tsp	salt	1 mL
1/4 tsp	freshly ground black pepper	1 mL

1. In a serving bowl, combine green onions, carrots, cabbage and parsley.

2. In a small bowl, whisk together mayonnaise, yogurt, honey, vinegar, mustard, salt and pepper. Pour over cabbage mixture and toss to coat well. Serve immediately, or cover and refrigerate for up to 4 hours.

Nutrition Tip

Cabbage is in very good company with broccoli, cauliflower, Brussels sprouts, kale, bok choy, arugula, radishes, rutabaga and many other vegetables that belong to the cruciferous family of vegetables. Cruciferous vegetables contain fiber, phytochemicals, vitamins and minerals, as well as sulfur-containing chemicals that give them a distinct aroma and assertive flavor. These chemicals may help reduce the risk of cancer. Health authorities recommend eating several servings of cruciferous vegetables per week to take advantage of their health benefits and for disease prevention.

Nutrition info per 1 cup (250 mL)

Calories	106
Carbohydrate	16 g
Fiber	3 g
Protein	3 g
Fat	5 g
Saturated fat	1 g
Cholesterol	4 mg
Sodium	281 mg

Food Choices
1/2 Carbohydrate
1 Fat

White Bean and Wheat Berry Salad

This hearty salad keeps well in the fridge for 2 days, so it's great to serve for next day's lunch.

- - - - - - - - - - - - - - - -

Tip

For instructions on cooking the white beans and wheat berries, see the cooking charts on pages 316 and 318.

2 cups	thinly sliced carrots	500 mL
1	red bell pepper, finely chopped	1
1/2	small red onion, thinly sliced	1/2
2 cups	cooked white beans (such as navy or Great Northern)	500 mL
2 cups	cooked wheat berries (see tip, at left)	500 mL
2 cups	broccoli or cauliflower florets	500 mL
1/2 cup	chopped fresh flat-leaf (Italian) parsley or cilantro	125 mL
1/4 cup	dried cranberries	60 mL

Dressing

1	clove garlic, minced	1
1 1/2 tsp	dried oregano	7 mL
1/2 tsp	ground cumin	2 mL
1/2 tsp	freshly ground black pepper	2 mL
1/4 tsp	salt	1 mL
1/3 cup	light (5% M.F.) sour cream	75 mL
1 tbsp	grated orange zest	15 mL
1/4 cup	freshly squeezed orange juice	60 mL
2 tbsp	red wine vinegar	30 mL
4 tsp	extra virgin olive oil	20 mL

1. In a serving bowl, combine carrots, red pepper, red onion, beans, wheat berries, broccoli, parsley and cranberries.

2. *Dressing:* In a small bowl, whisk together garlic, oregano, cumin, pepper, salt, sour cream, orange zest, orange juice, vinegar and oil.

3. Pour dressing over salad and toss gently to coat. Serve at room temperature.

Nutrition info per 1 1/2 cups (375 mL)

Calories	231
Carbohydrate	42 g
Fiber	10 g
Protein	10 g
Fat	4 g
Saturated fat	1 g
Cholesterol	3 mg
Sodium	158 mg

Food Choices
1 1/2 Carbohydrate
1 Meat & Alternatives
1 Fat

Whole-Grain Orzo Pasta Salad with Creamy Basil Pesto

Tiny orzo pasta is shaped like grains of rice. It is excellent in soups and pasta dishes, and in salads such as this one, with lots of vegetables and a tasty basil pesto with feta cheese.

Tip

Assemble salad up to 4 hours ahead, cover and refrigerate. Let stand at room temperature for 1 hour before serving.

1 cup	whole-grain orzo pasta	250 mL
3	green onions, thinly sliced	3
1	yellow bell pepper, diced	1
2 cups	cherry tomatoes, halved	500 mL
1 cup	diced English cucumber	250 mL
¾ cup	Creamy Basil Pesto (see recipe, opposite)	175 mL
¼ tsp	salt	1 mL
¼ tsp	freshly ground black pepper	1 mL

1. In a large saucepan of boiling water, cook orzo for 8 minutes or until al dente. Drain in a fine sieve and chill under cold water. Drain well.

2. In a serving bowl, combine pasta, green onions, yellow pepper, tomatoes and cucumber. Add pesto and season with salt and pepper; toss to coat. Serve at room temperature.

Nutrition Tip

Choosing low-GI foods is an effective way to reduce your blood glucose and help prevent or manage diabetes. (See page 58 for details about the glycemic index.) Pastas have a low or medium GI, meaning the carbohydrate causes only a gradual rise and fall of blood glucose levels. However, when overcooked, pasta becomes high-GI. Always cook pasta until al dente, meaning just tender to the bite, not soft and overcooked. For extra fiber, use whole-grain or whole wheat pastas in your favorite recipes.

Nutrition info per 1 cup (250 mL)

Calories	183
Carbohydrate	30 g
Fiber	5 g
Protein	8 g
Fat	5 g
Saturated fat	1 g
Cholesterol	3 mg
Sodium	218 mg

Food Choices
1 Carbohydrate
1 Meat & Alternatives
1 Fat

Creamy Basil Pesto

The classic Italian sauce gets a low-fat makeover, with creamy yogurt replacing most of the olive oil and feta cheese standing in for Parmesan and pine nuts.

- - - - - - - - - - - - - - - -

Tip

The pesto can be stored in an airtight container in the refrigerator for up to 2 days or in the freezer for up to 1 month.

● **Food processor**

2	cloves garlic, coarsely chopped	2
1½ cups	lightly packed fresh basil leaves	375 mL
⅓ cup	crumbled light feta cheese	75 mL
⅓ cup	nonfat plain yogurt	75 mL
4 tsp	extra virgin olive oil	20 mL
	Freshly ground black pepper	

1. In food processor, combine garlic, basil and feta; process until basil is finely chopped. Scrape down sides. Add yogurt and oil; process until smooth.

Variation

Mixed Herb Pesto: Instead of basil, use 1 cup (250 mL) lightly packed fresh parsley sprigs, ¼ cup (60 mL) lightly packed fresh oregano leaves and ¼ cup (60 mL) chopped fresh chives.

Nutrition info per 2 tbsp (30 mL)

Calories	57
Carbohydrate	2 g
Fiber	1 g
Protein	3 g
Fat	4 g
Saturated fat	1 g
Cholesterol	3 mg
Sodium	113 mg
Food Choices	
1 Fat	

Warm Barley Salad with Roasted Beets and Greens

Roasting brings out beets' natural sweetness and concentrates the flavor. In this salad, accented with lemon and dill, beets are partnered with wholesome barley, an excellent source of soluble fiber. Like oats, barley helps lower blood cholesterol levels.

- - - - - - - - - - - - - - -

Tip

Buy a bunch of beets with leaves. Trim the leaves, discarding the stems and any tough center ribs. Wash leaves and drain well, then shred.

- Preheat oven to 400°F (200°C)
- 8-inch (20 cm) square metal baking pan

1 lb	small beets, scrubbed, stem and root ends trimmed	500 g
¾ cup	pot barley, rinsed	175 mL
2¼ cups	water	550 mL
2 cups	shredded beet green tops (see tip, at left)	500 mL
4 tsp	extra virgin olive oil	20 mL
2 tsp	grated lemon zest	10 mL
2 tbsp	freshly squeezed lemon juice	30 mL
1 tsp	Dijon mustard	5 mL
¼ tsp	salt	1 mL
¼ tsp	freshly ground black pepper	1 mL
4	green onions, sliced	4
3 tbsp	chopped fresh dill or parsley, divided	45 mL
¼ cup	crumbled light feta cheese	60 mL

1. Wrap beets in foil and place in baking pan. Bake in preheated oven for 50 to 60 minutes or until tender when pierced with a knife (larger beets will take slightly longer). When cool enough to handle, peel and cut into thin wedges.

2. Meanwhile, in a medium saucepan, combine barley and water. Bring to a boil over high heat. Reduce heat to medium-low, cover and simmer, stirring occasionally, for 40 to 45 minutes or until barley is just tender and liquid is absorbed (add more water if liquid evaporates before barley is tender). Stir in beet greens and remove from heat.

Nutrition info per 1½ cups (375 mL)

Calories	234
Carbohydrate	40 g
Fiber	9 g
Protein	6 g
Fat	7 g
Saturated fat	2 g
Cholesterol	3 mg
Sodium	391 mg

Food Choices
1½ Carbohydrate
1 Fat

If beets with leaves aren't available, replace the leaves with other greens, such as spinach, Swiss chard or kale.

3. In a bowl, whisk together oil, lemon zest, lemon juice, mustard, salt and pepper.

4. In a shallow serving bowl, combine barley mixture, green onions and 2 tbsp (30 mL) of the dill. Pour dressing over salad and toss to coat. Arrange beet wedges around outside edge of bowl. Sprinkle with feta and the remaining dill. Serve warm or at room temperature.

Nutrition Tip

Barley is one of the grains with the greatest health benefits. Its slow-release carbohydrates help keep blood glucose levels stable. As a low-GI grain, it contains both soluble and insoluble fiber and, like oat bran, it helps lower blood cholesterol levels.

Whole-Grain Bulgur and Citrus Salad

This delicious recipe combines the nutty goodness of bulgur with the sweet tang of orange and cumin.

- - - - - - - - - - - - - - - - -

Tips

Bulgur is crushed wheat berries that have been partially steamed and dried, and needs only to be soaked in water to soften before it is added to salads. Coarse-grind whole-grain bulgur takes an hour to soften. If using a fine- to medium-grind bulgur, let soak for 30 minutes in step 1.

Section the oranges over a bowl to capture juice to use in the dressing.

Nutrition info per 1 cup (250 mL)	
Calories	195
Carbohydrate	34 g
Fiber	6 g
Protein	5 g
Fat	5 g
Saturated fat	1 g
Cholesterol	0 mg
Sodium	261 mg

Food Choices
1½ Carbohydrate
1 Fat

● **Food processor or blender**

Salad

1 cup	coarse whole-grain bulgur (see tip, at left)	250 mL
3	seedless oranges, peeled and sectioned	3
2	red bell peppers, finely chopped	2
½	English cucumber, diced	½
½	small red onion, thinly sliced	½

Dressing

1½ cups	lightly packed fresh parsley leaves	375 mL
1 tsp	ground cumin	5 mL
½ tsp	salt	2 mL
¼ tsp	freshly ground black pepper	1 mL
2 tbsp	extra virgin olive oil	30 mL
1 tbsp	grated orange zest	15 mL
3 tbsp	freshly squeezed orange juice	45 mL
2 tbsp	red wine vinegar	30 mL
4 tsp	honey-Dijon mustard	20 mL

1. *Salad:* Place bulgur in a bowl and add enough cold water to cover; soak for 1 hour. Drain in a fine sieve and squeeze out excess moisture by handfuls. Return to clean bowl and add oranges, red peppers, cucumber and red onion.

2. *Dressing:* In food processor, combine parsley, cumin, salt, pepper, oil, orange juice, vinegar and mustard; process, scraping down sides occasionally with a spatula, until parsley is finely chopped. Transfer dressing to a bowl and stir in orange zest.

3. Pour dressing over salad and toss well to coat. Cover and refrigerate for 4 hours, until chilled, or for up to 1 day.

Quinoa Tabbouleh

Makes 6 servings

Versatile quinoa, with its mild, nutty taste, goes well in salads, soups and side dishes. Here, it stands in for bulgur in this popular Middle Eastern salad. Thanks to quinoa's complete protein content, this tasty salad can stand on its own as a vegetarian dish, or it can be served as a side dish with chicken or fish.

Tip

When you purchase quinoa, it has usually been rinsed and air-dried to remove the naturally occurring bitter saponins, a resin-like coating. However, rinse it again before use, to remove any powdery residue that may remain.

1 cup	quinoa, rinsed	250 mL
2 cups	water	500 mL
1	clove garlic, minced	1
¼ tsp	ground cumin	1 mL
¼ tsp	paprika	1 mL
¼ tsp	salt	1 mL
¼ tsp	freshly ground black pepper	1 mL
2 tbsp	extra virgin olive oil	30 mL
2 tbsp	freshly squeezed lemon juice	30 mL
4	green onions, sliced	4
2	large tomatoes, diced	2
½	English cucumber, diced	½
½ cup	chopped fresh parsley	125 mL

1. In a medium saucepan, combine quinoa and water. Bring to a boil over high heat. Reduce heat to medium-low, cover and simmer for 15 minutes or until quinoa is tender and water is absorbed. Uncover and fluff with a fork. Transfer to a serving bowl and let cool.

2. In a small bowl, whisk together garlic, cumin, paprika, salt, pepper, oil and lemon juice.

3. Add green onions, tomatoes, cucumber and parsley to quinoa. Pour dressing over salad and toss to coat. Serve immediately or cover and refrigerate for up to 4 hours.

Nutrition info per 1 cup (250 mL)

Calories	166
Carbohydrate	24 g
Fiber	4 g
Protein	5 g
Fat	6 g
Saturated fat	1 g
Cholesterol	0 mg
Sodium	112 mg

Food Choices
1 Carbohydrate
1 Fat

Variation

Bulgur Tabbouleh: Replace the quinoa with ¾ cup (175 mL) fine- or medium-grind bulgur. Instead of cooking, place bulgur in a bowl and add enough cold water to cover; soak for 30 minutes. Drain in a fine sieve and squeeze out excess moisture by handfuls. Continue with step 2.

Classic Salad Dressing

Makes ½ cup (125 mL)

Why buy expensive bottled salad dressings when it's so easy to make a double batch of this great-tasting salad dressing and have it on hand in your fridge?

- - - - - - - - - - - - - - -

Tip

The dressing can be stored in the refrigerator for up to 2 weeks.

1	small clove garlic, minced (or 1 tbsp/15 mL minced shallots)	1
1 tsp	dried fines herbes	5 mL
¼ tsp	freshly ground black pepper	1 mL
¼ cup	freshly squeezed orange juice	60 mL
2 tbsp	red or white wine vinegar	30 mL
4 tsp	extra virgin olive oil	20 mL
1 tbsp	light mayonnaise	15 mL
1 tbsp	Dijon mustard	15 mL

1. In a jar, shake together garlic, fines herbes, pepper, orange juice, vinegar, oil, mayonnaise and mustard.

Variation

Italian Balsamic Dressing: Use balsamic vinegar instead of wine vinegar and substitute ½ tsp (2 mL) each dried basil and oregano for the fines herbes.

Nutrition info per 2 tbsp (30 mL)	
Calories	65
Carbohydrate	3 g
Fiber	0 g
Protein	0 g
Fat	6 g
Saturated fat	1 g
Cholesterol	1 mg
Sodium	119 mg
Food Choices 1 Fat	

Buttermilk Herb Dressing

Buttermilk adds a pleasant tang and creaminess to this dressing, which also makes a delicious dip for raw vegetables.

Tips

If you have fresh herbs, such as basil or dill, on hand, add 2 tbsp (30 mL) chopped fresh herbs to the dressing instead of using dried.

The dressing can be stored in an airtight container in the refrigerator for up to 1 week.

- **Food processor**

1	large green onion, coarsely chopped	1
1	clove garlic, coarsely chopped	1
1 tsp	dried fines herbes, tarragon or dillweed	5 mL
1/8 tsp	salt	0.5 mL
	Freshly ground black pepper	
1/2 cup	well-shaken buttermilk	125 mL
1/3 cup	light sour cream	75 mL
4 tsp	extra virgin olive oil	20 mL
2 tsp	white wine vinegar	10 mL
1/2 tsp	Dijon mustard	2 mL
2 tbsp	chopped fresh parsley	30 mL

1. In food processor, combine green onion, garlic, fines herbes, salt, pepper to taste, buttermilk, sour cream, oil, vinegar and mustard; process until smooth.

2. Transfer to a bowl and stir in parsley.

Nutrition Tip

Buttermilk's name and thick, creamy texture suggest that it contains a lot of fat. In fact, buttermilk is calcium-rich, like milk, and is low in fat if you buy the 1% version. Its tangy flavor makes it a great addition to cold soups, sauces and salad dressings, and it gives tenderness to baked goods.

**Nutrition info per
2 tbsp (30 mL)**

Calories	39
Carbohydrate	2 g
Fiber	0 g
Protein	1 g
Fat	3 g
Saturated fat	1 g
Cholesterol	3 mg
Sodium	72 mg

Food Choices
1/2 Fat
1 Extra

Healthy Oils and Their Culinary Uses

There are many healthy cooking oils to choose from, from kitchen favorites such as extra virgin olive oil and canola oil to specialty oils such as walnut, avocado, hemp and flaxseed oil.

The flavor of oils, especially specialty and unrefined oils, diminishes over time, so buy only small quantities or keep only a few kinds of oil on hand at any given time and rotate your selection. Once an oil is opened, keep it tightly sealed and use it within 6 months. Most oils can be stored in a cool, dry place, away from light, which can damage their quality and shelf stability. Flaxseed, hempseed, sesame, almond and walnut oils must be refrigerated to prevent rancidity, and you should also refrigerate or freeze any oil you don't use very often. If a refrigerated oil gets cloudy, let it stand at room temperature for a short time, until clear.

Beware of rancid oils, which will have an off taste and smell. Rancidity in oils, nuts, seeds and whole grains is a sign of oxidization, which causes free radicals to form. Free radicals can increase your risk of developing certain diseases, such as cancer and heart disease, over the long term.

Some oils are well suited to cooking at higher heats, while others are best used as a flavoring (for steamed vegetables, for example) or in dips and salad dressings, as heat can destroy their delicate flavor. Oils have different smoking points — the temperature at which they begin to break down and lose flavor and nutritional value. As a general rule, when heating oil in a skillet or saucepan, watch closely to prevent it from overheating. If the oil gets too hot and begins to smoke, remove the skillet from the heat, let it cool and discard the oil. All oils are high in calories and should be used in moderation.

Here is a list of healthy oils and their culinary uses:

- *All-purpose cooking oils:* Corn, safflower, soy and sunflower oils are neutral-flavored vegetable, legume and seed oils sold in supermarkets. These healthy oils are well suited to higher-heat cooking.
- *Almond oil:* This nut oil can be used in higher-heat cooking, although the heat will diminish its delicate, light toasted almond flavor. It is delicious in baking, dips and salad dressings. Store in the refrigerator.
- *Avocado oil:* Extracted from the flesh of avocados, the oil has a slightly nutty, full-bodied flavor. It's suited for higher-heat cooking, and is also wonderful in dips and salad dressings.
- *Canola oil:* High in both monounsaturated and polyunsaturated fats, including omega-3s, canola oil can be used in higher-heat cooking and in salad dressings.
- *Flaxseed oil:* Nutty and rich-tasting, and high in omega-3 fats, flaxseed oil is not recommended in cooking but is a healthy addition to dips and salad dressings. Store in the refrigerator.

- *Grapeseed oil:* Pressed from grape seeds and a good source of vitamin E, grapeseed oil is suited for higher-heat cooking
- *Hazelnut oil:* Light golden in color, full-bodied in flavor and aromatic, hazelnut oil is suited for higher-heat cooking and can be used in baking, dips and salad dressings.
- *Hempseed oil:* With its subtly nutty taste, hempseed oil is high in omega-3 fats and is a good choice for dips and salad dressings. It is not recommended for cooking. Store in the refrigerator.
- *Olive oil:* Olive oil is high in monounsaturated fat. The term "extra virgin" means it has been minimally processed, retaining the oil's natural flavor and its high levels of protective polyphenols and vitamin E. Extra virgin olive oil can be used for cooking at up to medium-high heat. If desired, use a less expensive olive oil for everyday cooking (as it has been refined, it can be used for high-heat cooking) and reserve extra virgin olive oil for salad dressings and marinades.
- *Peanut oil:* Made from pressed, steamed-cooked peanuts, this neutral all-purpose oil can be used for higher-heat cooking.
- *Pumpkin seed oil:* With a rich, nutty flavor, pumpkin seed oil is high in omega-3 fats, and is ideal for dips and salad dressings. It is not recommended for cooking.
- *Sesame oil (toasted):* This golden brown oil with an intensely nutty flavor is used as a seasoning to flavor Asian dishes and not as a cooking oil. Store in the refrigerator.
- *Walnut oil:* With its intense nutty flavor and aroma, walnut oil is high in omega-3 fats and is a great choice for dips and salad dressings. It is not recommended for cooking. Store in the refrigerator.

Note: Coconut oil, with its sweet, nutty taste, can be used in place of other saturated fats, such as butter, in high-heat cooking.

Stovetop Cooking Tip

We recommend using a nonstick skillet in our recipes, as it reduces the amount of fat needed in cooking. Flimsy nonstick skillets overheat quickly and often have an inferior coating that can break down over time. Today there are many quality nonstick pans to choose from, made with newer materials and heavier bottoms to better regulate the heat and safely cook foods. Consider investing in a new skillet and follow the manufacturer's directions on how to use the cookware correctly.

Sesame Ginger Dressing

Makes ¾ cup (175 mL)

This is an ideal salad dressing to toss with shredded napa cabbage, shredded carrots, blanched snow peas and red pepper strips. It also makes an excellent dressing for whole wheat or soba noodles, brown rice or other grains, such as quinoa, tossed with an array of fresh vegetables.

Tips

There are two types of rice vinegar available. Read the labels and buy the unseasoned version, as seasoned rice vinegar is loaded with sodium and added sugar.

The dressing can be stored in an airtight container in the refrigerator for up to 1 week.

Nutrition info per 2 tbsp (30 mL)	
Calories	40
Carbohydrate	2 g
Fiber	0 g
Protein	1 g
Fat	3 g
Saturated fat	0 g
Cholesterol	0 mg
Sodium	123 mg

Food Choices
½ Fat
1 Extra

● **Food processor**

4 oz	silken tofu	125 g
1	clove garlic, coarsely chopped	1
2 tbsp	coarsely chopped gingerroot	30 mL
1 tsp	granulated sugar	5 mL
4 tsp	reduced-sodium soy sauce	20 mL
1 tbsp	toasted sesame oil	15 mL
1 tbsp	natural unseasoned rice vinegar	15 mL
½ tsp	Asian chili sauce	1 mL

1. In food processor, combine tofu, garlic, ginger, sugar, soy sauce, oil, vinegar and chili sauce; process until smooth.

Nutrition Tip

When purchasing a store-bought salad dressing, choose one that is low in fat and sodium. Check the Nutrition Facts table: there should be no more than 5 grams of fat and less than 140 milligrams of sodium per 2 tbsp (30 mL) — enough dressing to toss with 2 cups (500 mL) of salad greens with vegetables. (See page 160 for a list of suggestions for creating your own salads.)

Beef, Lamb and Pork

Sunday Roast Beef with Wine Gravy

Makes 8 servings

A standing rib roast always makes dinner extra-special, whether it's a family Sunday supper or a gathering of friends. In this recipe, the thyme-pepper rub and red wine enhance the gravy, imparting a rich flavor to the meat.

- - - - - - - - - - - - - - - -

Tip

You should never be deprived of enjoying your favorite meals — including red meats, such as roast beef with gravy, on occasion. The key is to always select lean cuts of meat, trim off as much visible fat as possible and moderate portion sizes.

Nutrition info per serving

Calories	202
Carbohydrate	3 g
Fiber	0 g
Protein	24 g
Fat	9 g
Saturated fat	4 g
Cholesterol	55 mg
Sodium	199 mg

Food Choices
3 Meat & Alternatives
1 Extra

- **Preheat oven to 450°F (230°C)**
- **Shallow roasting pan**

3 lb	bone-in beef prime rib roast	1.5 kg
2	cloves garlic, cut into slivers	2
2 tbsp	Dijon mustard	30 mL
1 tsp	dried thyme	5 mL
1 tsp	coarsely ground black pepper	5 mL

Wine Gravy

½ cup	red wine or additional broth	125 mL
1½ cups	low-sodium or no-salt-added ready-to-use beef broth	375 mL
1 tbsp	cornstarch	15 mL
2 tbsp	water	30 mL
1 tbsp	Worcestershire sauce	15 mL
	Freshly ground black pepper	

1. Make small slits in roast and insert garlic slivers. In a bowl, combine mustard, thyme and pepper. Spread over roast.

2. Place roast, rib side down, in shallow roasting pan. Roast in preheated oven for 15 minutes. Reduce heat to 350°F (180°C) and roast for 1¼ to 1½ hours or until a meat thermometer inserted in the thickest part registers 145°F (63°C) for medium-rare. Transfer to a carving board, cover loosely with foil and let rest for 15 minutes.

3. *Wine Gravy:* Meanwhile, skim fat from drippings in pan. Place pan over medium heat and stir in wine. Cook, scraping up brown bits from bottom of pan, for about 2 minutes or until reduced by half. Stir in broth.

4. Strain sauce through a fine sieve into a saucepan. Bring to a boil over high heat. Boil, stirring often, for 5 minutes or until slightly reduced.

5. In a small bowl, combine cornstarch, water and Worcestershire sauce. Add to pan and return to a boil, stirring constantly, until sauce thickens. Season to taste with pepper.

6. Cut beef across the grain into thin slices and serve with gravy.

Pan-Seared Beef with Red Wine

Dressed up with wine, garlic and herbs, this steak is a special dish for when you're entertaining friends. Serve with Creamy Mashed Potatoes with Cauliflower (page 335).

- - - - - - - - - - - - - - -

Tips

Herbes de Provence is a blend of French herbs that often includes thyme, rosemary, basil and sage. If you can't find this blend, substitute a generous pinch of each of these herbs.

When purchasing broth, be sure to check the sodium content and choose one with 140 mg or less per 1 cup (250 mL).

2	well-trimmed boneless beef strip loin steaks (each 8 oz/250 g)	2
½ tsp	coarsely ground black pepper	2 mL
2 tsp	extra virgin olive oil	10 mL
2 tsp	butter	10 mL
1	large clove garlic, minced	1
¼ cup	finely chopped shallots	60 mL
¼ tsp	dried herbes de Provence (see tip, at left)	1 mL
⅓ cup	red wine (or additional broth)	75 mL
½ cup	low-sodium or no-salt-added ready-to-use beef broth	125 mL
1 tbsp	Dijon mustard	15 mL
2 tbsp	chopped fresh parsley	30 mL

1. Season steaks with pepper. Heat a large, heavy nonstick skillet over medium-high heat until hot. Add oil and butter. Brown steaks for about 1 minute per side. Reduce heat to medium and cook steaks for 2 to 4 minutes (depending on thickness) for medium-rare or to desired doneness. Transfer to a cutting board and tent with foil.

2. Add garlic, shallots and herbes de Provence to skillet; cook, stirring, for 1 minute. Stir in red wine and cook, scraping up any brown bits from bottom of pan, until liquid has almost evaporated. Stir in broth, mustard and parsley. Cook, stirring, for about 2 minutes or until slightly reduced.

3. Thinly slice steaks, across the grain and on the diagonal, into thin strips. Arrange on serving plates and spoon sauce over top. Serve immediately.

Nutrition info per serving

Calories	237
Carbohydrate	5 g
Fiber	1 g
Protein	26 g
Fat	11 g
Saturated fat	4 g
Cholesterol	60 mg
Sodium	173 mg

Food Choices
3 Meat & Alternatives
1 Fat

Old-Fashioned Slow Cooker Beef Stew

What's more comforting than a satisfying stew? With the welcoming herb-infused aroma that wafts through your kitchen, the first forkful confirms that this stew is comfort food at its best.

- - - - - - - - - - - - - - - -

Tips

When purchasing broth, be sure to check the sodium content and choose one with 140 mg or less per 1 cup (250 mL).

Four ounces (125 g) raw beef yields 3 oz (90 g) cooked beef (3 Meat & Alternatives Choices).

Nutrition info per 2 cups (500 mL)

Calories	367
Carbohydrate	38 g
Fiber	6 g
Protein	26 g
Fat	12 g
Saturated fat	3 g
Cholesterol	47 mg
Sodium	467 mg

Food Choices
1½ Carbohydrate
3 Meat & Alternatives
1 Fat

- **Large (minimum 5-quart) slow cooker**

1½ lbs	lean stewing beef, cut into 1-inch (2.5 cm) cubes	750 g
6 tbsp	all-purpose flour, divided	90 mL
6 tsp	canola oil, divided	30 mL
2	onions, chopped	2
3	cloves garlic, minced	3
1	bay leaf	1
1 tsp	dried thyme	5 mL
1 tsp	dried marjoram	5 mL
¾ tsp	salt	3 mL
½ tsp	freshly ground black pepper	2 mL
½ cup	red wine (or additional broth)	125 mL
⅓ cup	no-salt-added tomato paste	75 mL
2 cups	low-sodium or no-salt-added ready-to-use beef broth, divided	500 mL
2	stalks celery, thickly sliced	2
1½ lbs	potatoes (about 5 medium), peeled and quartered	750 g
1 lb	carrots (about 5 medium), peeled and cut into thick slices	500 g
12 oz	green beans, ends trimmed, cut into 2-inch (5 cm) lengths	375 g
¼ cup	chopped fresh parsley (see tip, at right)	60 mL

1. Pat meat dry with paper towels. In a bowl, toss beef with 2 tbsp (30 mL) of the flour to lightly coat.

2. In a large pot, heat 2 tsp (10 mL) of the oil over medium-high heat. Add half the beef and cook until nicely browned on all sides. Transfer to slow cooker stoneware. Repeat with 2 tsp (10 mL) oil and the remaining beef.

3. Reduce heat to medium and add the remaining oil to the pot. Add onions, garlic, bay leaf, thyme, marjoram, salt and pepper; cook, stirring, for 5 minutes or until onions are softened. Add wine and tomato paste; cook, scraping up any brown bits from bottom of pot. Stir in 1½ cups (375 mL) of the broth.

Tip

When parsley is called for in a recipe, you can use either curly leaf or the more strongly flavored flat-leaf (Italian) variety, depending on your preference. Either way, rinse it well, in plenty of water, to remove dirt. Dry parsley in a salad spinner and wrap in paper towels. Or let drain, then wrap it in a clean dry towel. Place in a plastic storage bag and refrigerate. The drier the parsley, the longer it lasts in the refrigerator.

4. Transfer onion mixture to stoneware and add celery, potatoes and carrots. Cover and cook on Low for 8 hours or until beef is tender.

5. In a bowl, stir together the remaining flour and the remaining broth until smooth. Stir into stew, along with beans. Cover and cook on High for 30 minutes or until slightly thickened and vegetables are tender. Discard bay leaf. Stir in parsley.

Stovetop Method

Prepare stew as directed in steps 1 to 3, transferring the browned beef to a plate in step 2. After step 3, return beef and any accumulated juices to pot and bring to a boil. Reduce heat to medium-low, cover and simmer, stirring occasionally, for 1 hour. Stir in celery, potatoes and carrots; cover and simmer for 30 minutes.

In a bowl, stir together the remaining flour and the remaining broth until smooth. Stir into stew and simmer, stirring, for about 2 minutes or until slightly thickened. (It may be necessary to add $1/2$ to 1 cup/125 to 250 mL more broth or water, if sauce is too thick.)

Stir in beans, cover and simmer for 30 minutes or until beef and vegetables are tender. Discard bay leaf. Stir in parsley.

Terrific Chili

Every cook has their own special version of chili. Here's one where the beans nicely absorb the spices and rich tomato flavor — it's sure to become your favorite.

Tips

The flavor of the chili hinges on the quality of chili powder used. Most powders are a blend of dried ground mild chiles, as well as cumin, oregano and garlic. However, they can contain a hefty dose of salt. Read the list of ingredients. If salt is one of the first ingredients, select a lower-sodium brand.

When purchasing broth, be sure to check the sodium content and choose one with 140 mg or less per 1 cup (250 mL).

Nutrition info per 1⅓ cups (325 mL)	
Calories	206
Carbohydrate	23 g
Fiber	6 g
Protein	16 g
Fat	7 g
Saturated fat	2 g
Cholesterol	30 mg
Sodium	318 mg

Food Choices
½ Carbohydrate
2 Meat & Alternatives

12 oz	lean ground beef	375 g
2	carrots, diced	2
1	large onion, chopped	1
3	cloves garlic, finely chopped	3
2 tbsp	chili powder	30 mL
1½ tsp	dried oregano	7 mL
1 tsp	ground cumin	5 mL
¼ to ½ tsp	hot pepper flakes (or to taste)	1 to 2 mL
1	can (28 oz/796 mL) no-salt-added tomatoes, with juice, chopped	1
1 cup	low-sodium or no-salt-added ready-to-use beef broth	250 mL
1	large green bell pepper, chopped	1
2 cups	well-rinsed drained canned pinto or red kidney beans	500 mL
¼ tsp	salt	1 mL
⅓ cup	chopped fresh cilantro or parsley	75 mL

1. In a large pot, cook beef over medium-high heat, breaking it up with a wooden spoon, for about 5 minutes or until no longer pink. Transfer to a sieve and drain off any fat.

2. Return beef to pan and reduce heat to medium. Add carrots, onion, garlic, chili powder, oregano, cumin and hot pepper flakes; cook, stirring often, for 5 minutes or until vegetables are softened.

3. Stir in tomatoes with juice and broth; bring to a boil over high heat. Reduce heat to medium-low, cover and simmer, stirring occasionally, for 30 minutes.

4. Stir in green pepper, beans and salt; cover and simmer for 15 minutes.

5. Ladle chili into warm bowls and sprinkle with cilantro.

Orange Ginger Beef and Vegetable Stir-Fry

Makes 4 servings

Here's a fast stir-fry that doesn't require a lot of chopping, thanks to the excellent assortment of frozen vegetables found in supermarkets. Serve with brown basmati rice or whole wheat pasta, such as linguine.

- - - - - - - - - - - - - - - -

Tip

Asian vegetable mixes often include carrots, broccoli, red bell pepper and snow or snap peas. However, any assortment of frozen vegetables can be used. Or use 4 cups (1 L) prepared fresh vegetables.

1 lb	boneless top sirloin steak, cut into very thin strips	500 g
2	cloves garlic, minced	2
1 tbsp	grated gingerroot	15 mL
1 tbsp	hoisin sauce	15 mL
2 tsp	cornstarch	10 mL
2 tsp	grated orange zest	10 mL
1/3 cup	freshly squeezed orange juice	75 mL
2 tbsp	rice vinegar	30 mL
4 tsp	reduced-sodium soy sauce	20 mL
1 tbsp	liquid honey	15 mL
1/4 tsp	hot pepper flakes (optional)	1 mL
1 tbsp	peanut or canola oil	15 mL
4 cups	frozen Asian mixed vegetables (16-oz/500 g package)	1 L
3	green onions, sliced	3

1. In a bowl, toss beef strips with garlic, ginger and hoisin sauce. Set aside.

2. In a glass measuring cup, stir together cornstarch, orange zest, orange juice, vinegar, soy sauce, honey and hot pepper flakes (if using) until smooth. Set aside.

3. In a large nonstick skillet, heat oil over medium-high heat. Add beef mixture and stir-fry for 3 to 4 minutes or until no longer pink. Transfer to a bowl.

4. Add vegetables and orange juice mixture to skillet. Increase heat to high, cover and cook, stirring occasionally, for 2 to 4 minutes or until vegetables are just tender-crisp.

5. Return beef and any accumulated juices to skillet. Add green onions and stir-fry for about 1 minute or until just heated through. Serve immediately.

Nutrition info per 1½ cups (375 mL)

Calories	278
Carbohydrate	23 g
Fiber	5 g
Protein	28 g
Fat	9 g
Saturated fat	3 g
Cholesterol	56 mg
Sodium	410 mg

Food Choices
½ Carbohydrate
3 Meat & Alternatives
1 Fat

Classic Meatloaf

This delicious meatloaf packed with great flavor is sure to become a favorite. Instead of ketchup as the traditional accompaniment, serve it with Classic Tomato Salsa (page 189.)

Tip

Double the recipe and wrap the extra cooked meatloaf in plastic wrap, then in foil, and freeze for up to 2 months. Let thaw overnight in the refrigerator.

- **Preheat oven to 350°F (180°C)**
- **9- by 5-inch (23 by 13 cm) metal loaf pan**

1	large egg	1
1	onion, grated	1
1	carrot, grated	1
1	clove garlic, minced	1
¼ cup	finely chopped fresh parsley	60 mL
1 tsp	dried basil	5 mL
1 tsp	dried marjoram	5 mL
¼ tsp	salt	1 mL
¼ tsp	freshly ground black pepper	1 mL
2 tbsp	ketchup	30 mL
2 tsp	Worcestershire sauce	10 mL
1½ lbs	lean ground beef	750 g
½ cup	oat bran or quick-cooking rolled oats	125 mL

1. In a large bowl, beat egg. Stir in onion, carrot, garlic, parsley, basil, marjoram, salt, pepper, ketchup and Worcestershire sauce. Crumble beef over mixture and sprinkle with oat bran. Gently mix until evenly combined. Press mixture lightly into loaf pan.

2. Bake in preheated oven for 50 to 60 minutes or until a meat thermometer inserted in the center registers 160°F (71°C). Let stand for 5 minutes. Drain off pan juices, turn loaf out onto a plate or cutting board and cut into thick slices.

Variation

You can replace the ground beef with lean ground turkey or chicken. Bake until a meat thermometer inserted in the center registers 165°F (74°C).

Nutrition info per serving

Calories	235
Carbohydrate	10 g
Fiber	2 g
Protein	24 g
Fat	12 g
Saturated fat	5 g
Cholesterol	90 mg
Sodium	245 mg

Food Choices
3 Meat & Alternatives
1 Extra

Tip

To reheat leftovers, cut into slices and place in a saucepan. Moisten with $\frac{1}{4}$ to $\frac{1}{2}$ cup (60 to 125 mL) low-sodium or no-salt-added ready-to-use beef or chicken broth, cover and heat over medium heat until piping hot. Or place meatloaf and broth in a casserole dish, cover and microwave on Medium-High (70%) until heated through.

Nutrition Tip

One of the challenges of reducing sodium in cooking is what to do with your family's favorite recipes. Rather than doing away with recipes you enjoy, compare them with the lower-sodium recipes we provide in this book. Little changes to your recipes will add up to healthier eating. Meatloaf is a great example, and here are six easy steps to modify your recipe:

1. The most important step is to cut back on the amount of salt you add. Use no more than $\frac{1}{2}$ tsp (2 mL) — and $\frac{1}{4}$ tsp (1 mL) is better — for every $1\frac{1}{2}$ lbs (750 g) of meat.
2. Increase the fresh and dried herbs and ground pepper to boost flavor.
3. Condiments such as ketchup and barbecue sauce contain a generous amount of sodium. You don't need to eliminate them; just reduce the amount you use by half. (Contrary to popular belief, Worcestershire sauce is not high in sodium; it contains just 55 mg per teaspoon (5 mL), so it makes an great flavor enhancer in ground meat dishes.)
4. Add a grated carrot, as we did in the recipe opposite, for a touch of sweetness.
5. Instead of bread crumbs — especially dry bread crumbs — which are loaded in sodium, use oat bran as a binder.
6. Skip the cheese and sausage meat, and any other ingredients that have a lot of fat and sodium.

Meatballs

Makes 64 meatballs

Who doesn't love meatballs? Whether as an appetizer or as part of a pasta dish, everyone always enjoys these tasty morsels.

- - - - - - - - - - - - - - -

Tips

Serve 8 meatballs per main course serving, or 3 meatballs per appetizer serving.

Cooked meatballs can be stored in an airtight container in the refrigerator for up to 1 day. To freeze, place meatballs in a single layer on trays; when frozen, transfer to airtight containers and freeze for up to 2 months. To defrost quickly, place 32 meatballs (to serve 4) in a casserole dish and microwave on High for 4 to 5 minutes, stirring once, until just warmed through.

Nutrition info per 8 meatballs	
Calories	224
Carbohydrate	4 g
Fiber	1 g
Protein	23 g
Fat	12 g
Saturated fat	5 g
Cholesterol	106 mg
Sodium	246 mg

Food Choices
3 Meat & Alternatives

- **Preheat oven to 375°F (190°C)**
- **2 rimmed baking sheets, lined with foil**

2	large eggs	2
2	cloves garlic, minced	2
1	onion, grated	1
½ tsp	salt	2 mL
½ tsp	dried thyme or oregano	2 mL
½ tsp	freshly ground black pepper	2 mL
2 lbs	extra-lean ground beef, chicken, turkey or pork	1 kg
1 cup	soft fresh whole wheat bread crumbs	250 mL

1. In a large bowl, beat eggs. Stir in garlic, onion, salt, thyme and pepper. Crumble beef over mixture and sprinkle with bread crumbs. Gently mix until evenly combined.

2. Shape beef mixture by level tablespoonfuls (15 mL) into balls. Arrange 2 inches (5 cm) apart on prepared baking sheets.

3. Bake in preheated oven, rearranging meatballs and rotating baking sheets once, for 15 to 18 minutes or until no longer pink inside. Transfer to a tray lined with paper towels to drain.

Sweet-and-Sour Pineapple Meatballs

Here's an updated classic with lots of family appeal. This dish comes together quickly, so start by cooking brown rice or quinoa to accompany it, then begin chopping the vegetables.

- - - - - - - - - - - - - - - - -

Tip

When draining the canned pineapple, reserve the juice to make the sauce. If using fresh pineapple, use the orange juice instead.

Variation

Use any combination of fresh vegetables, including broccoli, red pepper and snow peas, or frozen vegetables. You'll need 4 cups (1 L) vegetables.

Nutrition info 1½ cups (375 mL) sauce, including 8 meatballs	
Calories	350
Carbohydrate	27 g
Fiber	3 g
Protein	25 g
Fat	16 g
Saturated fat	5 g
Cholesterol	106 mg
Sodium	447 mg

Food Choices
1 Carbohydrate
3 Meat & Alternatives
1 Fat

4 tsp	packed brown sugar	20 mL
2 tsp	cornstarch	10 mL
¼ cup	unsweetened canned pineapple juice or freshly squeezed orange juice (see tip, at left)	60 mL
¼ cup	low-sodium or no-salt-added ready-to-use beef broth	60 mL
4 tsp	reduced-sodium soy sauce	20 mL
4 tsp	balsamic vinegar	20 mL
1 tbsp	canola oil	15 mL
1	onion, halved lengthwise and thinly sliced	1
2	cloves garlic, minced	2
1 tbsp	minced gingerroot	15 mL
2	carrots, thinly sliced on the diagonal	2
1	zucchini, halved lengthwise and sliced	1
1	large red bell pepper, cut into thin 2-inch (5 cm) long strips	1
32	Meatballs (see recipe, page 254)	32
1 cup	well-drained canned pineapple tidbits (see tip, at left) or diced fresh pineapple	250 mL
⅓ cup	coarsely chopped fresh cilantro (optional)	75 mL

1. In a large glass measuring cup or bowl, stir together brown sugar, cornstarch, pineapple juice, broth, soy sauce and vinegar until smooth. Set aside.

2. In a wok or large nonstick skillet, heat oil over medium-high heat. Stir-fry onion, garlic and ginger for 30 seconds or until fragrant. Add carrots, zucchini and red pepper; stir-fry for 2 minutes.

3. Stir reserved sauce mixture and add to wok; bring to a boil. Boil, stirring, for about 1 minute or until thickened. Stir in meatballs and pineapple; cook, stirring, for 2 to 3 minutes or until piping hot and vegetables are tender-crisp. Sprinkle with cilantro (if using). Serve immediately.

Grilled Lamb Chops with Rosemary Mustard Baste

Lamb chops are wonderful au naturel, but even more delicious with a mustard glaze flavored with rosemary. Here's a quick and tasty way to dress up lamb chops for the barbecue.

Tips

The marinade is also fantastic with lamb kabobs, as well as with chicken and pork.

It may be helpful to use a food scale to weigh portions of meat, poultry, seafood and cheese to ensure accuracy, especially if you are concerned about weight loss or are strictly monitoring your diet to manage your blood glucose levels.

Nutrition info per serving	
Calories	132
Carbohydrate	2 g
Fiber	0 g
Protein	18 g
Fat	5 g
Saturated fat	2 g
Cholesterol	68 mg
Sodium	86 mg

Food Choices
2 Meat & Alternatives

- **Preheat barbecue grill or stovetop grill pan to medium**

2	cloves garlic, minced	2
1 tbsp	chopped fresh rosemary	15 mL
¼ tsp	freshly ground black pepper	1 mL
2 tbsp	honey-Dijon mustard	30 mL
2 tbsp	balsamic vinegar	30 mL
8	lamb loin chops (1 inch/2.5 cm thick), trimmed (1½ lbs/750 g total)	8

1. In a shallow glass dish, combine garlic, rosemary, pepper, mustard and vinegar. Add lamb and turn to coat. Marinate at room temperature for 15 minutes, or cover and refrigerate, turning occasionally, for up to 8 hours.

2. Remove lamb from marinade, discarding marinade, and place on preheated grill. Cook for 6 to 7 minutes per side for medium-rare, or to desired doneness.

Nutrition Tip

Trimmed lean lamb, whether domestic or imported, is lower in fat than many people think: about 6 grams of fat per 3-oz (90 g) serving.

Spicy Lamb Stew

Makes 6 servings

Sometimes you crave a dish that explodes with spicy flavors. This spice-infused lamb stew satisfies that craving with its blend of aromatic seasonings. Serve with brown basmati rice and Cucumber Mint Raita (see recipe, page 271).

Tips

Buy a 3-lb (1.5 kg) leg of lamb or shoulder roast to get 1½ lbs (750 g) boneless lamb.

When purchasing broth, be sure to check the sodium content and choose one with 140 mg or less per 1 cup (250 mL).

Four ounces (125 g) raw lamb yields 3 oz (90 g) cooked lamb (3 Meat & Alternatives Choices).

Nutrition info per ¾ cup (175 mL)

Calories	303
Carbohydrate	7 g
Fiber	1 g
Protein	31 g
Fat	16 g
Saturated fat	6 g
Cholesterol	108 mg
Sodium	272 mg

Food Choices
3 Meat & Alternatives
2 Fat

4 tsp	canola oil, divided	20 mL
1½ lbs	lean boneless lamb, cut into 1-inch (2.5 cm) cubes	750 g
1	large onion, chopped	1
2	cloves garlic, minced	2
1 tbsp	minced gingerroot	15 mL
1 tsp	ground cumin	5 mL
1 tsp	ground coriander	5 mL
½ tsp	ground cinnamon	2 mL
½ tsp	salt	2 mL
¼ tsp	hot pepper flakes (or to taste)	1 mL
Pinch	ground cloves	Pinch
1 tbsp	all-purpose flour	15 mL
½ cup	plain low-fat yogurt	125 mL
1	large tomato, chopped	1
½ cup	Low-Sodium Chicken Stock (page 204) or low-sodium or no-salt-added ready-to-use chicken broth	125 mL
¼ cup	chopped fresh cilantro or parsley	60 mL

1. In a large saucepan, heat half the oil over medium-high heat. Add half the lamb and cook until nicely browned on all sides. Transfer to a plate. Repeat with the remaining oil and lamb.

2. Reduce heat to medium. Add onion, garlic, ginger, cumin, coriander, cinnamon, salt, hot pepper flakes and cloves; cook, stirring, for 2 minutes or until onion is lightly browned.

3. Sprinkle with flour and stir in yogurt. Cook, stirring, for 1 minute or until thickened.

4. Return lamb and any accumulated juices to pan and stir in tomato and broth. Bring to a boil. Reduce heat to medium-low, cover and simmer for 45 minutes or until lamb is tender. Sprinkle with cilantro before serving.

Variation
Spicy Beef Stew: Substitute an equal amount of lean stewing beef for the lamb, and increase the cooking time to 1½ hours or until beef is tender.

Jamaican Jerk Pork with Pineapple Pepper Salsa

Makes 4 servings

This streamlined recipe for a Jamaican classic uses a dried herb and spice blend that includes allspice and thyme — essential ingredients in jerk seasoning.

- - - - - - - - - - - - - - - -

Tip

Four ounces (125 g) raw pork yields 3 oz (90 g) cooked pork (3 Meat & Alternatives Choices).

- **Preheat oven to 350°F (180°C)**
- **13- by 9-inch (33 by 23 cm) metal baking pan or glass baking dish with a metal rack**

1	pork tenderloin (1 lb/500 g)	1
4 tsp	canola oil, divided	20 mL
1 tbsp	Dry Jerk Seasoning (see recipe, opposite)	15 mL
2 cups	Pineapple Pepper Salsa (see recipe, page 191)	500 mL

1. Place pork on a plate and brush with half the oil. Coat evenly with jerk seasoning.

2. In a large nonstick skillet, heat the remaining oil over medium heat. Add pork and cook until browned on all sides, about 5 minutes. Place pork on rack set in baking pan.

3. Roast in preheated oven for 18 to 22 minutes or until a meat thermometer inserted in the center registers 145°F (63°C). Transfer pork to a cutting board and let rest for 5 minutes.

4. Cut pork into ½-inch (1 cm) diagonal slices. Serve with Pineapple Pepper Salsa.

Nutrition info per serving (with salsa)	
Calories	233
Carbohydrate	8 g
Fiber	1 g
Protein	28 g
Fat	10 g
Saturated fat	2 g
Cholesterol	64 mg
Sodium	53 mg

Food Choices
3 Meat & Alternatives
1 Fat
1 Extra

Dry Jerk Seasoning

Dry seasoning rubs are a great, easy way to season meats, chicken and fish. Commercial rubs are often high in sodium, but when you make your own, you control the amount of salt. This convenient seasoning mix rivals the commercial jerk seasonings found in supermarkets, at a fraction of the cost.

Tips

Use 2 to 3 tsp (10 to 15 mL) of the jerk seasoning on boneless chicken breast and turkey cutlets, boneless pork loin chops or steaks.

Adjust the heat level by adding more or less cayenne, according to your preference.

1 tbsp	garlic powder	15 mL
1 tbsp	onion powder	15 mL
1½ tsp	ground allspice	7 mL
1½ tsp	dried thyme	7 mL
1½ tsp	dried oregano	7 mL
½ tsp	cayenne pepper (or to taste)	2 mL
½ tsp	ground cinnamon	2 mL
¼ tsp	freshly grated nutmeg	1 mL

1. In a small jar or airtight container, combine garlic powder, onion powder, allspice, thyme, oregano, cayenne, cinnamon and nutmeg. Store in a cool, dark place for up to 3 months. Shake before use.

Nutrition Tip

There is a wide range of no-salt-added seasoning blends in supermarkets. When shopping, you might come across salt substitutes containing potassium. Potassium may pose a health risk for those with kidney disease, so do not add a potassium-based salt substitute to your diet without first consulting your health care provider. Salt substitutes don't really resolve the craving for salt. By gradually reducing your intake of salt, you will get used to lower amounts.

Nutrition info per 1 tbsp (15 mL)

Calories	2
Carbohydrate	0 g
Fiber	0 g
Protein	0 g
Fat	0 g
Saturated fat	0 g
Cholesterol	0 mg
Sodium	0 mg

Pork Stuffed with Apples and Bread Crumbs

Whole-grain bread crumbs, apples and dried prunes combine to create a simple and succulent stuffing for pork tenderloin. The recipe is deal for entertaining, as it can be assembled ahead and the stuffed pork put into the oven to roast when guests arrive.

- - - - - - - - - - - - - - -

Tip

Prepare a second stuffed pork tenderloin for the freezer. Complete steps 1 to 3, using only fresh (not previously frozen) pork. Wrap well in plastic wrap, then in foil. Freeze for up to 1 month. Thaw in the refrigerator overnight. Increase the roasting time by 5 to 10 minutes.

Nutrition info per serving	
Calories	255
Carbohydrate	14 g
Fiber	2 g
Protein	28 g
Fat	10 g
Saturated fat	2 g
Cholesterol	64 mg
Sodium	217 mg

Food Choices
1 Carbohydrate
3 Meat & Alternatives
1 Fat

- Preheat oven to 375°F (190°C)
- Shallow roasting pan or glass baking dish

4 tsp	extra virgin olive oil, divided	20 mL
1 cup	finely diced apple (unpeeled)	250 mL
½ cup	finely chopped onion	125 mL
3 tbsp	chopped dried prunes, apricots, currants or raisins	45 mL
1 tsp	dried herbes de Provence, divided	5 mL
⅓ cup	fresh whole-grain bread crumbs	75 mL
1	pork tenderloin (1 lb/500 g)	1
¼ tsp	salt	1 mL
¼ tsp	freshly ground black pepper	1 mL

1. In a nonstick skillet, heat half the oil over medium heat. Add apple, onion, prunes and ½ tsp (2 mL) of the herbes de Provence; cook, stirring often, for 8 minutes or until tender. Transfer to a bowl and stir in bread crumbs. Let cool.

2. Cut tenderloin in half lengthwise, being careful not to cut all the way through. Open flat, like a book, and place on a work surface. Cover with plastic wrap. Using a meat mallet or rolling pin, pound until flattened into a rectangle about 10 by 8 inches (25 by 20 cm). Season with salt and pepper.

3. Spread stuffing evenly over pork, leaving a 1-inch (5 cm) border all around. Pat stuffing down lightly. Starting at a long end, roll up pork to enclose the filling. Secure with toothpicks. Place pork in roasting pan.

4. In a small bowl, combine the remaining herbes de Provence and the remaining oil. Brush over pork.

5. Roast in preheated oven for 35 to 40 minutes or until a meat thermometer inserted in the center registers 155°F (68°C). Transfer to a carving board, tent with foil and let rest for 5 minutes.

6. Remove toothpicks and cut crosswise into ½-inch (1 cm) thick slices.

Pork Chops with Honey and Thyme

Simple, tasty and reliable — count on this recipe to become a favorite way to cook fast-fry pork chops. Try it with thin turkey or chicken cutlets, too. Serve with a grain, such as brown rice, bulgur or quinoa, and a steamed vegetable, such as broccoli or green beans.

- - - - - - - - - - - - - - -

Tip

When purchasing broth, be sure to check the sodium content and choose one with 140 mg or less per 1 cup (250 mL).

Nutrition info per 2 chops with sauce	
Calories	206
Carbohydrate	6 g
Fiber	0 g
Protein	23 g
Fat	10 g
Saturated fat	3 g
Cholesterol	65 mg
Sodium	62 mg

Food Choices
3 Meat & Alternatives
½ Fat
1 Extra

½ cup	Low-Sodium Chicken Stock (page 204) or low-sodium or no-salt-added ready-to-use chicken broth	125 mL
1 tbsp	liquid honey	15 mL
1 tbsp	cider or white wine vinegar	15 mL
1 tsp	cornstarch	5 mL
1 lb	thin boneless loin pork chops (about 8), trimmed	500 g
	Freshly ground black pepper	
2 tsp	canola oil	10 mL
3	green onions, sliced	3
1 tsp	chopped fresh thyme (or ½ tsp/2 mL dried)	5 mL

1. In a bowl, combine broth, honey, vinegar and cornstarch. Set aside.

2. Pat pork chops dry with paper towels. Season with pepper. In a large nonstick skillet, heat oil over medium-high heat. Add pork and cook for 1 to 2 minutes per side or until lightly browned. Transfer to a plate.

3. Reduce heat to medium. Add green onions and thyme to skillet and cook, stirring, for 30 seconds. Stir reserved broth mixture and add to skillet; cook, stirring, for 1 minute or until sauce boils and thickens.

4. Return pork and any accumulated juices to skillet. Cover and simmer for 2 minutes or until just a hint of pink remains in pork. Season sauce to taste with pepper, if desired.

Pork Stir-Fry with Peppers and Spicy Peanut Sauce

Stir-frying streamlines dinner prep in this easy pork and pasta dish with a classic Asian-flavored peanut sauce.

Tips

Divide extras into portions and freeze in airtight containers for up to 2 months, for individual meals to reheat on the stovetop or in the microwave.

To clean leeks, trim off dark green tops. Cut leek down center almost to root end and slice crosswise, discarding root end. Rinse sliced leek in a sink full of cold water to remove any sand; scoop up leek and place in colander to drain, or use a salad spinner.

Nutrition info per 1½ cups (375 mL)	
Calories	401
Carbohydrate	43 g
Fiber	6 g
Protein	26 g
Fat	16 g
Saturated fat	4 g
Cholesterol	46 mg
Sodium	336 mg

Food Choices
2 Carbohydrate
2 Meat & Alternatives
2 Fat

4 tsp	canola oil, divided	20 mL
1 lb	lean boneless pork loin or tenderloin, cut into thin strips	500 g
3	bell peppers (assorted colors), cut into thin 2-inch (5 cm) long strips	3
2	cloves garlic, minced	2
1	leek (white and light green parts only), thinly sliced	1
¾ cup	Spicy Peanut Sauce (see recipe, opposite)	175 mL
8 oz	whole wheat spaghetti	250 g
½ cup	coarsely chopped fresh cilantro or parsley	125 mL

1. In a wok or large nonstick skillet, heat half the oil over medium-high heat. Stir-fry pork for 2 to 3 minutes or until browned on all sides. Transfer to a plate.

2. Add the remaining oil to the wok. Stir-fry bell peppers, garlic and leek for 2 minutes.

3. Return pork and any accumulated juices to wok and stir in Spicy Peanut Sauce; cook, stirring, for 1 to 2 minutes, or until just a hint of pink remains inside pork and vegetables are tender-crisp.

4. Meanwhile, in a large pot of boiling water, cook pasta according to package directions until al dente. Drain well and return to pot.

5. Add pork mixture and cilantro to pasta, tossing to coat. Serve immediately.

Variation

Substitute boneless skinless chicken breasts, cut into thin strips, for the pork.

Spicy Peanut Sauce

Double or triple this popular sauce and have it handy in your fridge for quick chicken, pork and tofu stir-fries. Dinner will be ready in no time.

- - - - - - - - - - - - - - -

Tips

The sauce keeps well for up to 1 month in an airtight container in the refrigerator.

Soy sauce is a popular condiment and ingredient, but it is also high in sodium. Choose reduced-sodium soy sauce. Brands vary, but there is typically about 1000 milligrams of sodium in 1 tablespoon (15 mL) of regular soy sauce and 500 milligrams in the same amount of reduced-sodium soy sauce.

1	clove garlic, minced	1
1 tbsp	minced gingerroot	15 mL
1 tbsp	packed brown sugar	15 mL
1 tsp	cornstarch	5 mL
⅓ cup	water	75 mL
2 tbsp	reduced-sodium soy sauce	30 mL
1 tbsp	freshly squeezed lime juice	15 mL
½ tsp	Asian chili sauce	2 mL
¼ cup	unsalted smooth peanut butter	60 mL

1. In a small saucepan, whisk together garlic, ginger, brown sugar, cornstarch, water, soy sauce, lime juice and chili sauce until smooth. Cook over medium-high heat, stirring, until sauce comes to a boil and thickens slightly. Reduce heat to low and simmer for 1 minute. Remove from heat and whisk in peanut butter.

Nutrition Tip

There is a wide selection of commercial sauces available that can save you time when preparing meals. However, many are loaded in sugar and sodium, so reduce the amount by half in your favorite recipes.

Nutrition info per 2 tbsp (30 mL)

Calories	86
Carbohydrate	6 g
Fiber	1 g
Protein	3 g
Fat	6 g
Saturated fat	1 g
Cholesterol	0 mg
Sodium	184 mg

Food Choices
1 Fat
1 Extra

Southwestern Pork Stew

Here's a great-tasting one-pot meal that is best made a day ahead to allow the rich stew flavors to blend. It also freezes well.

- - - - - - - - - - - - - - - -

Tips

When purchasing broth, be sure to check the sodium content and choose one with 140 mg or less per 1 cup (250 mL).

Four ounces (125 g) raw pork yields 3 oz (90 g) cooked pork (3 Meat & Alternatives Choices).

4 tsp	extra virgin olive oil, divided	20 mL
1 lb	lean stewing pork, cut into 3/4-inch (2 cm) cubes	500 g
2	onions, chopped	2
3	cloves garlic, minced	3
4 tsp	chili powder	20 mL
1 1/2 tsp	dried oregano	7 mL
1 tsp	ground cumin	5 mL
1/2 tsp	hot pepper flakes (or to taste)	2 mL
1/4 tsp	salt	1 mL
3 tbsp	all-purpose flour	45 mL
1	can (28 oz/796 mL) tomatoes, with juice, chopped	1
2 cups	low-sodium or no-salt-added ready-to-use beef or chicken broth	500 mL
2	bell peppers (assorted colors), chopped	2
2 cups	well-rinsed drained canned kidney beans or black beans	500 mL
2 cups	frozen corn kernels	500 mL
1/3 cup	coarsely chopped fresh cilantro	75 mL

1. In a large pot, heat half the oil over medium-high heat. Cook pork until browned on all sides. Transfer to a plate.

2. Add the remaining oil to the pot and reduce heat to medium. Add onions, garlic, chili powder, oregano, cumin, hot pepper flakes and salt; cook, stirring, for 4 minutes or until onions are softened.

3. Sprinkle with flour and stir in tomatoes with juice and broth. Bring to a boil, stirring.

4. Return pork and any accumulated juices to pot. Reduce heat to medium-low, cover and simmer for 1 hour or until pork is tender.

Nutrition info per 1 1/2 cups (375 mL)	
Calories	337
Carbohydrate	40 g
Fiber	9 g
Protein	24 g
Fat	11 g
Saturated fat	3 g
Cholesterol	47 mg
Sodium	526 mg

Food Choices
1 1/2 Carbohydrate
3 Meat & Alternatives
1/2 Fat

Tip

For 2 cups (500 mL) of beans, you will need one 19-oz (540 mL) can. Always pour beans and their liquid into a sieve and rinse the beans thoroughly under cold water. This reduces the sodium by up to 40%.

Variations

Substitute lean stewing beef for the pork.

For a vegetarian dish, use 1 lb (500 g) firm tofu, cut into small cubes, in place of the pork. Brown tofu in pot as directed in step 1 and add with the beans and vegetables in step 5.

5. Stir in bell peppers, beans and corn; simmer, covered, for 15 minutes or until vegetables are tender. Let cool slightly, cover tightly (or transfer to airtight containers) and refrigerate overnight to blend the flavors. (Or, if preferred, serve immediately, sprinkled with cilantro.)

6. Return stew to pot and heat over medium heat, stirring occasionally, for 10 minutes or until piping hot.

7. Ladle stew into bowls and sprinkle with cilantro.

Freezing and Reheating Soups, Stews and Casseroles

- Cooked soups, stews and casseroles can be kept safely for 2 to 3 days in the refrigerator, or frozen for up to 2 months.
- To freeze soups, chilis and stews, pack into rigid airtight containers and label with date and reheating information.
- To freeze layered casseroles, such as lasagna, wrap well in plastic wrap, then foil, or place in a heavy plastic freezer bag, removing air. Label with date and reheating information.
- Thaw soups, chilis and stews in the refrigerator overnight. Thaw casseroles in the refrigerator for up to 48 hours, depending on density.
- Reheat soups, chilis and stews in a saucepan over medium heat, stirring occasionally, until piping hot.
- Reheat casseroles in a 350°F (180°C) oven for 35 to 55 minutes or until piping hot in the center. Or microwave, covered, on Medium-High (70%) for 9 to 15 minutes (depending on amount), stirring occasionally, until heated through. For single servings, microwave, covered, on Medium-High (70%) for 3 to 5 minutes.

Recommended Cooking Methods to Limit Exposure to AGEs

Advanced glycation end products (AGEs) contribute to chronic diseases, such as diabetes, heart disease and kidney disease. Our bodies produce AGEs, and they are also present in some foods. Because they are difficult to break down, they can build up in our cells and cause damage. Foods high in protein and fat, and those combining protein and sugar, are the main sources of AGEs, especially when they are cooked at a high temperature or for a long time.

Reducing the amount of AGEs in the foods we consume and controlling blood glucose levels may delay or decrease AGE-related complications in diabetes. Here's how to reduce your exposure to AGEs:

- Eat fewer foods that are high in animal-based protein and fat. Instead, opt for vegetable-based proteins, such as legumes.

- Cut off all visible fat from meats and poultry before cooking.

- Limit your intake of meat, poultry or seafood cooked using high-temperature methods, such as grilling, broiling and frying. Instead, try steaming, poaching, braising, stewing or roasting with liquids. These methods use a lower temperature, add moisture to foods and use little or no added fat.

- If you do use a higher-heat cooking method, first marinate the meat, poultry or seafood with a marinade containing an acidic ingredient (such as lemon juice or vinegar) to tenderize the food and reduce the cooking time. To avoid charring, do not add sugar to marinades. Keep sodium down by omitting salt.

- When barbecuing, marinate foods first, then cook at a lower temperature. Meat, poultry and seafood should be cooked enough to eliminate harmful bacteria without producing char.

- Avoid overcooking foods. Cut off and discard any blackened (burnt) areas.

- Limit the amount of processed foods you eat, as they are often exposed to high temperatures during processing and may contain AGEs.

- Include seven to ten fruit and vegetable servings in your daily diet. Fruits and vegetables are low in AGEs and contain protective compounds, such as antioxidants, that can decrease the damage done by AGEs.

Chicken, Turkey, Fish and Seafood

- -

Thyme-Roasted Chicken

Rubbing herbs and seasonings under the bird's skin produces a succulent, flavorful roast chicken — and wonderful aroma! Despite the large amount of garlic, it imparts only a subtle flavor to the gravy.

- - - - - - - - - - - - - - -

Tips

The skin on a whole chicken or turkey helps the meat retain moisture while the bird is roasting, providing succulent, moist results. But always remove the skin before serving, as it's very high in fat.

Skimming off all of the fat from the pan juices before making the gravy results in a low-fat gravy.

Nutrition info per serving (about 3 oz/ 90 g cooked chicken with gravy)	
Calories	159
Carbohydrate	3 g
Fiber	0 g
Protein	26 g
Fat	4 g
Saturated fat	1 g
Cholesterol	79 mg
Sodium	198 mg

Food Choices
3 Meat & Alternatives
1 Extra

- Preheat oven to 350°F (180°C)
- Roasting pan with rack

4 lb	whole roasting chicken	2 kg
1	onion, quartered	1
10	cloves garlic, peeled	10
1 tbsp	chopped fresh thyme (or 1½ tsp/7 mL dried)	15 mL
¼ tsp	salt	1 mL
¼ tsp	freshly ground black pepper	1 mL
1⅓ cups	Low-Sodium Chicken Stock (page 204) or low-sodium or no-salt-added ready-to-use chicken broth (approx.), divided	325 mL
½ cup	white wine or additional stock or broth	125 mL
1 tbsp	all-purpose flour	15 mL

1. If included, remove giblets and neck from chicken. Remove any visible fat from the cavity opening. Rinse chicken under cold water, then pat dry inside and out with paper towels. Place onion and 2 garlic cloves inside cavity. Starting at cavity opening, gently lift skin and rub thyme, salt and pepper over breasts and legs. Tie legs together with kitchen string; tuck wings under back.

2. Add the remaining garlic, ⅔ cup (150 mL) stock and wine to roasting pan. Place rack in pan and place chicken, breast side up, on rack.

3. Roast in preheated oven, basting every 30 minutes and adding more stock if pan juices evaporate, for 2 to 2½ hours or until juices run clear when a thigh is pierced and a meat thermometer inserted in the thigh registers 170°F (77°C). Transfer to a platter, tent with foil and let stand for 10 minutes before carving.

Tips

This recipe calls for a large chicken, but smaller families can take advantage of leftovers, using them in sandwiches and salads for lunch the next day.

When purchasing broth, be sure to check the sodium content and choose one with 140 mg or less per 1 cup (250 mL).

4. Meanwhile, strain pan juices into a measuring cup, pressing down firmly to mash garlic into juices; skim off fat. Add enough of the remaining stock to make ¾ cup (175 mL).

5. In a small saucepan, stir together flour and 2 tbsp (30 mL) pan juices; cook, stirring, over medium heat for 1 minute. Gradually whisk in remaining pan juices; cook, stirring, until boiling and thickened.

6. Remove skin from chicken and cut into serving-size pieces. Serve with gravy.

Nutrition Tip

Deli products such as roast chicken and turkey are very high in sodium. If you wish to have cooked chicken on hand for salads and sandwiches, roast an additional whole chicken or chicken parts, such as chicken breasts, legs or thighs. (For parts, reduce the roasting time to 45 to 50 minutes or until a meat thermometer inserted in the thickest part registers 170°F/77°C.) Chicken can also be poached; follow the recipe for Low-Sodium Chicken Stock on page 204. Once the chicken is cooked, remove the skin and slice or cube the chicken. Pack into freezer storage bags in individual portions. Label and freeze for up to 1 month. Thaw in the refrigerator.

Tandoori Chicken with Cucumber Mint Raita

Ginger, cumin, coriander and cayenne pepper are signature ingredients in Indian cooking. Not only do they make chicken taste wonderful, but the spicy yogurt marinade keeps it moist and tender.

- - - - - - - - - - - - - - -

Tips

If you have time, let the chicken marinate for several hours or overnight to intensify the flavors.

For food safety reasons, discard any leftover marinade.

Double the recipe and place half the uncooked chicken with marinade in a storage container. Freeze for up to 1 month. Let thaw in the refrigerator overnight before cooking as directed.

Nutrition info per serving (with raita)	
Calories	164
Carbohydrate	6 g
Fiber	1 g
Protein	29 g
Fat	2 g
Saturated fat	1 g
Cholesterol	69 mg
Sodium	271 mg

Food Choices
3 Meat & Alternatives
1 Extra

- Food processor
- 13- by 9-inch (33 by 23 cm) glass baking dish with a metal rack, rack sprayed with vegetable oil cooking spray

1	large green onion, coarsely chopped	1
1	clove garlic, quartered	1
1	1-inch (2.5 cm) piece gingerroot, coarsely chopped	1
½ tsp	ground cumin	2 mL
½ tsp	ground coriander	2 mL
¼ tsp	ground turmeric	1 mL
¼ tsp	salt	1 mL
⅛ tsp	cayenne pepper (optional)	0.5 mL
⅓ cup	nonfat plain yogurt	75 mL
1 tbsp	no-salt-added tomato paste	15 mL
1 lb	boneless skinless chicken breasts (2 large)	500 g
½ cup	Cucumber Mint Raita (opposite)	125 mL

1. In food processor, combine green onion, garlic, ginger, cumin, coriander, turmeric, salt, cayenne (if using), yogurt and tomato paste; process until smooth.

2. On a cutting board, cut each chicken breast lengthwise to make two thinner halves. Arrange in a shallow glass dish and coat both sides with yogurt mixture. (Can be covered and refrigerated for up to 1 day.)

3. Preheat oven to 375°F (190°C).

4. Remove chicken from marinade, discarding marinade. Place chicken on rack in baking dish. Bake for 20 to 25 minutes or until chicken is no longer pink inside. Serve with Cucumber Mint Raita.

Cucumber Mint Raita

This cooling Indian yogurt sauce is excellent served with chicken or fish, as well as curried dishes.

Tip

The raita can be stored in an airtight container in the refrigerator for up to 5 days.

¾ cup	grated English cucumber (unpeeled)	175 mL
2 tbsp	chopped fresh mint or cilantro	30 mL
¼ tsp	ground cumin	1 mL
⅛ tsp	salt	0.5 mL
Pinch	cayenne pepper	Pinch
1 cup	nonfat plain yogurt	250 mL

1. Place cucumber in a sieve and squeeze out excess water. Wrap in paper towels or a clean kitchen towel and squeeze out excess moisture.

2. In a bowl, combine cucumber, mint, cumin, salt, cayenne and yogurt.

Nutrition info per 2 tbsp (30 mL)	
Calories	19
Carbohydrate	2 g
Fiber	0 g
Protein	1 g
Fat	1 g
Saturated fat	0 g
Cholesterol	2 mg
Sodium	46 mg
Food Choices	
1 Extra	

Chicken Cacciatore

To survive the six o'clock weeknight rush, batch-cook stews and sauce-based meals on weekends and keep them in the fridge for 2 to 3 days or freeze for easy reheating.

Tips

Sun-dried tomatoes sold dry in packages are more economical than those packed in oil. To reconstitute, place in a bowl and cover with boiling water. Let stand for 10 minutes or until softened.

If using sun-dried tomatoes packed in oil, drain oil, place tomatoes in a bowl and cover with boiling water. Drain well and blot dry to remove excess oil clinging to tomatoes.

Nutrition info per 2 thighs plus sauce	
Calories	238
Carbohydrate	12 g
Fiber	2 g
Protein	25 g
Fat	10 g
Saturated fat	2 g
Cholesterol	86 mg
Sodium	352 mg

Food Choices
3 Meat & Alternatives
1 Fat

3 tbsp	all-purpose flour	45 mL
2 lbs	bone-in skinless chicken thighs	1 kg
4 tsp	olive oil, divided	20 mL
1	small onion, chopped	1
2	cloves garlic, minced	2
3 cups	sliced mushrooms	750 mL
½ cup	white wine, Low-Sodium Chicken Stock (page 204) or low-sodium or no-salt-added ready-to-use chicken broth	125 mL
1	can (14 oz/398 mL) no-salt-added diced tomatoes, with juice	1
⅓ cup	chopped sun-dried tomatoes (see tip, at left)	75 mL
½ tsp	salt	2 mL
¼ tsp	freshly ground black pepper	1 mL
¼ cup	chopped fresh basil or parsley, or a combination	60 mL

1. Place flour in a shallow bowl. Coat chicken in flour, shaking off excess. Discard excess flour.

2. In a large saucepan, heat half the oil over medium-high heat. Brown chicken on all sides. Transfer to a plate.

3. Add the remaining oil to pan. Add onion, garlic and mushrooms; cook, stirring, for 5 minutes or until softened. Stir in wine.

4. Return chicken and any accumulated juices to pan. Stir in tomatoes with juice and sun-dried tomatoes; bring to a boil. Reduce heat to medium-low, cover and simmer for 35 minutes or until chicken is tender and juices run clear when chicken is pierced. Season with salt and pepper. Stir in basil.

Chicken Stir-Fry with Rice Noodles and Vegetables

Makes 4 servings

Quick-cooking rice noodles streamline dinner prep, as they need only to be soaked in hot water rather than boiled like traditional pasta. In this delicious stir-fry, chicken and rice noodles get dressed up in a curry, soy and hoisin sauce with lots of fresh vegetables.

- - - - - - - - - - - - - - - - -

Tip

Four ounces (125 g) raw chicken yields 3 oz (90 g) cooked chicken (3 Meat & Alternatives Choices).

5 oz	brown rice vermicelli	150 g
2 tsp	cornstarch	10 mL
2 tsp	curry powder	10 mL
6 tbsp	water, divided	90 mL
4 tsp	reduced-sodium soy sauce	20 mL
1 tbsp	hoisin sauce	15 mL
1 tbsp	balsamic or rice vinegar	15 mL
1/2 tsp	Asian chili sauce	2 mL
4 tsp	peanut or canola oil, divided	20 mL
1 lb	boneless skinless chicken breasts (2 large), cut into thin strips	500 g
3	carrots, cut into 2-inch (5 cm) long matchsticks	3
2	cloves garlic, minced	2
1 tbsp	minced gingerroot	15 mL
2 cups	snow peas, trimmed and halved	500 mL
3	green onions, thinly sliced	3
1/3 cup	chopped fresh cilantro	75 mL

1. Place vermicelli in a bowl and cover with hot water; let stand for 3 minutes or until softened. Drain well. Using scissors, cut noodles into 3-inch (7.5 cm) lengths. Set aside.

2. In a small bowl, stir together cornstarch, curry powder, 4 tbsp (60 mL) of the water, soy sauce, hoisin sauce, vinegar and chili sauce until smooth. Set aside.

3. In a wok or large nonstick skillet, heat half the oil over medium-high heat. Stir-fry chicken for 2 to 3 minutes or until browned on all sides. Transfer to plate.

4. Add the remaining oil to wok. Stir-fry carrots, garlic and ginger for 1 minute. Add the remaining water, cover and steam for 2 minutes or until carrots are tender-crisp.

5. Return chicken and any accumulated juices to wok. Stir in snow peas and soy sauce mixture; bring to a boil. Boil, stirring, until thickened.

6. Add rice noodles and stir-fry for 2 minutes or until piping hot. Stir in green onions and cilantro.

Nutrition info per 1½ cups (375 mL)

Calories	363
Carbohydrate	43 g
Fiber	6 g
Protein	32 g
Fat	7 g
Saturated fat	1 g
Cholesterol	67 mg
Sodium	341 mg

Food Choices
2 Carbohydrate
3 Meat & Alternatives
1 Fat

Parmesan Chicken Strips

When you come home from a day at work, it's a big help to have these tasty chicken strips stashed away in your freezer. Round out the meal with brown rice and a steamed vegetable, such as broccoli, for a dinner that's on the table in 30 minutes.

- - - - - - - - - - - - - - -

Tip

If making batches of chicken strips to freeze, use fresh (not defrosted) chicken breasts. Prepare recipe through step 3, placing unbaked strips on a rack set on baking sheet. Freeze until firm, then transfer to a storage container. Can be frozen for up to 1 month. There's no need to defrost them before baking; simply increase the baking time to 19 to 25 minutes.

Nutrition info per 4 chicken strips	
Calories	186
Carbohydrate	7 g
Fiber	1 g
Protein	25 g
Fat	6 g
Saturated fat	2 g
Cholesterol	96 mg
Sodium	223 mg

Food Choices
3 Meat & Alternatives
1 Extra

- **Preheat oven to 400°F (200°C)**
- **Food processor**
- **Baking sheet with rack, rack sprayed with vegetable oil cooking spray**

16	whole wheat soda crackers, broken into pieces	16
1/3 cup	freshly grated Parmesan cheese	75 mL
1/2 tsp	dried basil	2 mL
1/2 tsp	dried marjoram	2 mL
1/2 tsp	paprika	2 mL
1/4 tsp	freshly ground black pepper	1 mL
1 lb	boneless skinless chicken breasts (2 large)	500 g
1	large egg	1
1	clove garlic, minced	1

1. In food processor, combine crackers, Parmesan, basil, marjoram, paprika and pepper. Process to make fine crumbs. Transfer to a shallow bowl.

2. Cut chicken breasts in half lengthwise to make 2 thin pieces. Cut each piece diagonally into 5 strips.

3. In a bowl, beat egg and garlic. Add chicken strips. Using a fork, dip chicken strips, a few at a time, in crumb mixture until lightly coated. Arrange on rack set on baking sheet, spacing strips 1 inch (2.5 cm) apart. Discard any excess egg and crumbs.

4. Bake in preheated oven for 14 to 18 minutes or until chicken is no longer pink inside.

Nutrition Tip

Supermarkets display a wide assortment of tempting crumb-coated frozen chicken and fish products. While they may be time-saving, the majority of these products are loaded with fat and sodium. Processed foods are also often exposed to high temperatures in processing, and may contain AGEs.

Cilantro Chicken Patties

These moist and juicy patties are so flavorful and simple to make. If desired, serve Cucumber Mint Raita (page 271) alongside.

- - - - - - - - - - - - - - - - -

Tip

Double the recipe and make an extra batch of patties (using fresh, not previously frozen chicken). Place uncooked patties on a tray lined with parchment paper and freeze until firm. Wrap each patty individually in plastic wrap and place in a freezer bag or airtight container. Freeze for up to 1 month. Defrost patties in the refrigerator before cooking.

● **Preheat oven to 200°F (100°C)**

1	large egg	1
2	green onions, finely chopped	2
¼ cup	chopped fresh cilantro or parsley	60 mL
1 tsp	ground coriander	5 mL
1 tsp	grated lemon zest	5 mL
¼ tsp	salt	1 mL
¼ tsp	freshly ground black pepper	1 mL
1 lb	lean ground chicken or turkey	500 g
¼ cup	unseasoned dry bread crumbs	60 mL
2 tsp	peanut or canola oil	10 mL

1. In a large bowl, using a fork, beat egg. Stir in green onions, cilantro, coriander, lemon zest, salt and pepper. Mix in chicken and bread crumbs until evenly combined. With wet hands, shape into five ½-inch (1 cm) thick patties.

2. In a large nonstick skillet, heat half the oil over medium heat. Cook three of the patties, turning once, for 5 to 6 minutes per side or until patties are nicely browned and no longer pink in the center. Transfer patties to an ovenproof plate and keep warm in preheated oven. Wipe out skillet. Repeat with the remaining oil and patties. Serve immediately.

Nutrition info per patty

Calories	182
Carbohydrate	5 g
Fiber	0 g
Protein	22 g
Fat	11 g
Saturated fat	3 g
Cholesterol	109 mg
Sodium	220 mg

Food Choices
2 Meat & Alternatives
½ Fat
1 Extra

Chicken Shepherd's Pie

Makes 4 servings

Here's an updated shepherd's pie with the winning combination of mashed sweet potatoes and a savory chicken and mushroom filling.

- - - - - - - - - - - - - -

Tips

To make mashed sweet potatoes to accompany a stew or roast, follow the method outlined in steps 1 and 2.

The casserole can be prepared through step 5 up to 1 day ahead. Cover and refrigerate. Increase the baking time by 15 minutes.

Nutrition info per 1½ cups (375 mL)

Calories	404
Carbohydrate	47 g
Fiber	9 g
Protein	29 g
Fat	12 g
Saturated fat	4 g
Cholesterol	103 mg
Sodium	365 mg

Food Choices
2 Carbohydrate
3 Meat & Alternatives
½ Fat

- ● **Preheat oven to 375°F (190°C)**
- ● **Steamer basket**
- ● **Food processor**
- ● **8-cup (2 L) casserole dish, greased**

Mashed Sweet Potato Topping

1½ lbs	sweet potatoes, peeled and cubed	750 g
2 tbsp	light cream cheese or light sour cream	30 mL

Filling

1 lb	lean ground chicken or turkey	500 g
1	onion, chopped	1
2 cups	sliced mushrooms	500 mL
1 tsp	dried poultry seasoning or sage	5 mL
¼ tsp	freshly ground black pepper	1 mL
1 tbsp	cornstarch	15 mL
1½ cups	Low-Sodium Chicken Stock (page 204) or low-sodium or no-salt-added ready-to-use chicken broth	375 mL
1 tbsp	reduced-sodium soy sauce	15 mL
2 cups	frozen peas	500 mL
2	green onions, thinly sliced	2

1. *Topping:* Pour enough water into a large saucepan to come 1 inch (2.5 cm) up the side. Place steamer basket in pan, cover and bring to a boil over high heat. Add sweet potatoes and reduce heat to medium-low; cover and steam for 15 minutes or until tender. Drain well.

2. In food processor, combine sweet potatoes and cream cheese; process until smooth. Set aside.

3. *Filling:* In a large nonstick skillet, cook chicken over medium-high heat, breaking it up with a wooden spoon, for about 5 minutes or until no longer pink. Transfer to a sieve and drain off any fat. Reduce heat to medium. Add onion, mushrooms, poultry seasoning and pepper; cook, stirring often, for 5 minutes or until mushrooms are softened.

Tip

Soy sauce is a popular condiment and ingredient, but it is also high in sodium. Choose reduced-sodium soy sauce. Brands vary, but there is typically about 1000 milligrams of sodium in 1 tablespoon (15 mL) of regular soy sauce and 500 milligrams in the same amount of reduced-sodium soy sauce.

Variation

Substitute lean ground beef for the chicken.

4. In a measuring cup or bowl, whisk together cornstarch, stock and soy sauce until smooth. Stir into skillet and bring to a boil. Reduce heat and simmer, stirring occasionally, for 5 minutes or until sauce is thickened and flavors are blended.

5. Spoon chicken mixture into casserole dish and top with peas. Spread sweet potato mixture evenly over top. Sprinkle with green onions.

6. Bake in preheated oven for 35 to 40 minutes or until filling is bubbly around edges and center is piping hot.

Nutrition Tip

A generous potassium intake can help lower blood pressure, but most people don't get enough. Potassium is found in many plant foods — especially potatoes, sweet potatoes, squash, avocados, dark green leafy vegetables, beans and lentils, wheat bran and wheat germ, bananas, oranges and nuts — and also in dairy products.

Turkey Scaloppini with Mushrooms

Lean turkey cutlets are sautéed with assorted mushrooms and rosemary, with sun-dried tomatoes added to enhance the delectable sauce.

- - - - - - - - - - - - - -

Tips

Vary the flavor by using different dried herbs, such as herbes de Provence, fines herbes or tarragon, in place of the rosemary.

When purchasing broth, be sure to check the sodium content and choose one with 140 mg or less per 1 cup (250 mL).

Four ounces (125 g) raw turkey yields 3 oz (90 g) cooked turkey (3 Meat & Alternatives Choices).

Nutrition info per serving	
Calories	220
Carbohydrate	9 g
Fiber	2 g
Protein	28 g
Fat	7 g
Saturated fat	1 g
Cholesterol	65 mg
Sodium	312 mg

Food Choices
3 Meat & Alternatives
1 Fat

1 lb	boneless skinless turkey breast or chicken breasts	500 g
2 tbsp	all-purpose flour	30 mL
4 tsp	canola oil	20 mL
2 cups	assorted sliced mushrooms (such as shiitake, oyster and cremini)	500 mL
1/4 cup	chopped shallots	60 mL
1 tsp	chopped fresh rosemary (or 1/2 tsp/2 mL dried)	5 mL
1 cup	Low-Sodium Chicken Stock (page 204) or low-sodium or no-salt-added ready-to-use chicken broth	250 mL
1/4 cup	chopped sun-dried tomatoes (see tips, page 272)	60 mL
1/4 tsp	salt	1 mL
	Freshly ground black pepper	
2 tbsp	chopped fresh parsley	30 mL

1. On a cutting board, using a sharp knife, cut turkey into 8 thin cutlets. Place flour in a shallow bowl. Lightly coat turkey in flour, shaking off excess. Discard excess flour.

2. In a large nonstick skillet, heat half the oil over medium-high heat. Add half the turkey and cook for 2 minutes per side or until lightly browned. Transfer to a plate. Repeat with the remaining oil and turkey.

3. Reduce heat to medium and add mushrooms, shallots and rosemary to skillet; cook, stirring often, for 3 minutes or until softened. Add stock and bring to a boil. Boil for 1 minute or until slightly reduced.

4. Return turkey and any accumulated juices to skillet. Stir in sun-dried tomatoes and salt. Season with pepper to taste. Reduce heat to medium-low, cover and simmer for 2 to 3 minutes or until turkey is no longer pink inside and sauce is slightly thickened. Serve sprinkled with parsley.

Turkey Bulgur Meatloaf

This meatloaf includes bulgur, a healthy whole grain, as well as apples and mushrooms to keep it moist and juicy. Consider doubling the recipe, and freeze the second cooked meatloaf to have on hand for another meal.

- - - - - - - - - - - - - - -

Tips

To save time, chop the onion, mushrooms and apple in a food processor, using the pulse function.

When purchasing broth, be sure to check the sodium content and choose one with 140 mg or less per 1 cup (250 mL).

Nutrition info per serving

Calories	276
Carbohydrate	21 g
Fiber	4 g
Protein	27 g
Fat	10 g
Saturated fat	3 g
Cholesterol	102 mg
Sodium	265 mg

Food Choices
1 Carbohydrate
3 Meat & Alternatives
½ Fat

- **Preheat oven to 350°F (180°C)**
- **9- by 5-inch (23 by 12.5 cm) metal loaf pan, sprayed with vegetable oil cooking spray**

2 tsp	olive or canola oil	10 mL
1	onion, finely chopped	1
1 cup	finely chopped mushrooms (6 to 8)	250 mL
1 cup	finely diced apple (unpeeled)	250 mL
2 tsp	dried rubbed sage	10 mL
1 tsp	dried thyme	5 mL
½ cup	fine or medium bulgur	125 mL
⅔ cup	Low-Sodium Chicken Stock (page 204) or low-sodium or no-salt-added ready-to-use chicken broth	150 mL
2	large eggs	2
½ tsp	freshly ground black pepper	2 mL
¼ tsp	salt	1 mL
1 lb	lean ground turkey or chicken	500 g

1. In a medium saucepan, heat oil over medium heat. Add onion, mushrooms, apple, sage and thyme; cook, stirring often, for 5 minutes or until vegetables are softened.

2. Stir in bulgur and stock; bring to a boil. Reduce heat to low, cover and simmer for 10 minutes or until bulgur is tender and liquid is absorbed. Uncover and let cool for 10 minutes.

3. In a large bowl, lightly beat eggs, pepper and salt. Stir in bulgur mixture and turkey until thoroughly combined. Spoon into loaf pan and pack down lightly.

4. Bake in preheated oven for 55 to 60 minutes or until a meat thermometer inserted in the center registers 165°F (74°C). Remove from oven and let stand for 5 minutes. Drain off pan juices. Run a knife around edge of pan and turn meatloaf out onto a plate. Cut into thick slices.

Crispy Almond Baked Fish

Here's an easy, practical way to cook fish fillets, such as sole, catfish, tilapia, haddock or turbot. Unlike stovetop methods, where fish fillets, due to their size, often need to be cooked in more than one batch, all the fish is baked (and ready) at the same time.

- - - - - - - - - - - - - - - - -

Tip

Fresh fish should have a mild, pleasant odor but shouldn't smell "fishy." Cook fish as soon as possible after purchase, to enjoy it at its peak of freshness. If you need to store it, wrap fresh fish in plastic wrap or place in an airtight container and refrigerate for no more than 2 days.

Nutrition info per serving

Calories	170
Carbohydrate	5 g
Fiber	1 g
Protein	24 g
Fat	6 g
Saturated fat	1 g
Cholesterol	60 mg
Sodium	126 mg

Food Choices
3 Meat & Alternatives
1 Fat

- **Preheat oven to 425°F (220°C)**
- **Food processor**
- **Rimmed baking sheet, lined with parchment paper**

½ cup	soft fresh whole wheat bread crumbs	125 mL
⅓ cup	sliced blanched almonds	75 mL
½ tsp	dried tarragon or basil	2 mL
½ tsp	grated orange or lemon zest	2 mL
1 lb	skinless fish fillets	500 g
	Freshly ground black pepper	
	Lemon wedges	

1. In food processor, combine bread crumbs, almonds, tarragon and orange zest. Pulse until almonds are finely chopped.

2. Pat fish dry with paper towels. Arrange fish in a single layer on baking sheet. Season with pepper. Sprinkle crumb mixture over fish and pat lightly.

3. Bake in preheated oven for 8 to 10 minutes or until fish is opaque and flakes easily when tested with a fork (time depends on thickness of fish; increase time as needed). Serve with lemon wedges.

Nutrition Tip

Fish have long been known as healthy foods, providing protein, iodine, copper, magnesium and selenium. They also contain omega-3 fats, which are important for heart health. The benefits to the heart may include reduced triglycerides, blood that is less sticky (that is, less likely to clot) and reduced inflammation in the blood vessels. Health authorities recommend eating at least two 3-ounce (90 g) servings of fish per week, preferably omega-3-rich fish (see page 67).

Mediterranean Cod

What to do with fresh fish from the market and ripe tomatoes plucked from your garden? Add some briny olives and capers, and make this delicious fish dish that bursts with the sunny flavors of the Mediterranean.

- - - - - - - - - - - - - - - -

Tips

If fresh fish is unavailable, rely on frozen cod loins or halibut steaks instead. Partially defrost before baking and increase baking time by 5 to 8 minutes.

Olives should be used judiciously in cooking because of their salt content, but a little goes a long way in adding a robust flavor to this vibrant dish. Always rinse olives before use to remove excess salt.

Nutrition info per serving	
Calories	146
Carbohydrate	4 g
Fiber	1 g
Protein	21 g
Fat	5 g
Saturated fat	1 g
Cholesterol	49 mg
Sodium	202 mg

Food Choices
3 Meat & Alternatives
1 Fat

- **Preheat oven to 425°F (220°C)**
- **Shallow baking dish**

1 lb	skinless cod or halibut fillet, cut into 4 pieces	500 g
	Freshly ground black pepper	
2	ripe tomatoes, diced	2
2	green onions, sliced	2
1	clove garlic, minced	1
¼ cup	kalamata olives, rinsed, pitted and cut into slivers	60 mL
2 tbsp	chopped fresh parsley or basil	30 mL
1 tbsp	drained capers, rinsed	15 mL
Pinch	hot pepper flakes (optional)	Pinch
1 tbsp	extra virgin olive oil	15 mL

1. Arrange cod in a single layer in baking dish. Season with black pepper.

2. In a bowl, combine tomatoes, green onions, garlic, olives, parsley, capers and hot pepper flakes (if using); season with black pepper. Spoon over fish fillets and drizzle with oil.

3. Bake in preheated oven for 18 to 20 minutes or until fish is opaque and flakes easily when tested with a fork.

4. Serve in warm, wide, shallow bowls and spoon pan juices over top.

Pan-Seared Halibut with Cucumber Dill Sauce

Halibut is such a delicious fish, it's often best to simply pan-fry it and serve a refreshing sauce on the side.

- - - - - - - - - - - - - - -

Tip

Cooking times depend on the type and thickness of the fish. For thicker pieces of fish, pan-sear until browned on both sides, then transfer to a glass pie plate and bake in a preheated 375°F (190°C) oven for 7 to 9 minutes or until fish flakes easily when tested with a fork.

4	halibut steaks (each 5 oz/150 g and ¾ inch/2 cm thick)	4
⅛ tsp	salt	0.5 mL
	Freshly ground black pepper	
1 tbsp	canola oil	15 mL
1 cup	Cucumber Dill Sauce (see recipe, opposite)	250 mL
	Lemon or lime wedges	

1. Pat halibut dry with paper towels. Season with salt and pepper.

2. In a large nonstick skillet, heat oil over medium-high heat. Add halibut and cook for 3 to 4 minutes per side or until fish flakes easily when tested with a fork. (Reduce heat to medium if fish is browning too quickly.)

3. Transfer to plates and accompany with Cucumber Dill Sauce and lemon wedges.

Variations

This simple cooking method also works with a variety of other fish, such as trout, salmon and tilapia fillets and cod loins.

For a change of pace, try serving the fish with Fresh Tomato Basil Sauce (page 289) instead of the Cucumber Dill Sauce.

Nutrition info per serving (with sauce)

Calories	209
Carbohydrate	6 g
Fiber	0 g
Protein	26 g
Fat	8 g
Saturated fat	2 g
Cholesterol	47 mg
Sodium	257 mg

Food Choices
3 Meat & Alternatives
1 Fat
1 Extra

Cucumber Dill Sauce

Makes about 1 cup (250 mL)

Cucumber, fresh dill and lemon zest combine to make this refreshing sauce. It's an ideal accompaniment for fish or chicken, or steamed asparagus or beans. It also makes a delicious dip for raw vegetables.

- - - - - - - - - - - - - -

Tip

The sauce can be stored in an airtight container in the refrigerator for up to 5 days.

¾ cup	grated English cucumber (unpeeled)	175 mL
2 tbsp	chopped fresh dill	30 mL
½ tsp	grated lemon zest	2 mL
⅛ tsp	salt	0.5 mL
Pinch	cayenne pepper	Pinch
1 cup	light (5%) sour cream	250 mL

1. Place cucumber in a sieve and squeeze out excess water. Wrap in paper towels or a clean kitchen towel and squeeze out excess moisture.

2. In a bowl, combine cucumber, dill, lemon zest, salt, cayenne and sour cream.

Nutrition info per 2 tbsp (30 mL)	
Calories	25
Carbohydrate	3 g
Fiber	0 g
Protein	1 g
Fat	1 g
Saturated fat	1 g
Cholesterol	5 mg
Sodium	60 mg
Food Choices	
1 Extra	

Baked Salmon with Ginger and Lemon

Makes 4 servings

Fresh ginger gives such a sparkling flavor to salmon — or any fish, for that matter. Dried ground ginger just doesn't impart the same crisp taste.

Tips

Buy gingerroot that is firm and unwrinkled, with a gingery aroma. Mature, thick-skinned ginger has a more intense flavor than tender, thin-skinned roots.

Store gingerroot in a sealable plastic bag in the refrigerator. It will keep for several weeks. Or peel the ginger and freeze it in a freezer bag. Grate what you need for a recipe while it's still frozen and return the rest to the freezer.

Nutrition info per serving

Calories	234
Carbohydrate	3 g
Fiber	0 g
Protein	23 g
Fat	14 g
Saturated fat	3 g
Cholesterol	64 mg
Sodium	329 mg

Food Choices
3 Meat & Alternatives
½ Fat

- **Preheat oven to 375°F (190°C)**
- **Shallow baking dish**

4	skinless salmon fillets (each 4 oz/125 g)	4
2	green onions	2
1	clove garlic, minced	1
1½ tsp	minced gingerroot	7 mL
1 tsp	granulated sugar	5 mL
2 tbsp	reduced-sodium soy sauce	30 mL
1 tsp	grated lemon zest	5 mL
1 tbsp	freshly squeezed lemon juice	15 mL
1 tsp	sesame oil	5 mL

1. Arrange salmon in a single layer in baking dish.

2. Thinly slice green onions and set aside green parts for garnish. In a bowl, combine white part of green onions, garlic, ginger, sugar, soy sauce, lemon zest, lemon juice and oil. Pour marinade over salmon. Let stand at room temperature for 15 minutes, or cover and refrigerate for up to 1 hour.

3. Bake, uncovered, in preheated oven for 17 to 20 minutes or until fish is opaque and flakes easily when tested with a fork.

4. Arrange salmon on serving plates and spoon sauce from dish over top. Sprinkle with reserved green onions.

Nutrition Tip

Salmon is high in omega-3 fatty acids, which are important for heart health. The fish highest in omega-3s are anchovies, herring, mackerel, sablefish (black cod), wild salmon, sardines and rainbow trout (farmed).

Salmon with Balsamic Maple Glaze and Ginger Mango Salsa

Makes 4 servings

Easy to prepare and readily available, salmon has become a dinner superstar for its many health benefits.

- - - - - - - - - - - - - - - -

Tips

Buy salmon fillets that are all the same thickness — either center-cut or tail pieces — so that all of the pieces are cooked at the same time.

Four ounces (125 g) raw fish yields 3 oz (90 g) cooked fish (3 Meat & Alternatives Choices).

Nutrition info per serving (with salsa)	
Calories	281
Carbohydrate	17 g
Fiber	1 g
Protein	23 g
Fat	13 g
Saturated fat	3 g
Cholesterol	64 mg
Sodium	130 mg

Food Choices
1 Carbohydrate
3 Meat & Alternatives

- **Preheat oven to 375°F (190°C)**
- **Rimmed baking sheet, lined with foil or parchment paper**

Ginger Mango Salsa

1	large mango, peeled and diced	1
1	green onion, finely sliced	1
2 tbsp	chopped fresh cilantro	30 mL
1 tsp	grated gingerroot	5 mL
½ tsp	grated orange zest	2 mL
2 tbsp	freshly squeezed orange juice	30 mL

Salmon

2 tbsp	balsamic vinegar	30 mL
1 tbsp	pure maple syrup	15 mL
2 tsp	Dijon mustard	10 mL
4	skinless salmon fillets (each 4 oz/125 g)	4

1. *Salsa:* In a bowl, combine mango, green onion, cilantro, ginger, orange zest and orange juice. Let stand until ready to serve, for up to 1 hour.

2. *Fish:* In a small saucepan, bring vinegar to a boil over medium-high heat. Boil until reduced by about two-thirds. Whisk in maple syrup and mustard; bring just to a boil. Remove from heat and let cool.

3. Place salmon on prepared baking sheet and brush evenly with glaze. Bake in preheated oven for 12 to 15 minutes or until fish is opaque and flakes easily when tested with a fork.

4. Arrange salmon on serving plates and accompany with Ginger Mango Salsa.

Salmon Cakes with Tartar Sauce

Makes 4 servings

Mashed sweet potato acts a binder in these popular fish cakes, imparting a pleasant sweet taste and color.

- - - - - - - - - - - - -

Tips

Gently run the blade of a knife along the outside of canned sardines to scrape off the skin. As with salmon, keep the calcium-rich bones. Lightly pat the salmon and sardines with paper towels to absorb excess moisture.

To prepare the sweet potato, place 1 1/3 cups (325 mL) cubed sweet potatoes in a steamer basket set over a saucepan of boiling water. Steam for 10 minutes or until tender. Drain and mash.

Nutrition info per 2 cakes (with sauce)

Calories	264
Carbohydrate	18 g
Fiber	2 g
Protein	15 g
Fat	15 g
Saturated fat	3 g
Cholesterol	72 mg
Sodium	498 mg

Food Choices
1 Carbohydrate
2 Meat & Alternatives
1 1/2 Fat

- **Preheat oven to 200°F (100°C)**

1	can (7 1/2 oz/213 g) sockeye salmon, drained and skin removed	1
2	cans (each 3 oz/84 g) water-packed sardines, drained and skin removed	2
1/2 cup	mashed cooked sweet potato (see tip, at left)	125 mL
3	green onions, thinly sliced	3
1	large egg, beaten	1
1 1/2 tsp	dried fines herbes	7 mL
1 tsp	grated lemon zest	5 mL
1/4 tsp	freshly ground black pepper	1 mL
1/2 cup	panko bread crumbs	125 mL
4 tsp	canola oil, divided	20 mL
1/2 cup	Tartar Sauce (see recipe, opposite)	125 mL

1. In a bowl, using a fork, mash together salmon, sardines and sweet potato. Stir in green onions, egg, fines herbes, lemon zest and pepper. Using your hands, shape into eight 2 1/2-inch (6 cm) round patties.

2. Place bread crumbs in a shallow bowl. Lightly coat both sides of patties in crumbs, pressing gently to adhere. Discard any excess crumbs.

3. In a large nonstick skillet, heat half the oil over medium-high heat. Add half the cakes and cook for 3 to 4 minutes per side or until golden and hot in the center. (Reduce heat to medium if cakes are browning too quickly.) Place on an ovenproof plate and keep warm in preheated oven.

4. Using a paper towel, wipe out skillet. Add the remaining oil to skillet and cook the remaining cakes the same way. Serve with Tartar Sauce.

Tartar Sauce

Makes ½ cup (125 mL)		

1	green onion, thinly sliced	1
2 tsp	drained capers, rinsed and chopped	10 mL
⅓ cup	nonfat sour cream	75 mL
2 tbsp	light mayonnaise	30 mL
1 tsp	grainy mustard	5 mL
	Freshly ground black pepper	

Tartar sauce is traditionally made with mayonnaise and chopped pickles. This lower-fat, lower-sodium version uses nonfat sour cream and capers.

- - - - - - - - - - - - - - -

Tip

The sauce can be stored in an airtight container in the refrigerator for up to 5 days.

1. In a bowl, combine green onion, capers, sour cream, mayonnaise and mustard. Season to taste with pepper.

Nutrition info per 2 tbsp (30 mL)

Calories	41
Carbohydrate	4 g
Fiber	0 g
Protein	1 g
Fat	2 g
Saturated fat	0 g
Cholesterol	2 mg
Sodium	172 mg

Food Choices
½ Fat
1 Extra

Grilled Salmon with Lemon Oregano Pesto

Makes 4 servings

This simple pesto sauce keeps the salmon extra-moist and adds a burst of fresh flavor.

- - - - - - - - - - - - - -

Tip

Double the quantity of the pesto ingredients. Use half to marinate the fish and refrigerate the other half to use as a quick baste when grilling chicken, pork or lamb. Pesto can be stored in an airtight container in the refrigerator for up to 2 days.

Broiler Method: Preheat broiler, with rack set 4 inches (10 cm) from heat. In step 3, arrange salmon on a broiler pan and broil for 5 minutes per side or until fish is opaque and flakes easily when tested with a fork.

Nutrition info per serving	
Calories	240
Carbohydrate	2 g
Fiber	1 g
Protein	21 g
Fat	16 g
Saturated fat	3 g
Cholesterol	58 mg
Sodium	63 mg

Food Choices
3 Meat & Alternatives
1 Fat

- Preheat greased barbecue grill to medium
- Food processor or mini chopper
- Shallow glass baking dish

1	clove garlic, chopped	1
½ cup	lightly packed fresh parsley sprigs	125 mL
2 tbsp	lightly packed fresh oregano (or 2 tsp/10 mL dried)	30 mL
2 tsp	grated lemon zest	10 mL
2 tbsp	freshly squeezed lemon juice	30 mL
4 tsp	olive oil	20 mL
¼ tsp	freshly ground black pepper	1 mL
4	skinless salmon fillets (each 4 oz/125 g)	4

1. In food processor, combine garlic, parsley, oregano, lemon zest and juice, oil and pepper; purée until very smooth.

2. Pat salmon dry with paper towels. Arrange in baking dish and coat both sides with pesto. Marinate at room temperature for 15 minutes, or cover and refrigerate for up to 1 hour.

3. Place salmon on preheated grill and cook for 5 to 7 minutes per side (depending on thickness) or until fish is opaque and flakes easily when tested with a fork.

Pan-Roasted Trout with Fresh Tomato Basil Sauce

Makes 4 servings

Here's a simplified cooking method for trout. It's served with a vibrant fresh tomato topping that is more popularly associated with bruschetta.

- - - - - - - - - - - - - - - -

Tip

Learn more about how to choose sustainable seafood by checking out these websites: Marine Stewardship Council (www. msc.org), Monterey Bay Aquarium Seafood Watch (www.seafoodwatch. org) or SeaChoice (www. seachoice.org).

Nutrition info per serving

Calories	212
Carbohydrate	4 g
Fiber	1 g
Protein	24 g
Fat	11 g
Saturated fat	2 g
Cholesterol	70 mg
Sodium	135 mg

Food Choices
3 Meat & Alternatives
1 Fat

Fresh Tomato Basil Sauce

2	large ripe red tomatoes, seeded and diced	2
½	clove garlic, minced	½
2 tbsp	minced green onion	30 mL
2 tbsp	chopped fresh basil	30 mL
⅛ tsp	salt	0.5 mL
	Freshly ground black pepper	
1 tbsp	balsamic vinegar	15 mL
1 tbsp	extra virgin olive oil	15 mL

Fish

1 tsp	extra virgin olive oil	5 mL
1 lb	trout fillets with skins	500 g

1. *Sauce:* Shortly before serving, in a bowl, combine tomatoes, garlic, green onion, basil, salt, pepper to taste, vinegar and oil.

2. *Fish:* Pat trout dry with paper towels. Brush a large nonstick skillet with oil and heat over medium-high heat. Place trout, skin side down, in skillet. Cook for 2 minutes, without turning. Reduce heat to medium-low, cover and cook for 3 to 5 minutes or until fish is opaque and flakes easily when tested with a fork (time depends on thickness of fish; increase time as needed).

3. Arrange fish on plates and top with sauce.

Variation

Substitute Mexico's famous pico de gallo (also called salsa fresca) for the fresh tomato basil sauce. The preparation is very similar; just use cilantro instead of basil, replace the vinegar with freshly squeezed lime juice, and add 1 minced jalapeño pepper.

Tilapia with Lemon Caper Sauce

Makes 4 servings

This garlicky lemon sauce is the perfect foil for quick-cooking fish fillets — not to mention pork or chicken cutlets (see variation, opposite). Serve with quinoa and steamed green beans or broccoli.

Tips

When purchasing broth, be sure to check the sodium content and choose one with 140 mg or less per 1 cup (250 mL).

Four ounces (125 g) raw fish yields 3 oz (90 g) cooked fish (3 Meat & Alternatives Choices).

Nutrition info per serving

Calories	189
Carbohydrate	6 g
Fiber	0 g
Protein	24 g
Fat	7 g
Saturated fat	1 g
Cholesterol	51 mg
Sodium	270 mg

Food Choices
3 Meat & Alternatives
1 Fat
1 Extra

● **Preheat oven to 200°F (100°C)**

1	clove garlic, finely chopped	1
1 tsp	dried fines herbes or tarragon	5 mL
1/3 cup	Low-Sodium Chicken Stock (page 204) or low-sodium or no-salt-added ready-to-use chicken broth	75 mL
1/3 cup	dry white wine or additional stock or broth	75 mL
1 tsp	grated lemon zest	5 mL
1 tbsp	freshly squeezed lemon juice	15 mL
2 tsp	drained capers, rinsed	10 mL
1 lb	skinless tilapia fillets	500 g
1/4 tsp	salt	1 mL
1/4 tsp	freshly ground black pepper	1 mL
3 tbsp	all-purpose flour	45 mL
4 tsp	extra virgin olive oil, divided	20 mL

1. In a glass measuring cup or bowl, combine garlic, fines herbes, stock, wine, lemon zest, lemon juice and capers. Set aside.

2. Pat tilapia dry with paper towels. Season with salt and pepper. Spread flour on a plate and lightly coat fish in flour, shaking off excess. Discard excess flour.

3. In a large nonstick skillet, heat half the oil over medium-high heat. Add half the fish and cook for 1 to 2 minutes per side or until fish is lightly browned and flakes easily when tested with a fork. Transfer fish to a serving plate and keep warm in preheated oven. Repeat with the remaining oil and fish.

Variation

Pork or Chicken with Lemon Caper Sauce: Replace the tilapia with 1 lb (500 g) thin pork loin, chicken or turkey cutlets pounded to an even thickness between sheets of plastic wrap. Cook as directed, but in step 4, return browned meat to skillet and cook in lemon caper sauce over medium heat for 2 to 3 minutes or until just a hint of pink remains inside pork or chicken is no longer pink inside.

4. Reduce heat to medium and add stock mixture to skillet; cook, stirring, for about 2 minutes or until sauce is reduced and slightly thickened. Pour over fish and serve immediately.

Nutrition Tip

In addition to eating omega-3-rich fish, such as salmon, enjoy a variety of other fish and shellfish, such as tilapia, cod, halibut and mussels. Fish has many important nutrients, including high-quality protein, and is low in saturated fats.

Creamed Seafood with Dill

This classic seafood sauce still has a rich, luxurious taste when you reduce the fat by using half-and-half cream instead of heavy cream.

- - - - - - - - - - - - - -

Tips

You can use only fish or, for a special occasion, only shellfish in this recipe.

As the moisture content of various kinds of fish and shellfish differs, the fish and shellfish are poached first so the sauce has correct thickness.

To make this dish ahead, cover and refrigerate cooked seafood and sauce separately for up to 1 day. Reheat sauce in a saucepan over medium heat, stirring, until piping hot, then continue with step 5.

Nutrition info per ¾ cup (175 mL)	
Calories	185
Carbohydrate	7 g
Fiber	1 g
Protein	24 g
Fat	6 g
Saturated fat	3 g
Cholesterol	124 mg
Sodium	234 mg

Food Choices
3 Meat & Alternatives
1 Fat
1 Extra

1 cup	Low-Sodium Chicken Stock (page 204) or low-sodium or no-salt-added ready-to-use chicken broth	250 mL
½ cup	dry white wine or additional stock or broth	125 mL
8 oz	skinless sole or other white fish, cut into 1-inch (2.5 cm) cubes	250 g
8 oz	small scallops	250 g
8 oz	cooked peeled small shrimp	250 g
1 tbsp	butter or soft margarine	15 mL
3	green onions, thinly sliced	3
1	red bell pepper, finely chopped	1
¼ cup	all-purpose flour	60 mL
½ cup	half-and-half (10%) cream	125 mL
2 tbsp	chopped fresh dill or parsley	30 mL
	Freshly ground white pepper	

1. In a medium saucepan, combine stock and wine. Bring to a boil over medium heat. Add sole and poach for 2 minutes (start timing as soon as fish is added to broth). Add scallops and poach for 1 to 2 minutes or until seafood is just opaque. Using a slotted spoon, transfer fish and scallops to a bowl. Add shrimp and set aside.

2. Strain poaching broth into large glass measuring cup. There should be 2 cups (500 mL); add water, if necessary. Let cool slightly.

3. In the same saucepan, melt butter over medium heat. Add green onions and red pepper; cook, stirring, for 2 minutes or until softened.

4. In a bowl, whisk together flour and ½ cup (125 mL) of the reserved broth until smooth. Add to saucepan, along with the remaining broth; bring to a boil, whisking. Boil, whisking, for 2 minutes or until sauce is very thick and smooth. Whisk in cream.

5. Add seafood and cook, stirring often, until heated through. Stir in dill and season to taste with white pepper. Serve immediately.

Tofu, Pasta, Legumes and Grains

Baked Sesame Tofu

Makes 3 servings

If you haven't cooked tofu very often (or it hasn't yet won you over), try this easy and delicious method for preparing it. The sesame ginger sauce will become indispensable in your kitchen.

- - - - - - - - - - - - - - -

Tips

Extra-firm tofu is preferred in this recipe, but firm and silken tofu also work well.

Not everyone having tofu for dinner? Use the all-purpose marinade with boneless chicken breasts or fish (such as tilapia). Place in another dish and bake until chicken is no longer pink inside or fish is opaque and flakes easily when tested with a fork.

Nutrition info per serving	
Calories	171
Carbohydrate	10 g
Fiber	1 g
Protein	13 g
Fat	10 g
Saturated fat	1 g
Cholesterol	0 mg
Sodium	252 mg

Food Choices
½ Carbohydrate
1½ Meat & Alternatives
1 Fat

- Preheat oven to 350°F (180°C)
- 11- by 7-inch (28 by 18 cm) glass baking dish

Sesame Ginger Sauce

1	clove garlic, minced	1
2 tsp	minced gingerroot	10 mL
1 tbsp	packed brown sugar	15 mL
½ tsp	cornstarch	2 mL
¼ cup	water	60 mL
4 tsp	reduced-sodium soy sauce	20 mL
1 tbsp	natural unseasoned rice vinegar or balsamic vinegar	15 mL
1 tsp	toasted sesame oil	5 mL

Tofu

12 oz	extra-firm tofu	375 g
1 tbsp	toasted sesame seeds	15 mL
1	green onion, sliced	1

1. *Sauce:* In a small saucepan, combine garlic, ginger, brown sugar, cornstarch, water, soy sauce and vinegar. Heat over medium heat, stirring, for 1 to 2 minutes or until thickened. Remove from heat and stir in oil.

2. *Tofu:* Cut tofu into 6 to 8 slices, each about ½ inch (1 cm) thick. Pat dry with paper towels. Arrange in a single layer in baking dish and pour sauce over top. Let marinate at room temperature for 15 minutes, or let cool, cover and refrigerate for up to 1 day.

3. Bake in preheated oven for 20 to 25 minutes or until tofu is nicely glazed with sauce. Serve sprinkled with sesame seeds and green onion.

Nutrition Tip

Like meat, tofu supplies protein, iron and zinc, and it is also a source of calcium and folate. In this stir-fry we call for firm tofu, which is more concentrated in protein than softer tofu.

Soba Noodles with Tofu and Greens

This Japanese-inspired dish, with a combination of greens and tofu, makes a terrific vegetarian meal, especially when made with soba noodles to provide a healthy amount of protein. The dish doesn't take long to cook, so have all the ingredients assembled and measured before you start.

- - - - - - - - - - - - - - - -

Tips

Buckwheat soba noodles are lower in carbs than regular pasta and also have a lower GI.

Look for tofu made with calcium sulfate, to help you meet your daily calcium needs.

Nutrition info per 1½ cups (375 mL)	
Calories	313
Carbohydrate	39 g
Fiber	9 g
Protein	19 g
Fat	13 g
Saturated fat	2 g
Cholesterol	0 mg
Sodium	445 mg

Food Choices
1½ Carbohydrate
2 Meat & Alternatives
1½ Fat

5 oz	soba noodles or whole wheat spaghetti	150 g
2 tbsp	reduced-sodium soy sauce	30 mL
2 tsp	toasted sesame oil	10 mL
1 tsp	granulated sugar	5 mL
½ tsp	Asian chili sauce	2 mL
12 oz	extra-firm tofu	375 g
4 tsp	peanut or canola oil, divided	20 mL
2	cloves garlic, minced	2
2 tbsp	minced gingerroot	30 mL
4	baby bok choy, halved lengthwise	4
3 cups	shredded kale, collard greens or Swiss chard leaves	750 mL
2 tbsp	water	30 mL
2	green onions, sliced	2

1. In a large pot of boiling water, cook noodles according to package directions. Drain well and return to pot.

2. Meanwhile, in a bowl, stir together soy sauce, sesame oil, sugar and chili sauce. Set aside.

2. Cut tofu into ¾-inch (2 cm) cubes and pat dry with paper towels. In a large wok, heat 3 tsp (15 mL) of the peanut oil over medium-high heat. Stir-fry tofu for 5 minutes or until golden. Transfer to a plate.

3. Add the remaining oil to wok and heat over medium-high heat. Stir-fry garlic and ginger for 30 seconds or until fragrant. Add bok choy and kale; stir-fry for 1 minute. Add water, cover and steam for 2 minutes or until tender-crisp. Stir in sauce.

4. Add tofu and greens to the noodles and toss. Transfer to a large serving bowl and sprinkle with green onions.

Roasted Vegetable Lasagna

Lasagna is always popular, and this updated version features plenty of healthy vegetables in a tomato-rich sauce, layered with ricotta cheese.

- - - - - - - - - - - - - - - -

Tip

To make lasagna ahead, prepare as directed, let cool, cover and refrigerate for up to 2 days or overwrap with foil and freeze for up to 2 months. Let thaw in the refrigerator for 24 hours.

Nutrition info per serving

Calories	386
Carbohydrate	41 g
Fiber	7 g
Protein	25 g
Fat	15 g
Saturated fat	7 g
Cholesterol	59 mg
Sodium	506 mg

Food Choices
1½ Carbohydrate
2½ Meat & Alternatives
1 Fat

- Preheat oven to 400°F (200°C)
- 2 rimmed baking sheets
- 13- by 9-inch (33 by 23 cm) glass baking dish, sprayed with vegetable oil cooking spray

2	small zucchini, diced	2
2	red bell peppers, finely chopped	2
1	onion, chopped	1
1	fennel bulb, diced	1
1½ tsp	dried Italian seasoning	7 mL
1 tsp	freshly ground black pepper, divided	5 mL
4 tsp	extra virgin olive oil	20 mL
9	whole wheat lasagna noodles	9
1	large egg	1
¼ cup	chopped fresh parsley	60 mL
2 cups	light ricotta cheese	500 mL
¼ cup	freshly grated Parmesan cheese	60 mL
3 cups	Tomato Pasta Sauce (page 298)	750 mL
1 cup	shredded part-skim mozzarella cheese	250 mL

1. In a large bowl, combine zucchini, red peppers, onion, fennel, Italian seasoning and ½ tsp (2 mL) of the pepper. Drizzle with oil and toss to coat. Spread in a single layer on baking sheets, dividing equally. Roast in preheated oven, stirring occasionally and switching the position of the sheets on the oven racks halfway through, for 20 minutes or until tender. Transfer roasted vegetables to a large bowl. Reduce oven temperature to 350°F (180°C).

2. Meanwhile, in a large pot of boiling water, cook noodles for 8 minutes or until almost tender. Drain, then chill under cold running water. Arrange in a single layer on a damp tea towel.

3. In a medium bowl, beat egg. Stir in parsley, the remaining pepper, ricotta and Parmesan.

4. Spread ¾ cup (175 mL) pasta sauce in prepared baking dish. Stir remaining sauce into roasted vegetables.

5. Layer 3 noodles in baking dish. Spread one-third of the vegetable mixture on top. Top with half the ricotta mixture. Repeat layers. Arrange the remaining noodles on top and spread with the remaining vegetable mixture. Sprinkle with mozzarella.

6. Cover loosely with foil and bake for 30 minutes. Uncover and bake for 20 to 25 minutes or until bubbly and top is golden. Let stand for 5 minutes before cutting.

Nutrition Tip

Choosing low-GI foods is an effective way to reduce your blood glucose and help prevent and manage diabetes. (See page 58 for details about the glycemic index.) Pastas have a low or medium GI, meaning the carbohydrate causes only a gradual rise and fall of blood glucose levels. However, when overcooked, pasta becomes high-GI. Always cook pasta until al dente, meaning just tender to the bite, not soft and overcooked. For extra vitamins, minerals and fiber, use whole-grain or whole wheat pastas in your favorite recipes.

Tomato Pasta Sauce

Keep this indispensable sauce on hand in your freezer to use as a base for your family's favorite pasta dishes. Packed with vitamins A and C, tomato sauces also contain lycopene, an antioxidant that helps protect against prostate cancer.

- - - - - - - - - - - - - - -

Tips

If making sauce ahead, do not add the basil. Let sauce cool, portion into airtight containers and refrigerate for up to 5 days or freeze for up to 2 months. Add basil when reheating.

Instead of fresh basil, add 2 tsp (10 mL) dried basil with the garlic, and stir in 1/3 cup (75 mL) chopped fresh parsley at the end of cooking.

1 tbsp	extra virgin olive oil	15 mL
1	onion, finely chopped	1
4	cloves garlic, minced	4
2	cans (each 28 oz/796 mL) tomatoes, with juice, chopped	2
1 tsp	granulated sugar	5 mL
1/2 tsp	freshly ground black pepper	2 mL
1/3 cup	chopped fresh basil	75 mL

1. In a large saucepan, heat oil over medium heat. Add onion and garlic; cook, stirring often, for 3 minutes or until softened.

2. Stir in tomatoes with juice, sugar and pepper; bring to a boil. Reduce heat to medium-low, cover, leaving lid ajar, and simmer for 35 to 45 minutes, stirring occasionally, until slightly thickened. Stir in basil.

Variation

Fresh Tomato Pasta Sauce: In summer, instead of canned tomatoes, make this sauce with 5 lbs (2.5 kg) fresh ripe tomatoes, preferably plum (Roma). To prepare, remove cores. Cut an X in the bottom of each tomato. In small batches, plunge into boiling water for 30 seconds to loosen skins. Chill in ice water, then drain. Slip off skins, cut tomatoes in half crosswise and squeeze out seeds. Finely chop.

Nutrition info per 1 cup (250 mL)	
Calories	80
Carbohydrate	14 g
Fiber	3 g
Protein	3 g
Fat	3 g
Saturated fat	0 g
Cholesterol	0 mg
Sodium	387 mg

Food Choices
1/2 Fat
1 Extra

Easy Macaroni and Cheese with Broccoli

Here's a tasty, streamlined mac and cheese that's as easy to assemble as the ubiquitous boxed dinners sold in supermarkets — and a far better nutritional choice.

- - - - - - - - - - - - - - -

Tip

If reheating leftovers on the stovetop or in a microwave, stir in additional milk until sauce is creamy.

3 tbsp	all-purpose flour	45 mL
2 cups	low-fat (1%) milk	500 mL
1½ cups	shredded lower-fat (<20% M.F.) Cheddar cheese	375 mL
¼ cup	freshly grated Parmesan cheese	60 mL
½ tsp	dry mustard	2 mL
⅛ tsp	cayenne pepper (or to taste)	0.5 mL
1¼ cups	whole wheat elbow macaroni	300 mL
4 cups	small broccoli florets and chopped peeled stems	1 L

1. In a large saucepan, whisk flour and ⅓ cup (75 mL) of the milk until smooth. Whisk in the remaining milk. Cook over medium heat, stirring, until mixture comes to a boil and thickens. Reduce heat to medium-low and cook, stirring, for 2 minutes. Stir in Cheddar, Parmesan, mustard and cayenne. Reduce heat to low and keep warm.

2. In a large pot of boiling water, cook macaroni for 6 minutes or until almost tender. Add broccoli and cook for about 2 minutes or until pasta is al dente and broccoli is tender-crisp. Drain well and stir into cheese mixture. Increase heat to medium and cook for 1 minute or until sauce coats the pasta. Serve immediately.

Nutrition info per 1¼ cups (300 mL)

Calories	364
Carbohydrate	42 g
Fiber	5 g
Protein	26 g
Fat	12 g
Saturated fat	7 g
Cholesterol	35 mg
Sodium	497 mg

Food Choices
2 Carbohydrate
2 Meat & Alternatives

Creamy Tuna Pasta Bake

This lightened-up version of tuna casserole includes a nutritional boost of broccoli in a creamy basil sauce. It's perfect for casual entertaining when serving a crowd.

Tips

When purchasing broth, be sure to check the sodium content and choose one with 140 mg or less per 1 cup (250 mL).

If fresh basil is unavailable, add 1½ tsp (7 mL) dried basil or Italian seasonings with the garlic and add ¼ cup (60 mL) chopped fresh parsley with the tomatoes.

Nutrition info per 1½ cups (375 mL)

Calories	333
Carbohydrate	42 g
Fiber	5 g
Protein	25 g
Fat	7 g
Saturated fat	3 g
Cholesterol	26 mg
Sodium	472 mg

Food Choices
2 Carbohydrate
2 Meat & Alternatives
½ Fat

- **Preheat oven to 350°F (180°C)**
- **13- by 9-inch (33 by 23 cm) glass baking dish, sprayed with vegetable oil cooking spray**

1 tbsp	canola oil	15 mL
4 cups	sliced mushrooms	1 L
1 cup	sliced green onions	250 mL
3	cloves garlic, minced	3
⅓ cup	all-purpose flour	75 mL
2 cups	low-fat (1%) milk	500 mL
1 cup	Low-Sodium Chicken Stock (page 204) or low-sodium or no-salt-added ready-to-use chicken broth	250 mL
3	tomatoes, seeded and diced	3
½ cup	freshly grated Parmesan cheese	125 mL
½ cup	chopped fresh basil	125 mL
½ tsp	freshly ground black pepper	2 mL
¼ tsp	salt	1 mL
3 cups	penne or spiral pasta	750 mL
4 cups	broccoli florets and chopped peeled stems	1 L
2	cans (each 6 oz/170 g) water-packed light tuna, drained and flaked	2
1 cup	fresh whole wheat bread crumbs	250 mL
1 cup	shredded light Gouda or Cheddar cheese	250 mL

1. In a large saucepan, heat oil over medium-high heat. Add mushrooms, green onions and garlic; cook, stirring occasionally, for 5 minutes or until softened.

2. In a bowl, whisk flour and 1 cup (250 mL) of the milk until smooth. Whisk in the remaining milk. Add to pan, along with stock, and bring to a boil, stirring. Boil, stirring, for 3 minutes or until sauce thickens. Remove from heat and stir in tomatoes, Parmesan, basil, pepper and salt.

Tip

The sauce can be prepared through step 2 the day before; let cool, cover and refrigerate. Assemble the dish no more than 4 hours ahead to prevent the pasta from soaking up the sauce; cover and refrigerate until ready to bake. Increase the baking time by 15 minutes.

Variations

Substitute 2 cups (500 mL) diced cooked chicken or turkey for the tuna.

For a vegetarian version, replace the tuna with 2 cups (500 mL) well-rinsed drained canned no-salt-added white kidney beans.

3. In a large pot of boiling water, cook pasta for 7 minutes or until almost tender. Add broccoli and cook for 1 to 2 minutes or until pasta is al dente and broccoli is bright green and still crisp. Drain and chill under cold running water. Drain well and return to pot. Stir in tuna and sauce. Spread in prepared baking dish.

4. In a bowl, combine bread crumbs and Gouda; sprinkle over top.

5. Bake in preheated oven for 40 to 45 minutes or until topping is golden and center is piping hot.

Nutrition Tip

Several varieties of tuna, including albacore, are sources of omega-3 fats. However, albacore, because it's a larger fish, is more susceptible to mercury contamination. For this reason, it is best to limit canned albacore tuna in your diet. Instead, select light skipjack tuna, a smaller species with a lower mercury content.

Curried Lentils with Vegetables

Heady with the fragrance of curry, this one-pot lentil stew makes for a substantial meal in a bowl. Accompany with Cucumber Mint Raita (page 271), if desired.

- - - - - - - - - - - - - - - -

Tips

The larger brown or green lentil varieties are preferred in this recipe.

When purchasing broth, be sure to check the sodium content and choose one with 140 mg or less per 1 cup (250 mL).

3 cups	water	750 mL
1 cup	dried green or brown lentils, rinsed	250 mL
1	bay leaf	1
1 tbsp	canola oil	15 mL
1	large onion, chopped	1
2	cloves garlic, minced	2
1 tbsp	minced gingerroot	15 mL
2 tsp	curry powder (or to taste)	10 mL
Pinch	cayenne pepper	Pinch
2 cups	diagonally sliced green beans	500 mL
1½ cups	diced peeled potatoes (about 2 medium)	375 mL
1½ cups	Low-Sodium Vegetable or Chicken Stock (page 205 or 204) or low-sodium or no-salt-added ready-to-use vegetable or chicken broth	375 mL
¼ cup	no-salt-added tomato paste	60 mL
1	red bell pepper, finely chopped	1
1 cup	fresh or frozen corn kernels	250 mL
½ tsp	salt	2 mL
¼ cup	coarsely chopped fresh cilantro or parsley	60 mL

1. In a large saucepan, bring water to a boil over high heat. Add lentils and bay leaf. Reduce heat to medium-low, cover and simmer for 25 to 30 minutes or until lentils are tender. Drain well and discard bay leaf.

2. In a large saucepan, heat oil over medium heat. Add onion, garlic, ginger, curry powder and cayenne; cook, stirring often, for 5 minutes or until onion is softened.

Nutrition info per 2 cups (500 mL)	
Calories	343
Carbohydrate	62 g
Fiber	12 g
Protein	17 g
Fat	5 g
Saturated fat	1 g
Cholesterol	0 mg
Sodium	377 mg

Food Choices
2½ Carbohydrate
2 Meat & Alternatives
1 Fat

Tip

Freeze extra portions in individual airtight containers for up to 1 month, for convenient lunches and dinners.

Variation

Curried Chickpeas with Vegetables: Omit the water, lentils and bay leaf. In step 4, add 2 cups (500 mL) well-rinsed drained no-salt-added canned chickpeas with the corn.

3. Stir in beans, potatoes, stock and tomato paste; bring to a boil. Reduce heat to medium-low, cover and simmer for 10 minutes.

4. Stir in lentils, red pepper and corn; cover and simmer, stirring occasionally, for 10 minutes or until vegetables are tender. (Add water, if necessary, to prevent lentils from sticking.) Season with salt and stir in cilantro.

Nutrition Tip

Legumes, including lentils, are an excellent food choice for people with diabetes. High in soluble fiber, they cause a slower release of glucose following a meal and less fluctuation in blood glucose levels.

Baked Italian White Beans

A simple combo of beans and vegetables makes for a terrific side dish or main course that will delight not only the vegetarians in the crowd but everyone else as well.

- - - - - - - - - - - - - - -

Tip

To make 1 cup (250 mL) fresh bread crumbs, process 2 slices of crusty whole wheat bread in a food processor until fine crumbs form.

- **Preheat oven to 350°F (180°C)**
- **8-cup (2 L) shallow glass baking dish, sprayed with vegetable oil cooking spray**

1 tbsp	extra virgin olive oil	15 mL
2 cups	chopped Spanish onions	500 mL
3	cloves garlic, finely chopped	3
2 cups	diced seeded tomatoes (about 5 medium)	500 mL
1 tbsp	chopped fresh thyme (or 1 tsp/5 mL dried)	15 mL
1/4 tsp	freshly ground black pepper	1 mL
1 tbsp	balsamic vinegar	15 mL
2	small zucchini, halved lengthwise and thickly sliced	2
1	red bell pepper, finely chopped	1
1	yellow bell pepper, finely chopped	1
2 cups	well-rinsed drained canned white kidney beans	500 mL

Crumb Topping

1	large clove garlic, minced	1
1 cup	fresh whole wheat bread crumbs (see tip, at left)	250 mL
2 tbsp	chopped fresh parsley	30 mL
1 tbsp	extra virgin olive oil	15 mL

1. In a large saucepan, heat oil over medium heat. Add onions and garlic; cook, stirring often, for 7 to 9 minutes or until lightly colored.

2. Stir in tomatoes, thyme, pepper and vinegar; bring to a boil. Reduce heat to medium-low, cover and simmer, stirring occasionally for 15 minutes.

Nutrition info per 1 cup (250 mL)	
Calories	183
Carbohydrate	29 g
Fiber	7 g
Protein	7 g
Fat	5 g
Saturated fat	1 g
Cholesterol	0 mg
Sodium	244 mg

Food Choices
1/2 Carbohydrate
1/2 Meat & Alternatives
1 Fat

Tip
Recipe can be prepared through step 3 up to 1 day ahead; cover and refrigerate. When ready to bake, continue with step 4. Increase the baking time by 10 to 15 minutes.

3. Stir in zucchini, red pepper and yellow pepper; cover and simmer for 5 minutes or until vegetables are tender-crisp. Gently stir in beans. Spoon into prepared baking dish.

4. *Topping:* In a bowl, combine garlic, bread crumbs, parsley and oil. Sprinkle over bean mixture.

5. Bake in preheated oven for 35 to 40 minutes or until bubbly and top is golden.

Nutrition Tip

Legumes provide a significant amount of fiber and are a valuable source of protein. Varieties include kidney beans, black beans, black-eyed peas, chickpeas, Great Northern beans, lentils, navy beans, pinto beans, soy beans and split peas. Try to eat five servings of legumes every week, in dishes such as dips and spreads, soups, salads, chilis and stews. Most canned legumes are canned with salt, so be sure to drain and rinse well.

Chickpea Patties with Tahini Parsley Sauce

These deliciously spiced chickpea patties, topped with a creamy parsley sauce, are sure to entice meat eaters to try more vegetarian dishes. Cook up an extra batch and stash them in the freezer so you have them on hand to pack in lunches and for quick dinners.

Tip

Panko bread crumbs are crisp and airy, perfect for coating foods such as fish and cutlets. They make an ideal substitute for traditional dry bread crumbs, which are much higher in sodium.

Nutrition info per 2 patties (with sauce)

Calories	257
Carbohydrate	35 g
Fiber	5 g
Protein	11 g
Fat	9 g
Saturated fat	1 g
Cholesterol	47 mg
Sodium	321 mg

Food Choices

2 Carbohydrate
1 Meat & Alternatives
1 Fat

- Food processor

4 tsp	extra virgin olive oil, divided	20 mL
1	small onion, minced	1
2	cloves garlic, minced	2
1 tsp	ground cumin	5 mL
1 tsp	ground coriander	5 mL
1/4 tsp	paprika	1 mL
Pinch	cayenne pepper	Pinch
2 cups	well-rinsed drained canned chickpeas	500 mL
1	large egg	1
2 tbsp	whole wheat flour	30 mL
1/2 cup	panko bread crumbs or unseasoned dry bread crumbs	125 mL
1/2 cup	Tahini Parsley Sauce (see recipe, opposite)	125 mL

1. In a large nonstick skillet, heat 1 tsp (5 mL) of the oil over medium heat. Add onion, garlic, cumin, coriander, paprika and cayenne; cook, stirring often, for 4 minutes or until onion is softened. Remove from heat.

2. In food processor, combine chickpeas, egg and flour; pulse to make a coarse mixture that holds together. Add onion mixture and pulse until just combined.

3. Transfer chickpea mixture to a bowl. With wet hands (to prevent sticking), form mixture into eight 1/2-inch (1 cm) thick patties.

4. Place bread crumbs in a shallow bowl. Coat patties in crumb mixture, lightly pressing so crumbs adhere.

5. Wipe out skillet. Heat 1 1/2 tsp (7 mL) oil over medium-high heat. Cook four of the patties, turning once, for about 3 minutes per side or until golden and hot inside. (Reduce heat if necessary to prevent burning.) Transfer patties to a serving plate. Wipe out skillet. Repeat with the remaining oil and patties.

6. Serve patties warm or at room temperature, with Tahini Parsley Sauce.

Tahini Parsley Sauce

Serve this versatile sauce with fish, chicken, pork or lamb, or as a topping for burgers.

Tips

Tahini is a smooth, thick paste made from ground sesame seeds. It is commonly used in Middle Eastern cooking and is available in the international food or health food section of large supermarkets.

The sauce can be stored in an airtight container in the refrigerator for up to 1 week.

1	small clove garlic, minced	1
1/4 cup	finely chopped fresh parsley	60 mL
1 cup	nonfat plain yogurt or sour cream	250 mL
1 tbsp	tahini (sesame seed paste)	15 mL
1 tsp	freshly squeezed lemon juice	5 mL
1/8 tsp	salt	0.5 mL

1. In a bowl, combine garlic, parsley, yogurt, tahini, lemon juice and salt.

Freezing and Reheating Chickpea Patties

The cooked patties freeze well. Let cool completely, then place in a freezer bag and freeze for up to 1 month. To serve warm, place 2 frozen patties on a plate lined with paper towels and microwave on High for 1 minute or until defrosted and heated through (increase time if reheating a larger amount of patties).

Nutrition info per 2 tbsp (30 mL)

Calories	27
Carbohydrate	3 g
Fiber	0 g
Protein	2 g
Fat	1 g
Saturated fat	0 g
Cholesterol	1 mg
Sodium	60 mg

Food Choices
1 Extra

Middle Eastern Couscous with Chickpeas

This impressive dish, featuring couscous and nutrition-packed chickpeas, is flavored with Middle Eastern spices of cumin, coriander and zesty orange.

- - - - - - - - - - - - - -

Tips

Extras can be stored in an airtight container in the refrigerator for 2 to 3 days or in the freezer for up to 1 month.

When purchasing broth, be sure to check the sodium content and choose one with 140 mg or less per 1 cup (250 mL).

Nutrition info per 1½ cups (375 mL)	
Calories	286
Carbohydrate	55 g
Fiber	10 g
Protein	9 g
Fat	4 g
Saturated fat	1 g
Cholesterol	0 mg
Sodium	303 mg

Food Choices
2½ Carbohydrate
½ Meat & Alternatives
½ Fat

1 cup	Low-Sodium Vegetable Stock (page 204) or low-sodium or no-salt-added ready-to-use vegetable broth	250 mL
1 cup	whole wheat couscous	250 mL
1 tbsp	extra virgin olive oil	15 mL
1	large onion, halved lengthwise and cut into thin strips	1
3	cloves garlic, minced	3
2 tbsp	minced gingerroot	30 mL
2 tsp	ground cumin	10 mL
1 tsp	ground coriander	5 mL
¼ tsp	salt	1 mL
⅛ tsp	cayenne pepper (or to taste)	0.5 mL
3	carrots, thinly sliced	3
2	small zucchini, halved lengthwise and sliced	2
1	large red bell pepper, finely chopped	1
2 tsp	grated orange zest	10 mL
⅓ cup	freshly squeezed orange juice	75 mL
2 cups	well-rinsed drained canned chickpeas	500 mL
⅓ cup	dried cranberries	75 mL
⅓ cup	chopped fresh parsley or cilantro	75 mL

1. In a small saucepan, bring stock to a boil. Stir in couscous and remove from heat. Cover and let stand for 5 minutes. Fluff with a fork. Set aside and keep warm.

2. Meanwhile, in a large nonstick skillet, heat oil over medium heat. Add onion, garlic, ginger, cumin, coriander, salt and cayenne; cook, stirring, for 4 minutes.

Variation

Middle Eastern Quinoa with Chickpeas: Omit the couscous. In step 1, in a saucepan, bring 1 cup (250 mL) rinsed quinoa, 1 cup (250 mL) stock and ¾ cup (175 mL) water to a boil over high heat. Reduce heat to low, cover and simmer for 15 minutes or until quinoa is tender and water is absorbed. Continue with steps 2 to 4, then stir quinoa and parsley into chickpea mixture.

3. Increase heat to medium-high and stir in carrots, zucchini, red pepper and orange juice. Cover and steam, stirring occasionally, for 5 minutes or until vegetables are tender-crisp.

4. Stir in orange zest, chickpeas and cranberries; cover and cook, stirring occasionally, for 3 minutes or until heated through.

5. Stir couscous and parsley into chickpea mixture.

Nutrition Tip

Chickpeas (also called garbanzo beans) hold their shape well when cooked, so they make a great addition to soups and salads, as well as a convenient snack. Like other legumes, they are nutritious and low in fat, helping to lower cholesterol and improve blood sugar levels. One half-cup (125 mL) of boiled or canned chickpeas — 1 Meat & Alternatives Choice — contains 4 grams of fiber, is an excellent source of folate and also supplies potassium, iron, magnesium, selenium and zinc.

Jamaican Rice and Peas

Rice and peas is a traditional dish served throughout the Caribbean. This Jamaican version calls for kidney beans, but canned pigeon peas or black-eyed peas can also be used.

- - - - - - - - - - - - - - -

Tips

Freeze extra portions in individual airtight containers for up to 1 month. For best flavor, add cilantro after reheating.

For 2 cups (500 mL) of beans, you will need one 19-oz (540 mL) can. Always pour beans and their liquid into a sieve and rinse the beans thoroughly under cold water. This reduces the sodium by up to 40%.

1	can (14 oz/398 mL) light coconut milk	1
2 tsp	canola oil	10 mL
1	large onion, chopped	1
3	cloves garlic, minced	3
1 tsp	dried thyme	5 mL
1/4 to 1/2 tsp	hot pepper flakes (or to taste)	1 to 2 mL
1 cup	long-grain brown rice, rinsed	250 mL
2 cups	well-rinsed drained canned red kidney beans	500 mL
1/4 tsp	salt	1 mL
3	green onions, sliced	3
1/3 cup	chopped fresh cilantro or parsley	75 mL

1. Pour coconut milk into large glass measuring cup. Add enough water to make $2\frac{1}{2}$ cups (625 mL). Stir to blend.

2. In a large saucepan, heat oil over medium heat. Add onion, garlic, thyme and hot pepper flakes; cook, stirring often, for 4 minutes or until softened.

3. Stir in rice and coconut milk; bring to a boil. Reduce heat to medium-low, cover and simmer for 35 minutes or until almost all of the liquid is absorbed.

4. Stir in beans, cover and simmer for 8 to 10 minutes or until rice is tender. Let stand, uncovered, for 5 minutes. Season with salt. Stir in green onions and cilantro just before serving.

Nutrition info per 3/4 cup (175 mL)	
Calories	253
Carbohydrate	42 g
Fiber	6 g
Protein	9 g
Fat	6 g
Saturated fat	4 g
Cholesterol	0 mg
Sodium	311 mg

Food Choices
2 Carbohydrate
1/2 Meat & Alternatives
1 Fat

Ginger Brown Basmati Rice

Ginger, herbs and spices enhance basmati's already wonderful aroma and flavor. Serve this side dish alongside a chicken, lamb or lentil curry.

- - - - - - - - - -

Tips

Rinsing basmati rice removes excess starch, resulting in less sticky rice.

To reheat, place refrigerated or frozen rice in a casserole dish, along with 1 tbsp (15 mL) water for every 1 cup (250 mL) cooked rice. Cover and microwave on High, stirring occasionally, until piping hot. Add cilantro after reheating.

2 tsp	canola oil	10 mL
½	onion, finely chopped	½
2 tsp	minced gingerroot	10 mL
1	3-inch (7.5 cm) cinnamon stick, broken in half	1
1	bay leaf	1
1 cup	brown basmati rice, rinsed	250 mL
2½ cups	water	625 mL
¼ tsp	salt	1 mL
2 tbsp	chopped fresh cilantro or chives	30 mL

1. In a medium saucepan, heat oil over medium heat. Add onion, ginger, cinnamon stick and bay leaf; cook, stirring, for 2 minutes or until onion is softened.

3. Stir in rice, water and salt; bring to a boil. Reduce heat to low, cover and simmer for 35 to 40 minutes or until liquid is absorbed. Remove from heat and let stand, uncovered, for 5 minutes. Fluff with a fork and discard cinnamon stick and bay leaf. Transfer to a serving dish and sprinkle with cilantro.

Nutrition Tip

Brown rice is a whole-grain rice with a delicious nut-like flavor. It contains the nutrient-dense bran layer, with fiber, vitamins (including B complex) and minerals. The oil present in the bran layer shortens its shelf life. Store brown rice in a cool, dry place for up to 6 months. Refrigerate or freeze for longer storage.

Nutrition info per ⅓ cup (75 mL)

Calories	98
Carbohydrate	18 g
Fiber	1 g
Protein	2 g
Fat	2 g
Saturated fat	0 g
Cholesterol	0 mg
Sodium	77 mg

Food Choices
1 Carbohydrate

Wild and Brown Rice Pilaf

The combination of wild and brown rice, flecked with red pepper, makes for a colorful side dish.

- - - - - - - - - - - - - - - -

Tips

Wild rice has a wonderful nutty flavor and a slightly chewy texture. It's not a true rice but rather the nutritious seed of an aquatic grass that grows in marshy areas of freshwater lakes and rivers in parts of Canada and the northern United States. It is low in fat and high in protein and fiber.

When purchasing broth, be sure to check the sodium content and choose one with 140 mg or less per 1 cup (250 mL).

Nutrition info per ¾ cup (175 mL)	
Calories	212
Carbohydrate	36 g
Fiber	3 g
Protein	8 g
Fat	4 g
Saturated fat	1 g
Cholesterol	14 mg
Sodium	227 mg

Food Choices
2 Carbohydrate
½ Fat

½ cup	wild rice, rinsed	125 mL
2¼ cups	Low-Sodium Chicken Stock (page 204) or low-sodium or no-salt-added ready-to-use chicken broth, divided	550 mL
2 tsp	canola oil	10 mL
1	onion, finely chopped	1
1 tsp	chopped fresh thyme (or ½ tsp/2 mL dried)	5 mL
½ cup	long-grain brown rice, rinsed	125 mL
1	small red bell pepper, finely chopped	1
¼ tsp	salt	1 mL
	Freshly ground black pepper	
2 tbsp	chopped fresh parsley	30 mL

1. In a medium saucepan, combine wild rice and 1 cup (250 mL) of the stock. Bring to a boil over high heat. Reduce heat to low, cover and simmer for 15 minutes or until most of the stock is absorbed. Transfer to a bowl.

2. In the same saucepan, heat oil over medium heat. Add onion and thyme; cook, stirring often, for 3 minutes or until onion is softened.

3. Stir in partially cooked wild rice, brown rice and the remaining stock; bring to a boil over high heat. Reduce heat to low, cover and simmer for 35 minutes or until rice is almost tender.

4. Stir in red pepper, cover and simmer for 5 minutes or until liquid is absorbed. Season with salt and pepper. Stir in parsley.

Mushroom Barley Pilaf

Barley has long been associated with hearty soup, but rarely is it considered as a side dish. Here, barley is paired with mushrooms for a great-tasting, wholesome dish your family will love. Freeze extra servings for another meal.

- - - - - - - - - - - - - - - -

Tips

Pot barley (aka Scotch barley) is preferred over pearl barley, as it is less refined and retains more of the bran layer.

Barley makes a great substitute for long-grain brown rice in most pilaf recipes, as it has the same cooking time. It may require a bit more liquid when cooking, so add a small amount of water to prevent it from sticking.

Nutrition info per ½ cup (125 mL)

Calories	134
Carbohydrate	23 g
Fiber	5 g
Protein	5 g
Fat	3 g
Saturated fat	1 g
Cholesterol	11 mg
Sodium	92 mg

Food Choices
1 Carbohydrate
½ Fat

2 tsp	canola oil	10 mL
8 oz	mushrooms, sliced	250 g
1	onion, chopped	1
2	cloves garlic, minced	2
¾ tsp	dried thyme or marjoram	3 mL
1 cup	pot barley, rinsed	250 mL
2½ cups	Low-Sodium Chicken or Vegetable Stock (page 204 or 205) or low-sodium or no-salt-added ready-to-use chicken or vegetable broth	625 mL
¼ cup	freshly grated Parmesan cheese	60 mL
2 tbsp	chopped fresh parsley	30 mL
	Freshly ground black pepper	

1. In a medium saucepan, heat oil over medium heat. Add mushrooms, onion, garlic and thyme; cook, stirring, for 5 minutes or until vegetables are softened.

2. Stir in barley and stock; bring to a boil over high heat. Reduce heat to low, cover and simmer, stirring occasionally, for 40 to 45 minutes or until barley is just tender. Stir in Parmesan and parsley. Season to taste with pepper.

Variation

Bulgur Mushroom Pilaf: Use whole-grain bulgur instead of barley, and reduce the stock to 1¾ cups (425 mL). In step 2, cook bulgur for 15 minutes or until tender and liquid is absorbed.

Quinoa with Sautéed Spinach

Makes 4 servings

Quinoa is fast becoming a staple in today's kitchens thanks to its slightly nutty taste and quick cooking time. As an added bonus, it's also gluten-free.

Tips

Quinoa is relatively high in polyunsaturated fats, so buy it in small amounts and store it in the fridge or freezer to prevent it from becoming rancid.

You can replace the spinach with other greens, such as shredded kale, beet greens, collard greens, rapini or Swiss chard. Depending on the greens, it may be necessary to cook them slightly longer, until tender.

1¾ cups	Low-Sodium Chicken Stock (page 204) or low-sodium or no-salt-added ready-to-use chicken broth	425 mL
1 cup	quinoa, rinsed	250 mL
2 tsp	extra virgin olive oil	10 mL
1	large onion, finely chopped	1
2	cloves garlic, minced	2
8 cups	lightly packed baby spinach (about 8 oz/250 g)	2 L
1 tsp	grated orange zest	5 mL
¼ tsp	salt	1 mL
¼ tsp	freshly ground black pepper	1 mL
¼ tsp	freshly grated nutmeg (see tip, page 348)	1 mL

1. In a medium saucepan, bring stock and quinoa to a boil over high heat. Reduce heat to low, cover and simmer for 15 minutes or until quinoa is tender and stock is absorbed. Remove from heat and let stand, covered.

2. In a large nonstick skillet, heat oil over medium-high heat. Add onion and cook, stirring often, for 3 minutes or until lightly colored. Add garlic and spinach; cook, stirring, for 3 minutes or until spinach is wilted and liquid is evaporated. Stir in orange zest and season with salt, pepper and nutmeg.

3. Transfer quinoa to a serving dish and top with spinach mixture.

Nutrition Tip

Quinoa originated in the Andes and is a grain-like crop grown for its edible seeds. It is highly nutritious, as it's a complete protein, containing all eight essential amino acids.

Nutrition info per 1 cup (250 mL)	
Calories	223
Carbohydrate	34 g
Fiber	6 g
Protein	11 g
Fat	6 g
Saturated fat	1 g
Cholesterol	11 mg
Sodium	264 mg

Food Choices
1½ Carbohydrate
1 Fat

Storing, Preparing and Cooking Legumes

Dried legumes, also called pulses, include peas, beans, lentils and chickpeas. They have a low glycemic index and are particularly beneficial for those with diabetes because they slow the release of glucose after a meal, minimizing fluctuations in blood glucose levels and insulin response.

How to Store Dried Legumes

Place legumes in an airtight container and store in a cool, dry, dark place for up to a year.

How to Prepare Dried Legumes for Cooking

Place legumes in a colander and sort to remove any small pebbles and discolored beans. Rinse well under cold water.

- *Cold soak method:* Place legumes in a stockpot and cover with three times their volume of cold water. Let stand for 12 hours in a cool place or refrigerate overnight to avoid fermentation. Drain and rinse.

- *Quick soak method:* Place legumes in a stockpot and cover with three times their volume of cold water. Place over medium-high heat and slowly bring to a full rolling boil. Boil for 2 minutes, then remove from heat. Cover and let stand for 1 hour. Drain and rinse.

How to Cook Dried Legumes

Place soaked legumes in a stockpot and cover with three times their volume of cold water. (Water should be 1 to 2 inches/2.5 to 5 cm above the top of the legumes.) Bring to a boil over high heat. Cover, reduce heat to medium-low and simmer gently until just tender and not mushy. Legumes are done when they can be easily mashed between two fingers and don't taste raw. Drain and use immediately, or let cool, transfer to airtight containers and refrigerate for up to 3 days or freeze for up to 3 months.

Legume Tips

- Change the soaking water two to three times during the cold soak method and always discard the soaking liquid to minimize intestinal gas. Drain and rinse before cooking.

- In general, do not cook different types of dried legumes together, as each variety has a different cooking time.

- Cook legumes thoroughly, because undercooked starch is harder to digest.

- To minimize spill-over when cooking, add 1 tsp (5 mL) vegetable oil to the water.
- Add salt or acidic ingredients such as vinegar and tomatoes toward the end of cooking, as these ingredients prevent beans from becoming tender.
- Give your digestive system a chance to adjust to an increased amount of legumes in your diet. Start with smaller servings and drink plenty of water to aid digestion.
- The complex sugars (oligosaccharides) found in legumes cause gas production. If you're bothered by excessive gas, look for digestive enzymes in pill or liquid form at pharmacies, health food stores or grocery stores.

Dried Legumes Cooking Chart

Cooking times vary depending on the type and age of the legumes. One cup (250 mL) of dried legumes yields 2 to 3 cups (500 to 750 mL) cooked.

Legume	Requires soaking?	Cooking time
Black beans	Yes	60–90 minutes
Black-eyed peas	No	60–90 minutes
Chickpeas (garbanzo beans)	Yes	60–90 minutes
Kidney beans (white or red)	Yes	60–90 minutes
Lentils (green or brown)	No	30–45 minutes
Lentils (red)	No	10–15 minutes
Lima beans (small)	Yes	1 hour
Lima beans (large)	Yes	45–60 minutes
Peas, whole	Yes	90 minutes
Pinto, pink or red beans	Yes	60–90 minutes
Soybeans	Yes	3 hours
Split peas, green or yellow	No	45 minutes
White, navy or Great Northern beans	Yes	45–60 minutes

Storing and Cooking Whole Grains

Whole grains gained prominence when health authorities in both the United States and Canada recommended that at least half of the daily grains we consume should be whole grains. Current scientific evidence indicates that whole grains play an important role in lowering the risk of chronic diseases such as coronary heart disease and cancer, and play a key role in blood glucose management in diabetes and diabetes prevention.

To qualify as a whole-grain product, 100% of the original kernel — all of the bran, germ and endosperm — must be present. To help consumers better identify whole-grain products, the Whole Grains Council initiated an official packaging symbol, called the Whole Grain Stamp, in 2005. In recent years, it has become widespread on many cereal, bread and snack products in the United States and Canada, as well as internationally.

Health experts recommend that we aim for three servings a day of whole grains. The amount of whole grains in a product is stated on all Whole Grain Stamps in two categories: those that contain 16 grams or more of whole-grain ingredients are considered to be one serving; those that contain between 8 and 16 grams are considered to be a half-serving.

How to Store Whole Grains

Whole-grain flours retain their healthful oils and are more susceptible to oxidation, so they need to be stored correctly. Refer to the package directions for storage instructions, and use before the best-before date. If buying in bulk, shop at stores with a high turnover. In general, most whole-grain flours can be stored in the refrigerator for 2 to 3 months, or in the freezer for 6 to 8 months. Store flours and grains in airtight containers so they won't pick up odors from other foods.

Whole grains, such as wheat berries and brown rice, do not oxidize as easily because their oil is sealed into the original grain kernel, so they keep much longer than flours. Most can be stored for several months in a room-temperature cupboard, or for up to a year in the freezer.

The sniff test is the best test of freshness for whole grains and flours. All grains should have a light sweetness or no scent at all. If you detect a moldy or off smell, the grain or flour may be rancid and should be discarded.

The best advice on storing grains and flours: buy what you'll use within 3 months, and label and date them when you purchase them.

How to Cook Whole Grains

In a large saucepan (or a large pot, if preparing a larger batch), combine grain and allotted water (see chart, page 318). Bring to a boil over high heat. Reduce heat to medium-low, cover and simmer for the allotted time, or until done to your liking. Remove from heat.

Grains can vary in cooking time depending on the age of the grain, the variety and the pan used to cook them. If a grain is not as tender as you like, add more water and continue cooking. Or, if the grain is tender before the allotted cooking time has expired and the liquid is not all absorbed, just drain off the excess.

If whole grains stick to the bottom of the pan, turn off the heat, add a very small amount of liquid, cover and let stand for a few minutes. The grain will easily loosen.

Cooked grains can be stored in an airtight container in the refrigerator for up to 3 days (2 days for rice), and take just minutes to warm up, with a little added water or broth, on the stovetop or in the microwave. Use leftovers for cold salads (just toss with chopped vegetables and dressing), or add to soups and stews. Most whole grains, such as wheat berries and brown rice, can also be frozen for up to 3 months.

Whole Grains Cooking Chart

Whole grain (1 cup/250 mL)	Amount of liquid	Cooking time	Cooked yield
Amaranth	2 cups (500 mL)	20–25 minutes	3½ cups (875 mL)
Barley, hulled (pot)	3 cups (750 mL)	45–60 minutes	3½ cups (875 mL)
Buckwheat	2 cups (500 mL)	20 minutes	4 cups (1 L)
Bulgur	2 cups (500 mL)	10–12 minutes	3 cups (750 mL)
Cornmeal (polenta)	4 cups (1 L)	25–30 minutes	2½ cups (625 mL)
Couscous, whole wheat	2 cups (500 mL)	10 minutes (off the heat)	3 cups (750 mL)
Kamut*	4 cups (1 L)	45–60 minutes	3 cups (750 mL)
Millet, hulled	2½ cups (625 mL)	25–35 minutes	4 cups (1 L)
Oats, steel-cut	4 cups (1 L)	20 minutes	4 cups (1 L)
Pasta, whole wheat	6 cups (1.5 L)	8–12 minutes	Depends on size of pasta
Quinoa	2 cups (500 mL)	12–15 minutes	3 cups (750 mL)
Rice, brown	2½ cups (625 mL)	25–45 minutes	3–4 cups (750 mL to 1 L)
Rye berries*	4 cups (1 L)	45–60 minutes	3 cups (750 mL)
Sorghum	4 cups (1 L)	25–40 minutes	3 cups (750 mL)
Spelt berries*	4 cups (1 L)	45–60 minutes	3 cups (750 mL)
Wheat berries*	4 cups (1 L)	45–60 minutes	3 cups (750 mL)
Wild rice	3 cups (750 mL)	45–55 minutes	3½ cups (875 mL)

* Before cooking, soak grains overnight in three times the volume of cold water and leave in a cool place; drain.

Source: The Whole Grains Council, www.wholegrainscouncil.org. Used with permission.

Vegetables

Roasted Asparagus

Makes 4 servings

Roasting brings out the best in many vegetables, including asparagus.

- - - - - - - - - - - - - - - -

Tip

The roasting time will depend on the thickness of the asparagus stalks.

- **Preheat oven to 400°F (200°C)**
- **Rimmed baking sheet or shallow roasting pan**

1 lb	asparagus	500 g
1 tbsp	extra virgin olive oil	15 mL
1 tbsp	balsamic or red wine vinegar	15 mL
	Freshly ground black pepper	

1. Snap off tough asparagus ends and peel any large stalks. Arrange in a single layer on baking sheet. Drizzle with oil and vinegar. Season with pepper.

2. Roast in preheated oven, stirring occasionally, for 14 to 18 minutes or until asparagus is glazed and tender-crisp. Serve immediately.

Nutrition Tip

One of the best reasons to eat vegetables is their high fiber content. Fiber does not raise blood glucose levels as starches and sugars do. When calculating your daily carbs, subtract the grams of fiber from the grams of total carbohydrate to give you the available carbohydrate ("net carbs") that affects your blood glucose level. Aim for 45 to 75 grams of net carbs per meal, based on 1600 calories per day.

Nutrition info per serving

Calories	45
Carbohydrate	3 g
Fiber	1 g
Protein	1 g
Fat	3 g
Saturated fat	0 g
Cholesterol	0 mg
Sodium	9 mg

Food Choices
½ Fat

Steamed Baby Bok Choy

Makes 4 servings

Bok choy is a wonderful-tasting vegetable and has become readily available in most supermarkets year-round. Hot pepper flakes enhance the bok choy's flavor and are a great salt substitute when you're cooking vegetables.

- - - - - - - - - - - - -

Tip

This steaming method can be used for a wide variety of vegetables, from greens, such as kale and Swiss chard, to broccoli, asparagus, sliced carrots, red pepper strips, snow peas, carrots and sliced butternut squash. Adjust the cooking time according to the vegetables — broccoli and carrots, for example, will take slightly longer.

Nutrition info per serving	
Calories	35
Carbohydrate	2 g
Fiber	2 g
Protein	2 g
Fat	2 g
Saturated fat	0 g
Cholesterol	0 mg
Sodium	36 mg
Food Choices	
½ Fat	

1 lb	baby bok choy (about 8)	500 g
2 tsp	peanut or canola oil	10 mL
2	cloves garlic, minced	2
⅛ tsp	hot pepper flakes (or to taste)	0.5 mL
2 tbsp	water	30 mL

1. Cut bok choy lengthwise into halves or quarters (depending on size).

2. In a wok or large nonstick skillet, heat oil over medium-high heat. Sir-fry garlic and hot pepper flakes for 15 seconds. Add bok choy and stir-fry for 30 seconds.

3. Add water, cover and steam for 1 to 2 minutes or until bok choy is bright green and still crisp. Serve immediately.

Nutrition Tip

The glycemic index (GI) measures how fast and how high blood glucose rises after we eat. Low- or medium-GI foods raise blood glucose slowly; whereas high-GI foods cause glucose levels to spike and contribute to health problems. Most vegetables, such as leafy greens, bok choy, eggplant, zucchini, bell peppers and tomatoes are low-GI, so enjoy them often.

Orange Broccoli with Red Pepper

This quick stir-fry with the lively taste of orange makes a great side dish to serve with roast chicken, beef or pork.

- - - - - - - - - - - - -

Variation

Any combination of vegetables can be used in this stir-fry, including bell peppers, mushrooms, snow peas, cauliflower, fennel strips, blanched green beans and sliced carrots.

1 tsp	grated orange zest	5 mL
1/4 cup	freshly squeezed orange juice	60 mL
1/2 tsp	cornstarch	2 mL
2 tsp	extra virgin olive oil	10 mL
1/4 cup	minced shallots	60 mL
4 cups	small broccoli florets	1 L
1	red bell pepper, cut into thin 2-inch (5 cm) long strips	1
1/8 tsp	salt	0.5 mL
	Freshly ground black pepper	

1. In a bowl, stir together orange juice and cornstarch until smooth. Set aside.

2. In a large nonstick skillet, heat oil over medium-high heat. Add shallots and cook, stirring, for 20 seconds. Add broccoli and red pepper; cook, stirring, for 1 minute.

3. Stir in orange juice mixture, cover and steam for 1 to 2 minutes or until vegetables are tender-crisp. Sprinkle with orange zest and season with salt and pepper. Serve immediately.

Nutrition info per 1 cup (250 mL)

Calories	76
Carbohydrate	12 g
Fiber	3 g
Protein	3 g
Fat	3 g
Saturated fat	0 g
Cholesterol	0 mg
Sodium	113 mg

Food Choices
1/2 Fat

Braised Brussels Sprouts

Brussels sprouts, with their delicate, nutty flavor, take on a pleasant sweetness in this easy-to-prepare recipe that can be doubled to serve a crowd.

- - - - - - - - - - - - - - -

Tips

The sprouts can be blanched up to 1 day ahead. Chill in ice water, then drain well and wrap in a clean, dry kitchen towel to absorb moisture. Refrigerate in an airtight container.

Like other vegetables in the cabbage family, the key is not to overcook Brussels sprouts. Serve them when they are tender-crisp and bright green.

When purchasing broth, be sure to check the sodium content and choose one with 140 mg or less per 1 cup (250 mL).

Nutrition info per ¾ cup (175 mL)	
Calories	71
Carbohydrate	10 g
Fiber	4 g
Protein	3 g
Fat	3 g
Saturated fat	1 g
Cholesterol	1 mg
Sodium	30 mg
Food Choices ½ Fat	

1 lb	Brussels sprouts, trimmed and halved	500 g
2 tbsp	Low-Sodium Chicken Stock (page 204) or low-sodium or no-salt-added ready-to-use chicken broth	30 mL
1 tsp	granulated sugar	5 mL
4 tsp	red wine vinegar	20 mL
2 tsp	extra virgin olive oil	10 mL
1	clove garlic, minced	1
	Freshly ground black pepper	

1. In a saucepan of boiling water, blanch Brussels sprouts for 2 minutes or until bright green and crisp. Drain well.

2. In a bowl, stir together broth, sugar and vinegar. Set aside.

3. In a large nonstick skillet, heat oil over medium-high heat. Stir-fry garlic for 20 seconds or until fragrant. Add Brussels sprouts and stir-fry for 2 minutes or until lightly browned.

4. Stir in broth mixture, reduce heat to medium and cook, stirring often, for 1 to 2 minutes or until sprouts are barely tender and are still bright green. Season to taste with pepper. Serve immediately.

Sweet and Spicy Cabbage

This easy stir-fry gives cabbage a sweet-sour-spicy flavor. As an added bonus, light cooking helps retain cabbage's many valuable vitamins and minerals.

- - - - - - - - - - - - - - -

Tip

Overcooking cabbage (along with other members of the cruciferous family, such as Brussels sprouts, kohlrabi and bok choy) releases sulfur compounds with a pungent odor. To avoid this odor and preserve the vegetable's nutrients, cook just long enough to brighten the color of the vegetable while retaining its crisp texture.

1	large pear or apple	1
1 tbsp	canola oil	15 mL
½	red onion, cut into thin wedges	½
¼ tsp	hot pepper flakes (or to taste)	1 mL
6 cups	finely shredded savoy or napa cabbage	1.5 L
2 tbsp	rice vinegar	30 mL
1 tbsp	liquid honey	15 mL
⅛ tsp	salt	0.5 mL

1. Cut pear into quarters and core (it's not necessary to peel it). Thinly slice quarters, then cut slices in half crosswise.

2. In a large nonstick skillet, heat oil over medium-high heat. Stir-fry pear, onion and hot pepper flakes for 1 minute. Add cabbage and stir-fry for about 1 minute or until wilted.

3. Stir in vinegar and honey; stir-fry for 30 seconds. Season with salt. Serve immediately.

Variation

Substitute regular cabbage, collard greens or kale for the savoy cabbage. Remove the tough stems and center ribs and finely shred the leaves. When adding the greens at the end of step 2, reduce the heat to medium and stir-fry for 3 to 4 minutes or until tender.

Nutrition info per 1 cup (250 mL)

Calories	112
Carbohydrate	20 g
Fiber	5 g
Protein	3 g
Fat	4 g
Saturated fat	0 g
Cholesterol	0 mg
Sodium	103 mg

Food Choices
1 Carbohydrate
1 Fat

Parsley Baby Carrots

Baby carrots make a terrific side dish to accompany a pot roast or roast chicken.

Tips

The carrots can be blanched up to 1 day ahead. Chill in ice water, then drain well and refrigerate in an airtight container.

You can prepare this dish earlier in the day, but do not add the parsley. Cover and refrigerate. Reheat carrots on the stovetop or in the microwave until piping hot. Sprinkle with parsley before serving.

If doubling the recipe, glaze the carrots in a large nonstick skillet to evaporate the broth quickly.

Nutrition info per ¾ cup (175 mL)	
Calories	80
Carbohydrate	12 g
Fiber	2 g
Protein	1 g
Fat	4 g
Saturated fat	2 g
Cholesterol	8 mg
Sodium	68 mg

Food Choices
½ Fat
1 Extra

1 lb	baby carrots	500 g
3 tbsp	Low-Sodium Chicken or Vegetable Stock (page 204 or 205) or low-sodium or no-salt-added ready-to-use chicken or vegetable broth	45 mL
2 tsp	packed brown sugar	10 mL
2 tsp	freshly squeezed lemon juice	10 mL
1 tsp	butter or soft margarine	5 mL
	Freshly ground black pepper	
2 tbsp	finely chopped fresh parsley or chives, or a combination	30 mL

1. In a medium saucepan of boiling water, blanch carrots for 5 to 7 minutes (start timing when water returns to a boil) or until just tender-crisp. Drain and return to saucepan.

2. Stir in broth, brown sugar, lemon juice and butter. Season to taste with pepper. Cook over medium heat, stirring often, for 3 to 5 minutes or until liquid has evaporated and carrots are nicely glazed. Sprinkle with parsley.

Variation

Replace the baby carrots with a combination of carrot and rutabaga strips.

Edamame and Corn Sauté

This colorful side dish is reminiscent of succotash and goes well with fish and chicken.

- - - - - - - - - - - - - -

Tips

Shelled edamame (green soybeans) are tasty and versatile. They can be added to stir-fries, salads, rice and grain dishes, or puréed into a spread (like hummus).

To cut corn kernels from cobs, stand the ears on end and cut straight down, using a small, sharp knife.

Fresh corn is preferred in this dish, but frozen kernels can be substituted. Add frozen corn in step 1, along with the edamame.

2 cups	frozen shelled edamame or baby lima beans	500 mL
1 tbsp	extra virgin olive oil	15 mL
4	green onions, sliced	4
1	clove garlic, minced	1
1	zucchini, diced	1
2 cups	fresh corn kernels	500 mL
2	ripe tomatoes, seeded and diced	2
¼ tsp	salt	1 mL
Pinch	granulated sugar	Pinch
	Freshly ground black pepper	
2 tbsp	chopped fresh basil, parsley or cilantro	30 mL

1. In a medium saucepan of boiling water, cook edamame for 1 minute. Drain.

2. In a large nonstick skillet, heat oil over medium-high heat. Add edamame, green onions, garlic, zucchini and corn; cook, stirring often, for 4 minutes.

3. Stir in tomatoes, salt, sugar and pepper to taste. Cook, stirring often, for 2 to 3 minutes or until tomatoes are softened and sauce-like. Sprinkle with basil.

Nutrition Tip

Most people don't get enough potassium in their diet, and this important nutrient can offer protection from high blood pressure and stroke. Vegetables are a source of potassium — another good reason to include several servings of vegetables in your diet each day.

Nutrition info per 1 cup (250 mL)

Calories	183
Carbohydrate	26 g
Fiber	6 g
Protein	9 g
Fat	7 g
Saturated fat	1 g
Cholesterol	0 mg
Sodium	161 mg

Food Choices
1 Carbohydrate
1 Meat & Alternatives
½ Fat

Steamed Sugar Snap Peas with Ginger

Here's a quick stir-fry with ginger and shallots that nicely complements the sweetness of emerald green sugar snap peas.

Tips

Keep fresh ginger on hand in your refrigerator and mince or grate it to use in a variety of dishes. Thanks to its vibrant taste, you'll find you can do away with salt in many dishes.

Snow peas can be prepared the same way. As they cook so quickly, reduce the steaming time to 1 minute or until bright green and crisp.

2 tsp	peanut or canola oil	10 mL
1/4 cup	minced shallots	60 mL
2 tsp	minced gingerroot	10 mL
1 lb	sugar snap peas, strings removed	500 g
2 tbsp	water	30 mL

1. In a wok or large nonstick skillet, heat oil over medium-high heat. Stir-fry shallots and ginger for 1 minute.

2. Add peas and water; cover and steam for 3 minutes or until peas are just tender-crisp. Serve immediately.

Nutrition info per 3/4 cup (175 mL)	
Calories	71
Carbohydrate	9 g
Fiber	3 g
Protein	4 g
Fat	3 g
Saturated fat	0 g
Cholesterol	0 mg
Sodium	5 mg

Food Choices
1/2 Fat

Rapini with Toasted Garlic Crumbs

Rapini is a nutritious vegetable that resembles a cross between broccoli and mustard greens. It has a wonderfully assertive taste and texture.

Tips

Other leafy greens, such as kale, mustard greens and dandelion leaves, can be cooked the same way.

The garlicky bread crumb topping also makes a great flavor enhancer for other steamed vegetables.

Depending on the season, rapini can have a more strongly bitter flavor. To eliminate some of its bitterness, blanch it in boiling water for 1 minute, drain and use as directed in recipe.

Nutrition info per serving	
Calories	90
Carbohydrate	6 g
Fiber	3 g
Protein	5 g
Fat	5 g
Saturated fat	1 g
Cholesterol	0 mg
Sodium	82 mg
Food Choices 1 Fat	

4 tsp	extra virgin olive oil, divided	20 mL
1/4 cup	fresh whole-grain bread crumbs	60 mL
3	cloves garlic, minced, divided	3
1	bunch rapini (about 1 1/4 lbs/625 g), tough stalks removed	1
1/4 tsp	hot pepper flakes (or to taste)	1 mL
3 tbsp	water	45 mL

1. In a large nonstick skillet, heat half the oil over medium heat. Add bread crumbs and half the garlic; cook, stirring, for 4 minutes, or until bread crumbs are nicely toasted and crisp. Transfer to a bowl. Wipe out skillet.

2. Add the remaining oil to the skillet and increase heat to medium-high. Add rapini, the remaining garlic and hot pepper flakes; cook, stirring often, for 2 minutes.

3. Add water, reduce heat to medium, cover and steam rapini for 5 to 7 minutes or until just tender.

4. Transfer rapini to a serving bowl and sprinkle with crumb mixture. Serve immediately.

How to Prepare Rapini

To prepare rapini, wash it well in cold water. Trim the tough stalk ends. Both the florets and leafy stems are used, but the thicker stalks may require peeling for faster cooking. Cook rapini as you would broccoli, but for less time. Be careful not to overcook, as rapini can quickly become soft and mushy.

Cherry Tomato and Zucchini Sauté

This colorful vegetable medley is a great summer side dish when markets are overflowing with squash and sweet tomatoes.

- - - - - - - - - - - - - -

Tip

To toast pine nuts, place nuts in a dry skillet over medium heat and cook, stirring, for 3 to 4 minutes or until fragrant and toasted. Watch carefully, as pine nuts burn easily.

2 tsp	extra virgin olive oil	10 mL
3	small zucchini, halved lengthwise and thinly sliced	3
2	green onions, sliced	2
2 cups	cherry tomatoes, halved	500 mL
$\frac{1}{2}$ tsp	ground cumin (optional)	2 mL
2 tsp	balsamic vinegar	10 mL
	Freshly ground black pepper	
2 tbsp	chopped fresh mint or basil	30 mL
2 tbsp	lightly toasted pine nuts (see tip, at left)	30 mL

1. In a large nonstick skillet, heat oil over medium-high heat. Add zucchini and cook, stirring, for 1 minute.

2. Add green onions, tomatoes, cumin (if using) and vinegar; cook, stirring, for 1 to 2 minutes or until zucchini is tender-crisp and tomatoes are heated through. Season to taste with pepper. Sprinkle with mint and pine nuts. Serve immediately.

Nutrition info per 1¼ cups (300 mL)	
Calories	50
Carbohydrate	7 g
Fiber	3 g
Protein	1 g
Fat	2 g
Saturated fat	0 g
Cholesterol	0 mg
Sodium	12 mg
Food Choices	
½ Fat	

Steamed Vegetables with Toasted Almonds

Put your steamer basket to good use when preparing vegetables, and use this recipe as a guideline. The recipe can be easily doubled when you're serving a crowd.

Tip

To toast sliced almonds, place in a small nonstick skillet over medium heat and cook, stirring often, for 4 to 5 minutes or until golden and fragrant. Transfer to a bowl and let cool.

- **Steamer basket**

2 cups	cauliflower florets	500 mL
2 cups	broccoli florets	500 mL
½	red bell pepper, chopped	½
½	yellow or orange bell pepper, chopped	½
2 tsp	butter	10 mL
1	clove garlic, minced	1
2 tsp	freshly squeezed lemon juice	10 mL
3 tbsp	toasted sliced almonds	45 mL
1 tbsp	chopped fresh parsley	15 mL

1. Pour enough water into a large saucepan to come 1 inch (2.5 cm) up the side. Place steamer basket in pan, cover and bring to a boil over medium-high heat. Add cauliflower, broccoli, red pepper and yellow pepper; cover and steam for 5 to 7 minutes or until tender-crisp. Drain and transfer to a serving bowl.

2. Meanwhile, in a small saucepan, melt butter over medium heat, swirling pan occasionally, until butter turns a rich golden color (do not overcook or butter will burn.) Add garlic and cook, stirring, for 20 seconds or until fragrant. Stir in lemon juice.

3. Drizzle butter mixture over vegetables and sprinkle with almonds and parsley. Serve immediately.

Nutrition info per 1 cup (250 mL)

Calories	83
Carbohydrate	9 g
Fiber	3 g
Protein	4 g
Fat	5 g
Saturated fat	1 g
Cholesterol	5 mg
Sodium	42 mg

Food Choices
1 Fat

Variation

Replace the cauliflower and broccoli with other vegetables you may have on hand, such as baby carrots, green beans, snap peas and zucchini. Estimate 1 cup (250 mL) raw vegetables per serving. Steam longer-cooking and denser vegetables, such as baby carrots, for 5 to 7 minutes or until almost fork-tender, then add the bell peppers and any shorter-cooking vegetables, such as snap peas, and steam for 3 to 5 minutes or until tender-crisp.

Ratatouille

Makes 6 cups (1.5 L)

This versatile French vegetable stew can be served as a side dish, as a pasta sauce, as a topping for baked fish or as a pizza topping (see page 195).

– – – – – – – – – – – – – – – –

Tips

To get the amount of tomatoes needed for this recipe, drain a 28-oz (796 mL) can, reserving the juice. Chop tomatoes and measure. Refrigerate or freeze the remaining tomatoes and juice for making soups and stews.

Ratatouille can be stored in an airtight container in the refrigerator for up to 5 days, or in the freezer for up to 2 months.

2 tbsp	extra virgin olive oil	30 mL
1	large onion, chopped	1
4	cloves garlic, finely chopped	4
1 tsp	dried oregano or thyme	5 mL
¼ tsp	hot pepper flakes	1 mL
1	eggplant (about 1 lb/500 g), diced	1
2	bell peppers (assorted colors), finely chopped	2
2	small zucchini (about 12 oz/375 g), diced	2
1¼ cups	drained no-salt-added canned tomatoes (see tip, at left), chopped	300 mL
¼ cup	chopped fresh parsley	60 mL
1 tbsp	balsamic vinegar	15 mL

1. In a large saucepan, heat oil over medium-high heat. Add onion, garlic, oregano and hot pepper flakes; cook, stirring often, for 2 minutes or until softened.

2. Stir in eggplant and cook, stirring often, for 5 minutes.

3. Stir in bell peppers, zucchini and tomatoes. Reduce heat to medium-low, cover and simmer, stirring occasionally, for about 20 minutes or until vegetables are tender. Remove from heat and stir in parsley and vinegar.

Nutrition Tip

When buying canned tomatoes, always check the Nutrition Facts table, as the amount of salt added varies by brand. One 28-oz (796 mL) can might contain as much as ½ tsp (2 mL) salt (1200 milligrams of sodium or 350 milligrams per cup/250 mL), whereas tomatoes canned without salt have less than 20 milligrams of sodium per cup (250 mL). Choose lower-sodium brands whenever possible.

Nutrition info per 1 cup (250 mL)	
Calories	97
Carbohydrate	14 g
Fiber	3 g
Protein	2 g
Fat	5 g
Saturated fat	1 g
Cholesterol	0 mg
Sodium	12 mg

Food Choices
1 Fat

Roasted Root Vegetables with Rosemary

Makes 4 servings

Oven-roasting sweetens and concentrates the flavor of sturdy root vegetables — you'll be amazed by the results. For holiday meals, double the recipe and roast vegetables earlier in the day. Reheat in a covered casserole in the oven or microwave until piping hot.

Tips

Roast other vegetables, such as winter squash, beets and cauliflower, in the same manner.

If you don't have a heavy rimmed baking sheet, stack 2 lighter-weight baking sheets together for more even heat distribution.

Nutrition info per 1 cup (250 mL)	
Calories	150
Carbohydrate	26 g
Fiber	5 g
Protein	3 g
Fat	5 g
Saturated fat	1 g
Cholesterol	0 mg
Sodium	57 mg

Food Choices
1 Carbohydrate
1 Fat

- **Preheat oven to 400°F (200°C)**
- **Heavy rimmed baking sheet or large shallow roasting pan, greased**

4	small carrots (about 12 oz/375 g)	4
2	parsnips (about 10 oz/300 g)	2
2	white turnips or $\frac{1}{2}$ small rutabaga (about 10 oz/300 g)	2
1	red onion, cut into wedges	1
8	cloves garlic (unpeeled)	8
2 tsp	chopped fresh rosemary or thyme	10 mL
$\frac{1}{4}$ tsp	freshly ground black pepper	1 mL
$\frac{1}{4}$ cup	Low-Sodium Chicken or Vegetable Stock (page 204 or 205) or low-sodium or no-salt-added ready-to-use chicken or vegetable broth	60 mL
4 tsp	extra virgin olive oil	20 mL
1 tbsp	red wine vinegar or balsamic vinegar	15 mL
2 tsp	liquid honey	10 mL
2 tbsp	chopped fresh parsley	30 mL

1. Peel carrots, parsnips and turnips, and cut into $2\frac{1}{2}$- by $\frac{1}{2}$-inch (6 by 1 cm) strips. (You should have 8 cups/2 L vegetables.) Arrange on baking sheet, along with onion wedges and garlic cloves. Sprinkle with rosemary and season with pepper.

Tips

If doubling the recipe, spread vegetables on 2 baking sheets and switch the positions of the sheets on the oven racks halfway through roasting.

When purchasing broth, be sure to check the sodium content and choose one with 140 mg or less per 1 cup (250 mL).

2. In a small bowl, combine broth, oil, vinegar and honey. Drizzle over vegetables and toss to coat. Spread out in an even layer.

3. Roast in preheated oven for 35 to 40 minutes, stirring occasionally, until vegetables are tender and lightly colored. Serve sprinkled with parsley.

Nutrition Tip

Frozen vegetables, or those canned with no added salt, are a healthier option than regular canned vegetables, which contain significant amounts of sodium.

Roasted Butternut Squash with Onion and Sage

Roasting brings out the best in winter squash. Most supermarkets now offer convenient packages of peeled, cubed ready-to-cook butternut squash in the produce department, making this fall dish a breeze to whip together.

Tip

Vegetable oil cooking sprays are sold in aerosol cans and pump sprays at supermarkets. We suggest buying a spray pump mister, available at specialty kitchen shops. This non-aerosol dispenser can be filled with any kind of oil. We recommend using canola oil, as it's an all-purpose oil for both baking and roasting.

Nutrition info per ½ cup (125 mL)	
Calories	91
Carbohydrate	18 g
Fiber	3 g
Protein	2 g
Fat	2 g
Saturated fat	0 g
Cholesterol	0 mg
Sodium	80 mg

Food Choices
½ Carbohydrate
½ Fat

- Preheat oven to 375°F (190°C)
- 11- by 7-inch (28 by 18 cm) glass baking dish, sprayed with vegetable oil cooking spray

4 cups	cubed butternut squash (about 1 lb/500 g, cut into ¾-inch/2 cm cubes)	1 L
1	small onion, cut into thin wedges	1
1 tbsp	finely chopped fresh sage	15 mL
⅛ tsp	salt	0.5 mL
	Freshly ground black pepper	
2 tsp	extra virgin olive oil	10 mL

1. In baking dish, combine squash, onion, sage, salt and pepper to taste. Drizzle with oil and toss to coat. Spread out in an even layer.

2. Roast in preheated oven for 30 to 35 minutes, stirring occasionally, until squash is just tender when pierced with a fork.

Variation

Roasted Butternut Squash with Sweet Spices: Replace the sage with ¼ tsp (1 mL) each ground cinnamon and ground cumin.

Creamy Mashed Potatoes with Cauliflower

At holiday celebrations, if you're craving a mound of creamy mashed potatoes with the roast beef or turkey, you won't feel deprived when you indulge in this delicious side dish that delivers all of the same great taste and appeal of traditional mashed potatoes, but with the added bonus of cauliflower, a powerful cancer-fighting vegetable.

- - - - - - - - - - - - - - - -

Tip

Do not use a food processor to mash the potatoes and cauliflower together, or you'll end up with a gooey mixture.

Nutrition info per 1 cup (250 mL)

Calories	123
Carbohydrate	20 g
Fiber	3 g
Protein	4 g
Fat	4 g
Saturated fat	2 g
Cholesterol	8 mg
Sodium	195 mg

Food Choices
1 Carbohydrate
½ Fat

- **Steamer basket**
- **Food processor**

5 cups	cauliflower florets (about 1 lb/500 g)	1.25 L
4	small russet potatoes, peeled and quartered (about 1 lb/500 g)	4
1 tbsp	butter or soft margarine	15 mL
¼ cup	warm milk (approx.)	60 mL
¼ tsp	salt	1 mL
¼ tsp	freshly grated nutmeg	1 mL

1. Pour enough water into a large saucepan to come 1 inch (2.5 cm) up the side. Place steamer basket in pan, cover and bring to a boil over medium-high heat. Add cauliflower; cover and steam for 10 to 12 minutes or until very tender. Drain well.

2. Transfer cauliflower to food processor and purée. Set aside.

3. Add another 1 inch (2.5 cm) of water to the saucepan. Place steamer basket in pan, cover and bring to a boil over medium-high heat. Add potatoes; cover and steam for 20 to 25 minutes or until fork-tender. Drain well and return to saucepan. Place over low heat and dry for 1 minute.

4. Using a potato masher or an electric hand mixer on low speed, mash potatoes until very smooth. Mash in cauliflower purée, butter and enough of the milk to make a smooth mixture. Season with salt and nutmeg.

5. Return pan to medium-low heat and reheat mash, stirring often, until piping hot.

Fork-Mashed New Potatoes with Fresh Herbs

Waxy new potatoes are low on the glycemic index compared to baking potatoes such as russets. In this novel preparation, the potatoes are coarsely mashed and flavored with fresh herbs.

- - - - - - - - - - - - - - - -

Tip

It is not necessary to peel the potatoes. With the peel, you get the added bonus of fiber and other essential nutrients, such as vitamin C, vitamin B and iron.

1 lb	small new potatoes	500 g
	Cold water	
1 tbsp	chopped fresh basil or parsley	15 mL
1 tbsp	chopped fresh chives	15 mL
¼ tsp	salt	1 mL
	Freshly ground black pepper	
2 tbsp	light sour cream	30 mL
½ tsp	Dijon mustard	2 mL

1. Place potatoes in a medium saucepan and add enough cold water to cover. Bring to a boil over high heat. Reduce heat to medium, cover and gently boil for 20 minutes or until potatoes are tender. Drain and cut into quarters.

2. Place potatoes in a shallow bowl and add basil, chives, salt, pepper to taste, sour cream and mustard. Using a fork, roughly mash until potatoes are somewhat smooth but some lumps remain. Serve immediately.

Nutrition Tip

Potatoes can be part of a healthy meal so long as you stick to a reasonable portion size and add a minimum of fat, especially saturated fat from butter, sour cream or cheese. If you enjoy eating potatoes, choose new potatoes more often, as they have a low to medium glycemic index (versus high-GI storage potatoes, such as russets, used for mashing and baking). Choosing low GI-foods is an effective way to reduce your blood glucose and help prevent and manage diabetes.

Nutrition info per ½ cup (125 mL)	
Calories	92
Carbohydrate	20 g
Fiber	2 g
Protein	2 g
Fat	1 g
Saturated fat	0 g
Cholesterol	2 mg
Sodium	175 mg

Food Choices
1 Carbohydrate

Sweet Potato Oven Fries

Makes 6 servings

The key to great oven fries is to cut sweet potatoes into thin strips and roast them in a single layer at a high temperature. Thickly cut fries steam instead of crisping properly.

- - - - - - - - - - - - - - - -

Variation

Instead of preparing the spice blend, sprinkle the sweet potatoes with 2 tsp (10 mL) chopped fresh rosemary or 1 tsp (5 mL) dried crumbled rosemary, along with the salt and pepper.

- **Preheat oven to 425°F (220°C), with rack placed in upper third**
- **Large rimmed baking sheet, lined with parchment paper or foil**

1 tsp	packed brown sugar	5 mL
½ tsp	chili powder	2 mL
¼ tsp	ground cumin	1 mL
¼ tsp	paprika	1 mL
¼ tsp	salt	1 mL
¼ tsp	freshly ground pepper	1 mL
2	sweet potatoes (about 1½ lbs/750 g)	2
2 tbsp	extra virgin olive oil	30 mL

1. In a small bowl, combine brown sugar, chili powder, cumin, paprika, salt and pepper,

2. Peel sweet potatoes and cut lengthwise into ½-inch (1 cm) slices. Cut slices into ½-inch (1 cm) thick strips. Place in a bowl. Drizzle with oil and sprinkle with spice mixture. Toss to coat evenly. Arrange in a single layer on prepared baking sheet.

3. Roast in preheated oven for 30 to 35 minutes, turning fries occasionally with a spatula, until golden and edges are crisp. Serve immediately.

Nutrition info per serving

Calories	130
Carbohydrate	21 g
Fiber	3 g
Protein	2 g
Fat	5 g
Saturated fat	1 g
Cholesterol	0 mg
Sodium	131 mg

Food Choices
1 Carbohydrate
1 Fat

Parmesan Two-Potato Bake

Sweet potatoes team with regular potatoes in this pleasing dish, ideal with roast chicken or pork.

- - - - - - - - - - - - - - -

Tips

Vegetable oil cooking spray can be purchased in aerosol cans and pump sprays at supermarkets. A recommended alternative is to buy a spray pump mister, available at specialty kitchen shops. This easy-to-use tool is a non-aerosol dispenser you fill with any kind of oil you have in your kitchen. We recommend using canola oil, as it's an all-purpose oil for both baking and roasting.

When purchasing broth, be sure to check the sodium content and choose one with 140 mg or less per 1 cup (250 mL).

Nutrition info per serving

Calories	91
Carbohydrate	18 g
Fiber	2 g
Protein	3 g
Fat	1 g
Saturated fat	1 g
Cholesterol	3 mg
Sodium	82 mg

Food Choices
1 Carbohydrate

- **Preheat oven to 375°F (190°C)**
- **13- by 9-inch (33 by 23 cm) glass baking dish, sprayed generously with vegetable oil cooking spray**

1 lb	russet potatoes (3 medium), peeled and thinly sliced	500 g
1 lb	sweet potatoes (2 small), peeled and thinly sliced	500 g
2	cloves garlic, minced	2
1 tsp	chopped fresh thyme or rosemary	5 mL
¼ tsp	freshly ground black pepper	1 mL
1 cup	Low-Sodium Chicken or Vegetable Stock (page 204 or 205) or low-sodium or no-salt-added ready-to-use chicken or vegetable broth	250 mL
¼ cup	freshly grated Parmesan cheese	60 mL

1. In prepared baking dish, arrange potatoes and sweet potato in alternating layers.

2. In a glass measuring cup, combine garlic, thyme, pepper and stock; pour over potatoes. Sprinkle with Parmesan.

3. Bake in preheated oven for 50 to 55 minutes or until potatoes are tender and top is golden brown.

Nutrition Tip

Use half or all sweet potatoes instead of russet potatoes in your favorite recipes. Russet potatoes have a high glycemic index, meaning the carbohydrate quickly converts to sugar in the body and can spike blood glucose levels. Sweet potatoes have a lower glycemic index and release glucose more slowly into the bloodstream.

Breads, Muffins and Cookies

Banana Bran Bread

Makes 1 loaf (14 slices)

Everyone has a favorite recipe for banana bread in their files. Here's an easy-to-assemble version that relies on banana, honey and yogurt to keep the bread moist for several days.

- - - - - - - - - - - - - - -

Tip

Have leftover ripe bananas on your counter but no time to bake? Simply freeze whole bananas in their peel. (To use, let partially thaw at room temperature, then peel.) Alternatively, peel and mash bananas, pack into containers and freeze for up to 2 months. Thaw at room temperature. Frozen banana purée may darken slightly, but this will not affect the delicious baked results.

- **Preheat oven to 325°F (160°C)**
- **9- by 5-inch (23 by 12.5 cm) metal loaf pan, sprayed with vegetable oil cooking spray and bottom lined with parchment paper**

1½ cups	whole wheat flour	375 mL
¾ cup	natural wheat bran	175 mL
2 tsp	ground cinnamon	10 mL
1 tsp	baking soda	5 mL
½ tsp	baking powder	2 mL
1	large egg	1
1 cup	mashed ripe bananas (about 3)	250 mL
½ cup	liquid honey	125 mL
½ cup	nonfat plain yogurt	125 mL
3 tbsp	canola oil	45 mL
1 tsp	grated orange zest	5 mL

1. In a medium bowl, stir together flour, wheat bran, cinnamon, baking soda and baking powder.

2. In a large bowl, whisk egg. Whisk in bananas, honey, yogurt, oil and orange zest.

3. Stir egg mixture into flour mixture until just combined. Spoon batter into prepared loaf pan.

4. Bake in preheated oven for 50 to 55 minutes or until a tester inserted in the center comes out clean. Let cool in pan on a wire rack for 15 minutes. Run a knife around edges of pan, turn loaf out onto rack and let cool completely.

Nutrition info per slice

Calories	137
Carbohydrate	26 g
Fiber	3 g
Protein	3 g
Fat	4 g
Saturated fat	0 g
Cholesterol	13 mg
Sodium	113 mg

Food Choices
1½ Carbohydrate
½ Fat

Nutrition Tip

Cinnamon adds a wonderful flavor boost to recipes, and it also contains several beneficial nutrients, including polyphenols, a potent antioxidant. Although there has been a great deal of media attention about the potential benefits of using cinnamon to help regulate blood sugar levels in people with type 2 diabetes, more research is needed.

Orange Pumpkin Loaf

Makes 1 loaf (16 slices)

This bread is much easier to bake than pumpkin pie, but still loaded with all the spice-scented flavors we love.

Tip

Like all orange vegetables, pumpkin is very high in antioxidant carotenoids. One half-cup (125 mL) of canned pumpkin contains 4 grams of fiber and is an excellent source of vitamin K and a good source of vitamin E.

- **Preheat oven to 350°F (180°C)**
- **9- by 5-inch (23 by 12.5 cm) metal loaf pan, sprayed with vegetable oil cooking spray, bottom lined with parchment paper**

1¾ cups	whole wheat flour	425 mL
½ cup	natural wheat bran	125 mL
2 tsp	baking powder	10 mL
½ tsp	baking soda	2 mL
2 tsp	ground cinnamon	10 mL
¼ tsp	ground cloves	1 mL
¼ tsp	ground allspice	1 mL
2	large eggs	2
½ cup	packed brown sugar	125 mL
1 cup	homemade thick pumpkin or squash purée (see box, page 219) or canned pumpkin purée (not pie filling)	250 mL
2 tsp	grated orange zest	10 mL
½ cup	freshly squeezed orange juice	125 mL
¼ cup	canola oil	60 mL
2 tbsp	raw green pumpkin seeds (pepitas)	30 mL

1. In a large bowl, stir together flour, wheat bran, baking powder, baking soda, cinnamon, cloves and allspice.

2. In a medium bowl, whisk eggs. Whisk in brown sugar, pumpkin, orange zest, orange juice and oil.

3. Stir egg mixture into flour mixture until just combined. Spoon batter into prepared loaf pan and sprinkle top with pumpkin seeds.

4. Bake in preheated oven for 50 to 55 minutes or until a tester inserted in the center comes out clean. Let cool in pan on a wire rack for 15 minutes. Run a knife around edges of pan, turn loaf out onto rack and let cool completely.

Nutrition info per slice	
Calories	130
Carbohydrate	20 g
Fiber	3 g
Protein	3 g
Fat	5 g
Saturated fat	1 g
Cholesterol	23 mg
Sodium	90 mg

Food Choices
1 Carbohydrate
1 Fat

Whole-Grain Buttermilk Biscuits

Light and flaky, these biscuits are perfect accompaniments to soups or stews. They also make a great base for shortcakes: spread them with nonfat Greek yogurt and juicy sliced strawberries.

Tip

To make ahead, place biscuits in sealable plastic freezer bag and freeze for up to 1 month. Thaw at room temperature. Place on a plate lined with paper towels and microwave on Medium (50%) until warmed through.

- Preheat oven to 400°F (200°C)
- 2½-inch (6 cm) round cookie cutter
- Baking sheet, lined with parchment paper

1½ cups	whole wheat flour, divided	375 mL
½ cup	5- or 7-grain cereal mix or large-flake (old-fashioned) rolled oats	125 mL
2 tbsp	granulated sugar	30 mL
1½ tsp	baking powder	7 mL
½ tsp	baking soda	2 mL
¼ tsp	salt	1 mL
¾ cup	well-shaken buttermilk	175 mL
2 tbsp	butter or soft margarine, melted	30 mL

Topping

1 tbsp	well-shaken buttermilk or low-fat (1%) milk	15 mL
2 tbsp	5- or 7-grain cereal mix or large-flake (old-fashioned) rolled oats	30 mL

1. In a large bowl, stir together 1⅓ cups (325 mL) of the flour, cereal mix, sugar, baking powder, baking soda and salt. Make a well in the center and add buttermilk and butter to the well. Stir to make a soft, slightly sticky dough.

2. Sprinkle a cutting board with the remaining flour. Turn dough out onto board and, with floured hands, gently knead three or four times, adding more flour if required to prevent dough from sticking to board. Pat dough out to ¾-inch (2 cm) thickness. Dip cookie cutter in flour, then cut out rounds of dough and place 2 inches (5 cm) apart on prepared baking sheet. Dust board with additional flour, if necessary to prevent sticking, gather dough scraps into a ball and flatten. Continue cutting dough into rounds.

Nutrition info per biscuit	
Calories	125
Carbohydrate	21 g
Fiber	3 g
Protein	4 g
Fat	3 g
Saturated fat	2 g
Cholesterol	7 mg
Sodium	212 mg

Food Choices
1 Carbohydrate
½ Fat

Tip

Today's cultured buttermilk is slightly thick and rich and is low in fat, so it is ideal to use in baking. Because of its acidity, it produces tender baked results when combined with leavening ingredients. If you don't have buttermilk on hand, sour milk can be substituted. For this recipe, add 2 tsp (10 mL) lemon juice or white vinegar to a measuring cup and pour in enough low-fat (1%) milk to measure ¾ cup (175 mL). Let stand for 2 minutes, and the sour milk will slightly curdle and thicken.

3. *Topping:* Brush tops of rounds with buttermilk and sprinkle with cereal mix.

4. Bake in preheated oven for 15 to 18 minutes or until golden. Transfer biscuits to a wire rack. Best served warm from the oven.

Baking Tips

- Store whole grains such as flours, bran and wheat germ in airtight containers in a cool, dark place. Refrigerate or freeze for longer storage, to prevent rancidity.
- Store nuts in an airtight container and refrigerate or freeze to keep them fresh.
- To measure dry ingredients correctly, spoon them into a dry metal or plastic measure (not a glass measuring cup, which is used to measure liquids). Use a knife to level the top. For flour, give it a quick stir before measuring, as it tends to become compact during storage. Do not pack the dry measure down by tapping it on the countertop; this increases the amount.
- For best results, always use the correct pan size.
- Line the bottom of baking pans with parchment paper (not waxed paper) or greased heavy-duty foil to prevent mixtures from sticking to the bottom of the pan.
- Position the oven rack in the center of the oven to ensure that breads, cakes and cookies bake uniformly.
- Unless directed in a recipe, do not cut bars and squares when warm. Set the baking pan on a rack to cool, then place in the freezer until partially frozen. Run a sharp knife around the edges, then cut into bars or squares.

Cheese Cornbread

Makes 9 squares

Serve this tempting savory cornbread with a bowl of warm chili, soup or salad.

- - - - - - - - - - - - - - -

Tip

You can double the recipe and bake in a 13- by 9-inch (33 by 23 cm) metal baking pan. Increase the baking time to 25 to 30 minutes.

- Preheat oven to 375°F (190°C)
- 8-inch (20 cm) square metal baking pan, sprayed with vegetable oil cooking spray and bottom lined with parchment paper

½ cup	whole wheat flour	125 mL
½ cup	cornmeal	125 mL
1 tbsp	granulated sugar	15 mL
1½ tsp	baking powder	7 mL
¼ tsp	salt	1 mL
⅓ cup	shredded lower-fat (<20% M.F.) Cheddar cheese	75 mL
1	large egg	1
⅔ cup	low-fat (1%) milk	150 mL
2 tbsp	canola oil	30 mL

1. In a large bowl, stir together flour, cornmeal, sugar, baking powder and salt. Stir in cheese.

2. In a small bowl, whisk together egg, milk and oil. Pour over flour mixture and stir until combined. Pour batter into prepared pan.

3. Bake in preheated oven for 20 to 24 minutes or until top springs back when lightly touched in center. Transfer pan to a wire rack, cut into 9 squares and serve warm.

Variation

Jalapeño Cheese Cornbread: Add 1 tbsp (15 mL) minced seeded jalapeño pepper with cheese.

Nutrition info per square

Calories	116
Carbohydrate	14 g
Fiber	1 g
Protein	4 g
Fat	5 g
Saturated fat	1 g
Cholesterol	24 mg
Sodium	161 mg

Food Choices
1 Carbohydrate
1 Fat

Buttermilk Bran Muffins

Nicely moistened with molasses, these muffins will become a morning favorite. High in insoluble fiber, wheat bran adds extra bulk to our diet, making us feel full, and helps food pass through the digestive tract more quickly.

Tips

Buttermilk has a tendency to separate, so give it a quick shake to blend it together before measuring.

Always measure the oil before measuring sticky sweeteners such as molasses or honey. For recipes that don't call for oil, spray the measure with vegetable oil cooking spray or lightly coat it with oil. Every last drop of sweetener will easily pour out.

Nutrition info per muffin

Calories	174
Carbohydrate	29 g
Fiber	4 g
Protein	4 g
Fat	6 g
Saturated fat	1 g
Cholesterol	32 mg
Sodium	205 mg

Food Choices
1½ Carbohydrate
1 Fat

- **Preheat oven to 400°F (200°C)**
- **12-cup nonstick muffin pan, generously sprayed with vegetable oil cooking spray**

1¼ cups	whole wheat flour	300 mL
1 cup	natural wheat bran	250 mL
1 tsp	baking soda	5 mL
½ tsp	baking powder	2 mL
¼ tsp	salt	1 mL
2	large eggs	2
⅓ cup	packed brown sugar	75 mL
1 cup	well-shaken buttermilk	250 mL
¼ cup	vegetable oil	60 mL
¼ cup	light (fancy) molasses	60 mL
½ cup	raisins or chopped dried apricots or dates	125 mL

1. In a large bowl, stir together flour, bran, baking soda, baking powder and salt.

2. In a medium bowl, whisk eggs. Whisk in brown sugar, buttermilk, oil and molasses.

3. Stir egg mixture into flour mixture until just combined. Fold in raisins. Divide batter evenly among prepared muffin cups.

4. Bake in preheated oven for 20 to 24 minutes or until tops spring back when lightly touched. Let cool in pan on a wire rack for 5 minutes, then transfer muffins to rack to cool.

Blueberry Oat Bran Muffins

Makes 12 muffins

The goodness of oat bran not only helps lower your cholesterol, but also keeps blood glucose levels in check.

- - - - - - - - - - - - -

Tip

If using frozen blueberries when making muffins and breads, do not thaw. Toss the frozen berries with about 1/4 cup (60 mL) of the flour mixture to prevent them from bleeding their juices and turning the batter blue. Continue with recipe as directed.

- Preheat oven to 400°F (200°C)
- 12-cup nonstick muffin pan, generously sprayed with vegetable oil cooking spray

1¼ cups	whole wheat flour	300 mL
1 cup	oat bran	250 mL
2½ tsp	baking powder	12 mL
½ tsp	freshly grated nutmeg (see tip, page 348)	2 mL
¼ tsp	salt	1 mL
1	large egg	1
½ cup	packed dark brown sugar	125 mL
¾ cup	low-fat (1%) milk	175 mL
¼ cup	butter or soft margarine, melted	60 mL
1 tsp	grated lemon zest	5 mL
1½ cups	fresh or frozen blueberries	375 mL

1. In a large bowl, stir together flour, oat bran, baking powder, nutmeg and salt.

2. In a medium bowl, whisk egg. Whisk in brown sugar, milk, butter and lemon zest.

3. Stir egg mixture into flour mixture until just combined. Gently fold in blueberries. Divide batter evenly among prepared muffin cups.

4. Bake in preheated oven for 20 to 24 minutes or until tops spring back when lightly touched. Let cool in pan on a wire rack for 5 minutes, then transfer muffins to rack to cool.

Nutrition info per muffin

Calories	153
Carbohydrate	27 g
Fiber	3 g
Protein	4 g
Fat	5 g
Saturated fat	3 g
Cholesterol	26 mg
Sodium	157 mg

Food Choices
1½ Carbohydrate
1 Fat

Nutrition Tip

The ingredients used in baked goods and desserts — sugars, flours, fats, nuts, dried fruits — all add up to calories, so enjoy them as a special occasion treat and limit the portion size.

Spiced Applesauce Flax Muffins

Makes 12 muffins

Wholesome and nutritious, these delectable muffins are great for breakfast or as a snack.

Tip

Prepare a double batch and freeze muffins in an airtight container or sealable plastic storage bag for up to 1 month. To quickly defrost and reheat, wrap each muffin in a paper towel and microwave on High for 20 seconds or until warmed through.

Nutrition info per muffin

Calories	164
Carbohydrate	31 g
Fiber	5 g
Protein	5 g
Fat	3 g
Saturated fat	0 g
Cholesterol	16 mg
Sodium	145 mg

Food Choices
2 Carbohydrate
1/2 Fat

- **Preheat oven to 375°F (190°C)**
- **12-cup nonstick muffin pan, generously sprayed with vegetable oil cooking spray**

1 1/3 cups	whole wheat flour	325 mL
1/2 cup	ground flax seeds (flaxseed meal)	125 mL
1/2 cup	wheat germ	125 mL
1 tsp	baking soda	5 mL
1/2 tsp	baking powder	2 mL
1 tsp	ground cinnamon	5 mL
1/4 tsp	ground cloves	1 mL
1/4 tsp	ground allspice	1 mL
1/3 cup	finely chopped dates or dried apricots	75 mL
1	large egg	1
1/2 cup	packed brown sugar	125 mL
1 cup	unsweetened applesauce	250 mL
1/2 cup	nonfat sour cream	125 mL

1. In a large bowl, stir together flour, flax seeds, wheat germ, baking soda, baking powder, cinnamon, cloves and allspice. Stir in dates until evenly distributed.

2. In a medium bowl, whisk egg. Whisk in brown sugar, applesauce and sour cream.

3. Stir egg mixture into flour mixture until just combined. Divide batter evenly among prepared muffin cups.

4. Bake in preheated oven for 20 to 24 minutes or until tops spring back when lightly touched. Let cool in pan on a wire rack for 5 minutes, then transfer muffins to rack to cool.

Morning Glory Muffins

These popular, wholesome muffins combine the chewy texture of carrots with the wonderful flavors of apple, raisins, coconut and spices. They're a perfect way to start the day — or enjoy one as a snack!

Tip

Whole nutmeg may be sold still encased in a brittle brown shell, or the shell may be removed. If necessary, remove the shell using a nutcracker. Use a rasp grater, such as a Microplane, to grate fresh nutmeg. It has an incredible aroma and imparts a much more pronounced and exotic flavor to foods than the ground nutmeg sold in the spice section.

Nutrition info per muffin	
Calories	194
Carbohydrate	31 g
Fiber	4 g
Protein	6 g
Fat	6 g
Saturated fat	2 g
Cholesterol	16 mg
Sodium	168 mg

Food Choices
2 Carbohydrate
1 Fat

- Preheat oven to 375°F (190°C)
- 12-cup nonstick muffin pan, generously sprayed with vegetable oil cooking spray

1½ cups	whole wheat flour	375 mL
½ cup	wheat germ	125 mL
1 tsp	baking powder	5 mL
1 tsp	baking soda	5 mL
1½ tsp	ground cinnamon	7 mL
½ tsp	freshly grated nutmeg (see tip, at left)	2 mL
1 cup	grated carrots (about 2 medium)	250 mL
1 cup	grated apple	250 mL
⅓ cup	unsweetened shredded coconut	75 mL
⅓ cup	raisins or chopped dried apricots or figs	75 mL
2	large egg whites	2
1	large egg	1
½ cup	packed brown sugar	125 mL
¾ cup	nonfat plain yogurt	175 mL
3 tbsp	canola oil	45 mL

1. In a large bowl, stir together flour, wheat germ, baking powder, baking soda, cinnamon and nutmeg. Stir in carrots, apple, coconut and raisins.

2. In a medium bowl, whisk egg whites and egg. Whisk in brown sugar, yogurt and oil.

3. Stir egg mixture into flour mixture until just combined. (Batter will be thick.) Divide batter evenly among prepared muffin cups, filling almost to the top.

4. Bake in preheated oven for 20 to 24 minutes or until tops spring back when lightly touched. Let cool in pan on a wire rack for 5 minutes, then transfer muffins to rack to cool.

Granola Spice Cake

When you crave a little indulgence, this moist spiced cake with the goodness of granola and apple hits the spot.

- - - - - - - - - - - - - - -

Tips

Wrap individual pieces of cake in plastic wrap and store at room temperature for up to 2 days, or place in sealable freezer bags and freeze for up to 1 month.

Vegetable oil cooking sprays are sold in aerosol cans and pump sprays at supermarkets. We suggest buying a spray pump mister, available at specialty kitchen shops. This non-aerosol dispenser can be filled with any kind of oil. We recommend using canola oil, as it's an all-purpose oil for both baking and roasting.

Nutrition info per serving	
Calories	142
Carbohydrate	24 g
Fiber	2 g
Protein	4 g
Fat	4 g
Saturated fat	1 g
Cholesterol	16 mg
Sodium	96 mg

Food Choices
1½ Carbohydrate
1 Fat

- **Preheat oven to 350°F (180°C)**
- **8-inch (20 cm) square metal baking pan, sprayed with vegetable oil cooking spray, bottom lined with parchment paper**

1 cup	Multigrain Granola with Walnuts and Dried Fruit (page 172)	250 mL
½ cup	whole wheat flour	125 mL
⅓ cup	wheat germ	75 mL
1 tsp	baking powder	5 mL
1 tsp	ground cinnamon	5 mL
½ tsp	baking soda	2 mL
½ tsp	ground ginger	2 mL
¼ tsp	ground cloves	1 mL
1	large egg	1
½ cup	packed brown sugar	125 mL
½ cup	grated apple	125 mL
½ cup	nonfat plain yogurt	125 mL
2 tbsp	canola oil	30 mL
2 tbsp	wheat germ	30 mL

1. In a large bowl, combine granola, flour, ⅓ cup (75 mL) wheat germ, baking powder, cinnamon, baking soda, ginger and cloves.

2. In another bowl, whisk egg. Whisk in brown sugar, apple, yogurt and oil.

3. Stir egg mixture into granola mixture until just combined. Spread evenly in prepared pan. Sprinkle top evenly with 2 tbsp (30 mL) wheat germ.

4. Bake in preheated oven for 25 to 28 minutes or until a tester inserted in the center comes out clean. Let cool completely in pan on a wire rack. Cut into 12 pieces.

Granola Power Bars

This recipe shows how easy it is to make your own healthy snack bars. Wrap each one individually in plastic wrap and store in the freezer to have handy to add to lunch bags or for a mid-day snack.

- - - - - - - - - - - - -

Tips

We use unsalted peanut butter rather than light peanut butter in our recipes. Although it has a higher fat content, the peanut flavor is more pronounced and flavorful when used in recipes.

Store these bars in an airtight container at room temperature for up to 5 days, or wrap individually in plastic wrap, place in a sealable plastic freezer bag and freeze for up to 1 month.

Nutrition info per bar	
Calories	137
Carbohydrate	18 g
Fiber	2 g
Protein	4 g
Fat	6 g
Saturated fat	1 g
Cholesterol	0 mg
Sodium	12 mg

Food Choices
1 Carbohydrate
1 Fat

- **Preheat oven to 350°F (180°C)**
- **9-inch (23 cm) square metal baking pan, lined with foil, with ends extending slightly over edge of pan, foil sprayed with vegetable oil cooking spray**

2	large egg whites	2
1/3 cup	unsalted peanut butter or almond butter	75 mL
1/3 cup	liquid honey	75 mL
1 tsp	vanilla extract	5 mL
1 1/3 cups	Multigrain Granola with Walnuts and Dried Fruit (page 172)	325 mL
1/4 cup	ground flax seeds (flaxseed meal)	60 mL

1. In a large bowl, whisk egg whites until frothy. Stir in peanut butter, honey and vanilla until smooth. Stir in granola and flax seeds until combined. Spread in prepared pan.

2. Bake in preheated oven for 18 to 22 minutes or until set in the middle and light brown around the edges. Using edges of foil, lift out of pan and transfer to a cutting board. While warm, cut into 12 bars. Let cool completely.

Nutrition Tip

If you are looking for a high-protein cereal, energy bar, prepared/frozen meal or protein powder, keep in mind that 7 grams of protein is equal to the amount of protein in 1 ounce (30 g) of meat. A high-protein snack should therefore have at least 7 grams of protein (and no more than 30 grams of carbohydrate). A prepared meal should have at least 14 grams of protein. A protein powder (to stir into cereal or a smoothie) should have at least 7 grams of protein per serving. If there is carbohydrate in the powder, remember to count it.

Oatmeal Chocolate Chip Cookies

Makes 3 dozen cookies

Everyone loves home-baked cookies as an occasional treat, especially moist and chewy ones like these, made with wholesome oats and wheat germ.

- - - - - - - - - - - - - -

Tip

Store cookies in an airtight container at room temperature for up to 5 days or in the freezer for up to 1 month.

Nutrition info per cookie

Calories	99
Carbohydrate	12 g
Fiber	1 g
Protein	2 g
Fat	5 g
Saturated fat	3 g
Cholesterol	19 mg
Sodium	64 mg

Food Choices
½ Carbohydrate
1 Fat

- **Preheat oven to 350°F (180°C)**
- **Baking sheets, lined with parchment paper**

1 cup	whole wheat flour	250 mL
⅓ cup	wheat germ	75 mL
½ tsp	baking soda	2 mL
¼ tsp	salt	1 mL
¾ cup	packed brown sugar	175 mL
⅔ cup	butter, softened	150 mL
2	large eggs	2
1 tsp	vanilla extract	5 mL
1½ cups	large-flake (old-fashioned) rolled oats	375 mL
¾ cup	semisweet chocolate chips	175 mL

1. In a small bowl, stir together flour, wheat germ, baking soda and salt.

2. In a large bowl, using an electric mixer on low speed, cream brown sugar and butter until light and fluffy. Beat in eggs, one at a time, and vanilla. Beat in flour mixture until incorporated. Using a wooden spoon, stir in oats and chocolate chips.

3. Drop by rounded tablespoonfuls about 2 inches (5 cm) apart on prepared baking sheets and flatten with a fork.

4. Bake one sheet at a time in preheated oven for 12 to 14 minutes or until edges are golden. Transfer cookies to a wire rack to cool.

Variation

Replace the chocolate chips with dried fruit, such as raisins, dried cranberries or chopped dried apricots, or a combination.

Hazelnut and Dried Cranberry Biscotti

Makes 40 cookies

These crunchy morsels, served with a glass of low-fat milk, make for a simple, satisfying dessert or snack. Dried cranberries add a sweet-tart flavor.

- - - - - - - - - - - - - -

Tips

To toast and skin hazelnuts, place nuts on a rimmed baking sheet in a preheated 325°F (160°C) oven for 8 to 10 minutes or until fragrant and lightly browned. Place in a clean, dry towel and rub off most of the skins.

Store biscotti in an airtight container at room temperature for up to 5 days or in the freezer for up to 1 month.

Nutrition info per 2 cookies	
Calories	135
Carbohydrate	20 g
Fiber	2 g
Protein	3 g
Fat	6 g
Saturated fat	2 g
Cholesterol	27 mg
Sodium	76 mg

Food Choices
1 Carbohydrate
1 Fat

- **Preheat oven to 325°F (160°C)**
- **Large baking sheet, lined with parchment paper**

2 cups	whole wheat flour	500 mL
1 tsp	baking powder	5 mL
1½ tsp	ground cinnamon	7 mL
¼ tsp	ground cloves	1 mL
¼ tsp	ground allspice	1 mL
¼ tsp	salt	1 mL
¾ cup	packed brown sugar	175 mL
⅓ cup	butter, softened	75 mL
2	large eggs	2
½ cup	dried cranberries or raisins	125 mL
½ cup	hazelnuts, toasted, skinned and coarsely chopped (see tip, at left)	125 mL

1. In a medium bowl, stir together flour, baking powder, cinnamon, cloves, allspice and salt.

2. In a large bowl, using an electric mixer on low speed, cream brown sugar and butter until light and fluffy. Beat in eggs, one at time. Using a wooden spoon, stir in flour mixture to make a soft dough. Stir in cranberries and hazelnuts.

3. With floured hands, gather dough in a ball and divide in half. On a lightly floured board, pat dough into two logs, each about 10 inches (25 cm) long and 2½ inches (6 cm) wide. Arrange logs about 2 inches (5 cm) apart on prepared baking sheet.

4. Bake in preheated oven for 24 to 28 minutes or until firm to the touch. Remove from oven, leaving oven on, and let cool on baking sheet for 10 minutes. Using a long spatula, transfer logs to a cutting board. Using a serrated knife, cut each log on the diagonal into ½-inch (1 cm) slices.

5. Place cookies upright, ½ inch (1 cm) apart, on baking sheet (use two sheets, if necessary). Bake for 20 minutes or until dry and light brown. Transfer cookies to a wire rack to cool.

Desserts

People with diabetes were once told to avoid sweets entirely. However, you can enjoy them occasionally; the key is to monitor total carbs when eating dessert with your meal. Simply sub in a small portion of dessert in place of bread, pasta, rice or crackers with a similar amount of carbohydrate. Rather than selecting empty-calorie sweets, choose a dessert that is low in fat and contains fiber and other valuable nutrients. Many of the desserts included here provide a good dose of calcium. Others are high in fiber, and many also contain fruit. The bottom line: everything in moderation!

Peach Cake

Here's a light and moist cake to serve for a special-occasion dessert or afternoon coffee.

- - - - - - - - - - - - - - -

Tip

To peel peaches, plunge them in a saucepan of rapidly boiling water for 15 to 30 seconds to loosen skins. Place in a bowl of cold water to chill quickly. Drain, peel and slice. Use immediately to prevent darkening.

- **Preheat oven to 350°F (180°C)**
- **9-inch (23 cm) springform pan, bottom and sides sprayed with vegetable oil cooking spray, bottom lined with parchment paper**

1¼ cups	all-purpose flour	300 mL
⅓ cup	granulated sugar	75 mL
1 tsp	baking powder	5 mL
½ tsp	baking soda	1 mL
1	large egg	1
⅔ cup	nonfat artificially sweetened vanilla-flavored yogurt	150 mL
3 tbsp	butter, melted	45 mL
1 tsp	grated lemon zest	5 mL
3	peaches or nectarines, peeled and thinly sliced	3

Topping

¼ cup	sliced blanched almonds	60 mL
1 tbsp	granulated sugar	15 mL
¾ tsp	ground cinnamon	3 mL

1. In a large bowl, stir together flour, sugar, baking powder and baking soda.

2. In a medium bowl, whisk together egg, yogurt, butter and lemon zest.

3. Stir egg mixture into flour mixture to make a smooth, thick batter. Spread evenly in prepared pan. Arrange peaches on top in a circular fashion.

4. *Topping:* In a small bowl, combine almonds, sugar and cinnamon. Sprinkle over peaches.

5. Bake in preheated oven for 35 to 40 minutes or until a tester inserted in the center comes out clean. Let cool in pan on a wire rack. Run a knife around edge of pan and remove sides. Using a metal spatula, transfer cake from springform base to a plate for serving.

Nutrition info per serving

Calories	201
Carbohydrate	31 g
Fiber	2 g
Protein	5 g
Fat	7 g
Saturated fat	3 g
Cholesterol	35 mg
Sodium	169 mg

Food Choices
2 Carbohydrate
1 Fat

Variation
Replace the peaches with 2 cups (500 mL) thinly sliced apples or pears.

Blueberry Lemon Upside-Down Cake

This quick, delicious dessert can be served as a cake or as a pudding warm from the oven. Serve topped with a dollop of nonfat Greek yogurt.

- - - - - - - - - - - - - - - -

Tip

If using frozen berries, place in a fine sieve and quickly rinse under cold water to remove any ice crystals. Spread on a plate lined with paper towels to drain. Do not let berries completely thaw.

- **Preheat oven to 350°F (180°C)**
- **8-inch (20 cm) square glass baking dish, bottom and sides sprayed with vegetable oil cooking spray, bottom lined with parchment paper**

2 cups	fresh blueberries (see tip, at left)	500 mL
2 tbsp	packed brown sugar	30 mL
1 cup	all-purpose flour	250 mL
1 tsp	baking powder	5 mL
Pinch	salt	Pinch
1/3 cup	granulated sugar	75 mL
1/4 cup	butter or soft margarine, softened	60 mL
1	large egg	1
1 tsp	grated lemon zest	5 mL
1/2 cup	low-fat (1%) milk	125 mL

1. Rinse blueberries and spread on paper towels to drain. Sprinkle brown sugar over bottom of prepared baking dish. Spread blueberries evenly in bottom of dish.

2. In a small bowl, stir together flour, baking powder and salt.

3. In a large bowl, using a wooden spoon, cream granulated sugar and butter until light and fluffy. Beat in egg and lemon zest. Add flour mixture alternately with milk, making two additions of each and stirring to make a smooth batter. Spoon evenly over blueberries and smooth the top.

4. Bake in preheated oven for 25 to 30 minutes or until a tester inserted in the center comes out clean. Remove from oven and run a knife around edges of pan. Place a serving plate on top of pan and carefully invert cake onto serving plate. Let cool completely.

Nutrition info per serving

Calories	189
Carbohydrate	29 g
Fiber	2 g
Protein	3 g
Fat	7 g
Saturated fat	4 g
Cholesterol	39 mg
Sodium	114 mg

Food Choices
2 Carbohydrate
1 Fat

Peach Cherry Gingerbread Cobbler

A biscuit topping with all the old-fashioned flavor of gingerbread marries well with summery ripe peaches and cherries in this recipe. For convenience, use frozen fruit to streamline the preparation time.

- **Preheat oven to 400°F (200°C)**
- **8-cup (2 L) casserole dish, sprayed with vegetable oil cooking spray**

Fruit Filling

2 cups	sliced fresh or frozen peaches	500 mL
2 cups	fresh or frozen sweet or tart cherries	500 mL
1½ tsp	grated orange zest	7 mL
	Granulated artificial sweetener equivalent to ⅓ cup (75 mL) granulated sugar	
1 tbsp	cornstarch	15 mL
2 tbsp	orange juice	30 mL

Biscuit Topping

1 cup	whole wheat flour	250 mL
1 tsp	baking powder	5 mL
¾ tsp	ground ginger	3 mL
½ tsp	baking soda	2 mL
½ tsp	ground cinnamon	2 mL
¼ tsp	ground allspice	1 mL
1	large egg	1
⅔ cup	light sour cream	150 mL
¼ cup	liquid honey	60 mL
2 tbsp	canola oil	30 mL
2 tbsp	sliced almonds	30 mL

1. *Filling:* In casserole dish, combine peaches, cherries, orange zest and artificial sweetener.

2. In a small bowl, combine cornstarch and orange juice; stir into fruit mixture.

3. Bake in preheated oven for 20 to 25 minutes (30 to 40 minutes if using frozen fruit) or until fruit mixture is bubbling around the edges. Remove from oven, leaving oven on.

Nutrition info per serving

Calories	165
Carbohydrate	33 g
Fiber	4 g
Protein	5 g
Fat	3 g
Saturated fat	1 g
Cholesterol	28 mg
Sodium	108 mg

Food Choices
2 Carbohydrate
½ Fat

4. *Topping:* Meanwhile, in a large bowl, stir together flour, baking powder, ginger, baking soda, cinnamon and allspice.

5. In a small bowl, whisk together egg, sour cream, honey and oil until smooth.

6. Stir egg mixture into flour mixture to make a smooth batter. Drop spoonfuls of batter evenly over hot fruit and smooth with back of spoon. Sprinkle with almonds.

7. Bake for 25 to 30 minutes or until top is golden and fruit is bubbly. Let cool on a wire rack for 15 minutes. Serve warm or at room temperature.

Nutrition Tip

Fruit is an important part of a healthy diet. It's a great source of antioxidants, vitamins, minerals and fiber, which helps lower blood glucose levels. We have provided up to three servings of fruit a day in our menus (pages 148–155), including several of our low-fat, high-fiber desserts, like this one.

Apple Tart

Makes 8 servings

Intimidated by the thought of making homemade pastry? Try this simple free-form tart with a low-fat pastry dough that's a breeze to make and roll out. The stunning dessert looks like it came from a pastry shop.

- - - - - - - - - - - - - - -

Tip

For the apples, try a variety such as Golden Delicious, Spy or Granny Smith.

Variation

Use Italian prune plums or pears instead of apples.

Nutrition info per serving	
Calories	191
Carbohydrate	31 g
Fiber	1 g
Protein	4 g
Fat	6 g
Saturated fat	4 g
Cholesterol	15 mg
Sodium	121 mg

Food Choices
2 Carbohydrate
1 Fat

- **Food processor**
- **Baking sheet, lined with parchment paper**

Pastry

1¼ cups	all-purpose flour	300 mL
1 tbsp	granulated sugar	15 mL
¼ tsp	salt	1 mL
¼ cup	cold butter, cut into pieces	60 mL
½ cup	nonfat plain Greek yogurt	125 mL

Filling

1 tbsp	cornstarch	15 mL
4 cups	peeled thinly sliced firm cooking apples (about 3)	1 L
¼ cup	granulated sugar	60 mL
¼ cup	finely chopped pecans or walnuts	60 mL
1 tsp	ground cinnamon	5 mL

1. *Pastry:* In food processor, combine flour, sugar, salt and butter; pulse until crumbly. Add yogurt and process until dough just holds together.

2. Gather dough into a ball and flatten to a 5-inch (12.5 cm) circle. Wrap in plastic wrap and refrigerate for 1 hour.

3. Preheat oven to 375°F (190°C).

4. On a lightly floured surface, roll pastry out to a 13-inch (33 cm) round. Transfer to prepared baking sheet. Using a sharp knife, trim pastry edge to form an even circle.

5. *Filling:* Place cornstarch in a sieve and sift over pastry. Starting 2 inches (5 cm) from edge of pastry, overlap apple slices in a circle. Arrange another overlapping circle of apples in the center.

6. In a bowl, combine sugar, pecans and cinnamon; sprinkle over apples. Fold pastry rim over apples to form a 2-inch (5 cm) edge.

7. Bake for 35 minutes or until pastry is golden and apples are tender. Let cool on pan on a wire rack. Using a spatula, carefully slide pie onto a serving plate.

Cinnamon Apple Slices with Dried Cranberries

This quick dessert sauce is like enjoying a baked apple without the extra effort of baking the fruit in your oven.

- - - - - - - - - - - - - - -

Tip

Use apples that hold their shape after cooking, such as Cortland, Granny Smith or Golden Delicious, or Bartlett or Bosc pears.

4 cups	sliced cooking apples or pears (unpeeled)	1 L
1/4 cup	dried cranberries	60 mL
2 tbsp	packed brown sugar or pure maple syrup	30 mL
1/2 cup	water, divided	125 mL
1 tsp	cornstarch	5 mL
1 tsp	ground cinnamon	5 mL
	Stevia extract or artificial sweetener	

1. In a medium saucepan, combine apples, cranberries, brown sugar and half the water. Cook over medium heat, stirring occasionally, for 6 to 8 minutes or until apples are almost tender.

2. In a small bowl, combine cornstarch and cinnamon. Stir in the remaining water until smooth. Pour over apple mixture and cook, stirring, for 1 minute or until thickened. Stir in stevia to taste (how much you need will depend on the tartness of the apples). Serve warm or let cool, transfer to an airtight container and refrigerate for up to 3 days.

**Nutrition info per
1/2 cup (125 mL)**

Calories	74
Carbohydrate	19 g
Fiber	2 g
Protein	0 g
Fat	0 g
Saturated fat	0 g
Cholesterol	0 mg
Sodium	3 mg

Food Choices
1 Carbohydrate

Bumbleberry Oat Crisp

Makes 6 servings

Bumbleberry is a favorite fruit filling that is mixture of several berries and may also include apple or rhubarb, if you wish.

- - - - - - - - - - - - - - -

Tip

If you have a favorite fruit crisp recipe you enjoy making and would like to modify it, use this high-fiber, low-sugar topping and reduce the amount of sugar added to the fruit layer.

- Preheat oven to 350°F (180°C)
- Six 6-oz (175 mL) ramekins or custard cups
- Rimmed baking sheet

3 tbsp	granulated sugar	45 mL
4 tsp	cornstarch	20 mL
1 tsp	grated orange zest	5 mL
1	bag (20 oz/600 g) assorted frozen berries (see tip, at right)	1
½ cup	large-flake (old-fashioned) rolled oats	125 mL
⅓ cup	oat bran	75 mL
3 tbsp	whole wheat flour	45 mL
3 tbsp	packed brown sugar	45 mL
¾ tsp	ground cinnamon	3 mL
Pinch	freshly grated nutmeg (see tip, page 348)	Pinch
2 tbsp	butter, melted	30 mL

1. In a small bowl, combine granulated sugar, cornstarch and orange zest.

2. Place berries in a large bowl. Sprinkle sugar mixture over fruit and toss lightly. Divide fruit evenly among ramekins and place ramekins on baking sheet.

3. In a bowl, combine oats, oat bran, flour, brown sugar, cinnamon and nutmeg. Pour in butter and toss to combine. Sprinkle evenly over fruit.

Nutrition info per serving	
Calories	190
Carbohydrate	38 g
Fiber	5 g
Protein	3 g
Fat	5 g
Saturated fat	3 g
Cholesterol	10 mg
Sodium	31 mg

Food Choices
2 Carbohydrate
1 Fat

Tip

Use a combination of frozen berries, such as blueberries, strawberries, raspberries and/or blackberries. If you wish to use fresh fruit, use 5 cups (1.25 L).

4. Bake in preheated oven for 25 to 30 minutes or until fruit is bubbly and topping is golden. Let cool on a wire rack for 15 minutes. Serve warm or at room temperature.

Cutting Back on Sugar in Baking

Refined sugars, such as granulated and brown sugar, don't just provide sweetness; they also make baked goods moist and tender, and aid in browning. Many traditional recipes contain a lot of sugar, but you can reduce the amount by up to a third in most recipes without sacrificing quality.

While granulated artificial sweeteners can be used in baking, they don't produce baked goods of the same quality as those made with real sugar. If using a granulated artificial sweetener that can be used cup for cup in place of granulated sugar, experiment with using half sugar and half artificial sweetener in your favorite recipes.

Pomegranate and Spice Poached Pears

Here's a classic preparation for pears that makes an impressive end to a special meal.

- - - - - - - - - - - - - - - -

Tips

Select pears that are not overly ripe so they will hold their shape when poached.

Poach pears a day ahead. They are best served well chilled.

1½ cups	unsweetened pomegranate juice or pure cranberry juice	375 mL
4	whole cloves	4
3	2-inch (5 cm) strips orange peel	3
1	3-inch (7.5 cm) cinnamon stick, broken in half	1
6	small Bartlett or Anjou pears, peeled, halved lengthwise and cored	6
	Stevia extract or artificial sweetener	
⅓ cup	nonfat plain Greek yogurt	75 mL
2 tsp	liquid honey	10 mL
	Freshly grated nutmeg	
	Mint sprigs (optional)	

1. In a medium, deep saucepan, combine pomegranate juice, cloves, orange peel and cinnamon stick. Bring to a boil over high heat. Add pears, reduce heat to medium-low, cover and simmer for 10 minutes or until pears are just tender when pierced with a knife (time depends on ripeness of pears). Using a slotted spoon, transfer pears to a bowl or storage container.

2. Return poaching liquid to a boil over medium-high heat; boil until reduced by about half. Strain through a sieve to remove spices. Add stevia to taste and let cool. Pour over pears, cover and refrigerate for at least 4 hours, until chilled, or for up to 2 days.

3. In a bowl, combine yogurt and honey. Arrange 2 pear halves in each of six dessert bowls. Spoon some of the syrup over top and add a dollop of yogurt mixture in the center. Sprinkle with nutmeg. Garnish with mint sprigs, if desired.

Nutrition info per serving	
Calories	122
Carbohydrate	30 g
Fiber	4 g
Protein	2 g
Fat	0 g
Saturated fat	0 g
Cholesterol	0 mg
Sodium	12 mg
Food Choices	
2 Carbohydrate	

Gingered Fresh Fruit Compote

Makes 6 servings

Candied ginger dresses up a simple homemade or store-bought fruit salad.

- - - - - - - - - - - - - - -

Tips

Use any combination of fruits, cut into bite-size pieces, including pears, peaches, plums, apples, pineapple and strawberries. Prepare the fruit mixture no more than 4 hours ahead of serving to prevent discoloration.

This compote is best served the same day it is made.

½ cup	orange juice	125 mL
2 tbsp	liquid honey	30 mL
4 tsp	finely chopped candied ginger	20 mL
1 tsp	grated orange zest	5 mL
3 cups	chopped fresh fruit (see tip, at left)	750 mL

1. In a small saucepan, combine orange juice, honey and ginger. Bring to a boil over medium heat; boil for 2 minutes. Remove from heat and stir in orange zest. Let cool to room temperature.

2. Place fruit in a serving bowl and pour ginger mixture over top. Cover and refrigerate for 2 hours or until well chilled.

Nutrition Tip

Honey is slightly sweeter than sugar, although the amount of carbohydrate is about the same: 4 grams. Both honey and sugar have 16 calories per teaspoon (5 mL). Try to cut back on all added sugars in your diet, regardless of type.

Nutrition info per ½ cup (125 mL)

Calories	74
Carbohydrate	19 g
Fiber	2 g
Protein	1 g
Fat	0 g
Saturated fat	0 g
Cholesterol	0 mg
Sodium	3 mg

Food Choices
1 Carbohydrate

Lemon Cream with Fresh Berries

Here's an easy-to-assemble dessert with a luscious lemon cream that hints of cheesecake and is layered with berries or fresh fruit.

Tips

For the berries, try raspberries, blackberries, blueberries and/or sliced strawberries.

To wash fresh berries, place them in a strainer and gently rinse under cold water. Drain and arrange in a single layer on a dry kitchen towel or paper towels to dry.

¼ cup	granulated sugar	60 mL
2 tsp	grated lemon zest	10 mL
¼ cup	freshly squeezed lemon juice	60 mL
2 tbsp	cold water	30 mL
1 tbsp	cornstarch	15 mL
½ cup	light cream cheese, softened	125 mL
1 cup	nonfat plain yogurt or artificially sweetened lemon-flavored or vanilla-flavored yogurt	250 mL
3 cups	assorted fresh berries	750 mL
	Additional berries and grated lemon zest	
	Fresh mint sprigs	

1. In a small saucepan, whisk together sugar, lemon juice, cold water and cornstarch until smooth. Cook over medium heat, whisking constantly, for 2 to 3 minutes or until mixture comes to a full boil and thickens. Remove from heat and whisk in cream cheese and lemon zest until smooth. Whisk in yogurt. Cover and refrigerate for at least 4 hours, until chilled and slightly thickened, or for up to 1 day.

2. Arrange half the berries in four parfait glasses or large wine glasses. Top with half the lemon mixture. Layer with the remaining berries and lemon cream. Serve immediately or cover and refrigerate for up to 4 hours. Just before serving, garnish with whole berries, lemon zest and mint sprigs.

Nutrition info per serving	
Calories	208
Carbohydrate	34 g
Fiber	5 g
Protein	7 g
Fat	6 g
Saturated fat	3 g
Cholesterol	18 mg
Sodium	127 mg

Food Choices
2 Carbohydrate
1 Fat

Raspberry Panna Cotta with Fresh Berries

Deliciously light and creamy, panna cotta is an Italian eggless custard made with gelatin and served with fruit. It's so easy to make and, best of all, it can be made in advance.

- - - - - - - - - - - - - - - -

Tips

For the assorted berries, try raspberries, blueberries and/or sliced strawberries.

Nutrition info per serving	
Calories	165
Carbohydrate	36 g
Fiber	3 g
Protein	6 g
Fat	1 g
Saturated fat	0 g
Cholesterol	1 mg
Sodium	100 mg

Food Choices
2 Carbohydrate

● **Six 6-oz (175 mL) ramekins or custard cups, sprayed with vegetable oil cooking spray**

3 cups	frozen raspberries, thawed	750 mL
2 tbsp	water	30 mL
1	package (¼ oz/7 g) unflavored gelatin powder	1
2 tbsp	granulated sugar	30 mL
1½ cups	nonfat artificially sweetened vanilla-flavored yogurt	375 mL
1 cup	nonfat sour cream	250 mL
2 tbsp	liquid honey	30 mL
3 cups	assorted fresh berries	750 mL

1. Using a wooden spoon, press raspberries through a fine sieve into a bowl, extracting as much of the pulp as possible; discard seeds. Measure raspberry sauce; you should have 1 cup (250 mL). Add water, if necessary.

2. Place water in a small saucepan and sprinkle with gelatin; let stand for 2 minutes to soften. Stir in sugar and ⅓ cup (75 mL) of the raspberry sauce. Heat over medium heat, stirring, for about 1 minute or until sauce is hot and gelatin and sugar are dissolved (do not let boil). Transfer to a medium bowl.

3. Stir yogurt and sour cream into hot raspberry sauce. Pour into prepared ramekins, cover and refrigerate for at least 4 hours, until set, or for up to 2 days.

4. In a small bowl, combine the remaining raspberry sauce and honey. Cover and refrigerate until serving time.

5. Run a paring knife around edge of each panna cotta to loosen. Place hot tap water in a shallow bowl. Dip the bottom of each ramekin in hot water for 15 seconds to loosen. Wipe ramekins dry and carefully invert panna cottas onto serving plates. Spoon about 2 tbsp (30 mL) sauce around each dessert and top with fresh berries.

Pumpkin Spice Custard

Makes 6 servings

Reminiscent of pumpkin pie, this simple dessert is made using canned or homemade pumpkin purée, or another puréed squash, such as butternut.

Tip

If using homemade pumpkin or squash purée, make sure to drain off excess liquid as directed on page 219. The purée should be quite thick, to resemble the thickness of canned pumpkin.

- ● **Preheat oven to 350°F (180°C)**
- ● **Six 6-oz (175 mL) ramekins or custard cups, sprayed with vegetable oil cooking spray**
- ● **13- by 9-inch (33 by 23 cm) metal baking pan**

2	large eggs	2
2	large egg whites	2
¼ cup	packed brown sugar	60 mL
½ tsp	ground cinnamon	2 mL
½ tsp	ground ginger	2 mL
½ tsp	grated orange zest	2 mL
¼ tsp	freshly grated nutmeg (see tip, page 348)	1 mL
1 cup	canned pumpkin purée (not pie filling) or homemade pumpkin or squash purée (see box, page 219)	250 mL
1 cup	canned evaporated skim milk	250 mL
	Additional ground cinnamon	

1. In a bowl, whisk eggs and egg whites. Whisk in brown sugar, cinnamon, ginger, orange zest, nutmeg, pumpkin and milk.

2. Pour pumpkin mixture into prepared custard cups and arrange in baking pan. Add enough hot water to pan to come halfway up sides of custard cups.

3. Bake in preheated oven for 30 to 35 minutes or until a toothpick inserted in center comes out clean. Remove from water bath and let cool slightly, then refrigerate for at least 4 hours, until chilled, or for up to 2 days.

4. Using a fine sieve, sprinkle tops with cinnamon before serving.

Nutrition info per serving

Calories	113
Carbohydrate	18 g
Fiber	1 g
Protein	7 g
Fat	2 g
Saturated fat	1 g
Cholesterol	64 mg
Sodium	93 mg

Food Choices
1 Carbohydrate
½ Meat & Alternatives

Nutrition Tip

Like all orange vegetables, pumpkin is very high in antioxidant carotenoids. One half-cup (125 mL) of canned pumpkin contains 4 grams of fiber and is an excellent source of vitamin K and a good source of vitamin E.

Vanilla Pudding

A bowl of creamy, smooth vanilla pudding is pure comfort food. Enjoy this easy dessert hot, at room temperature or cold. Top with sliced strawberries or any berries you have on hand, if desired.

3 tbsp	cornstarch	45 mL
2 tbsp	granulated sugar	30 mL
1	large egg	1
2 cups	low-fat (1%) milk	500 mL
2 tsp	vanilla extract	10 mL
	Stevia extract or artificial sweetener (optional)	

1. In a bowl, whisk together cornstarch and sugar. Gradually whisk in egg and milk. Strain through a fine sieve into a medium saucepan to remove any bits of egg white.

2. Place saucepan over medium heat and cook, whisking constantly, for about 3 minutes or until pudding comes to a full boil and thickens.

3. Remove from heat and stir in vanilla. Sweeten with stevia to taste, if desired.

4. Pour into four serving bowls. Serve warm or let cool slightly, cover top of pudding with plastic wrap and refrigerate for at least 2 hours, until chilled, or for up to 2 days.

Nutrition Tip

Low-fat dairy products are an excellent fit in a diabetes menu. They are a great source of protein, calcium, vitamin A, vitamin B_{12}, folate, riboflavin, potassium, magnesium and zinc. Be aware that 1 cup (250 mL) of milk and ¾ cup (175 mL) of plain yogurt each contain 12 grams of carbohydrate.

Nutrition info per ½ cup (125 mL)

Calories	123
Carbohydrate	18 g
Fiber	0 g
Protein	6 g
Fat	2 g
Saturated fat	1 g
Cholesterol	53 mg
Sodium	70 mg

Food Choices
1 Carbohydrate

Creamy Chocolate Banana Pudding

This creamy pudding makes for a nutritious and economical treat that is incredibly easy to whip up for dessert or a snack. It's an ideal recipe to get kids cooking!

¼ cup	unsweetened cocoa powder	60 mL
3 tbsp	cornstarch	45 mL
2 tbsp	granulated sugar	30 mL
2 cups	low-fat (1%) milk	500 mL
	Granulated artificial sweetener equivalent to 2 tbsp (30 mL) granulated sugar	
2 tsp	vanilla extract	10 mL
2	bananas, sliced	2

1. Using a fine sieve or sifter, sift cocoa powder, cornstarch and sugar into a medium saucepan. Gradually whisk in milk until smooth. Cook over medium heat, whisking constantly, for about 3 minutes or until mixture comes to a full boil and thickens. Remove from heat and stir in artificial sweetener and vanilla.

2. Pour into four serving bowls. Serve warm or let cool slightly, cover top of pudding with plastic wrap and refrigerate for at least 2 hours, until chilled, or for up to 2 days. Just before serving, top pudding with banana slices.

Nutrition info per ½ cup (125 mL) plus ½ banana

Calories	171
Carbohydrate	35 g
Fiber	3 g
Protein	6 g
Fat	2 g
Saturated fat	1 g
Cholesterol	6 mg
Sodium	56 mg

Food Choices
2 Carbohydrate

Nutrition Tip

Chocolate comes from cacao beans, which are rich in antioxidants called flavanols, known for their heart-healthy effects. The darker the chocolate, the higher the cacao content and amount of flavanols. Unsweetened cocoa powder is an especially high source. One tablespoon (15 mL) of unsweetened cocoa powder has about 20 calories and 5 grams of carbohydrate. Enjoy it in a Mocha Latte (page 182) or blend it into a banana smoothie or cold milk; sweeten lightly with a bit of sugar or artifical sweetener.

Lemon Mango Sorbet

Mango and lemon make an ideal pair in this refreshing tropical dessert.

- - - - - - - - - - - - - - -

Tips

The sorbet can be stored in the freezer for up to 2 weeks.

If you have an ice cream maker, in step 3 pour the mango mixture into the ice cream maker and freeze according to manufacturer's instructions.

● **Food processor**

2 tbsp	granulated sugar	30 mL
¼ cup	water	60 mL
4 cups	diced fresh or frozen mangos (3 to 4 medium)	1 L
2 tsp	grated lemon zest	10 mL
2 tbsp	freshly squeezed lemon juice	30 mL
1 cup	nonfat plain yogurt	250 mL
	Stevia extract or artificial sweetener	

1. In a small saucepan, bring sugar and water to a boil over medium heat, stirring until sugar is dissolved. (Or place in glass measuring cup and microwave on High for 1 minute.) Let cool.

2. In food processor, combine sugar mixture, mangos, lemon zest and lemon juice; purée until smooth. Add yogurt and process until blended. Sweeten with stevia to taste.

3. Pour mango mixture into a shallow metal pan and freeze for 2 to 3 hours or until partially frozen. Return to food processor and purée to break up ice crystals. Transfer to an airtight container and freeze until firm.

4. To serve, place container in the refrigerator for 1 hour to allow sorbet to soften for easy scooping.

Nutrition info per ½ cup (125 mL)

Calories	83
Carbohydrate	20 g
Fiber	2 g
Protein	2 g
Fat	0 g
Saturated fat	0 g
Cholesterol	1 mg
Sodium	24 mg

Food Choices
1 Carbohydrate

Nutrition Tip

Refreshing, colorful mangos are very high in vitamin C and a source of fiber.

Appendix 1:
Food and Activity Journal

Before you can start changing your lifestyle for the better, you need to know where you stand. Photocopy the journal below (or create your own version) and use it to record everything you eat and drink, and all your activity, for one week. You could add rows for sleep or anything else you are interested in tracking. Once you have completed the journal, review your habits. Remember, there is no right or wrong here, just information. Be objective about where you are now and where you would like to go in the future. If you decide you want to change something, set a SMART goal (see page 135). Then use clean copies of the journal to measure your progress. It is well known that it is much easier to change behavior if you can measure it.

	Day 1	Day 2	Day 3	
Breakfast				
Lunch				
Dinner				
Snacks				
Exercise or activity				

Day 4	Day 5	Day 6	Day 7

Appendix 2: Quitting Smoking

When you started smoking, perhaps as a young adult, you likely did it to be cool or to fit in. You never imagined you would be smoking all these years later. You never imagined that smoking would cost you many thousands of dollars. As a young person, you didn't care that smoking was bad for your health. You also didn't know or care that nicotine is one of the most difficult addictions to beat.

That was then, this is now.

A diagnosis of diabetes or prediabetes is a game-changer. Your blood vessels are now very vulnerable to atherosclerosis, dramatically increasing your risk of heart attack, stroke, blindness, kidney failure and amputation. Then there are the "usual suspects" associated with smoking: mouth, lung and pancreatic cancers, emphysema, pneumonia, erectile dysfunction and poor wound healing.

Quitting smoking is very tough, but it can be done. Smoking is now at an all-time low in Canada and the United States. Some people quit cold turkey, while others use quitting aids, such as nicotine patches or gum, medication or hypnosis. For many people, it takes several tries before they successfully quit.

Here are some tips from past smokers:

1. Make a list of all the reasons you want to quit smoking.

2. Set a quit date.

3. Familiarize yourself with stop smoking resources and quitting aids, and use as many as you need. These include:

- your state, provincial or national "Quitline" — trained counselors are waiting at the end of the phone to guide and encourage you

- stop smoking apps for your phone or other gadget

- online resources such as www.helpguide.org (search on "smoking cessation"), www.quitnet.com (an online community of past smokers and people trying to quit), the On the Road to Quitting program (available at Health Canada's website, www.hc-sc.gc.ca) and www.smokefree.gov

- support from your friends and family

- medications recommended by your health care provider

- nicotine replacement gums, patches or inhalers

- alternative approaches such as hypnosis, acupuncture or laser therapy (these have less "proof" of effectiveness but have helped some people)

- lifestyle changes, such as replacing smoking with a new habit — taking walks, reading, chewing gum, knitting, woodworking — anything that takes your mind off nicotine cravings

4. Ask yourself if you need a replacement for the "tactile" aspect of smoking. After all, smoking involves opening the pack, lighting up and holding the cigarette. Some people find that having something to do with their hands makes quitting easier. You can fiddle with a straw, a cinnamon stick (which is also nice to nibble on), a nicotine inhaler, a squeeze ball or a pen.

5. Remove all ashtrays from your home. Do not allow anyone to smoke in your house or car (including you, though you can still smoke outside until your quit date).

6. Anticipate some challenging nicotine cravings in the beginning. The worst of these cravings usually only last three days, so know that if you can just push through those three days, it will get better. When a nicotine craving hits, it can be helpful to hold your breath for 10 seconds or do a cardio-intensive activity such as jumping jacks until you are out of breath.

7. Some people also crave sugar. Be prepared with a supply of sugar-free gums and mints, and low-carb ice pops and beverages. Treat yourself to small portions of sweets (try 100-calorie-portion packs) until the cravings pass.

Join the growing number of nonsmokers and reclaim your health. You *can* quit smoking!

FAQ

Q. I smoke when I'm tense, and I'm tense when I don't smoke. What can I do?

A. One of the reasons cigarettes are hard to quit is because, yes, they make you feel better on many levels. Nicotine withdrawal can cause tension, moodiness, headaches and sugar cravings. Fortunately, there are a variety of tools available to help you manage nicotine withdrawal. But you also need to develop new coping methods for when life just isn't going your way. Cigarettes have been there to turn to when you're feeling lonely, angry, depressed, bored or anxious. When you are a nonsmoker, you are still going to have bad days, but you'll no longer use cigarettes as a crutch. Think about how you will help yourself feel better. There are many healthy and effective ways to cope with stress and negative emotions. See page 112 for ideas.

Resources

Websites provide a great deal of written information, and many now also offer interactive health assessment and tracking tools. Some will even "coach" you toward your goals. Imagine, support and ideas delivered right to your inbox or smartphone!

Academy of Nutrition and Dietetics: www.eatright.org

American Diabetes Association: www.diabetes.org; 1-800-DIABETES (1-800-342-2383)

American Heart Association: www.heart.org

Better Together: http://bettertogetherbc.ca

Canadian Diabetes Association: www.diabetes.ca or www.diabetesgps.ca; 1-800-BANTING (1-800-226-8464)

Dairy Council of California: www.healthyeating.org, click on "Eat Better, Eat Together"

Diabète Quebec: www.diabete.qc.ca

Diabetes Exercise and Sports Association: www.diabetes-exercise.org

Dietitians of Canada: www.dietitians.ca

Health Canada Quit Now: http://hc-sc.gc.ca/hc-ps/tobac-tabac/quit-cesser/now-maintenant/index-eng.php; 1-866-366-3667

Heart and Stroke Foundation: www.heartandstroke.com

Joslin Diabetes Centre: www.joslin.org

National Diabetes Education Program: www.ndep.nih.gov or www.yourdiabetesinfo.org; 1-888-693-NDEP (1-888-693-6337)

National Weight Control Registry: www.nwcr.ws

Public Health Agency of Canada: Download a copy of *Your Guide to Diabetes* (2011) from www.phac-aspc.ca or order at 1-800-O-Canada (1-800-622-6232)

Smokefree.gov: http://smokefree.gov; 1-800-QUIT-NOW

References

Sources Used Throughout

American Diabetes Association. Nutrition recommendations and interventions for diabetes: A position statement of the American Diabetes Association. *Diabetes Care* 2008 Jan;31(Suppl 1): S61–S78.

American Diabetes Association. Standards of medical care in diabetes — 2013. *Diabetes Care* 2013 Jan; 36(Suppl 1):S11–S66.

Canadian Diabetes Association. *Beyond the Basics: Lifestyle Choices for Diabetes Prevention and Management.* 2007.

Canadian Diabetes Association. *Beyond the Basics: Meal Planning for Healthy Eating, Diabetes Prevention and Management.* 2006.

Canadian Diabetes Association Clinical Practice Guidelines Expert Committee. Clinical practice guidelines for the prevention and management of diabetes in Canada. *Canadian Journal of Diabetes* 2008;32(Suppl 1):S1–S201.

Garber AJ, Handelsman Y, Einhorn D, et al. Diagnosis and management of prediabetes in the continuum of hyperglycemia: When do the risks of diabetes begin? A consensus statement from the American College of Endocrinology and the American Association of Clinical Endocrinologists. *Endocrine Practice* 2008 Oct;14(7):933–46.

Health Canada. *Eating Well with Canada's Food Guide — A Resource for Educators and Communicators.* 2011.

Institute of Medicine of the National Academies of Science. A Report of the Panel on Macronutrients, Subcommittees on Upper Reference Levels of Nutrients and Interpretation and Uses of Dietary Reference Intakes, Standing Committee on the Scientific Evaluation of Dietary Reference Intakes. *Dietary Reference Intakes for Energy, Carbohydrate, Fiber, Fat, Fatty Acids, Cholesterol, Protein, and Amino Acids (Macronutrients).* Washington, DC: The National Academies Press, 2005.

Inzucchi S, Bergenstal R, Buse J, et al. Management of hyperglycemia in type 2 diabetes: A patient-centered approach. Position Statement of the American Diabetes Association (ADA) and the European Association for the Study of Diabetes (EASD). *Diabetes Care* 2012 Jun;35(6):1364–79.

National Diabetes Information Clearinghouse (NDIC). *National Diabetes Statistics, 2011.* Available at www.diabetes.niddk.nih.gov/dm/ pubs/statistics. Accessed February 4, 2013.

U.S. Department of Agriculture. *USDA Food Guidance System (MyPlate).* Available at www.choosemy plate.gov. Accessed February 4, 2013.

U.S. Department of Agriculture. *USDA National Nutrient Database for Standard Reference* (Releases 21 to 25).

U.S. Department of Agriculture and U.S. Department of Health and Human Services. *Dietary Guidelines for Americans, 2010,* 7th ed. Washington, DC: U.S. Government Printing Office, 2010.

Introduction

Canadian Diabetes Association. *Diabetes Facts.* Available at www.diabetes.ca/diabetes-and-you/ what/facts. Accessed February 4, 2013.

International Diabetes Federation. *Global Atlas,* 5th ed. Available at www.idf.org/diabetesatlas/5e/ the-global-burden. Accessed February 4, 2013.

Chapter 1: Understanding Diabetes

American College of Obstetricians and Gynecologists Committee on Obstetric Practice. ACOG Committee Opinion No. 435: Postpartum screening for abnormal glucose tolerance in women who had gestational diabetes mellitus. *Obstetrics and Gynecology* 2009;113(6):1419–21.

American Diabetes Association. *Living with Diabetes: Women.* Available at www.diabetes.org/living-with-diabetes/women/?loc=DropDownLWD-women. Accessed February 4, 2013.

Chiasson JL, Josse RG, Gomis R, et al. Acarbose for prevention of type 2 diabetes mellitus: The STOP-NIDDM randomised trial. *Lancet* 2002 Jun 15;359(9323):2072–77.

De Luca C, Olefsky J. Inflammation and insulin resistance. *FEBS Letters* 2008 Jan 9;582(1):97–105.

Diabetes Prevention Program Research Group. 10-year follow-up of diabetes incidence and weight loss in the Diabetes Prevention Program Outcomes Study. *Lancet* 2009 Nov; 374(9702):1677–86.

Hsu D. Canadian Diabetes Association National Nutrition Committee technical review: Advanced glycation end-products in diabetes management. *Canadian Journal of Diabetes* 2010;34(2):136–40.

Knowler WC, Barrett-Connor E, Fowler SE, et al. Reduction in the incidence of type 2 diabetes with lifestyle intervention or metformin. *New England Journal of Medicine* 2002 Feb 7; 346(6):393–403.

Kosaka K, Noda M, Kuzuya T. Prevention of type 2 diabetes by lifestyle intervention: A Japanese trial in IGT males. *Diabetes Research and Clinical Practice* 2005 Feb;67(2):152–62.

Li G, Zhang P, Want J, et al. The long-term effect of lifestyle interventions to prevent diabetes in the China Da Qing Diabetes Prevention Study: A 20-year follow-up study. *Lancet* 2008 May 24; 371(9626):1783–89.

Lindstrom J, Louheranta A, Mannelin M, et al. The Finnish Diabetes Prevention Study (DPS): Lifestyle intervention and 3-year results on diet and physical activity. *Diabetes Care* 2003 Dec;26(12):3230–36.

National Diabetes Information Clearinghouse (NDIC). *Diagnosis of Gestational Diabetes.* Available at http://diabetes.niddk.nih.gov/dm/pubs/diagnosis/#5. Accessed February 4, 2013.

National Diabetes Information Clearinghouse (NDIC). *Insulin Resistance and Diabetes.* Available at http://diabetes.niddk.nih.gov/dm/pubs/insulinresistance. Accessed February 4, 2013.

Pan XR, Li GW, Hu YH. Effects of diet and exercise in preventing NIDDM in people with impaired glucose tolerance: The Da Qing IGT and Diabetes Study. *Diabetes Care* 1997 Apr;20(4):537–44.

Smiley T. The role of declining beta cell function in the progression of type 2 diabetes: Implications for outcomes and pharmacological management. *Canadian Journal of Diabetes* 2003;27(3):277–86.

Chapter 2

Health Canada. *Estimated Energy Requirements.* Available at www.hc-sc.gc.ca/fn-an/food-guide-aliment/basics-base/1_1_1-eng.php. Accessed February 4, 2013.

Health Canada. *Nutrition Labelling.* Available at www.hc-sc.gc.ca/fn-an/label-etiquet/nutrition/index-eng.php. Accessed February 4, 2013.

Holick M, Binkley N, Bischoff-Ferrari H, et al. Evaluation, treatment, and prevention of vitamin D deficiency: An Endocrine Society clinical practice guideline. *Journal of Clinical Endocrinology and Metabolism* 2011 Jul;96(7):1911–30.

Hypertension Canada. Sodium — the silent additive. Detailed Sodium Backgrounder. Updated November 2011.

Institute of Medicine. *Dietary Reference Intakes for Calcium and Vitamin D.* Washington, DC: The National Academies Press, 2011.

U.S. Food and Drug Administration. *Nutrition Facts Label Programs and Materials.* Available at www.fda.gov/Food/ResourcesForYou/Consumers/NFLPM/default.htm. Accessed February 4, 2013.

Chapter 3

American Diabetes Association. *Saturated vs. Unsaturated: Why Some Fats are Healthier Than Others.* Available at www.diabetes.org/news-research/research/research-discoveries/recent-advances/saturated-vs-unsaturated.html. Accessed February 4, 2013.

Canadian Diabetes Association. *Sugars and Sweeteners.* Available at www.diabetes.ca/files/en_sweeteners_final.pdf. Accessed February 4, 2013.

Cappuccio F, D'elia L, Strazzullo P, Miller M. Quantity and quality of sleep and incidence of type 2 diabetes: A systematic review and meta-analysis. *Diabetes Care* 2010;33(2):414–20.

Gardner C, Wylie-Rosett J, Gidding S, et al. Nonnutritive sweeteners: Current use and health perspectives — a scientific statement from the American Heart Association and the American Diabetes Association. *Diabetes Care* 2012 Aug; 35(8):1798–1808.

Gibbs N. *The Magic of the Family Meal.* Available at www.time.com/time/magazine/article/0,9171,1200760-3,00.html. Accessed February 4, 2013.

Heart and Stroke Foundation. *Healthy Waists.* Available at www.heartandstroke.on.ca/site/c.pvI3IeNWJwE/b.4018281/k.8698/Healthy_Waists.htm. Accessed February 4, 2013.

Jenkins D, Wolever T, Taylor R, et al. Slow release dietary carbohydrate improves second meal tolerance. *American Journal of Clinical Nutrition* 1982 Jun;35(6):1339–46.

Johnson RK, Appel LJ, Brands M, et al. Dietary sugars intake and cardiovascular health: A scientific statement from the American Heart Association. *Circulation* 2009 Sep 15;120(11):1011–20.

Knutson K, Ryden A, Mander B, Van Cauter E. Role of sleep duration and quality in the risk and severity of type 2 diabetes mellitus. *Archives of Internal Medicine* 2006 Sep 18;166(16):1768–74.

Oldways Preservation Trust. *Mediterranean Diet Pyramid.* Available at http://oldwayspt.org/resources/heritage-pyramids/mediterranean-pyramid/overview. Accessed February 4, 2013.

Paddon-Jones D, Westman E, Mattes RD. Protein, weight management, and satiety. *American Journal of Clinical Nutrition* 2008 May;87(5):1558S–61S.

Wikipedia. *Classification of Obesity.* Available at http://en.wikipedia.org/wiki/Classification_of_obesity. Accessed February 4, 2013.

Wolever T, Jenkins D, Ocana A, et al. Second-meal effect: Low-glycemic-index foods eaten at dinner improve subsequent breakfast glycemic response. *American Journal of Clinical Nutrition* 1988 Oct;48(4):1041–47.

Index

Library and Archives Canada Cataloguing in Publication

Burkhard, Johanna
    The diabetes prevention & management cookbook : your 10-step plan for nutrition & lifestyle / Johanna Burkhard and Barbara Allan.

Includes index.
ISBN 978-0-7788-0443-7

    1. Diabetes—Diet therapy—Recipes. 2. Cookbooks I. Allan, Barbara, dietitian II. Title.

RC662.B874 2013   641.5'6314   C2012-907542-6

- -

Burkhard, Johanna
    The diabetes prevention & management cookbook : your 10-step plan for nutrition & lifestyle / Johanna Burkhard and Barbara Allan.

Includes index.
ISBN 978-0-7788-0452-9

    1. Diabetes—Diet therapy—Recipes. 2. Cookbooks I. Allan, Barbara, dietitian II. Title.

RC662.B874 2013   641.5'6314   C2012-907542-6